THE NEW KEY
TO COSTA RICA

THE NEW KEY TO COSTA RICA

BEATRICE BLAKE
ANN BECHER

DEIRDRE HYDE
Illustrator

ALLAN SEIDEN
Photographer

ULYSSES PRESS

Published by: Ulysses Press
3286 Adeline Street, Suite 1
Berkeley, CA 94703

Library of Congress Catalog Card Number 92-60866
ISBN 0-915233-76-2

Printed in the U.S.A. by the George Banta Company

10 9 8 7 6 5 4 3 2

Publishers: Ray Riegert, Leslie Henriques
Managing Editor: Claire Chun
Editors: Sharilyn Hovind, Joanna Pearlman
Editorial Associates: Wendy Ann Logsdon, Laurie Greenleaf
Cartographers: Wendy Ann Logsdon, Phil Gardner
Cover Designers: Bonnie Smetts, Leslie Henriques
Indexer: Sayre Van Young

Illustrations on pages 59 and 60 by Anabel Maffioli
Fishing section text by Jerry Ruhlow

Distributed in the United States by Publishers Group West, in Canada by Raincoast Books, and in Great Britain and Europe by World Leisure Marketing

Printed on recycled paper

For
peace with justice
in harmony with nature

Acknowledgements

The present edition would not have been possible without the dedicated hard travelling of our researchers, Ronnie Cummins and Rose Welch, who took four months to cover the country, going places that our growing family could not reach. Many people would have liked to have their job, but very few people would have done it with the vision and purposefulness of Ronnie and Rose. As travel becomes the world's number one money-generating industry, they know the importance of developing a sustainable model of tourism that will be good not only for the environment, but for the people as well. They have traveled extensively throughout Central America doing the beautiful *Children of the World* book series, and see the people of other countries also looking to tourism as a way of bettering their economic situation. With this in mind, our intrepid researchers talked with people who work and live around tourism projects, to find out what they think is positive and negative for their communities. They also spent a lot of time consulting with hotel owners about sustainable tourism. Out of these discussions came our survey of eco-tourism businesses, with the resulting symbol, indicating the businesses that support sustainable tourism by making an effort to protect the environment, the local culture, and the economic development of their community. Thank you Ronnie and Rose, for all your ideas and hard work.

We are also grateful for the insight, knowledge, and support of Dr. Deirdre Evans-Pritchard, whose Sustainable Tourism Initiative brought community people, hoteliers, and conservationists together to start projects based on the above-mentioned principles. Many thanks to her and to Rick Holland, Director of TsuliTsuli/Audubon of Costa Rica, for their involvement in the formation and analysis of the survey. We are very pleased that TsuliTsuli will follow up on this work as they develop their "green rating" for eco-tourism operators in Costa Rica. Hugs and kisses to dear friends Alan Kirk and Ann Schauber who pointed out the clumsiness of our original survey and streamlined it based on their extensive experience with such things, thus guaranteeing greater response and greater accuracy.

We are grateful to Alvaro Ugalde, Director of Parques Nacionales, for his support of our project, to Gerardo Barboza of the Tempisque Conservation Area for his valuable input, and to Tania D'Ambrossio of the Costa Rican Tourism Institute for assistance with logistics. We also want to thank Anita Myketuk and Don Melton of Quepos, Philip and Marilyn Edwardes of Jacó, Todd and Laurel of Cahuita, Jack and Diane Ewing of Dominical, and Patricia and Lenny Iacono of Montezuma for helping to get the survey out to their neighbors. We'd also like to thank our friend, Charlotte Walters, for all her support. There were many people who made a special effort to help us learn what was going on in their areas: Patricia Cardenas of the Casa de Cultura in Liberia, Fernando Nietzen of Geoventuras, Magda Campos of Amigos de Lomas Barbudal in Guanacaste, Mauricio and Colocha Salazar and Paula Palmer of the Asociacion Talamanqueña de Ecoturism y Conservación, Amos Bien of Rara Avis, Mike and Susan Kalmbach of La Paloma Lodge, Jan Dankers of Hotel Flamboyant in Jacó, James Hamilton of Tilajari Resort Hotel in Muelle de San Carlos, Luis Wachong of Hotel del Cerro in Golfito, and Edna and Jacob Dases of the Pancana Restaurant in Tortuguero. Thank you all. We were sorry to learn of the recent death of Don Victor Quiros, with whom we spent a pleasant day in Las Juntas de Abangares, while he shared his vision of a revival of the history and traditions of his home town.

A special thank you goes out to the many readers who wrote with comments and corrections on information in the book, complaints and praise for different businesses, and entertaining stories of their travels. We were very fortunate to meet Steve Marquardt who generously shared his research on wheelchair accessibility in Costa Rica.

I'd also like to acknowledge the dedicated effort of the staff at Ulysses Press who have taken on the monumental task of reorganizing and clarifying this eleventh edition: Ray Riegert, Leslie Henriques, Sharilyn Hovind, Joanna Pearlman, Wendy Logsdon, Laurie Greenleaf, and Claire Chun.

Thanks to my husband, Dennis, and our children Danny and Elizabeth for "aguantaring" through yet another edition of this book, and for making me laugh. Thanks to our good friend Deirdre Hyde for her wonderful cover and illustrations.

Sincerest thanks go to my assistant, Adita Molina for her constant, loving support, and to her father, Fernando Molina, for helping us out when we really needed him. Essential too has been the kindness of our neighbors, Martina Alvarez Gutierrez and family.

And deepest love and gratitude go to the strong, generous, and joyful spirit of my mother, Jean Wallace, who started the original version of the Key in 1978, in honor of this special little country in which she finally found her home.

Beatrice Blake
San José, Costa Rica
August 1, 1992

The New Key To Costa Rica
Sustainable Tourism Rating

This edition of *The New Key to Costa Rica* gives special recognition to those lodgings that are doing their best to protect nature, preserve local culture, and benefit their surrounding communities. These are three basic aspects of sustainable tourism: tourism that gives something back to the environment and to the people who are attracting the visitors in the first place.

In order to determine which lodgings were practicing sustainable tourism, our researchers traveled all over the country, talking not only with staff, but also with restaurants and tour companies and, as importantly, with the people who live in the communities surrounding tourism projects. We also received feedback from travelers we met along the way. Next, we sent a questionnaire to all the lodgings located on beaches and near national parks or private reserves, places whose business depends on their proximity to natural areas. We did not send questionnaires to hotels in urban areas, nor did we send them to towns whose original economic growth preceded tourism. For example, towns like Quepos, Puntarenas, Limón, and Liberia were not included, whereas Jacó, Playa del Coco, and Puerto Viejo de Talamanca were included, because their recent growth is primarily due to tourism. We limited our first survey to lodgings, excluding other kinds of projects.

Of the 225 places which were sent questionnaires, 25 percent responded. Of those, almost half made it onto our list of recommended businesses. Some of those who made it are tone tropical paradises, some are small, inexpensive family-run operations. Some that didn't get on the list scored high on ecologically sound practices like composting, recycling, and proper disposal of sewage, but fell short when it came to respect for local culture and contribution to local economies. Sometimes the reverse was true.

The lodgings that earned the sustainable tourism rating (❂) are not necessarily known for their elegant decor or classy amenities, although most of them are tastefully designed with the traveler's comfort in mind. Some of them are quite simple and small. But they are all places where you can learn about the real Costa Rica, with its problems as well as its beauties, and where you can relax more deeply, knowing that part of what you pay is going towards national or local ecological projects, and that the people serving you are probably happy to work there.

As you can see, this is a very partial list. We hope that in the future many more facilities will be added to our list, and that your support of these businesses will influence the direction of tourism in Costa Rica.

SUSTAINABLE TOURISM LODGINGS

CENTRAL VALLEY

Turrialba: Albergue de Montaña Pochotel *(page 136)*

ATLANTIC COAST

Puerto Viejo de Talamanca: Cabinas Chimuri *(page 151)*; Cabinas Jacaranda *(page 153)*

NORTHERN ZONE

Horquetas: Rara Avis *(page 166)*

Puerto Viejo de Sarapiquí: El Gavilán Lodge *(page 168)*

Arenal: Burío Inn *(page 173)*; Arenal Volcano Observatory *(page 174)*; Lago Coter Ecoadventure Lodge *(page 174)*

GUANACASTE PROVINCE

Playa Avellanas: Lagartillo Beach Hotel *(page 203)*

CENTRAL PACIFIC ZONE

Montezuma: Cabinas El Sano Banano *(page 218)*

Monteverde: El Sapo Dorado *(page 224)*; Hotel Fonda Vela *(page 225)*

Jacó: Hotel Club del Mar *(page 232)*

SOUTHERN ZONE

Dominical: Finca Brian y Milena *(page 251)*; Bella Vista Lodge *(page 251)*

Zancudo: Cabinas Sol y Mar *(page 258)*

Pavones: Tiskita Lodge *(page 259)*

Corcovado: Corcovado Tent Camp *(page 263)*

Drake Bay: Drake Bay Wilderness Camp *(page 266)*; El Caballito del Mar (page 266); La Paloma Lodge *(page 266)*; Cocalito Lodge *(page 266)*; Albergue Jinetes de Osa *(page 267)*

San Vito: Wilson Botanical Gardens *(page 269)*

Costa Rica:
Disarmed Democracy

At one point in its history, Costa Rica produced more bananas than any other country in the world, but it is far from being a "banana republic." Armyless, democratic, conservation-minded—people in many other developing countries are fighting for what Costa Rica has had for years. How did this come about?

Costa Rica acted progressively long before it became the general trend. The establishment of free, obligatory, tax-financed education in the constitution of 1869, the elimination of the death penalty in 1882, and the abolition of the army in 1948 all testify to Costa Rica's unique character and vision, and all helped to lay the groundwork for the present social order.

Historically, Costa Rica has almost always remained aloof from the conflicts that have shaken her sister republics. John L. Stephens, a North American archaeologist who visited in 1840, mentioned even then that Costa Rica was an island of tranquility compared to the rest of Central America. Although the national character tends to ignore or imagine itself above the problems of its neighbors, former president Oscar Arias (1986-1990) took a decisive and responsible role in waging peace, especially where Nicaragua was concerned. His unflagging efforts to bring warring parties to the conference table won him the 1987 Nobel Peace Prize. At the same time, many Costa Ricans resented his concentration on international issues and wished he would pay more attention to the economic problems at home.

Costa Rican family trees show that 75 percent of the leading figures in her history were descended from only four *conquistadores* and, of course, their indigenous consorts. The native people of Costa Rica were never completely dominated by the Spanish colonizers, so the class divisions that exist to this day in other Latin American countries did not develop to the same degree here. The few indigenous groups not decimated by war and disease moved away to isolated mountain regions, where they still live. Costa Rica's poverty and isolation led colonial families to fend for themselves, resulting in the establishment of more egalitarian values than in other Latin countries.

When it was discovered in the 1830s that coffee grew well in the highlands of Central America and fetched a high price in European markets, the powerful elites of most of the newly independent nations on the isthmus forced *campesinos* from the land in order to create large coffee plantations. Not so in Costa Rica. Small farmers were encouraged to grow coffee and sell the beans to central *beneficios* or processing plants owned by wealthier farmers, who would prepare the beans for export. Thus rich and poor participated together in the coffee-growing process, each small farmer caring for his bushes in a personal way. (Coffee plants demand a lot of attention, and Costa Rican coffee has always been known as one of the finest on the international market.) The *beneficio* policy gave stability and importance to the small farmer, and allowed him to grow subsistence crops for his family.

The development of the educational and electoral systems during the late 1800s provided the basis for a participatory democracy. By the end of the 19th century, political violence was on the decline and the budget of the police force exceeded that of the army. When the victorious forces of the 1948 civil war decided to constitutionally abolish the army, a *de facto* situation that had been evolving since the beginning of the century was legally ratified.

Costa Ricans, by nature, seek to avoid conflict, so being armyless fits in with the national character. Abolishing the army has had several functions: it inhibits the formation of a military group capable of gaining autonomy; it frees public funds for development; it makes elections the only route to power; it establishes Costa Rica's neutrality in the region—a militarily weak country cannot be attacked without provoking international condemnation of the aggressor; and it shows the illegitimacy of armed opposition toward a state that has renounced the use of force.

The pragmatic thinkers who brought about the abolition of the army recognized the United States as the dominant superpower of the region, and their ally and friend. Implied in the army's abolishment is the belief that the U.S. would come to Costa Rica's rescue if it were attacked. During the years of Sandinista arms build-up in Nicaragua, many Costa Ricans longed for the United States to invade and put an end to the regime. Then-president Arias faced as much internal opposition to his peace plan as he did external. In fact, it was not until he won the Nobel Prize in 1987 that his critics started to let up a bit. Similarly, the vast majority of Costa Ricans lauded the U.S. invasion of Panamá. Disarmament does not necessarily imply pacifism.

Costa Ricans view the military as an encumbrance to their political and social life as well as to the public budget. They prefer to channel their national resources into health and education. Because of their nationalized medical and social security systems, Costa Rican health care is on a par with that of industrialized nations. And, in an attempt to ensure the well-being of future generations, 27 percent of Costa Rica's territory is legally set aside for national parks, biological reserves, forest reserves and buffer zones, wildlife refuges, and Indian reserves. Having enough money to patrol and protect these areas is another story.

Even without an army, finding the money to pursue goals of social justice and ecological balance has become well-nigh impossible for Costa Rica as she fights an uphill battle against her tremendous deficit. The International Monetary Fund demands austerity from a government whose bureaucracy employs 20 percent of the work force. The developed countries pump in millions of dollars of aid, but the largest chunk of the country's budget—almost one-third—goes to service the same foreign debt!

Costa Rican currency is currently worth about one-sixteenth of its 1980 value. A respectable middle-range salary is still less than the equivalent of U.S.$300 per month, and the national average is about $150 per month. Recent studies show that the average family has to spend $125 per month on food alone. More than a third of Costa Rican families live below the poverty level.

Despite all this, Ticos, rich and poòr, actively support their democracy. On election day they honk horns, wave party flags, dress up in party colors, and proudly display their index fingers dipped in purple indelible ink to show they have voted. The communist parties, which have played an important role in Costa Rican history, won less than 1 percent of the vote in the last election. A whopping 80 percent of the electorate turns out to vote.

Even with the enthusiasm that turns their election day into a national fiesta, Costa Ricans are skeptical about politics and politicians. Their roots are still in the soil and in the unity of their families. Babies are the acknowledged rulers of the household. Mother's Day is one of the biggest national hol-

idays. Foreigners complain that it is hard to make deep friendships here because family ties are so strong. The united family that made it possible for early poverty-stricken farmers to survive is perhaps still the real basis of Costa Rican stability.

At the same time, women are a solid 50 percent of the work force, and are rapidly increasing their numbers in such traditionally male-dominated roles as doctors, lawyers, and government officials. Dr. Victoria Garrón became the first woman vice president of the Republic in 1986, and Dr. Rosemary Karpinski the first woman president of the Legislative Assembly.

Costa Ricans' love for the beauty and freedom of their country is almost palpable. At 6:00 p.m. each September 14, the eve of their Independence Day, everyone drops what they are doing to sing the national anthem. In corner stores and homes across the country, everyone joins in. It's a rousing hymn in tribute to peace, hard work, and the generosity of the earth, but it's also a warning that if these things are threatened, Costa Ricans will "convert their rough farming tools into arms," as they did when William Walker tried to invade in the 19th century.

Now Costa Rica faces another kind of invasion. The increasing popularity of "eco-tourism" has opened the country to a huge influx of visitors, attracted by her incredible ecological diversity. Convinced that the "clean industry" of tourism will be a source of much-needed foreign exchange, the government is offering incentives for large tourism projects that will provide hotel rooms to keep up with the demand. No one is listening to the voices of the *campesinos* who still have not been paid for their land, which was made part of a biological reserve, or to those of the dairy workers who cannot afford to buy more pasture for their animals because the price of land has gone up due to foreign and local speculation, or the coastal dwellers who suddenly find there's no room on the bus to town because it's filled with surfboards. A more serious threat is the kind of touristic development that regards local people merely as a pool of potential maids, waiters, gardeners, and laundresses, and nothing more. The traditional values of the small independent farmers who are the backbone of Costa Rican democracy could be lost in the process.

On the other hand, most Costa Ricans are proud to share the beauty of their land with visitors, and know how to make foreigners feel at home. Some programs are trying to incorporate native skills into tourism and ecology: young men who were raised hunting turtles are now being trained to help visitors understand the ancient ritual of turtle nesting; sharp-eyed *campesinos* are learning to be taxonomists in the national parks; men and women from the dry Guanacaste region are reviving the ancient pottery-making techniques of their ancestors; indigenous women from Talamanca have written a book to explain their beliefs about conserving the forest and its wildlife.

Even though the *campesino* and the ox cart are powerful symbols in Costa Rican life, almost half the population of the country now lives in urban areas. Cramped housing developments cover the fertile soil of the Central Valley. As happens everywhere, the city dwellers quickly forget their roots. Hopefully, visitors like you will take time to meet Costa Rica's rural inhabitants and learn to value their knowledge, cultures, and lifestyles, as well as support the small businesses they have created.

Beatrice Blake
Anne Becher
November 1992

Table of Contents

ONE

Costa Rica: A Brief History

To understand the unique character of the Costa Rican people today, it helps to know something of their history. Over the centuries, Costa Rica has taken some decidedly different turns from her Central American sister states.

PRE-COLUMBIAN COSTA RICA

The largest and most developed pre-Columbian population in Costa Rica was that of the Chorotegas, whose ancestors had migrated from Southern Mexico to the Nicoya Peninsula, probably in the 13th century. They were running away from enemies who wanted to enslave them—their name translates as "fleeing people."

Much of the information we have about the Chorotegas was collected by Gonzalo Fernández de Oviedo, a Spanish explorer who lived with them for a short period in 1529.

Outstanding farmers, the Chorotegas managed three harvests of corn per year. They also grew cotton, beans, fruits, and cacao, which they introduced to Costa Rica and whose seeds they used as currency. Land was communally owned and the harvest was divided according to need, so that old people and widows with children could be cared for.

The Chorotegas lived in cities of as many as 20,000 people, which had central plazas with a marketplace and a religious center. Only women could enter the market. Women wore skirts, the length of which depended upon their social level. Men could go naked, but often wore a large cloth or a woven and dyed sleeveless cotton shirt.

Women worked in ceramics, producing vessels painted in black and red, decorated with plumed serpents (the symbol for unity of matter and spirit), jaguars, monkeys, and crocodiles. They carved stylized jade figures in human and animal shapes. The figures may have been used in fertility ceremonies or to bring good luck in the hunt. They wrote books on deerskin parchment and used a ritual calendar.

1

War was institutionalized. A permanent military organization fought to obtain land and slaves, who were used as human sacrifices. Eating someone who had been sacrificed to the gods was a purification rite. The Chorotegas also sacrificed virgins by throwing them into volcano craters.

The Chibcha people from Colombia migrated to the South Pacific region of Costa Rica, where they lived in permanent, well-fortified towns. Their concern with security could have arisen from their possession of gold—which they fashioned into human and animal figures (especially turtles, armadillos, and sharks). Both women and men fought for the best lands and for prisoners, who were used as slaves or as human sacrifices. They believed in life after death; vultures performed a vital role in transporting people to the other world by eating their corpses.

These people probably made the granite spheres that lie in linear formations in the valley of the Río Térraba and on the Isla del Caño off the coast of the Península de Osa. These spheres range in diameter from 7.5 centimeters (the size of an orange) to 1.8 meters. Their almost perfect roundness and careful placement make them one of Costa Rica's pre-Columbian mysteries.

Peoples from the jungles of Brazil and Ecuador migrated to the lowland jungles of the Costa Rican Atlantic Coast. They lived semi-nomadically, hunting, fishing, and cultivating yuca, pejibaye, pumpkin, and squash. Their chief's nobility was hereditary, passed down through the female line of the family.

Social prestige was gained by good warriors. Apparently, decapitated heads of enemies were war trophies. Their stone figurines represent warriors with a knife in one hand and a head in the other.

They worshipped the sun, the moon, and the bones of their ancestors and believed that all things had souls. During religious festivals there was a ritual inebriation with a fermented *chicha* made from *yuca* or *pejibaye*. The burial mounds of these people have yielded the greatest number of pre-Columbian artifacts in the country.

COLONIAL COSTA RICA

On September 18, 1502, during his fourth and last voyage to the New World, Christopher Columbus anchored in the Bay of Cariari (now Limón) after a violent tempest wrecked his ships. During the 17 days that he and his crew were resting and making repairs, they visited a few coastal villages. The native people treated them well, and they left with the impression that Veragua (a name that Columbus used for the Caribbean Coast between Honduras and Panamá) was a land rich in gold, whose gentle and friendly inhabitants could be easily conquered.

A few years later, in 1506, King Ferdinand of Spain sent a governor to colonize Veragua. Governor Diego de Nicuesa and his colonizers received a different welcome. First, their ship went aground on the coast of Panamá, and they had to walk up the Atlantic shore. Food shortages and tropical diseases reduced the group by half. Then they met the Indians, who burned their crops rather than feed the invaders. The Spanish realized that their task was not going to be easy. There was no centralized empire to conquer and sack, and the scattered tribes were at home in a climate and terrain that the explorers found devastating. This first attempt at colonization was a miserable failure.

After Vásco Núñez de Balboa discovered the Pacific Ocean in 1513, the Spaniards started exploring the west coast of Veragua. In 1522, an exploratory land expedition set out from northern Panamá. Despite sickness, starvation, and tropical weather, the survivors of the long, hazardous trip called it a success: they had obtained gold and pearls, and their priest claimed he had converted more than 30,000 Indians to Catholicism between Panamá and Nicaragua.

More explorers and would-be colonizers arrived. There were attempted settlements on both coasts, but they ended in tragedy for the settlers, who died of hunger, were driven out by the Indians, or fought among themselves and dissolved their communities.

Juan Vásquez de Coronado arrived as governor in 1562. He found a group of Spaniards and Spanish-Indian *mestizos* living inland from the Pacific Coast. Coronado explored Costa Rica, treating the Indians he met more humanely than had his predecessors. He decided that the highlands were more suitable for settlement, so he moved the settlers to the Cartago Valley, where the climate was pleasant and the soils were rich from the lava deposited by Volcán Irazú. In 1563, Cartago was established as the capital of Costa Rica.

In contrast to most other Spanish colonies, there was no large exploitable work force in Costa Rica. The Indian population had been decimated early on by war and disease. Because it had no riches and was difficult to reach from Guatemala, the seat of Spain's Central American empire, Costa Rica was left free from foreign intrusion. Forgotten by its "mother country," Costa Rica was almost self-sufficient in its poverty. At one point, even the governor was forced to work his own small plot of land to survive.

Costa Rica's Spanish population remained small and its lifestyle humble through the 17th century. In 1709, Spanish money became so scarce that settlers used cacao beans as currency, just like the Chorotegas. Women wore goat-hair skirts; soldiers had no uniforms. Volcán Irazú erupted in 1723, almost destroying Cartago. Nevertheless, the Spanish survived, and the area settled by Spaniards actually increased during the 1700s. Three new cities were founded in the Meseta Central (Central Valley): Cubujuquí (Heredia) in 1706, Villanueva de la Boca del Monte (San José) in 1737, and Villa Hermosa (Alajuela) in 1782.

INDEPENDENCE

In October 1821, word arrived from Guatemala that Spain had granted independence to its American colonies on September 15th. It had taken the news one month to travel through the mountains and valleys to Costa Rica. After a period of internal strife, Costa Rica declared itself a state in the short-lived Federal Republic of Central America.

The first president of free Costa Rica, Juan Mora Fernández, built roads and schools and gave land grants to anyone who would plant coffee. This epoch was one of the most influential in the evolution of Costa Rican democracy, because small farmers were encouraged to grow coffee and sell the beans to wealthier farmers, who would prepare the beans for export. Thus, rich and poor each had an important place in the coffee-growing process, and mutual respect was developed.

By the mid-1800s, coffee was Costa Rica's principal export, and coffee growers were a powerful and wealthy elite. They built a road to transport coffee from the Meseta Central to Costa Rica's port, Puntarenas. They exported first to Chile, then later to Germany and England. By mid-century, European money was entering the pockets of Costa Rican coffee growers, and Europeans were arriving en masse at this tropical frontier. Costa Rica was becoming cosmopolitan. A university was founded in 1844 to disseminate European thinking, and Costa Rican politicians sported European liberal ideologies.

By 1848, the coffee elite was influential enough to elect its own representative for president, Juan Rafael Mora. He was a self-made man who had become one of the most powerful coffee growers in the country. He was charismatic, astute, and respected by the coffee elite and the *campesinos* alike. He became a veritable national hero by leading an "army" of Costa Ricans to defend his country when it was invaded by one of the most detested figures in Central American history, the North American William Walker.

THE SAGA OF WILLIAM WALKER

A study of William Walker's early life gives one little indication of how he would later come to be the scourge of Central America. Walker was graduated from the University of Nashville at the age of 14. By the time he was 19, he held both a law and a medical degree from the University of Pennsylvania. He followed this memorable academic record with two years of post-graduate study in Paris and Heidelberg.

His success stopped there. Returning from Europe, Walker quickly failed as a doctor, lawyer, and journalist. He had an ill-fated courtship with a beautiful deaf-mute New Orleans socialite, then in 1849 turned up as a gold miner in California. He didn't fare well in this occupation either, and soon started working as a hack writer in several California cities.

At this point, something happened in the mind of William Walker, and he launched himself on a career as a soldier of fortune. From then on, he succeeded in creating chaos wherever he took his five-foot, three-inch, one-hundred-pound frame.

In the early 1850s, Walker sailed with several hundred men on a "liberating expedition" to the Baja California Peninsula and México. The expedition was financed by the Knights of the Golden Circle, a movement bent on promoting the "benefits" of slavery. Walker spent a year in Mexico, during which time he awarded himself the military title of colonel and proclaimed himself "President of Sonora and Baja California."

Back in the United States after several encounters with the Mexican army, he was arrested for breaking the Neutrality Act of 1818. His acquittal of the charge gained him fame and willing followers. His next expedition was to Nicaragua.

Walker went with two main goals. One was to convert Central America into slave territory and annex it to the southern United States; the other was to conquer Nicaragua and ready it for the construction of a trans-isthmic canal. The new riches that were being discovered in California attracted many Easterners, but crossing the United States by land was slow and difficult. Walker had made contacts with a group of economically powerful North Americans who thought that a sea route could be more efficient and profitable. Southern Nicaragua would be a perfect site for the isthmus crossing; ships could sail up the San Juan River, which formed the Nicaragua–Costa Rica border, cross Lake Nicaragua, then pass through a to-be-built 18-mile canal from the lake to the Pacific Ocean.

Walker's contacts arranged for an invitation from the Liberal Party of Nicaragua, which at the time was embattled with the Conservatives. In June 1855, he landed in Nicaragua with 58 men. After losing his first encounter

La Casona,
scene of Walker's defeat

with the Conservatives, Walker managed to hold out until several hundred reinforcements arrived from California, bringing new model carbines and six-shooters. They soon overpowered the Conservatives, and, after an "open" election, Walker became "President of the Republic of Nicaragua."

Central Americans from throughout the isthmus rose to fight Walker and his band of *filibusteros*. In February 1856, President Juan Rafael Mora of Costa Rica declared war on Walker, but not on Nicaragua. Mora raised an army of 9000 in less than a week. This "army," led by Mora and his brother-in-law José María Cañas, was composed of *campesinos,* merchants, and government bureaucrats ill-dressed for combat and armed only with farm tools, machetes, and old rifles. They marched for two weeks to Guanacaste, where they found 300 *filibusteros* resting at the Santa Rosa hacienda (now a national monument in Santa Rosa National Park). Having invaded Costa Rica, the *filibusteros* were preparing to conquer San José. The Costa Rican army, by then diminished to 2500 men, attacked the *filibusteros*, who fled back to Nicaragua after only 14 minutes of battle.

Two thousand Costa Ricans followed Walker up to Nicaragua and, in a generally masterful campaign, fought him to a standstill. The turning point came in Rivas, Nicaragua. Walker and his band were barricaded in a large wooden building from which they could not be dislodged. Juan Santamaría, a drummer boy, volunteered to set fire to the building and succeeded in forcing Walker's retreat. In his action, Santamaría lost his life, and became Costa Rica's national hero.

Walker's attempt to convert Nicaragua and the rest of Central America into slave territory was backed by U.S. President James Buchanan, and his failure angered the president. When Walker confiscated the trans-isthmic transportation concession that U.S. financier Cornelius Vanderbilt had already started installing, Vanderbilt began to finance some of Walker's enemies. This was the beginning of the end of Walker's career.

After another engagement in late 1856 on Lake Nicaragua, where the Costa Rican army brilliantly cut Walker off from his support troops, the rag-tag *filibustero* forces were near defeat. On May 1, 1857, Walker surrendered to a U.S. warship.

The adventurer traveled to Nicaragua again in late 1857, but this time he was taken prisoner before he could wreak any havoc. When he was released in 1860, he sailed to Honduras, where, upon landing, he seized the custom house. This brought a British warship to the scene, upon which Walker, pursued by the Hondurans, eventually took refuge. Offered safe conduct into U.S. hands by the British commander, Walker insisted he was the rightful president of Honduras. The British therefore put Walker ashore again, where he was taken by the Hondurans and promptly shot.

The net result of Walker's Central American marauding was the death of some 20,000 men. The inscription on William Walker's tombstone reads,

"Glory to the patriots who freed Central America of such a bloody pirate! Curses to those who brought him and to those who helped him."

Juan Rafael Mora is now acclaimed for having saved Central America from Walker and the interests he represented, but he wasn't that popular when he returned from battle. People accused Mora of having been too ambitious and blamed him for an epidemic of cholera that infected Costa Rican soldiers in Nicaragua and spread to kill almost 10 percent of the population.

Mora manipulated the 1859 election to win despite massive opposition. In August 1859, his enemies overthrew him. A year later, Mora led a coup d'etat against the new president, also a member of the coffee elite. His attempt failed, and he was shot by a firing squad in 1860—an inglorious end for a man who is now a national hero. All through the 1860s, quarrels among the coffee growers helped to put presidents in power and later depose them. Nevertheless, most presidents during these years were liberal and intellectual civilians. Despite the political instability of the decade, the country managed to establish a well-based educational system. This was a time when new schools were founded, European professors were brought over to design academic programs, and the first bookstores in San José opened their doors.

THE ATLANTIC RAILROAD AND UNITED FRUIT

By the mid-1800s, Costa Rica realized it needed an Atlantic port to facilitate coffee export to Europe. When Tomás Guardia declared himself Chief of State in 1871, he decided to build a railway to Limón. He contracted Henry Meiggs, a North American who had built railways in Chile and Perú. Meiggs went to England to secure loans for the project. He obtained 3.4 million sterling pounds, of which only 1 million actually arrived. These loans created the first foreign debt in Costa Rica's history.

Costa Rica's population wasn't large enough to provide the project with the necessary labor force, so thousands of Jamaican, Italian, and Chinese workers were recruited. After an optimistic start, it soon became evident that it was going to be a slow, dangerous, and costly process. Construction of the railroad claimed some 4000 workers' lives, cost the equivalent of 8 million dollars, and lasted 19 years. The jungle proved itself a formidable and deadly barrier.

Meiggs' nephew, Minor C. Keith, became the director a few years after the project started. The railroad he inherited was constantly beleaguered by severe shortages of funds, so he started experimenting with banana production and exportation as a way to help finance the project. When he realized that the banana business could yield very profitable results, Keith made a deal with the new president, Bernardo Soto, in 1884. In return for a grant from the Costa Rican government of 800,000 acres of untilled land along the tracks, tax-free for 20 years, and a 99-year lease on the railroad, Keith would renegotiate the project's pending debts to England, and complete construction at his own expense.

By 1886, Keith had settled the financial problems with England. He spent the next four years laying the last 52 miles of track that climbed through the steep, treacherous valley of the Reventazón River. Relations between Keith and the labor force weren't good. In 1888, Italian workers organized the first strike in Costa Rica's history, demanding prompt payments and sanitary working and living conditions.

The railroad was completed in 1890. Until 1970, it was the only route from the Meseta Central to Limón. And, until the line was closed in late 1990, it was still the major means of transportation for many of the people who lived in the tiny towns it passed. Children took the train to school; it served as an ambulance for the sick and as a hearse for the dead.

After they finished the railway, many Italian workers settled in Costa Rica's highlands. Chinese workers settled in various parts of the country. The Jamaicans stayed on the Atlantic Coast and started working on the banana plantations that Keith established on his free acres. The development of banana plantations where there had once been jungles forced the native peoples to move up into the mountains.

In 1899, Keith and a partner founded the United Fruit Company. *La Yunai,* as it was called, quickly became a legendary social, economic, political, and agricultural force in many Latin American countries. Costa Rican author Carlos Luis Fallas describes work conditions on the steamy plantations in his book *Mamita Yunai,* and Gabriel García Márquez tells what it did to the imaginary town of Macondo in *One Hundred Years of Solitude.* Although Costa Rica was the smallest country where it operated, United possessed more land here than anywhere else. Costa Rica became the world's leading banana producer.

Keith ended up a very wealthy man and married the daughter of one of the presidents of Costa Rica. Most profits from the banana industry went to the foreign owners of the production, shipping, and distribution networks that made export possible.

United's peak year in Costa Rica was in 1907. By 1913 the company was facing serious problems. Panamá disease had infected banana trees, and United's employees were protesting unfair working conditions. A 1913 strike was broken by the Costa Rican government—two strike leaders were chased into the plantations and killed.

United initiated a new policy: it would lease company land to independent growers and buy bananas from them. Tensions with workers grew; a 1934 strike led by two young San José communists, Manuel Mora and Jaime Cerdas, finally brought better working and living conditions. They maintained the original demands of 1913 and added to the list regular payment of salaries, free housing, medical clinics on plantations, and accident insurance. United wouldn't talk with the strikers, but the planters leasing land from United did, and convinced United to sign an agreement.

In the late 1930s, a new disease, *Sigatoka*, infected banana trees up and down the coast. In 1938, United decided to pick up and move west to the Pacific lowlands around Golfito, where banana remained king until violent labor conflicts and dwindling Pacific markets compelled the company to abandon its installations in 1985.

Now bananas are again becoming big business on the Atlantic lowlands, as huge projects buy up land, cutting down whatever forest remains in their way and forcing small farmers out of the area. The 32,000 hectares currently planted in bananas are expected to increase to 45,000 by 1995. Pesticide use tops three million kilos per year. In the 1970s, thousands of workers were made sterile by contact with a pesticide that had been banned in the U.S. Even now, the pesticides used on banana plantations make it impossible to grow other crops on the same land, because of the high level of chemicals that persist in the soil.

LIBERALISM ARRIVES IN COSTA RICA

The 1880s saw an increasing split between a traditional, conservative church and a liberalizing state. The bishop of Costa Rica criticized the European ideas that were becoming popular with the elite and the politicians. The bishop was summarily expelled from the country in 1884, and in 1885 there was an official denouncement of an earlier church-state concord that had declared Catholicism the state religion. Public outcry at the government's treatment of the church was minimal.

The first truly democratic election, characterized by real public participation, took place in 1889. Liberals saw it as the result of their efforts to educate and raise democratic consciousness in the people. In fact, their efforts worked so well that the public gave their overwhelming support to the liberals' opposition. Supporters of the liberals threatened not to recognize the new president, so 10,000 armed opposition members flooded the streets of San José. The liberals then demonstrated their firm commitment to democracy by recognizing the new, rightfully elected president.

Costa Rica's democratic tradition has endured until today, with only a few exceptions. One was in 1917, when the Minister of War and the Navy, Federico Tinoco, overthrew an unpopular president. Tinoco's brutal and repressive dictatorship lasted through 30 months of widespread opposition. Finally, Tinoco fled the country. A provisional president held office for a year until normalcy was reached, and Costa Rica resumed its democratic tradition with a fair presidential election.

ROOTS OF THE 1948 CIVIL WAR

Rafael Angel Calderón Guardia was the legally elected president between 1940 and 1944. A profoundly religious Catholic, Calderón's political ideology was Social Christian. One of his first actions was to reinstate religious education in public schools. Another was to found the University of Costa Rica. He initiated many social reforms that still exist today, including social security, workers' rights to organize, land reform, guaranteed minimum wage, and collective bargaining. These reforms earned Calderón the adoration of the poor and the opposition of the upper classes.

Calderón ran a puppet candidate, Teodoro Picado, in the 1944 election. Picado won, but the election was widely criticized as fraudulent. Young, middle-class intellectuals, as well as traditionally anticommunist Costa Ricans distrustful of church-state involvement, resented Calderón's grasping for power and criticized the odd alliance he had made with Catholic Archbishop Monseñor Víctor Sanabria and Manuel Mora of the Communist Party.

Farmers, businesspeople, *campesinos,* liberal labor unions, and young intellectuals organized against Calderón. Calderón's allies were the government, the church, the communist labor unions, and the army.

In the 1948 election, Calderón ran against Otilio Ulate, who represented the unified opposition. Ulate won the election by a small margin, but the government demanded a recount. Disagreement was complicated by a fire that destroyed half the ballots the day after the election. Government forces refused to yield to Ulate, and Teodoro Picado remained in power.

Pepe Figueres, a coffee grower and outspoken opponent of Calderón who had been exiled in Mexico, had returned to Costa Rica before the elections. On March 12, 1948, he and his men captured the airport at San Isidro de El General. Foreign arms were airlifted in quickly, due to Figueres' advance planning. Armed groups, trained by Guatemalan military advisors, were formed throughout the country. President Picado declared a state of siege, using borrowed Nicaraguan soldiers and mobilized banana workers from the communist unions. Unaccustomed to the cool climate of San José, they wore blankets over their shoulders, Mexican style, to keep warm. For this reason, Calderón supporters were called *mariachis.* After 40 days of civil war, during which more than 2000 people died, a negotiated treaty was signed. Picado stepped down and Figueres took over as provisional president.

Figueres governed for 18 months, long enough to draft a new constitution. Prohibition of presidential reelection, banning of communist labor unions and parties, abolition of the army, the right to vote for women and blacks, and the establishment of a neutral body that would oversee elections were some of the new constitutional laws. Banks and insurance companies were nationalized, and 10 percent of all bank funds were seized for reconstruction. All of Calderón's social reforms were maintained. In 1949, Figueres turned the country over to Ulate, the rightful president.

Costa Rica elected Figueres president twice, once in 1953 and then again in 1970. "Don Pepe" died June 8, 1990, and was mourned by people of all political persuasions as the defender of Costa Rican democracy and development.

The 1948 revolutionaries formed the National Liberation Party (PLN). Almost without fail, Costa Ricans have alternated their presidents—one from the PLN, the next from the opposition. There have been only two exceptions to this pattern in the 11 peaceful national elections that have been held since 1948. Costa Rican voters have a deep distrust of power being concentrated in one party's hands for too long.

The opposition is an odd coalition of wealthy business owners, who see the PLN's social democratic direction as harmful to their interests, and poor people, who generally side with the party that is out of power. The Partido Unidad Social Cristiana was consolidated during the 1980s under the leadership of Rafael Angel Calderón Fournier, son of Calderón Guardia. He lost the 1982 and 1986 elections to PLN candidates, but finally won in 1990, and was inaugurated as president 50 years to the day after his father assumed power.

SINCE 1948

Costa Rica fortified its progressive social policies during the three decades following 1948, and enjoyed a gradual upward economic trend. The policy of the 1960s and 1970s was to try to become more self-sufficient agriculturally and industrially, which actually led to a heavier dependence on imported pesticides, fertilizers, raw materials, machinery, and oil. Costa Rica and many other Third World countries accepted large First World loans for infrastructure projects like bridges, hydroelectric dams, and roads. When the price of oil rose in the early 1970s, the economy could no longer do without it. Then coffee, banana, and sugar prices went down on the world market, the loans came due, and Costa Rica found itself entering the 1980s with its economy in shambles.

The instability of neighboring countries like Nicaragua and El Salvador impeded cooperation in the Central American Common Market and made Costa Ricans feel insecure. From 1978 to 1979, under President Rodrigo Carazo,

northern Costa Rica served as a virtual base for Sandinista operations. Costa Ricans had no sympathy for the Somoza dynasty and were hopeful that the Nicaraguans could make a go of democracy. But after Somoza was deposed, the Sandinista arms build-up and Marxist-Leninist doctrine disillusioned many Costa Ricans. This led them to lend tacit support to the Contras, who were operating out of Costa Rica despite the government's official neutrality policy under PLN President Luis Alberto Monge.

Costa Rica elected a president in February 1986 from the younger generation of the PLN. Oscar Arias, an economist, lawyer, and author of several books on the Costa Rican economy and power structure, campaigned on the promise to work for peace in Central America. The first part of his task was to enforce Costa Rica's declared neutrality policy, and to stand up to the United States and the politicians within his own party who were supporting Contra activity in Costa Rica (such as the secret airstrip that figured in the Iran-Contra scandal).

As the world knows by now, Arias' untiring efforts to fulfill his promise won him the 1987 Nobel Peace Prize. While the peace process has met with skepticism and even ennui in the First World press, for many Central Americans it signifies a coming of age—a chance to unite and shape their future in a new way. Even though the process has been slower than scheduled, much more communication has taken place between warring factions than ever before. The first democratic elections in Nicaragua's history, held February 25, 1990, were largely a result of the peace plan and saw the Sandinistas defeated.

The economic and social problems at the root of Central America's conflicts are deep and require not just talk, but concerted action. Hopefully, as East-West tensions continue to ease, Central Americans who demand social and economic justice in their countries will no longer be labeled communists and will be able to enter into the political process without risking their lives.

Costa Rica's economic crisis of the early 1980s has been overcome in some ways. Tourism has become the country's third largest source of income. Nontraditional exports such as ornamental plants and flowers, strawberries, and oranges are bringing in as much money now as the traditional exports of bananas, coffee, sugarcane, and meat. Unfortunately, the new agro-industries demand high start-up costs and are not labor-intensive, making them unavailable to small farmers. In addition, because of the high costs of imported fertilizers and pesticides, it costs less for Costa Rica to import basic grains like corn, beans, and rice from the United States than it does to grow them here. So government policy has led away from support for the small, independent, subsistence farmer, forcing *campesinos* off the land and threatening the very basis of Costa Rica's stability and democracy.

The Unidad government of Rafael Angel Calderón Fournier has promised to address these problems, while at the same time resolving the country's enormous deficit. If he does so, Calderón will undoubtedly run up against the same economic powers that challenged his father's liberal policies during the 1940s. How successful he'll be at handling the enormous challenges ahead of him, only time will tell.

TWO

The Ecological Picture

Costa Rica is part of a land bridge between North and South America. Her geographical and climatic conditions make it possible for flora and fauna characteristic of both continents—as well as the Antilles—to coexist, thus creating incredibly diverse ecosystems.

Costa Rica measures only 300 kilometers (185 miles) across at her widest point, but four mountain ranges divide her like a backbone. Mount Chirripó, at 3820 meters (12,500 feet), is the highest point in southern Central America. It is part of Costa Rica's oldest and southernmost mountain range, the Cordillera de Talamanca, which extends into Panamá. The Central Volcanic Range is made up of volcanoes Turrialba, Irazú, Barva, and Poás. More than half of Costa Rica's three million inhabitants live in the Central Valley, whose fertile soil was created by the activity of these volcanoes over the last two million years. To the northwest is the nonvolcanic Tilarán range, which reaches 1700 meters (5500 feet) at Monteverde. Farthest northwest, toward the Nicaraguan border, is the Guanacaste Range, which boasts five active volcanoes, including Rincón de la Vieja, Miravalles (now being used to generate geothermal energy), and Volcán Arenal. The most ancient rocks in the area are more than 100 million years old and occur in the "Nicoya complex," low mountains that crop up here and there along the Pacific.

ECOLOGICAL ZONES

Costa Rica's 20,000-square-mile territory offers a great diversity of ecological zones, from subalpine dwarfed vegetation to rich rainforest to beautiful tropical beaches. Cloud forests like the one at Monteverde are filled with plants that are specifically adapted to gather water and promote condensation and precipitation. These high, misty forests are responsible for Costa Rica's rich water resources. Augmenting the water-gathering function of the trees themselves are epiphytes, plants that live on trees in order to have growing space or to better reach the light. Unlike parasites, epiphytes filter their own food from water, dust particles, and organic matter accumulated

15

around their roots. They add to the diversity of the forest by adapting themselves to conditions that are impossible for other plants. Costa Rica has 1100 different species of orchids, 95 percent of which are epiphytes. The 200 species of bromeliads, much more commonly seen than orchids, are also epiphytes. Epiphytes, vines, and the treetops create a canopy that helps to maintain the humidity inside the forest and provides a home for many small animals whose feet may never touch the ground.

The dry tropical forests of Guanacaste—like those found in Santa Rosa National Park—feature huge deciduous trees that burst into bloom at the beginning of the dry season. The scarlet *poró* tree, the orange-red flame-of-the-forest, the purple jacaranda, the pink-and-white meadow oak, and the yellow *corteza amarilla* are like huge bouquets on the landscape. Other plants flower during the rainy season, thus keeping active a large number of different pollinating insects and birds.

Six species of mangroves exist in Costa Rica's Pacific saltwater swamps, forming a complex community with marine animals and plants.

The rainforests of the Pacific, like Corcovado National Park on the Osa Península, are some of the most complex ecological systems on the planet. They maintain species similar to those found in the Atlantic rainforests, but because of a short dry season, they also shelter some species common to dry forests.

ECOSYSTEMS

Its 850 bird species, more than there are in the entire North American continent, make this tiny country a birdwatcher's paradise. Keep your eyes open on a walk through any of Costa Rica's wild places, and you'll see the wonderful ways birds, insects, frogs, and reptiles have evolved to protect themselves. Some imitate leaves, flowers, and stems of plants; others are indistinguishable from rocks or tree bark. Other animals, who are poisonous or taste very bad, warn potential predators with their bright coloring (red, blue, metallic green). Several butterflies have a disagreeable taste to birds. Other, tastier butterflies imitate the coloring of the bad-tasting butterflies to gain protection. Some animals hide their brightly colored parts and only display them if attacked. One butterfly's outer wings resemble a dry leaf, but its underwings flash two huge, glinting owl eyes.

Due to her complex ecosystems, Costa Rica abounds in cases of highly specialized interspecies relationships. In many cases, both participating species co-evolve by modifying themselves to meet the needs of the other. Many flowers are designed to attract only the animals that can complete their pollination process. Birds, butterflies, and insects—and even bats—can act as pollinizing agents. Bright colors attract a pollinizing agent with a strong sense of sight, like hummingbirds. If the pollinizing agent has a stronger sense of smell, as do flies and some butterflies, the flower will be fragrant. Some of the most fragrant flowers emit their scent only at night to attract animals with nocturnal habits, such as bats.

DEFORESTATION

The ecological relationships that are so fascinating to observe in Costa Rica are a lesson for humans in how to live cooperatively with nature, rather than exploiting, exterminating, and controlling, as people are prone to do now. Despite the richness of its forests, Costa Rica takes first place in Latin America for percentage of deforested land. In 1950, 72 percent of Costa Rica was covered in forest. In 1973, it was 49 percent; in 1978, 34 percent; and in 1985, 26 percent. At this rate, Costa Rica's unprotected forests will be destroyed by the year 2000.

One sees evidence of deforestation constantly. Huge trucks piled with massive tree trunks rumble along the highways from Talamanca, Osa, and Sarapiquí, all areas recently opened to roads. A flight to Tortuguero will show you the facts—a thin border of rich tropical forest lines the shore, and inland, where nobody sees, the land is naked. Only a few tall trees remain from the forest that is rapidly disappearing. Part of the Guanacaste region has become a desert due to four centuries of cattle raising and slash-and-burn agriculture.

According to a 1987 study, the reasons for this destruction are the following: Spontaneous, unplanned expansion of agricultural frontiers, often in response to foreign credit possibilities (in the 1960s, millions of dollars in loans were given to Costa Ricans by the U.S. to stimulate beef production); lumbering activity, which often destroys large areas of forest to extract certain profitable (and often endangered) species of trees, leaving the rest to rot; a population that doubled between 1950 and 1970; the concentration of the best agricultural lands into large properties, forcing *campesinos* to clear and work land on hillsides for subsistence; laws that defined clearing of forest for agriculture as proof that the land was being "improved," a requirement for obtaining land titles; and the government's inability to enforce deforestation laws.

The cattle raising encouraged by banks during the 1960s, and the subsequent conversion of large tracts of forest to erosion-prone pasture, have had particularly harmful ecological effects. It has been estimated that Costa Rica loses 2.5 tons of topsoil to erosion for every kilo of meat exported. (Much of this meat ends up as hamburgers in North American fast-food restaurants.)

As a consequence of this deforestation, Costa Rica faces not only erosion, but flooding, long-term hydroelectric shortages, sedimentation in canals and rivers, destruction of beautiful coral reefs from silt, climatic destabilization, loss of forest wildlife and valuable wood resources, loss of genetic reserves of incalculable value, scarcity of drinking water in some areas during the dry season, and, of course, loss of natural beauty.

Most government reforestation efforts are directed toward planting fast-growing trees that can be sold in a few years for lumber or firewood. Although this form of reforestation is extremely valid and useful, it is important to understand that rain or cloud forests, and the habitats they support, cannot be reproduced by simple reforestation. Hundreds of years are needed to re-generate an ecologically viable rainforest. Very little effort is being made to replace the precious hardwoods found in natural rainforest, because in-vestors would have to wait generations to reap the profits.

A CODE OF ENVIRONMENTAL ETHICS FOR NATURE TRAVEL

Tourists can be valuable allies in the fight to conserve natural resources. In fact, one of the ideas behind eco-tourism is to prove that the forest is worth more economically in its virgin state than cut down and converted to pastureland.

The Audubon Society of Costa Rica has outlined a code of environmental ethics for nature travel. Most responsible eco-tourism agencies try to follow the code as closely as possible. If you experience instances where this code is being violated, you can write to the Audubon Society (address below).

1. **Wildlife and natural habitats must not be needlessly disturbed.** Visitors should stay on the trails, avoid using machetes, and not col-lect plants. Some ecosystems, such as coral reefs, are particularly sensitive, and special care should be taken to avoid damaging them.

Visitors should keep their distance from wildlife so it is not com-pelled to take flight. Animal courtship, nesting, or feeding of young must not be interrupted. Bird nests should be observed from a safe distance through binoculars. Nesting sea turtles should be viewed only with the assistance of a trained guide. Photographers also should keep their distance: foliage should not be removed from around nests, and animals should not be molested for the sake of a picture.

Monkeys and other wild animals should not be fed, because this al-ters their diet and behavior.

2. **Waste should be disposed of properly.** Tour operators should set a good example for visitors by making sure that all garbage is confined to the proper receptacles. Boats and buses must have trash cans. Special care should be taken with plastic. No littering of any kind should be tolerated. When possible, tourists and tour groups should use returnable or reusable containers.

3. **Tourism should be a positive influence on local communities.** Tourists and tour operators should make every reasonable effort to allow communities near natural areas to benefit from tourism. By hiring local guides, patronizing locally owned restaurants and lodges, and buying local handicrafts, tourists can help convince residents that wild places are worth saving.

4. **Tourism should be managed and sustainable.** Tour operators should encourage managers of parks and reserves—including the Costa Rican government, to develop and implement long-term man-

agement plans. These plans should prevent deterioration of ecosystems, prevent overcrowding, distribute visitors to underutilized areas, and consider all present and future environmental impacts.

5. Tourism should be culturally sensitive. Tour operators should give visitors an opportunity to enjoy and learn from Costa Rica's mix of cultures. Tourism should serve as a bridge between cultures, allowing people to interact and enrich their understanding of how other people live. Tours should be designed to take advantage of and not conflict with local cultural traditions.

6. There must be no commerce in wildlife, wildlife products, or native plants. There are strict international laws prohibiting the purchase or transport of endangered or migratory wildlife. Tourists should be discouraged from buying or collecting any wildlife or plants, even if they are legal. Audubon does not tolerate trade in wild birds, feathers, stuffed birds or animals, sea turtle products of any kind, snakes and lizards or their skins, coral, furs, or orchids and other plants (except those commercially grown).

7. Tourists should leave with a greater understanding and appreciation of nature, conservation, and the environment. Visits to parks and refuges should be led by experienced, well-trained, and responsible naturalists and guides. Guides should be able to provide proper supervision of the visitors, prevent disturbances to the area, answer questions of the visitors regarding flora and fauna, and describe the conservation issues relevant to the area.

8. Tourism should strengthen the conservation effort and enhance the natural integrity of places visited. Tour operators should collaborate with conservation organizations and government agencies in finding ways of putting the economic resources generated by tourism to work improving Costa Rica's environmental programs. Equally important, tourism's human resources, including visitors, should be linked with active conservation. Visitors should be made aware of Costa Rica's great conservation achievements as well as the problems.

The best tour operators will find ways for interested tourists to demonstrate their support of conservation programs: by contributing money, volunteering to work in a park or in ecological organizations, writing letters of support, planting a tree, or becoming involved in one of the other creative outlets for concerned activism.

HOW TO HELP

Despite the bleak ecological picture, many people are working to reverse the situation, and visitors who admire Costa Rica's beauty are important collaborators in these efforts.

APREFLOFAS (Asociación Preservacionista de Flora y Fauna Silvestre) (Apdo. 917, 2150 Moravia; 40-6087) organizes volunteers to patrol wilderness areas to report illegal hunting, fishing, and logging to the appropriate authorities. They urgently need volunteers, vehicles, and funds.

Arbofilia (Apdo. 512, 1100 Tibas; 35-5470) is a grass-roots organization in which Costa Rican tree-lovers are helping campesinos reforest one of the most environmentally degraded areas of the country. Biologists provide seedlings and voluntary expertise in grafting, planting, and greenhouse management. In return, the *campesinos* provide voluntary labor and make a *"compromiso con la naturaleza"* (commitment to nature), by vowing not to cut trees by water sources, not to burn fields, and not to hunt endangered birds or animals. The group uses the term "ecological regeneration" rather than "reforestation" because they plant only native species and try to observe the patterns in which trees are found in nature. Jungle Trails (55-3486), a nature-tour company, takes visitors on a one-day trip to the Puriscal region to see Arbofilia in action. The tour fee includes the cost of a seedling, which a visitor can plant.

ASCONA (Apdo. 8-3790, 1000 San José; 22-2296, 22-2288), one of Costa Rica's oldest environmental groups, works to promote the development of the country through the rational use of natural resources in order to achieve progress without destruction. ASCONA appreciates donations and help from volunteers, especially if they have technical or scientific backgrounds. U.S. tax-deductible donations can be made through World Wildlife Fund.

The **Audubon Society of Costa Rica** (Apdo. 4910, 1000 San José; 40-8775) is involved in the restoration of Costa Rica's rivers, preservation of habitat of migratory birds, and in "Bananamigo," a proposal to establish criteria for environmentally friendly banana production. Its tourism committee wrote the environmental ethics code above.

CEDARENA (Centro de Derecho Ambiental y de los Recursos Naturales) (Apdo. 134, 2050 San Pedro; 25-1019) researches laws pertaining to such areas as urban air pollution, forestry, solid-waste management, land tenure and use, and coastal and marine resources, in order to untangle the web of outdated or unenforced legislation. It maintains an information bank on environmental law, which will be used to help plan an investment and development strategy for the World Bank, other lending agencies, and the Costa Rican government. They willingly accept volunteers interested in environmental law.

The **Fundación de Parques Nacionales** (Apdo. 1008, 1002 San José; 20-1744, 32-0008, 32-1182, 31-7961) promotes management, protection and development of national parks and reserves. Much of the territory designated as such is still unpaid for and could revert back to private ownership. Donations are matched with endowment funds in Costa Rican government bonds and through debt-for-nature swaps.

Fundación Neotrópica promotes conservation and sustainable development in communities near national parks and other protected areas. Artisanry by people living in those communities is sold at their Nature Store at Volcán Poás National Park. Their Editorial Heliconia publishes a bilingual photographic guide to the parks in paperback ($12 including postage), a coffee-table version (Boza, *Costa Rica National Parks,* 1992—$45 including postage), and a map showing park locations with photographs ($10 including postage). British artist Deirdre Hyde's beautiful posters of the flora and fauna of the parks are published by Heliconia and are favorite souvenirs ($7 each including postage). (All items are cheaper when purchased in Costa Rica.) A $25 annual fee entitles members to a quarterly newsletter and a 10 percent discount at the Nature Store (Apdo. 236, 1002 San José; 53-2130). They are located across from the Colegio de Arquitectos y Ingenieros on the road to Curridabat. Tax-deductible contributions can be made through the Nature Conservancy.

Grupo Ecologico Yiski receives all kinds of recyclable materials, which they sell to the appropriate recyclers in order to fund various ecological projects. Call them at 36-3823 for pickup.

The **Organization for Tropical Studies** (Apdo. 676, San José; 40-6696, 40-5033), **Tropical Science Center** (Apdo. 8-3870, 1000 San José; 53-3308), **Monteverde Conservation League** (Apdo. 10165, 1000 San José; 61-2953), **Caribbean Conservation Corp.** (P.O. Box 2866, Gainesville, FL 32602, USA, 904-373-6441; Costa Rica phone: 24-9215), **Friends of Lomas Barbudal** (691 Colusa Avenue, Berkeley, CA 94707, USA; 510-526-4115), and **Fundación Gran Carara** (Apdo. 469, 1011 CR; 34-1867, fax: 53-6338) are active in research, training, environmental education, and stewardship of the forest and wildlife reserves they maintain in La Selva, Monteverde, Tortuguero, Lomas Barbudal, and Carara, respectively. The CCC needs volunteer turtle taggers during the March-September nesting season. If you have a background in biology you can be a research assistant for free room and board. Lay people must pay a minimum fee for lodging.

In the United States, tax-deductible donations can be made to support the efforts of some of the above groups through the following organizations:

ASCONA, Gran Carara
World Wildlife Fund
1250 24th Street NW
Washington, DC 20037, USA
202-293-4800

Conservation International
1015 18th Street NW
Suite 1000
Washington, DC 20036, USA
202-429-5660

Rainforest Alliance
270 Lafayette Street, Suite 512
New York, NY 10012, USA
212-941-1900

Fundación Neotrópica
The Nature Conservancy
International Program
1815 North Lynn Street
Arlington, VA 22209, USA
703-841-5300

Monteverde Cloud Forest
National Audubon Society
950 Third Avenue
New York, NY 10002, USA
212-546-9100

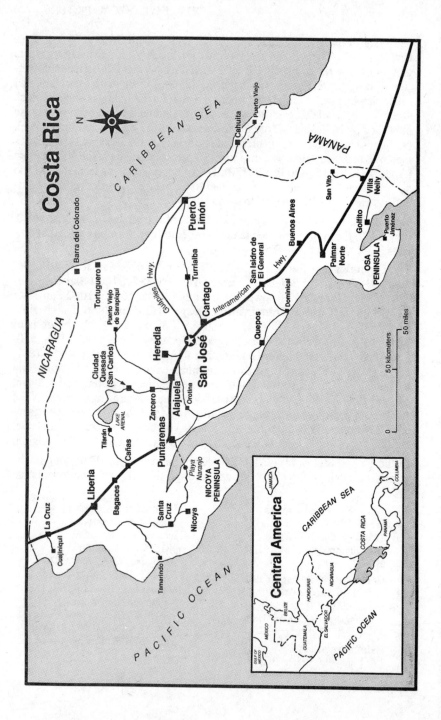

THREE

Planning Your Trip

WHEN TO GO

In Costa Rica, the tourist season is Christmas through Easter, which corresponds to the dry season. You can almost depend on clear, sunny weather, but there are occasional unseasonal storms from the north, which can last for several days. The rainy season usually takes awhile to get started in May, and often diminishes for a couple of weeks in July. The rains dwindle down in November.

There are certain advantages to coming during the off-season: The mornings are almost invariably clear and warm. The scenery is fresher and greener. The days are cooled by the rains, which for some people is a blessing, especially at the beach. The clouds usually clear in time for a magnificent sunset. Many hotels offer substantial discounts during the off-season, sometimes as much as 50 percent. All places are less crowded, more peaceful. Less harm is done to the ecosystems in the parks when fewer people come trooping through at one time.

Since Costa Rica's tourist infrastructure is struggling to keep up with increased demand, many hotels are completely booked during the dry season, even small backpacker hotels and pensiones. This can add a bit of tension and disappointment to a "let's just explore and see what happens" kind of vacation. So be warned—if you decide to come during the dry season, plan way ahead.

CLIMATE

Given Costa Rica's latitude—between 8 and 12 degrees north of the Equator—day length and temperature do not change drastically with the seasons. The sun rises around 5 a.m. and sets around 6 p.m. year-round. Temperature differences are experienced by changing altitude. The misty highlands are in the 10°-13°C (50°-55°F) range, while the Central Valley, at 1200 meters (3800 feet), averages 22°C (72°F). At sea level, the temperature is 26°C (80°F), tempered by sea breezes on the coast. Slight variations occur in December,

23

January, and February, due to cold winds from the North American winter. These cooler temperatures bring on the dry season or "summer," as Central Americans call it, which lasts from December through April. Temperatures start to rise as the sun approaches a perpendicular position over Costa Rica. This causes increased evaporation and brings on the rainy season, or "winter," which lasts from May through November, except for a two-week dry season, a time called *el veranillo de San Juan* (the "little summer"), which occurs sometime in July.

Costa Rica's weather pattern is changing and is not as predictable as it used to be. Now there are many dry days during the "winter" and a few storms during the "summer." A new rule of thumb is: The more gloriously sun-drenched the morning during the rainy season, the harder it will rain in the afternoon. Conversely, on a cloudy morning there will be less evaporation, and thus a generally drier day.

The Atlantic Coast has always been an exception to the rule. Trade winds laden with moisture from the Caribbean approach Costa Rica from the northeast. As the moisture rises to the chilly heights of the Cordilleras, it condenses into rain on their eastern slopes. For this reason, there is no definite dry season in the Atlantic zone, but the beaches tend to be sunnier than the mountains. In a similar phenomenon, trade winds from the southeast discharge their moisture against the mountains that separate the Osa Peninsula from the rest of the country. The Atlantic plains and the Osa both receive 4000 to 7000 millimeters (150 to 300 inches) of rain a year, compared to an average of 2500 millimeters (100 inches) in the Central Valley.

One of the most surprising things for newcomers to the Central Valley is that it's not as warm as they thought it would be. The truly hot months are at the end of the dry season, March and April. December, January, and February are usually rain-free, but the weather can be downright chilly, especially at night or if a wind is blowing. During the rainy season, May to November, the days tend to start out warm and sunny and cloud over by noon. The downpour usually starts around 2 or 3 p.m. and it can get pretty cold then, too. Usually a sweater and long pants are enough to keep you warm. When it rains, it *really rains*, but afternoon downpours are usually short-lived. If you go down in altitude from San José's 3800 feet, you'll be able to wear the kind of clothes you hoped you could wear in the tropics.

HOLIDAYS

Costa Rica has 17 official *feriados* (holidays) per year, and they are taken quite seriously. Do not expect to find government offices, banks, professional offices, or many stores open on *feriados*. Two times during the year, the whole country shuts down completely. These are *Semana Santa* (the week before Easter) and the week between Christmas and New Year's Day. Transportation stops totally on Holy Thursday and Good Friday, making

Wednesday's buses very crowded. Good Friday is the most important day of Holy Week in Costa Rica and is a day of mourning throughout the country.

Easter week is the time to see picturesque religious processions in the countryside. There are also large nonreligious parades in San José on Labor Day, Independence Day, and during Christmas week. *The Tico Times* will tell you where the most interesting events are. It's best to avoid visiting the beach during Easter week because it's the last holiday young Ticos have before their school starts, and they're all at the beach with their radios.

Following is a list of Costa Rica's *feriados*:

January 1   New Year's Day

March 19   Feast of Saint Joseph (San José's patron saint)

April 11   Anniversary of the Battle of Rivas

Holy Thursday through Easter Sunday

May 1   Labor Day, Corpus Christi

June 29   Saint Peter and Saint Paul

July 25   Annexation of Guanacaste Province

August 2   Our Lady of the Angels

August 15   Assumption Day, Mother's Day

September 15   Independence Day

October 12   Día de la Raza (Columbus Day, Carnaval in Limón)

December 8   Immaculate Conception

December 24 and 25   Christmas Eve and Christmas Day

The following are a few of the celebrated special events and fiestas.

JANUARY

Santa Cruz: Tico-style bullfights and lively regional folk dancing are the main attractions at the **Santa Cruz Fiestas.**

San José: Top junior tennis players from around the world compete in the week-long **Copa del Café.**

FEBRUARY

San Isidro de El General: A cattle show, agricultural and industrial fair, and orchid show are highlight this town's **fiestas.**

Rey Curré: See a re-creation of the struggle between the Indians and the Spaniards at the time of the conquest during the **Fiesta of the Diablitos** held each year in this small Indian village near Buenos Aires in the Southern Zone.

MARCH

San Antonio de Escazú: **Día del Boyero** (Ox-Cart Driver's Day) is celebrated with a parade of brightly colored carts and the blessing of the animals and crops.

San José: March is a busy month in San José. You'll find the **National Orchid Show**, featuring more than 500 species, as well as the **Bonanza Cattle Show**, the biggest event of the year for cattlemen (but many visitors come for the Wild-West fun of the rodeos and horseraces). There's also a **Craft Fair** in town, offering the wares of more than 200 local artisans. The **Carrera de la Paz** marathon attracts as many as a thousand runners.

Ujarras: The ruins of the first colonial church in Costa Rica in Ujarras, is the destination of a **religious procession**.

APRIL

Alajuela: Fiestas are held in honor of Costa Rica's national hero in this, his home town, on **Juan Santamaría Day**.

MAY

Limón: May 1, celebrated as **International Labor Day** all over Costa Rica, is a day for picnics, dances, and cricket matches.

San Isidros: Any town of this name—and there are several—is likely to be celebrating **San Isidro Labrador** on May 15 (this saint's day) with festivities that include a blessing of the animals.

San José: The University of Costa Rica marks **University Week** with parades, dances, and cultural events.

San Juan: San Juan Day sees the running of the **Carrera de San Juan**, the year's biggest marathon.

JUNE

On June 29th, **Saint Peter and Saint Paul's Day** is celebrated throughout the country.

JULY

Liberia: Fiestas and rodeos are the highlight of the celebration commemorating the **Annexation of Guanacaste** to Costa Rica in 1824.

Puntarenas: Don't miss the regatta of beautifully decorated fishing boats and yachts celebrating the **Fiesta of the Virgin of the Sea**.

AUGUST

Cartago: The old capital is the destination of an annual national pilgrimage honoring Costa Rica's patron saint, the **Virgin of Los Angeles,** known for her miracles.

San José: **International Black People's Day** is the focal point of **Semana Cultural Afro-Costarricense** (Afro-Costa Rican Culture Week), and features lectures, panels, and displays on Black culture.

San Ramón: All the saints from neighboring towns are brought on a pilgrimage for **Día De San Ramón** in the town named for this saint. Fiestas follow the parade.

SEPTEMBER

Guanacaste: Playa Hermosa is the site of **Festival Marino,** featuring such outdoor events as sandcastle making and jet- and waterskiing.

San José: In the capital and the rest of the country, **Independence Day** is celebrated with parades and the singing of the National Anthem.

OCTOBER

Puntarenas: The annual **Regatta** is an international event held at the Costa Rica Yacht Club.

Limón: The yearly **Columbus Day Carnival** is the Limonese version of Rio, with brightly costumed dancers parading through the streets all night, concerts and general merrymaking.

NOVEMBER

From an **International Surf Tourney** to special services in honor of **All Soul's Day,** there are events taking place all across the country this month.

Central Valley: Harvest time for one of Costa Rica's major crops is marked by a **Coffee-Picking Tournament.**

DECEMBER

Christmas celebrations begin early in the month everywhere in Costa Rica with music and special foods like *rompope* (eggnog) and *chicha* (a homemade corn liquor).

Boruca: This Indian village hosts **Fiesta de Los Negritos,** honoring the village's patron saint with ancient Indian rituals.

Guanacaste: Nicoya is the site of **Fiesta de la Yeguita,** with a procession, foods made from corn, music, bullfights, and fireworks.

San José: December 15 is the start of **Las Posadas,** a Christmas tradition where children, musicians, and carolers go door-to-door re-creating Mary

A THUMBNAIL GUIDE TO TOURING

Central Valley	Birdwatching	Botany	Crafts	Fishing	Hiking	Water Sports	Wildlife	Good for Kids	Camping	Days for Trip	Tours
Ojo de Agua						●		●		½	
La Guácima							●	●		½	✓
Zarcero					●					1	✓
Grecia					●	●		●		½	
Sarchí			●							½	✓
Poás	●	●	●		●			●		½	✓
Heredia					●				●	½	✓
Braulio Carrillo	●	●			●					½	✓
Rancho Redondo					●					½	
Cartago								●		½	✓
Irazú & Prusia					●			●		½	✓
Orosi				●	●	●		●		½	✓
Tapantí	●	●		●	●	●	●	●		½	
Turrialba & Guayabo	●	●			●	●		●		1	✓

Atlantic Coast	Birdwatching	Botany	Crafts	Fishing	Hiking	Water Sports	Wildlife	Good for Kids	Camping	Days for Trip	Tours
Cahuita	●	●	●		●	●	●		●	3	✓
Hitoy Cerere	●	●			●		●			3	
Puerto Viejo	●	●		●	●	●	●		●	3	✓
Tortuguero	●	●				●	●	●		3	✓

Northern Zone	Birdwatching	Botany	Crafts	Fishing	Hiking	Water Sports	Wildlife	Good for Kids	Camping	Days for Trip	Tours
Puerto Viejo de Sarapiquí	●	●	●	●	●	●			●	2	✓
Rara Avis	●	●			●		●			3	✓
Arenal				●	●	●		●	●	2	✓

Guanacaste	Birdwatching	Botany	Crafts	Fishing	Hiking	Water Sports	Wildlife	Good for Kids	Camping	Days for Trip	Tours
Cañas & Lomas Barbudal	●	●			●	●	●	●		3	✓
Palo Verde	●						●		●	3	✓
Rincón de la Vieja	●	●			●		●		●	3	✓
Santa Rosa	●	●			●	●	●		●	3	
Guanacaste	●	●			●		●		●	3	

	Birdwatching	Botany	Crafts	Fishing	Hiking	Water Sports	Wildlife	Good for Kids	Camping	Days for Trip	Tours
Guanacaste											
Liberia Beaches				✓		✓		✓	✓	3	✓
Santa Cruz Beaches				✓		✓	✓	✓	✓	3	✓
Nicoya & Guaitil			✓							3	
Nosara	✓	✓		✓	✓	✓	✓	✓	✓	4	✓
Ostional							✓			4	
Sámara & Carrillo				✓		✓		✓	✓	4	✓
Barra Honda					✓		✓		✓	3	✓
Central Pacific											
Gulf of Nicoya	✓			✓		✓				1	✓
Curú	✓				✓	✓			✓	3	✓
Tambor				✓	✓	✓	✓	✓	✓	3	✓
Montezuma & Cabo Blanco	✓	✓			✓	✓	✓		✓	4	✓
Monteverde	✓	✓	✓		✓		✓	✓	✓	3	✓
Carara	✓	✓			✓		✓	✓		1	✓
Herradura & Jacó				✓		✓			✓	1	✓
Manuel Antonio	✓	✓		✓	✓	✓	✓			3	✓
Southern Zone											
Copey de Dota	✓			✓	✓					1	✓
San Gerardo	✓			✓	✓					1	✓
Chirripó	✓	✓			✓				✓	4	✓
Dominical	✓					✓		✓	✓	3	
Boruca			✓		✓					3	
Pavones						✓	✓		✓	4	✓
Zancudo				✓		✓				4	
Corcovado	✓	✓			✓		✓		✓	5	✓
Marenco	✓	✓			✓		✓			3	✓
Drake Bay	✓			✓	✓	✓	✓		✓	4	✓
Wilson Gardens	✓	✓			✓		✓			3	✓
La Amistad	✓	✓		✓	✓		✓		✓	4	✓
Isla del Coco	✓	✓		✓	✓	✓				4	✓

and Joseph's search for lodging. The week between Christmas and New Year's Day offers the biggest celebration of the year in San José, complete with a gigantic parade with floats, Tico-style bull fights, and El Tope, and a huge horse parade in the Sevillian tradition (elegantly clad riders showing off their purebred steeds). The fairground in Zapote turns into an amusement park. On New Year's Eve, there's a dance in San José's Central park to welcome the New Year.

COMING AND GOING

ENTRY REQUIREMENTS

When traveling with a passport, citizens of the United States, Canada, and most Latin American and European countries are entitled to stay in Costa Rica for 90 days. They must enter the country with at least $400 and a departure ticket. Citizens of some Latin American, Asian, African, and East European countries must obtain a visa from a Costa Rican consulate and pay a deposit upon entering the country, refundable when they leave. Check with the consulate nearest you for the latest information.

Always carry your ID: While in Costa Rica, if you don't want to carry your passport with you, get a copy of it made, but don't go anywhere without identification. You can get your passport copy *emplasticado* (covered with plastic) at various street stands in San José.

EXIT AND EXTENDED VISAS

All tourists must pay an airport tax of about $4 when they leave. To avoid waiting in line to do this at the airport, you might want to pay it at the airline office downtown when you reconfirm your return reservation.

In addition to the airport tax, if you overstay your 30- or 90-day visa, you will need an **exit visa** in order to leave the country. An exit visa is good for 30 days from the date it is issued, so it is an automatic 30-day extension of your visa. If you do not use your exit visa within 30 days, you must buy a new one. Any local travel agent can obtain an exit visa for you, but be sure to request it at least three working days before you are scheduled to depart. They charge a small fee for this service, well worth it compared to the hassle of getting the visa yourself. If you leave by air, an exit visa costs about $12. If you leave by land, the exit visa costs $30. Allow at least 48 hours for processing of exit visas. They cannot be processed on weekends or holidays.

If you have stayed beyond 90 days when you apply for your exit visa, you will be charged $2.50 for each month or part of a month that you stayed without a valid tourist card, plus extra charges totaling about $5.50, plus your exit visa.

You can stay legal by leaving the country for a few days every three months and coming back in with a new tourist card. If you leave the country while your tourist visa is still valid, you don't need an exit visa. **Longer stays** are only granted to those applying for student visas or residency.

After you've gotten your exit visa and are ready to leave, be sure to **confirm your departure** flight 72 hours in advance.

Get to the airport at least two hours ahead of flight time. Flights are often overbooked.

TRANSPORTATION

AIRLINES SERVING COSTA RICA

Usually the cheapest and most-direct flights to Costa Rica from the U.S. are through Miami, although flights also originate in Los Angeles, Dallas, Houston, New Orleans, Washington, DC, and New York. Until recently, **LACSA** was Costa Rica's only international airline. It is known for its almost accident-free record—and for jolly Costa Rica-bound flights where everyone gets tipsy on free wine or wired on Costa Rican coffee and returning Ticos applaud as the plane touches down. LACSA's toll-free number in the U.S. is 800-225-2272. In Canada, it's 800-663-2344; England: 01499-6731; Japan: 445-48-74; Taiwan: 02-704-94-38. **Aero Costa Rica** recently became LACSA's competitor for international flights. Their number in Miami is 800-237-6274.

American Airlines, United, and **Continental** also have flights to Costa Rica. Try to get a travel agent who is experienced in sending people to Costa Rica, because there are many alternatives. Regular travel agents might not have information about Central American airlines, which tend to be less expensive than the U.S.-based airlines but make more stops, usually in the capital of their homebase country and one other place, before arriving in San José. Following are the Central American airlines and their 800 numbers in Miami, so you can check for yourself: **Aviateca** of Guatemala (800-327-9832); **TACA** of El Salvador (800-535-8780); **SAHSA** of Honduras (800-327-1225). **Mexicana** (800-531-7921) also offers flights.

Whatever airline you take, make reservations several months ahead if you are coming during the dry season, and confirm your reservation 72 hours in advance, because schedules sometimes change. Get to the gateway airport at least two hours before flight time or allow two hours between connecting flights, unless you're going all the way with the same airline. Check-in lines are lengthy and documentation checks and payment of airport taxes may take time. You are required to pay a $28 airport tax in Miami. (If you have some time to spare, the **Hotel Mia** in the Miami airport has a health spa on the eighth floor with a swimming pool, sauna, jacuzzi, running track, and nautilus machines. A one-day membership costs $5. There is also a special nursery room with a changing table and stove in the airport near the LACSA desk.)

Airlines flying from Europe are **KLM** (via Curacao and Aruba), **LTU** (via San Andres), **Condor,** and **Iberia** (via Puerto Rico and Dominican Republic).

For information on **low-cost flights** to Costa Rica, contact the above airlines, or:

> **González Travel**
> 504-885-4058, fax: 504-469-7500
>
> **Americas Tours and Travel**
> 800-553-2513
> 206-623-8850, fax: 206-467-0454

CHARTER FLIGHTS   Canadians have been flocking to Costa Rica because of the availability of charter flights. **Fiesta Wayfarer Holidays** in Toronto, 416-498-5566; **Fiesta West** in Vancouver, 604-688-1102; and **Go Travel** in Montreal, 514-735-4526, charter planes from those cities year-round. Tourists have the option of staying one, two, or three weeks.

There are also charter flights from Germany via LTU.

DRIVING TO COSTA RICA

If you're driving, allow about three weeks from the time you enter Mexico to the time you reach Costa Rica. Avoid the highlands of Guatemala and El Salvador. For a detailed account of one such trip, read the October 18, 1991, tourism edition of *The Tico Times* ($1 including postage, Apdo. 4632, 1000 San José, fax: 33-6378).

PACKING

Tourists are permitted to bring binoculars, two cameras, and electrical items that are for personal use only, like a small radio, a hairdryer, a personal computer or electric typewriter, a video camera, etc. The most important thing to remember is that the items should not be in their original boxes and not look too new. They don't want tourists to "import" electronic items and sell them here.

In San José during the rainy season, people usually carry umbrellas—brightly colored *sombrillas* for women and black *paraguas* for men. In the mountains, a lightweight rain poncho is usually more convenient. You'll be glad to have high rubber boots if you go hiking in the rainforest, especially in Corcovado or Sarapiquí. You can buy good ones in Costa Rica for under $7 at provincial supply stores, and many places, like **Monteverde**, rent them to visitors for around $1. Bring boots with you from home only if you wear an especially large size.

When you go to the beach or rainforest, bring at least three changes of lightweight cotton or cotton-mix clothing protected inside a plastic bag in case of sudden downpours. Even if you are going to the steamy lowlands, you often have to pass through high mountains to get there—Cerro de la Muerte on the way to the Osa, Braulio Carrillo or Vara Blanca on the way to Sarapiquí. You'll be happier if you have a zippered sweatshirt, long pants, and socks that can be peeled off as you get to lower altitudes. The sweatshirt also makes a good pillow for long bus trips.

Many hotels will let you store excess luggage while you venture off. I can usually fit everything I need for a trip to the country in a day-pack. I start out in a bathing suit, jeans, a cotton overshirt, socks, and running shoes. In addition, I bring two bathing suits or leotards, two pairs of lightweight pants, extra socks, two long T-shirts (one to sleep in), flip-flops, the zippered sweatshirt, and a scarf, as well as insect repellent, a flashlight, a book, an umbrella or rain poncho, a towel, and toilet paper. If you are going to Irazú, Poás, Chirripó, or other high altitudes, you'll need a jacket on top of a thick sweater and warm socks.

Things that are not made in Costa Rica are sold with a 100 percent import tax, and therefore are much more expensive here than elsewhere. Following is a list of items that are imported or impossible to find. Bring them with you.

Film and camera equipment	Sunscreen
Cassette tapes	Anti-itch ointment
Binoculars	Water purifying device
Pocket alarm clock or watch	Small first-aid kit
Pocket calculator	Contact lens solution
Swiss army knife	Birth control items
Good walking shoes	Vitamins
Insect repellent	Earplugs
Sulfur powder (sprinkle on socks to deter chiggers)	A universal plug for bathroom sinks
	Beach towel and washcloth

If you are traveling on a tight budget, you will also find the following items handy:

Your own cup	Towel, washcloth, and soap (Of course, most places, even cheap ones, supply towels and soap, but there is an occasional one that doesn't.)
Flashlight	
Toilet paper	
A cotton sheet or two (some hotels have nylon or polyester covers, which are uncomfortable in the humid heat at the beach)	
String and clothespins for hanging up wash	Late-night readers will want a small tensor lamp with a long extension cord and a 2-prong to 3-prong adapter.

ELECTRICITY

The electric current used in Costa Rica is 110 volts, AC. The sockets are American-style, but usually don't have a place for a grounding prong. American and Canadian appliances whose plugs don't have grounding prongs should work, but it's always a good idea to check with your hotel about the voltage *before* you plug anything in.

TRAVELING EXPENSES

Costa Rica is not as inexpensive for travelers as Mexico and other Central American countries. Although public transportation is cheap, restaurant and hotel prices are relatively high, but variable. If you are determined to spend as little money as possible, bring a tent and visit during the dry season, or visit during the rainy season and take advantage of the off-season rates. You can also find clean and decent rooms with shared baths for under $12 almost anywhere. Meals cost between $2 and $6, depending on the "atmosphere." Groceries cost about two-thirds as much as they do in the United States. Two people can travel for about $20/day each, including bus transportation, comfortable lodging (double occupancy), and restaurant meals. If you go to the least expensive places, you can get by for $15 each. Camping out is cheaper still, but you have the inconvenience of hauling around equipment and making sure your tent is guarded at all times.

CURRENCY AND BANKING

The currency unit is the *colón (¢)*. Bills come in denominations of ¢5 to ¢5000, and coins from 10 *céntimos* to ¢20. The current exchange rate is around ¢136 per U.S.$1. In March 1992, the government decided to "float" the *colón* against the dollar, so rates change from day to day.

CHANGING MONEY

You can change money at the airport until 5 p.m. Hotels are authorized to change money and travelers checks for their guests, but sometimes you get fewer *colones* than you do at the bank.

Banks are open 9 a.m. to 3 p.m., and there are some branches that stay open until 6 p.m. There is always a special window for changing dollars. Be sure to go there instead of waiting in the regular line. When you get to the dollar window, you are given a little slip of paper that you then must present at the regular window (after waiting in the regular line). In other words, try to change your money at your hotel. However, there might be a limit to how much your hotel can change for you. If you have to go to a bank, don't go on Mondays or Fridays, or the day after holidays, because the lines are longer.

The **Banco Mercantil** just opened a tiny office devoted to money changing only on Avenida 2 between Calles Central/2. (Open weekdays 9 a.m. to noon, 1 to 5:45 p.m.; 21-3841). Be sure to store your money away carefully before you leave.

It is best to change money in San José before going to the provinces, and to carry small bills with you (not just ¢1000s) because everyone has a problem stocking enough change.

Special note for Canadians: The banks that accept Canadian dollars are **BCT** (Calle Central, Avenidas 1/3; 33-6611), **Banex** (Calle Central, Avenida 1;

57-0522), **Lyon** (Calle 2, Avenidas Central/1; 21-2611), and **Banco de San José** (Calle Central, Avenidas 3/5; 21-9911).

CREDIT CARDS

Most tourism businesses accept major credit cards, but some don't, so check with them just to make sure. You can use a credit card to buy *colones* at banks if you have sufficient credit on your card. **Visa** (33-0044), **Mastercard** (23-8855), **American Express** (33-0044), and **Diners Club** (21-0078) all have local representatives. If your card is lost or stolen, you should contact your home office as well as the Costa Rican branch.

HEALTH PRECAUTIONS

INOCULATIONS

You should see your doctor before taking any foreign journey to be sure you're up to date on your regular vaccinations (tetanus, polio, measles, and so on). You probably won't need to get any special vaccinations or inoculations before traveling to Costa Rica, but it's a good idea to check for current recommendations by calling the **Centers for Disease Control** hotline in Atlanta at 404-332-4555.

WATER

Water is safe to drink in San José. Bottled water is recommended in the suburbs of Escazú and Santa Ana, in Puntarenas and Limón. *Soda* is the term to use when asking for carbonated mineral water. Orvian has recently started producing noncarbonated mineral water here, but it is not well distributed. Call **Aguas Minerales de Costa Rica** (42-1539) for more information.

AMOEBAS AND PARASITES

Even though Costa Rica's water is good in most places, visitors traveling in the provinces sometimes have intestinal problems. If symptoms are persistent, they might be due to *amibas* or *giardia*. If you get a strong attack of diarrhea, it's wise to take a stool sample to a local lab to have it analyzed. Put it in a clean glass jar, and deliver it immediately. Amoebas can't be found in samples that are a few hours old. The **Clínica Bíblica** lab is open weekends and holidays (23-6422). **Clínica Americana**, 22-1010, has a good lab, and Dr. Gil Grunhaus, across from Hospital San Juan de Dios, 22-9516, gives the most complete reports. Your results will be ready the same day, especially if you bring your sample before noon ($4 in advance). If results are negative, take up to three samples. Sometimes the offending organisms are not found the first time. The most dangerous one is *entamoeba histolytica*. This can migrate to your liver and cause damage later.

It is not necessary to go to a doctor unless you want to. A pharmacist can give you the needed drug based on your lab results. We have not found that natural methods cure amoebas. Even if you get over your diarrhea, the organisms can still be doing damage to your system unless you've taken medicine. Symptoms often show up as a tendency toward constipation and a feeling of depression and low energy. It's best to take the chemicals and be done with the bugs. Be sure to ask for the literature that goes with the medicine so you'll know about possible side effects. To avoid bugs when traveling outside San José, stay away from drinks made with local water or ice and fruits and vegetables that cannot be peeled.

CHOLERA

The cholera epidemic that has taken so many lives in Latin America has so far been held at bay in Costa Rica because of a strong public education campaign and a concerted effort on the part of health officials to identify and treat any cases imported from other countries. Cholera causes an extremely strong attack of watery diarrhea, sometimes accompanied by vomiting, which kills because victims quickly become dehydrated. The treatment is a simple oral rehydration solution, called *suero*, available for a few cents in any drugstore. If you do have frequent, copious, watery diarrhea without fever, don't wait to take a sample to a laboratory, get medical help right away. You can be sure that if there is an epidemic of cholera in Costa Rica, it will be all over the media, and the areas where it is occurring will be clearly defined. After observing the determination with which Costa Ricans have confronted this danger, we doubt the disease will reach epidemic proportions here.

SWIMMING POOLS AND RIVERS

Look for any visible signs of pollution before you jump into a river or pool, and always be sure to wash well with soap and water after you come out. To avoid fungus infections in the ears, clean them with rubbing alcohol and a swab after swimming.

INSECTS

Mosquitos can be a problem, even in breezy San José at night during the dry season. Anti-mosquito spirals can be bought at supermarkets and *pulperías* for about 40 cents a box. Smaller stores will often sell you just a pair for about 12 cents. Be sure to ask for the little metal stand (*soporte*) that goes with them. Light up the spiral and circle it several times over your bed, then put it as far away from your bed as possible, or even outside the window or door. They usually work pretty well.

On the Atlantic Coast, beware of **sandfly** bites that seem to become infected and grow instead of disappearing. This could be a sign of *papalomoyo* (Leishmaniasis), a disease that can be life-threatening if untreated. See a tropical disease specialist immediately.

Purrujas (no-see-ums) are perhaps the most aggravating of Costa Rican insects. They bite you without your even seeing or feeling them, then they itch for days. They like to hang out at the edge of the beach where the sand meets the trees. They also seem to be more active at dusk. Bring sulfur powder from home to sprinkle on your socks to discourage them. That means you should wear shoes and socks on the beach for your sunset walk. Dusk is generally the time when you have to apply insect repellent, too.

Some people have serious allergic reactions to **ant** bites. A person having an allergic reaction might begin to itch all over, then turn red and swell up. If that happens, get to a hospital as soon as possible. To avoid ant bites, wear closed shoes whenever you're in the jungle or on the beach.

Africanized bees have worked their way north from Brazil, and can attack humans with fatal results if their nests are disturbed. It is wise to be aware of this when exploring hot, dry areas, where bee colonies are ten times denser than in rainforests. If attacked, run as fast as you can in a zigzag direction, or jump into water. Bees don't see well over distances. Never try to take cover; don't crawl or climb into a precarious position from which you cannot make a quick exit. Throw something light-colored over your head to protect your eyes and nose; keep your mouth closed. If you know you are allergic to bee stings, talk with your doctor before you come to Costa Rica and carry the proper medication with you. For more detailed information, contact the OTS (40-9938, 40-5033).

SNAKES

If you want to be able to recognize a poisonous snake in case you run across one in the wild, visit the **Serpentorium** (second floor, open daily 10 a.m. to 7 p.m.; Avenida 1, Calles 9/11; $1 admission) in San José. Live native poisonous and nonpoisonous frogs, snakes, and reptiles are on exhibit here, along with some foreign snakes, such as the black cobra and a 19-foot python. At first we thought that the reptiles were very realistic plastic replicas because they move so little, but after awhile we saw that their positions had changed slightly, so they must be alive.

ACCOMMODATIONS IN COSTA RICA

Costa Rica is racing to build hotels to keep up with tourism demands, and existing hotels are often booked far in advance. Make reservations at least two months ahead for the dry season, and three months at Christmas or Easter. Most hotels have fax numbers, which we have tried to include as it's often easier to correspond by fax rather than by phone; for some without faxes we've listed a mailing address—an apartado, or Apdo. Some demand a deposit. Travel agents have told us that even if you have confirmed your reservation, you can still get bumped if you haven't sent a deposit.

Our hotel rates are based on *double* occupancy (unless otherwise indicated), and include a 16 percent tax. Please keep in mind that prices change, and although we try to be as accurate as possible, don't take it on faith that a hotel still charges what we said it charges—always ask. Rates will vary if you are alone or in a group, or if meals are included. In theory, the Tourism Institute (ICT) determines each year the rates hotels can charge. These rates are given in *colones*, and must be posted in each room. In practice, many hotels charge in dollars and maintain the dollar price even if it no longer matches the price in *colones*. You have a right to demand to pay the official price that is posted in your room.

You can find clean, fairly comfortable rooms almost anywhere for under $15 for two. Atmosphere costs more. If you can afford it, there are plenty of places with great atmosphere, equipment, and service. Our main complaint about many hotels, even some expensive ones, is that you're often subjected to noise pollution from somebody's high-powered sound system. Usually, the source is a nearby dance hall or neighbors with a loud radio. A place can seem perfectly *tranquilo* when you arrive during the day; the thumping disco across the river only comes on at night. The best solution is to get up and dance. Places that are owned by foreigners are generally quieter than places owned by Ticos, who regard loud music as *alegre*.

We should clarify the meaning of various terms that appear throughout the book referring to lodging.

Hotels usually have more than one story, but not always. *Cabinas* are the most common form of lodging at the beach or in the mountains. They may be separated, or connected in rows or duplexes. They roughly correspond to what a North American would call a "motel." However, here *motel* refers to a small number of establishments, mostly on the southeastern side of San José, which couples use for clandestine romantic trysts. The couples are often married, but not to each other. The motels rent by the hour. *Villas* and *chalets* are fancy cabinas, usually separated from each other. *Pensiones* and *hospedajes* are usually converted houses, and often serve family-style meals. A *posada* is an inn.

Beach and mountain hotels often give discounts in the rainy season. Weekly and monthly rates are common as well. If you are staying in one place for a while, consider renting a house. See *The Tico Times* for listings, or ask at a local *pulpería*.

Cold water means just that—that there is no hot water. However, showers at places near the beach are often "solar-heated" naturally, and it sometimes feels good to take a cool shower instead of a hot one when you are very hot.

Heated water refers to an electric device that warms the shower water as it comes out of the shower head. *Note:* These contraptions are usually set to come on when the water is turned on, but in some places you have to turn them on yourself. Check how yours works while you are still dry and have your shoes on. You don't want to be fooling around with it while you are wet and barefoot in the shower. If there is too little water pressure, the little buggers become too hot and can burn out, so be careful. Usually these things make for a pretty limp, lukewarm shower.

Hot water refers to water heated by a hot water tank.

Solar-heated water indicates the use of solar-heating devices.

Natural ventilation refers to places at the beach that, because of their location or construction, take advantage of ocean breezes and thus do not need fans.

NOTES FOR SENIOR TRAVELERS

Older travelers will certainly be able to find good company, comfortable traveling conditions and lodging, with the security that excellent health care is available if they should need it. Note: The bad condition of the sidewalks is a real problem in many places, and much care must be taken as a pedestrian.

Elderhostel, which sponsors inexpensive and interesting trips for people over 60 years of age, now includes Costa Rica in its itinerary. You may find out more by contacting Elderhostel at 75 Federal Street, Boston, MA 02110; 617-426-7788.

NOTES FOR DISABLED TRAVELERS

Unfortunately, very little has been done to make access easier for disabled people and parents pushing strollers. Streets and sidewalks are often in deplorable condition, some curbs are more than a foot high, and many roads do not have sidewalks at all, forcing everyone into the street. Despite all this, several disabled people we talked to said they felt conditions were better for them here than in the U.S. because of the climate, the relatively low cost of quality health care and hospitalization, and the low cost of maids and other helpers. Many neighborhoods do have sidewalks—you just have to do some searching.

It is best to get around by taxi. Taxi service is fairly reasonable, but you'll have better luck if you summon a taxi by phone instead of trying to hail one on the street. Taxi drivers seem to ignore the disabled if they have the opportunity to pick up others.

Although nowhere is perfect, the following hotels win our wheelchair access awards: Cabinas Grant in Puerto Viejo do Talamanca (Atlantic Coast), Cabinas Playa Hermosa in northern Guanacaste, Hotel Playa Nosara in southern Guanacaste, Hotel Fonda Vela in Monteverde, and Cabinas Espadilla in Manuel Antonio. For further information in Costa Rica contact CENARE (Centro Nacional de Rehabilitación, 32-8233 or 32-9749). The best person to talk to is Dr. Federico Montero. They also sponsor weekly wheelchair basketball games.

The only wheelchair-accessible bathrooms in San José are at the **Hotel Aurola Holiday Inn.**

For information in the U.S., contact the **Society for the Advancement of Travel for the Handicapped** (SATH) (26 Court Street, Brooklyn, NY 11242; 718-858-5483); **Travel Information Center** (Moss Rehabilitation Hospital, 1200 West Tabor Road, Philadelphia, PA 19141; 215-329-5715 ext. 9600); **Mobility International USA** (P.O. Box 3551, Eugene, OR 97403; 503-343-1284); or **Flying Wheels Travel** (143 West Bridge Street, P.O. Box 382, Owatonna, MN 55060; 800-535-6790). **Travelin' Talk** (P.O. Box 3534, Clarksville, TN 37043; 615-552-6670), a networking organization, also provides information.

NOTES FOR TRAVELING WITH CHILDREN

Ticos love children. You won't get dirty looks for bringing them along— only smiles and a helping hand when needed. Both men and women seem to be naturally sensitive to the needs of children, whether it be to spontaneously help you lift them on or off the bus, or to include the kids in conversation. If you have a baby (especially a fair-haired one), be prepared to be stopped in the street while people admire your little treasure.

When preparing for your trip, pack a junior first-aid kit with baby aspirin, thermometer, vitamins, diarrhea medicine, sunblock, bug repellent, tissues, and cold medicine.

Pack extra plastic bags for dirty diapers, cloth diapers for emergencies, a portable stroller and papoose-style backpack, a car seat if you plan to use a car, easy-to-wash clothes, swimsuits, a life jacket, beach toys, and picture books relating to Costa Rica.

Try to plan a flight during your child's nap time. Bring everything you need on board—diapers, food, toys, books, and extra clothing for kids and parents alike. It's also helpful to carry a few new toys, snacks, and books as treats if boredom sets in.

Pace your trip so your child can adapt to all the changes in routine. Don't plan exhausting whirlwind tours, and keep travel time to a minimum. You'll be a lot more comfortable if you splurge on a rental car rather than taking the buses. Seek out zoos, parks, plazas, outdoor entertainment, and short excursions to amuse your child. Costa Rica's marketplaces are more fascinating to some children than museums.

Bathrooms are hard to find sometimes, and it is perfectly acceptable for little ones to pee in the bushes or even against a building if you are in the city. Disposable diapers are readily available for trips, but you won't find many places with changing tables. People will help you find the best place to do what has to be done.

In San José, there are not a lot of organized activities for kids, but there are children's theater performances on Sundays and some arts and crafts stuff in the parks. The Friday edition of the "*Viva*" section in the daily *La Nación* lists whatever is happening for children over the weekend. There are not a lot of playgrounds either. Playgrounds, like Central American plumbing, seem to get trashed and ruined overnight. One place most kids will enjoy is the **Parque Nacional de Diversiones** (open Wednesday through Sunday, 9 a.m. to 6:30 p.m., and until 10 p.m. on Friday and Saturday; 31-2072, 31-6823), a large, clean, and well-run amusement park with all kinds of mechanical rides in La Uruca, west of San José. About $4.50 will entitle your kid to all the rides he or she can take in a day. All proceeds go to support the Children's Hospital. There are plenty of places to eat there, but they are all of the greasy fast-food variety, so bring your own snacks and juices. It's located a few kilometers west of Hospital Mexico, the large building you see on the left as you leave the western suburbs of San José heading for Puntarenas. In order to find it, you must get off the main highway and take the access road that runs parallel to the highway directly in front of the hospital.

In San José, Viajes Colón offers a **baby-sitting service** (21-3778, fax: 57-2367, 24-hour hotline: 25-2500).

NOTES FOR TRAVELING WITH PETS

People wishing to bring their cats and dogs into Costa Rica must write, in English, to Dr. Hugo Guzman, Departamento de Zoonosis, Apdo. 10123, 1000 San José, CR (23-0333, ext. 331), asking for an import permit. Include the animal's name, breed, size, color, age, and sex, your planned arrival date, the address where you'll be living in Costa Rica, $5 per animal to cover processing costs, and your current return address. Allow at least six weeks for the permit to be processed and returned to you before you leave.

The cat or dog must then be certified by a registered veterinarian as free of internal and external parasites. The pet must also be up-to-date and certified in its rabies, distemper, hepatitis, parovirus, and leptospirosis vaccinations. The rabies shot must be at least 30 days old, but no older than three years.

If the animal arrives in Costa Rica without these documents, it could be quarantined, refused entry, or destroyed. A month's grace period is allowed if the departure and arrival dates on the *Permiso de Importación* don't correspond with your trip's dates for some reason. Information on requirements for other animals is available from the above address.

People wishing to take cats and dogs out of Costa Rica must present a certificate from a registered Costa Rican veterinarian of a health examination and the animal's vaccination records to the Ministerio de Salud, where the documents will be stamped. They then go to the Banco Central for a *Permiso de Exportación* (export permit). This can be done up to 15 days before leaving the country.

Dogs are not regarded with the same affection as they are in North America and Europe, and are used as guards rather than as pets. Most Costa Ricans are scared to death of dogs. If there is a rabies epidemic, government agents go around feeding poisoned meat to dogs, especially in the countryside. Several friends have lost beloved pets in this way.

Another problem might be finding a temporary place to stay with your pet. In general, bed-and-breakfasts are more willing to take animals.

NOTES FOR STUDENT TRAVELERS

As well as being a full-service travel agency, OTEC (Calle 3, Avenidas 1/3, San José; 22-0866) is affiliated with the **International Youth Hostel Federation** (IYHF). If you are under 26 years old or have a student or teacher ID card, you can become a member for ¢1100 ($8) and a photograph. Affiliated youth hostels exist in San José, Lake Arenal, Rincón de la Vieja National Park, and Guayabo National Monument. An IYHF membership can get you discounts on international flights, and at stores, restaurants, and hotels in Costa Rica.

Viajes Colón gives a 15 to 30 percent discount year-round to students and teachers on tours all over the country, including fishing and white-water rafting. No IYHF membership is necessary. They also arrange hotel discounts for student groups and have a **baby-sitting service** (21-3778, fax: 57-2367, 24-hour hotline: 25-2500).

The **Toruma Youth Hostel** (Avenida Central, Calles 29/31; 24-4085) coordinates low-cost trips to other hostels in the country.

STUDENT DISCOUNTS   You can get a 40 percent discount on LACSA flights to Costa Rica with an International Student Identification Card. To apply for a card ($14) in North America, request a free Student Travel Catalog from the **Council on International Educational Exchange** (CIEE) (205 East 42nd Street, New York, NY 10017; 212-661-1414). The catalog has an application form. With card in hand, one can purchase the discounted ticket only through a student travel agency. Council Travel is a chain of U.S. student travel agencies affiliated with CIEE: a list of locations can be requested at the above address. **Travel Cuts** (187 College Street, Toronto, Ontario; 416-979-2406) is a Canadian student travel agency. Student/teacher/youth ID cards are also available at student travel agencies.

SPECIAL WAYS TO VISIT COSTA RICA

NATURE TOURS

The following agencies organize tours for nature lovers and birdwatchers. Bilingual naturalists accompany small groups into parks and reserves, and arrange for food, lodging, and transportation, which are all included in the trip price. The following Costa Rica-based groups will arrange jaunts for groups of two to ten people, once you are there. All the Costa Rica-based groups listed here donate from 1 to 10 percent of the price of each tour to various ecological and community organizations.

Caribbean Treks and Expeditions
Apdo. 363, San José, CR
23-2125, 33-3992, fax: 23-5785
Trekking, biking, surfing, rafting.

Costa Rica Expeditions
Apdo. 6941, San José, CR
22-0333, fax: 57-1665
Natural history and adventure travel, especially in Monteverde, Tortuguero, and Corcovado; rafting.

Costa Rica Sun Tours
Apdo. 1195, 1250 Escazú, CR
55-3518, 55-3418, fax: 55-4410
Specializing in Pavones and Arenal; bicycle tours of Orosi Valley.

Geotur
Apdo. 469 Y Griega

1011 San José, CR
34-1867, fax: 53-6338
Wildlife observation in Carara, Santa Rosa, Cahuita, and Braulio Carrillo.

Guanacaste Tours
Apdo. 55
5000 Liberia, CR
66-0306, fax: 66-0307
Visits to Arenal, Palo Verde, Santa Rosa, Tamarindo.

Horizontes
Apdo. 1780
1002 San José, CR
22-2022, fax: 55-4513
Nature, cultural, and educational tours to all locations; hiking tours. Can arrange conventions, seminars.

Interviajes
Apdo. 296
3000 Heredia, CR
Phone/fax: 38-1212
Low-cost tours to many locations.

Jungle Trails
Apdo. 5941
1000 San José, CR
55-3486, fax: 55-2782
Camping, hiking, birdwatching, and tree-planting trips, specializing in Volcán Barva. Personalized tour planning.

Temptress Cruises
U.S. phone: 800-336-8423
20-1679, fax: 20-2103
Week-long cruises to national parks on the Pacific with a naturalist guide; scuba diving; photography.

Tikal Tours
Apdo. 6398
1000 San José, CR
23-2811, fax: 23-1916
Visits to all locations.

U.S-BASED NATURE TOUR COMPANIES

Baja Expeditions
San Diego, CA
800-843-6967, 619-581-3311
fax: 619-581-6542

Betchart Expeditions
Cupertino, CA
800-252-4910, 408-252-4910
fax: 408-252-1444

Borderland Productions
Tucson, AZ
602-882-7650

Costa Rica Connection
San Luis Obispo, CA

800-345-7422, 805-543-8823
fax: 805-543-3626

Extraordinary Expeditions
Hailey, ID
800-234-1569
phone/fax: 208-788-2012

Forum Travel
Pleasant Hill, CA
510-671-2900, fax: 510-946-1500

Geo Expeditions
Sonora, CA
800-351-5041, 209-523-0152

Halintours
Austin, TX
512-450-0955, fax: 512-450-0958

Laughing Heart Adventures
Willow Creek, CA
800-541-1256, 916-629-3516

Osprey Tours
Martha's Vineyard, MA
508-645-9049, fax: 508-645-3244

Overseas Adventure Travel
Cambridge, MA
800-221-0814, 617-876-0533
fax: 617-876-0455

Voyagers International
Ithaca, NY
800-633-0299, 607-257-3091
fax: 607-257-3699

Wildland Journeys
Seattle, WA
800-345-4453
206-365-0686

Wings
Tucson, AZ
602-749-1967
fax: 602-749-3175

LANGUAGE LEARNING VACATIONS

Many people like the idea of learning Spanish on their Costa Rican vacation. There are many excellent language schools here, offering a variety of experiences. **Centro Lingüístico Conversa** (see below) has a new lodge overlooking the beautiful Santa Ana Valley with live-in instructors so that families and individuals can enjoy life in rural Costa Rica while studying. **Centro Lingüístico Latinoamericano** trains participants in international service programs, in addition to offering courses for tourists. **Instituto de Lengua Española** is primarily for missionaries, but accepts other students when space is available. It is one of the most intensive and least expensive schools. The **Centro Cultural** teaches Spanish and English (maximum ten students per class), and sponsors plays and concerts by Costa Rican and U.S. performers. They also have a large English-language library and a TV room for viewing CNN. Students must pass through security as they enter. The ICADS Spanish Immersion Program includes lectures and activities emphasizing environmental issues, women's studies, economic development, and human rights, with optional afternoon internships in grassroots organizations. ILISA guarantees a maximum of four students per class and will arrange for students to earn one semester credit for each week of Spanish study (20 hours) evaluated as specified by the Educational Testing Service at Princeton University. ICAI has several different fees for its Spanish courses, depending on the number of weekend tours involved. In addition to its affordable, conversation-oriented classes, **Mesoamerica** has a one-day class on "Survival Spanish for Tourists," which includes lunch and tips about travel and local customs ($60). The **Academia Costarricense de Lenguaje** offers cultural evenings focusing on Latin American customs, foods, and musical traditions, as well as optional courses in Spanish guitar and Latin American dancing!

Most schools arrange for students to live with Costa Rican families to immerse themselves in the language. They also set up weekend sightseeing trips for participants. Class size is small. Intensive conversational methods are used for four to six hours a day in programs lasting from one week to several months. Students are placed according to ability. All language schools assist their students in extending their tourist visas.

Academia Costarricense de Lenguaje
Apdo. 336, 2070 Sabanilla, CR
21-1624, 33-8914, fax: 33-8670

American Institute for Language and Culture
Apdo. 200, 1000 San José, CR
25-4313, fax: 24-4244

Centro Cultural Costarricense- Norteamericano
Apdo. 1489, 1000, San José, CR
25-9433, fax: 24-1480

Centro Lingüístico Conversa
Apdo. 17, Centro Colón, San José, CR
21-7649, fax: 33-2418

Centro Lingüístico Latinoamericano
Apdo. 151, Alajuela, CR
41-0261

Centro Panamericano de Idiomas
Apdo. 947, 1000 San José, CR
phone/fax: 38-0561; U.S. phone: 214-522-1090

Forester Instituto Internacional
Apdo. 6945, 1000 San José, CR
25-3155, fax: 25-9236

Instituto Bilingue Internacional
Apdo. 548, Y Griega, San José, CR
27-9763

**ICADS, Institute for Central American
Development Studies**
Dept. 826 P.O. Box 025216
Miami, FL 33102-5216, USA
In CR: 25-0508, fax: 34-1337

**ICAI, Central American Institute for
International Affairs**
Apdo. 10302, 1000, San José, CR
33-8571, fax: 21-5238

**ILISA, Instituto Latinoamericano
de Idiomas**
Apdo. 1001, 2050 San Pedro, CR
25-2495, 25-5413, 34-0104, fax: 25-4665
In U.S. and Canada: 800-377-2665

Instituto Británico
Apdo. 8184, 1000 San José, CR
34-9454, 25-0256, fax: 53-1894

Instituto de Lengua Española
Apdo. 100, 2350 San José, CR
27-7366, fax: 27-0211

Instituto Universal
Apdo. 219, 2120 San José, CR
57-0441, fax: 23-9917

Intensa
Apdo. 8110, 1000 San José, CR
25-6009, 24-6353, fax: 53-8912

Mesoamerica
Apdo. 300, 1002 San José, CR
33-7710, fax: 33-7221

STUDY PROGRAMS

Spanish, Latin American Culture, Politics, Economy, Literature, Tropical Biology, Ecology, International Relations, International Business—you can study nearly anything in Costa Rica. There are several options for university-level students who want to spend a semester or a year here, as well as shorter seminars for nonstudents. All programs require advance planning, so start thinking about it early. Also, since there are two decidedly different seasons, choose your months according to your preferred weather.

Associated Colleges of the Midwest (ACM) is a competitive program run by and primarily for several private midwestern colleges. However, students at any accredited university or college can apply. The Fall semester (from September to December) offers an intensive course in Spanish and the social sciences (the topic of the course changes each year). Students can do research in an area of their particular interest. The program's Spring semester (from February to May) gives students an opportunity to do two months of field research in the social or physical sciences with some excellent professors. Students live with Costa Rican families. For more information, write:

> Associated Colleges of the Midwest
> 18 South Michigan Avenue
> Suite 1010
> Chicago, IL 60603
> In Costa Rica: 25-0725, fax: 53-5790

Friends World Program of Long Island University maintains its Latin American Regional Center in San José. It focuses on understanding world problems through work and study in countries around the globe. Students in San José take Spanish classes and design their own projects. They may work in national ministries, with experimental agricultural projects, or in rural communities. Students receive credit based on a journal they keep during their projects. For information, write:

> Friends World Program
> Long Island University
> Southampton Campus
> Southampton, NY 11968
> In Costa Rica: phone/fax: 25-0289

The **University of Kansas** runs one-, two-, and three-semester study programs that are open to students who are at least sophomores at any U.S. college or university. Kansas students take full course loads at the University of Costa Rica (UCR) and live with Costa Rican families. The first-semester group arrives for an orientation period in February, a month before UCR classes begin. The second semester group arrives in July. Kansas students like their program for the flexibility it offers them in choosing courses and for the contact they have with Costa Rican students. For more information, write:

> Office of Studies Abroad
> 204 Lippincott Hall
> University of Kansas
> Lawrence, KS 66045

The **State University of New York** at Albany sponsors one- or two-semester programs open to college juniors and seniors with at least two years of college-level Spanish. Students live with Costa Rican families selected by program coordinators at the University of Costa Rica and enroll in regular university courses in any discipline at the UCR. For further information on this program, contact:

> Office of International Programs
> L1-84
> University at Albany
> State University of New York
> Albany, NY 12222

People who would like to enroll directly in the **University of Costa Rica** do so as "Special Students." All foreigners fall into this category for the first two years of their studies at the UCR. Admission fees are about double those for Costa Rican students, but the price is still quite low compared to U.S. standards. There is also the option of being an *oyente* (auditing a class). The first semester runs March through June, the second runs July to December. The office is on the west side of campus, near the Oficina del Registro.

During the December-March break there is a series of *cursos libres* on many subjects. They are open to the public for a nominal registration fee. For more information, contact:

> Oficina de Asuntos Internacionales
> Ciudad Universitaria Rodrigo Facio
> San José, CR
> 24-3660, fax: 25-5822

The **University for Peace** is located on a beautiful tract of forested farmland in Villa Colón, southwest of San José. The goal of the university is to create pilot projects for peace studies programs in universities around the world. By exploring different aspects of peace education and the most effective methods of teaching them to cross-cultural groups, the university hopes to foment fundamental change in the orientation of university programs and to establish peace education in unions, churches, and other community groups. Presently the University for Peace is offering two-year masters degree programs in International Relations, Ecology and Peace, and Human Rights and Peace Education. To request the university's bulletin write:

> University of Peace
> Apdo. 199, 1250 Escazú, CR
> To arrange a visit, call 49-1072
> fax: 49-1929

The **Monteverde Institute** provides educational programs on both local and international levels. It offers long and short courses in tropical ecology and biology for groups from abroad. Students take part in field trips, lectures, and Spanish language study led by core faculty, resident researchers, and scientists. As part of its Community Programs, the institute coordinates workshops and cultural and educational activities, lends support to women's groups in the area, and is responsible for the Volunteer Coordinating Center.

> Monteverde Institute
> Apdo. 10165
> 1000 San José, CR
> 61-1253

The **Organization for Tropical Studies** is a consortium of universities and research institutions dedicated to education, investigation, and conservation in the tropics. They offer "Tropical Biology: An Ecological Approach," a two-month lecture/field experience course, twice a year at their research stations in La Selva, Palo Verde, and Wilson Gardens, as well as several other courses. They also provide logistical support for dissertation research.

> OTS
> P.O. Box DM
> Duke Station
> Durham, NC 27706
> 919-684-5774, in Costa Rica: 40-6696

The **Institute for Central American Development Studies** offers a semester-abroad study program, including coursework and structured internship opportunities in Costa Rica, Nicaragua, and Belize. Subjects offered include Women's Studies, Environment/Ecology, Public Health, Journalism/Videography, and Agriculture. The internships help integrate theory with real-world experiences, and allow students to give something back to the host society through service projects. Fall, Spring, and Summer terms with credit. Noncredit internship placement also available.

> ICADS
> Dept. 826, P.O. Box 025216
> Miami, FL 33102-5216
> In Costa Rica: 25-0508, fax: 34-1337

The **Central American Institute for International Affairs** (ICAI) offers a course on "Central American Issues and Perspectives," including lectures on history, politics, the impact of *perestroika* in the region, environmental issues, and Costa Rica as a model for development. Students meet with government and opposition leaders in Nicaragua and Costa Rica.

Their ten-day seminar, "Investing and Living in Costa Rica," includes legal aspects of *pensionado* status, medical and insurance systems, real estate, rentals, and investments. The month-long seminar, "Spanish and International Business," takes people to industrial and shipping sites, chambers of commerce, and government agencies involved in fomenting exports, while helping them build the vocabulary needed to do business. Lectures dealing with current economic issues are also part of the course.

"Photographing the Natural Treasures of Costa Rica" takes amateur and professional photographers to La Selva Biological Reserve in Sarapiquí and to Puerto Viejo on the Caribbean coast. The week-long tour is offered five times a year.

> ICAI
> P.O. Box 5095
> Anaheim, CA 92814
> 714-527-2918, fax: 714-826-8752
> In Costa Rica: 33-8571, fax: 21-5238

ILISA offers an excellent two-week course, in English, on "Central American History and Culture." Starting with a lecture on the complex historical issues affecting the area, students visit coffee and banana plantations, museums, and the Central Bank, where foreign debt and structural adjustment issues affecting Third World countries are explained.

> ILISA
> Apdo. 1001, San Pedro 2050
> San José, CR
> 25-2495, 25-5413, 34-0104, fax: 25-4665
> In the U.S. and Canada: 800-377-2665

Mesoamerica (The Institute for Central American Studies) runs study tours to Nicaragua ($795, not including airfare) to promote a better understanding between U.S. citizens and the people of Central America. The 12-day tours include five days of orientation seminars in San José and seven days in Nicaragua. Participants meet with high-level government officials, opposition parties, journalists, religious leaders, and academics. There are visits to an agricultural cooperative, historic sites, and local artisan markets.

Mesoamerica's new "Environmental Seminar" topics include deforestation, reforestation, commercial agriculture and pesticide use, the future of the oceans, and the impact of U.S. policy on international environmental issues. Field trips include visits to a rainforest, a coastal national park, and a sustainable agriculture project, as well as a river-rafting trip to a proposed hydroelectric dam site. ICAS will plan special study seminars for interested groups on request.

For those interested in Central American politics, Mesoamerica is a great place to work as an intern. People who are fluent in Spanish and willing to volunteer for at least 20 hours a week for six months can read newspapers and journals, help maintain Mesoamerica's extensive clipping file, do research, and write articles for the monthly newsletter. Internships must be confirmed in advance. College credit can be arranged. Write:

> Mesoamerica
> The Institute for Central American Studies
> Apdo. 300, 1002, San José, CR
> 33-7112, fax: 33-7221

Lifestyle Explorations offers a 13-day tour for those interested in living here with trips to the Atlantic and Pacific coasts as well as San José residential areas. Long-time residents share their experiences.

Lifestyle Explorations
P.O. Box 57-6487
Modesto, CA 95355, USA
209-577-4081

ADDITIONAL TOUR INFORMATION

For other available tours contact:

Costa Rican Tourist Board
B.I.V. Tower, Suite 801
Miami, FL 33131, USA
800-327-7033, 305-358-2150
fax: 305-358-7951

View with sombrilla del pobre.

FOUR

Once You Arrive:
Getting Around in Costa Rica

STREET ADDRESS SYSTEM

As you can see from the Downtown San José map in Chapter 6, San José's streets are laid out in a very logical system: odd-numbered streets (*calles*) are east of Calle Central, even-numbered streets are west. Odd-numbered *avenidas* are north of Avenida Central and even-numbered avenues are south. So if an address is on Calle 17, Avenidas 5/7, it is in the northeastern part of the city.

However, most Ticos completely ignore the street numbering system. *Calles* and *avenidas* appear in the phone book, and that's about it. The accepted way to give directions is from *puntos cardinales* or landmarks. If you call for a taxi, you have to give the name of a church or a *pulpería* (corner store) or a well-known business (like Pollos Kentucky). Then you state how many *metros* you are from there and in what direction. *Cien* (100) *metros* roughly corresponds to one city block. These are some examples of typical ways of giving directions: *"De la pulpería La Luz, cien metros al norte y cincuenta al oeste."* ("From the La Luz grocery store one block north and half a block west.") *"De la Iglesia La Soledad, doscientos al sur y trescientos al este."* ("From the Soledad Church, two blocks south and three blocks east.")

TIQUISMOS—
HAVING FUN WITH COSTA RICAN SPANISH

Ticos are amused and delighted when foreigners try to speak Spanish, especially when they include *tiquismos*, expressions that are peculiar to Costa Rican or Central American culture.

Not only the vocabulary, but the way of using words is important. Spanish speakers use a lot of *muletillas* (fillers, literally "crutches") in their speech. They "address" the person with whom they are speaking more often than is done in English, and they do it in a way that English speakers might consider slightly offensive. It is common for women to be called *mamita, madre, mi hijita* (little mother, mother, my little daughter, all roughly corresponding to "honey"). Latins love to use salient physical characteristics as nicknames. Common ones are *gordo* (fatty), *flaco* (skinny), *macho* or *macha* (Costa Rican for fair-skinned or fair-haired), *negro* (dark-skinned), *chino* (it doesn't matter if you're Asian or just have slightly slanting eyes, your name is Chino), *gato* (blue or green eyes). You just have to be slightly *gordo* or *flaco* to merit those names. If you're really *gordo* or *flaco*, and people really like you, you get a special name like *repollito* (little cabbage) or *palito* (little stick). *Gordo* and *negro* are commonly used as terms of endearment, regardless of appearance.

Any male under 30 is usually called *maje* by his friends. This is a special Costa Rican measure of friendship, which literally means "dummy," but figuratively is more like pal or buddy. It is used widely as a *muletilla*. *Majes* have various expressions of approval—such as the famous *pura vida* (great, terrific), *tuanis* (cool), and *buena nota* (groovy). *Mala nota* is ungroovy, *furris* is uncool, and *salado* means "too bad for you." Expressions of extreme approval are *qué bruto*, *qué bárbaro*, and disapproval, *qué horror*, or *fatal, maje*.

The above expressions are the slang of urban youth. However, all Ticos are aware of polite, courteous, and respectful forms of speech. They make their world more pleasant by using little expressions of appreciation. For example, if someone helps you in a store or on the street, you say "*Muchas gracias, muy amable.*" ("Thank you very much, you are very kind."), and they will say "*Con mucho gusto.*" ("With much pleasure.")

It is customary in the morning to ask, "*¿Cómo amaneció?*" ("How did you wake up?") "*Muy bien, por dicha, ¿y usted?*" ("Very well, luckily, and you?") "*Muy bien, gracias a Dios.*" ("Very well, thank God.")

When talking about a future event or plan, Ticos will often include *si Dios quiere* ("if God wants" or "God willing"): "*Nos vemos el martes, si Dios quiere.*" ("We'll see each other Tuesday, God willing.")

If you are in the city and see someone on the other side of the street whom you know, you call "*¡Adiós!*" In the countryside, when you pass someone on the road, it is customary to say *adiós* even if you don't know them. In these situations, *adiós* means hello. It is only used to mean good-bye when you're going away for good. Everyday good-byes are *hasta luego* (until then, until later), and the other person might add "*Que Dios le acompañe.*" ("May God accompany you.")

Giving a coin to a beggar in the street often earns you a special blessing: he or she will say "*Dios se lo pague.*" ("May God repay you.")

Although "now" and "in a little while" have very different meanings in English, here they can be expressed with the same word: *ahora*. Perhaps this is the linguistic root of the *mañana* attitude that so frustrates gringos. If you want to express the idea of "right away," you can emphatically use the word *¡ya!* keeping in mind that *ya* can also can be used to mean already, later, and soon. Eskimos have 26 different words for snow. Latin Americans have the same words for many different time concepts, perhaps because time is not of such vital importance to their existence. It's what people love and hate about the tropics. Keep that in mind when dealing with the bureaucracy, or when deciding whether or not you have enough time to buy a cold drink when you've been told the bus is coming *ahorititica*.

Vos is a form of second person singular address used throughout Central America instead of *tú*. The verb form used with *vos* is made by changing the *r* on the end of an infinitive to *s* and accenting the last syllable. Thus with the verb *poder*, "*tú puedes*" becomes "*vos podés*," and with *sentirse*, "*tú te sientes*" becomes "*vos te sentís*." Much to the consternation of their Spanish and South American friends, more and more Ticos use the formal *usted* for everyone, probably because it's easier and safer.

Other fillers that are used commonly in Spanish are terms like *fíjate*, *imagínate*, and *vieras que*, for which there are no real equivalents in English. Roughly, they could be translated as "would you believe" or "just think!" These expressions are used to give emphasis to what the speaker is saying. For example: "*¡Fíjate vos que no me dejaron entrar!*" ("Would you believe it—they wouldn't let me in!") Or, you might say, "*Imagínese cómo me dió pena verla así.*" ("Imagine how bad I felt to see her like that.").

Vieras is often used the same way we use "sure" in English: "*¡Vieras qué susto me dió!*" ("I sure was scared!" or, "You should have seen how it scared me!")

Achará is another particularly Tico expression and indicates regret at a loss: "*Fíjese que el perro comió mis begonias. Achará mis florecitas.*" ("Would you believe it—the dog ate my begonias. My poor little flowers!")

When you come to someone's house, especially in the country, it is customary to stand on the ground near the porch and say "*¡Upe!*" as a way of letting

them know you're there. When they ask you to come in, as you enter the house you say "*Con permiso.*" ("With your permission."). If they offer you something to eat, it is much more polite to accept than not to accept. Giving makes people happy, and if you don't let them give to you, it hurts their feelings. People will ask you about your family, whether you're married, how many children you have. Most can't quite grasp the idea of people not being married or not having children. When you're sitting and talking and finally no one can think of anything else to say, you say, "*Pues, sí.*" ("Well, yes.").

Learn some of these expressions and practice them until you don't make any *metidas de pata* (literally, "putting your foot in it," or mistakes). Ticos will be glad to help you. If you do make a mistake, there is a word which is instant absolution: just say, "*¿Diay?*" That means, "Well, what can you expect?" or "What can be done about it?" As you get to know the Ticos, you'll find out that this little word comes in very handy.

FRUITS AND VEGETABLES

The abundance of fresh, delicious fruits and vegetables in Costa Rica is amazing. You can get an idea of it by elbowing your way through the **Mercado Borbón** (Calle 8, Avenidas 3/5), a two-level circus of fruit and vegetable vendors in a rough-and-tumble part of San José. Or you can go to any of the Saturday morning *ferias del agricultor*, where streets are shut off and truck farmers bring their fresh produce to the neighborhoods. In San José, the Saturday morning market is west of Plaza Víquez (Calles 7/9, Avenidas 16/20). There you will find fresh homemade whole wheat bread and pastries, eggs, chickens, fish, cheese, and honey, as well as every imaginable fruit and vegetable. Bring your own shopping bags. Many suburbs of San José also have their Saturday street markets: Escazú, Guadalupe, and Zapote, to name a few.

Unfortunately, pesticide use is still unregulated in Costa Rica, and most farmers are not aware of organic gardening. However, a small group of farmers from the Cartago area is experimenting with organic methods. Call 73-6079 for more information (Spanish only).

Here are some tips on how to identify and choose the best produce:

A ripe **papaya** will always be slightly soft, but a too-soft papaya should be avoided. It is customary for papaya vendors to cut a triangular piece out of the papaya to show you its color. Some people are fans of the rounder *amarilla* or yellow-orange papaya. Others will swear that only the more elongated and red-orange *cacho* papaya is worthy of the name. You don't have to buy a papaya just because the vendor cut a piece out of it for you. At least Ticos don't. Just make sure you feel it first.

Mangos should be slightly soft and red and yellow in color, without any brown or mushy spots. By far the most delicious are the large *mangas*, given feminine gender because of their voluptuous size. The neatest way to eat mangas is to slice them close around the flat oval seed to get two meaty halves. With the skin-side down, score each piece into one-inch divisions without cutting through the skin. Now gently turn each half inside out, and you will have a bunch of delicious bite-sized pieces offering themselves to you.

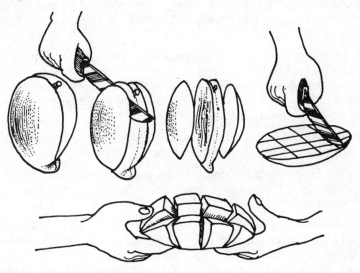

Ticos love to eat green mangos sliced and sprinkled with lemon and salt. Some people get a rash or irritation around their lips from eating mangos. This can be avoided by cutting off the part of the fruit nearest the stem, as the irritation is caused by the sap.

Ticos judge the ripeness of a **piña** (pineapple) by giving it a slap. A good piña should sound firm and compact. The yellow pineapple is best for eating. The white pineapple is more acid and is used in cooking and to tenderize meats. It produces a hollow sound when thumped. A green color on the outside does not necessarily mean the fruit is unripe. You should be able to pluck a leaf easily from the top of a ripe piña.

Sandías (watermelons) are considered sweeter if they produce a firm rather than a hollow sound. The best watermelons come from the hot coastal zones. One of the nicest parts of driving to Puntarenas is stopping at the fruit stands in Esparza for a delicious sandía.

Don't make the mistake of a friend of ours who, on a hot San José afternoon, came home with what he thought was a delicious, red, juicy watermelon. "And what a bargain!" he said as he thirstily cut into the *chiverre*, only to find a mass of whitish spaghetti-like pulp. Chiverre looks just like a watermelon from the outside. You'll see them sold on the roadsides during Semana Santa. Their pulp is candied with *tapa dulce* to make special Easter treats.

Melón (cantaloupe) is judged for sweetness by its firm sound, but a fragrant smell is the best indication of a fully ripe melón.

Moras (blackberries) are used mainly in *refrescos* and ice cream. You have to liquefy moras in a blender and then strain and add sugar and water to the sour juice.

Four types of **limones** (lemons) grow here. The seedless *verdelio* is rare. The *criollo* is small, juicy, and greener. The *bencino* is more the size of a North American lemon but is green and has much less juice than the criollo. The *limón mandarina* looks like a bumpy tangerine, and is very sour and juicy. It's good for making lemonade.

Guayabas (guavas) are plentiful in Costa Rica from September through November. Their pink fruit is used for jam or guava paste.

Cas is a little round fruit similar to the guayaba whose tart tropical flavor is popular in *refrescos* and sherbets. Try the *nieve de cas* at Pop's, a local ice cream chain.

Tamarindo is a tart and sweet *refresco* made from the seed pod of the tamarind tree. You will see the orange-sized balls of brown tamarindo seeds and pulp at the markets. The seeds are put in hot water so the sticky tamarindo washes off. Then sugar and cold water are added. The resulting light brown *refresco* is somewhat similar in flavor to apple juice.

Granadillas (passion fruit) are yellowish-red and slightly larger than an egg. They have a crisp, but easily broken shell. Inside are little edible seeds surrounded by a delicious, delicately flavored fruit, which is first slurped and then chewed.

Marañón is an unusual fruit. Its seed, the cashew nut, grows on top of it in a thick, rubbery shell. Don't try to bite open the shell; it's very bitter. Cashews must be roasted before they can be eaten; they are poisonous when raw. The ripe fruit can be eaten or made into a *refresco* or fermented into wine. The dried fruit is like a cross between a prune and a fig and is sold in supermarkets. You can make a quick and elegant dessert with half a dried marañón topped with a dollop of cream cheese and a cashew.

Avocados are called **aguacates**. They are usually a little less buttery and flavorful than their North American counterparts. They are soft when ripe, but if bought green can be left inside a paper bag to ripen.

Zapotes look like big brown avocadoes, and their texture is avocado-like, but their pulp is bright red-orange and sweet. Some places make zapote ice cream.

Fresh **coco** (coconut meat) can be found at fruit stands downtown. *Pipas* or green coconuts are popular with Ticos on hot days at the beach. They are sold whole, with a straw stuck through a hole in the outer shell so that the coconut water can be drunk.

The best way to get coconut meat out of its shell is to hack it open with a machete or a hammer and then heat the shells on top of the stove in a pan. This makes the meat shrink a little bit so that it is easier to remove.

Pejibaye, a relative of the coconut, is one of Costa Rica's most unusual treats. *Pejibayes* grow in clusters on palm trees, like miniature coconuts. The part that you eat would correspond to the fibrous husk, while the hard *pejibaye* seed, when cracked open, reveals a thin layer of bitter white meat around a hollow core. The bright orange or red pejibayes are delicious boiled in salted water, then peeled, halved and pitted and eaten alone or with mayonnaise. You'll see them sold on San José streets year-round. Their flavor is difficult to describe. They are not sweet, but more a combination of chestnut and pumpkin with a thick, fibrous texture. You can buy a *racimo* (bunch) of raw *pejibayes* at the Mercado Borbón and boil them up for parties, or you can buy them in the supermarkets peeled and canned to take home as souvenirs.

Palmito (palm heart) is another delicacy worth trying. It is sold raw in the supermarkets or tenderly pickled in jars or bags. It is the succulent inner core of small palm trees. Even though whole trees must be cut so that you can savor palmito, the trees are cultivated as a crop, so are replaced.

As human nature would have it, the most highly prized fruits in Costa Rica are imported apples, grapes, and pears. They signify the advent of the Christmas season, and Ticos pay big prices for them. Recently though, highland Ticos have started to grow a sweet-tart variety of apple that we think is much better than the Delicious. You also might enjoy the native **manzana de agua**, a dark-red, pear-shaped fruit which is light and refreshing to eat when ripe.

Mamones are little green spheres, which you can break open with your fingers or teeth to expose a large seed covered with a layer of fruit that tastes like a peeled grape.

Pejibaye

Mamón chino is the mamón's exotic cousin, sporting a red shell with soft spines growing all over it. It resembles a fat, round, red caterpillar and has an even larger delicious grapelike fruit inside its outrageous shell.

When you slice a yellow **carambola**, the pieces look like five-pointed stars. It makes a delicious *refresco*.

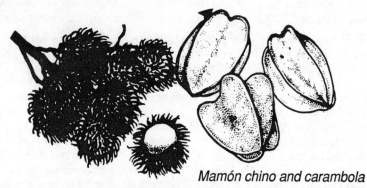

Mamón chino and carambola

COMIDA TÍPICA (NATIVE FOOD)

Those who expect to find spicy food anywhere south of the border will be disappointed in Costa Rican cuisine. It is quite bland for the most part and doesn't have a whole lot of variety. But, except for being a little heavy-handed with the grease, Ticos have a wholesome high-fiber diet, with rice and beans included in every menu. Lunch is the big meal of the day, and many businesses still give two hours off at lunchtime so that people can take the bus back to mama's for a substantial *casado*. People often content themselves with soup and toast in the evening. Those who stay in Costa Rica develop a certain affection for the noble bean, and a good *gallo pinto* is really a delight. Ticos who want to spice up their food usually have a jar of tiny pickled red and yellow chilies on the table. Be wary of these if you see them in a restaurant. They are pure fire!

Sodas are small restaurants where you can get inexpensive snacks and light meals. They line the streets of San José and fill the Mercado Central. These are some of the foods you'll run across at *sodas* or at the Fiesta de Maíz in La Garita in Alajuela.

> *arreglados*—sandwiches, usually made of meat, on a tasty but greasy bun
>
> *arroz con pollo*—rice with chicken and vegetables
>
> *cajeta de coco*—delicious fudge made of coconut, *tapa dulce*, and orange peel
>
> *casado*—a plate of rice, black beans, cabbage and tomato salad, meat or egg, *picadillo*, and sometimes fried plantains

ceviche—raw seabass cured in lemon juice with *culantro* (chinese parsley) and onions—delicious

chorreados—corn pancakes, sometimes served with *natilla*

cono capuchino—an ice cream cone dipped in chocolate

dulce de leche—a thick syrup made of milk and sugar

elote asado—roasted corn on the cob

elote cocinado—boiled corn on the cob

empanadas—corn turnovers filled with beans, cheese, or potatoes and meat

gallo pinto—the national breakfast dish of rice and beans fried together

gallos—meat, beans, or cheese between two tortillas

guiso de maíz—fresh corn stew

horchata—a sweet drink made of corn and cinnamon

masamorra—corn pudding

melcochas—candies made from raw sugar

milanes and tapitas—small, foil-wrapped, pure chocolate candies, available in corner stores and restaurants all over the country. Beware: these delicious little things are addictive

natilla—sour cream, often more liquid than North American sour cream

olla de carne—literally "pot of meat," but actually a meat soup featuring large pieces of *chayote* (a green, pear-shaped vegetable that grows on vines), *ayote* (a pumpkin-like squash), *yuca*, *plátano*, or other vegetables

palomitas de maíz—"little doves," or popcorn

pan bon—a dark, sweet bread with batter designs on top—a Limón specialty

pan de maíz—a thick, sweet bread made with fresh corn

patacones—fried, mashed green plantains, served like french fries with meals on the Atlantic Coast

patí—flour-based *empanadas* filled with fruit or spicy meat, sold on the Atlantic Coast

picadillo—a side dish of fried vegetables, often containing meat

plátanos—plantains. They look like large bananas, but cannot be eaten raw. Sweet and delicious when fried or baked. Also sold like potato chips. A Central American staple

queque seco—pound cake

refrescos—cold fruit drinks. Most refrescos are made with a lot of sugar. If you order a refresco that is not made in advance, like *papaya en agua, papaya en leche*, or *jugo de zanahoria* (carrot juice), you can ask for it *sin azúcar* (without sugar) and add your own to taste. Similarly, an *ensalada de frutas* (fruit salad) might come smothered in jello and ice cream. You can ask for it *sin gelatina, sin helados*

sopa de mondongo—tripe soup

sopa negra—soup made from bean gravy, with hard-boiled egg and vegetables added

tacos—a bit of meat topped with cabbage and tomato salad

tamal asado—a sweet cornmeal cake

tamal de elote—sweet corn tamales, wrapped in cornhusks

tamales—cornmeal, usually stuffed with pork or chicken, wrapped in banana leaves and boiled—a Christmas tradition

tapa dulce—native brown sugar, sold in a solid form that looks like an inverted flower pot. It's grated with a knife or boiled into a syrup from which is made *agua dulce*, a popular *campesino* drink

torta chilena—a many-layered cake filled with *dulce de leche*

tortas—sandwiches on bread rolls

tortilla—may mean the Costa Rican thin, small, corn tortilla, but also another name for an omelette

tortilla de queso—a large, thick tortilla with cheese mixed into the dough

yuca—manioc, a thick tuber, another staple of the Central American diet. *Enyucados* are *empanadas* made from a yucca-based dough.

SOUVENIRS

Tiny *huacas*, copies of pre-Columbian jewelry representing frogs, lizards, turtles, and humanesque deities, are relatively inexpensive and make lovely necklaces, earrings, and tiepins. Some nice copies of pre-Columbian jadework and ceramics are sold around the National Theater. Authentic pre-Columbian artifacts are not allowed to be taken out of the country, so don't believe anyone who tells you something is original. If it is original, the item has been stolen from an archeological site.

If you need lightweight souvenirs, there are T-shirts, or jewelry made of wood and metal. Colorful scarves, hats, blouses, bags, and sun visors with motifs of native flora and fauna are unusual souvenirs made by Go Bandannas. Their creative coloring and activity book, *Let's Discover Costa Rica*, is the answer for the kids on your souvenir list. They are sold almost everywhere.

If you're staying for a while, take advantage of the low prices and excellent work of local tailors and seamstresses. They make fine formal clothes, or can copy your favorite designs. Ask well-dressed Ticos whom they would recommend.

You can buy freshly ground coffee or coffee beans at the Central Market or in souvenir shops. It is usually ground finer than percolator coffee, for use in the *chorreador*, a filter bag that hangs from a wooden stand. There are percolator grinds available in supermarkets, where you'll find *Caferica*, a delicious coffee liqueur, as well as dried bananas, coconut twirls, macadamia nuts, cashews, and yummy El Angel jams, fruit leathers, and pastes. A *tapa dulce*, the native hard brown sugar, can be grated to add a rich flavor to baked goods or used on cereal and in coffee. We've heard of tourists who take home cases of **Salsa Lizano**, a tasty bottled sauce that Ticos love to sprinkle on their *gallo pinto*.

Be sure to stop by the **Tienda de la Naturaleza** at Volcán Poás. It sells delightful handicrafts made by people living near the national parks, thus helping the benefits of tourism to filter down to local *campesinos*.

An extraordinary woodworker is Paul Smith, one of the early settlers in Monteverde. His lovingly crafted bowed instruments are made of European wood aged for ten years. You can find Smith at his Grecia workshop (44-6990). (See the San José chapter for other talented woodcrafters.)

The capital of Costa Rican **woodcraft** is Sarchí, about an hour northwest of San José (see Chapter Seven). Everything from salad bowls to rocking chairs to miniature ox carts can be purchased there (the rocking chairs fold, and the ox carts come apart for easy transport). The capital of Costa Rican **leathercrafts** is Moravia, a suburb of San José, where there are couple a couple of blocks filled with souvenir shops near the main square. (Moravia buses leave frequently from Avenida 3, Calles 3/5, near Parque Morazán.)

If you are going to Monteverde, save some of your souvenir budget for CASEM, the women's crafts cooperative there, which specializes in embroidered and hand-painted clothing depicting cloud-forest wildlife. You'll see it on the right as you enter Monteverde. There is also a **crafts cooperative** on the main square in Ciudad Quesada. **Laurel's Creations** in Cahuita makes stunning hand-painted beach dresses and shirts. Don't miss them.

Wicker, raffia, and woven palm-leaf items should be spray varnished when you get home. Don't be tempted to but tortoise shell or alligator-skin goods—they are made from endangered animals that are internationally protected. Customs officials at your home-country airport will confiscate those items.

TIPPING

A 10 percent service charge and a 12 percent tax are included in your restaurant bill, so it is not customary to tip unless you really feel like it. It is not customary to tip taxi drivers either. In fact, a nice thing about Costa Rica is that people are not standing around with their hands out all the time—

partly because tourism is so new, partly because of a tradition of equality and pride. We hope that these qualities survive the influx of massive tourism here. You would be surprised to know how little the staff at most hotels, including luxury hotels, earns (usually less than $150/month), so a little gratuity here and there is certainly helpful, especially if you have appreciated the service received.

BUSINESS HOURS

Costa Ricans tend to start the day early. You'll find that stores are generally open from 8 or 9 a.m. until 6 or 7 p.m., six days a week (most businesses are closed Sunday). Many establishments still shut their doors sometime between 11:30 a.m. and 2:30 p.m. for a two-hour lunch. Core banking hours are 9 a.m. to 3 p.m.; government offices are open from 8 a.m. to 4 or 5 p.m.

METRIC CONVERSION

Costa Rica uses the metric system. Conversions are as follows: one mile = 1.6 kilometers; one pound = .45 kilos; one gallon = 3.8 liters; and 32° Fahrenheit = 0° Centigrade (freezing).

TIME ZONE

All of Costa Rica is on central standard time, which is six hours behind Greenwich mean time.

COMMUNICATIONS

While Costa Rica boasts more phones per capita than any other Latin American country, patience and perseverance are still key when dealing with the communications bureaucracies.

COUNTRY CODES

Throughout the text, Costa Rica phone numbers are listed without the country code, which is 506. Other country codes you may need are 505 for Nicaragua and 507 for Panamá.

TELEPHONES

Pay telephones take ¢5, ¢10, and ¢20 coins, so bring a stack of them. Put a coin in the groove at the top of the box. Pick up the receiver and dial. The phone will start to beep. When the person answers, the call is sometimes cut off. Go to another phone. This one probably has a long line of people waiting in front of it. They already know that the phone you tried to use is *malo*. When you finally get through, be prepared for a second series of beeps after a few minutes. These mean that you are about to be cut off. Drop in another coin if you still want to talk. It's wise to tell the person you're calling the number of your pay phone so they can call you back and you can talk uninterrupted. The number is often posted above the phone on a yellow sign. Good luck.

In rural areas, like Puerto Viejo or Monteverde, hotels and *pulperías* have phones to call out on. They do the dialing and charge you for the length of time you speak.

INTERNATIONAL CALLS

The access numbers for credit card calls are: 114 for ATT, 162 for MCI, and 163 for Sprint. If you have access to a private phone, direct dialing is easy from Costa Rica. The telephone directory has a list of codes for various countries. To dial the U.S. or Canada direct, for example, dial 001 first, then the area code and number. To call person-to-person or collect, dial 09 first, then the country code minus its zeros then the area code and number. The operator will then come on the line. For international information, dial 124. If you don't have access to a phone in San José, go to **Radiográfica** (open 7 a.m. to 10 p.m., Calle 1, Avenida 5) or **Telecomunicaciones Internacionales** (TI) (open 7 a.m. to 10 p.m., Avenida 2, Calles 1/3).

FAX SERVICES

The above two companies also offer telex and fax services. You can send or have faxes sent to you at their numbers: 23-1609 (Radiográfica) or 57-2272 (TI). Call Radiográfica (87-0513, 87-0511) to check whether you have received a fax, or Telecomunicaciones (55-0444), or tell your correspondent to include your number in the fax and you will be notified when it is received.

MAIL

In San José, the Main Post Office (Correo Central) is located on Calle 2, Avenidas 1/3. Mail letters from a post office. There are hardly any mailboxes on the streets, and they are seldom used.

Beware of having anything other than letters and magazines sent to you in Costa Rica. A high duty is charged on all items arriving by mail, in an attempt to keep foreign merchandise from entering illegally. Receiving packages can mean two trips to the *Aduana* (customs office) in Zapote, a suburb of San José. The first trip is to unwrap and declare what you have received. The second one, three to five days later, is to pay a customs charge on every item in the package before you can take it home. If the package contains food or cosmetics, it must be examined by the Ministry of Health and the process takes even longer.

Photographs can be received duty-free if just a few are sent at a time. Individually sent cassette tapes can also make it through. Usually anything that fits in a regular-sized or magazine-sized envelope will arrive duty-free. But you will have to pay outrageous fees for a box of blank checkbooks, or the cookies Grandma sends to remind you she cares—in short, beg your loved ones **not** to send you anything. Once the duty has been assessed, you can't even have the package sent back. It will be confiscated by the *Aduana*.

You can send most things from Costa Rica to North America or Europe with no problem, although postal rates for packages are pretty high. Mail packages from the entrance to the far left of the main entrance as you face the downtown San José Post Office. Surface mail (*marítimo*) is somewhat cheaper than *correo aéreo* (airmail), and takes four to six weeks to arrive.

There is a general delivery service (*Lista de Correos*). If you are planning to stay in Costa Rica for a while, you can rent a post office box (*apartado—Apdo.* for short), or have your mail sent to a friend's box, which is safer than having it sent to a street address. However, there have been a lot of complaints lately about mail theft in the government postal system. That is why we list fax numbers instead of *apartados* in this book whenever possible. Many people are turning to private mail services. You can sign up with **Interlink** (32-2544, 32-4725), which, for $15/month, gives you a post office box in Miami from which mail is delivered to you once a week in Costa Rica. Interlink also allows you to send or receive up to four pounds of mail per month, lets you subscribe to periodicals at U.S. resident prices, gives you access to catalog and toll-free ordering, and offers you a 10 percent discount on courier service.

LAUNDRY

Laundromats are uncommon in Costa Rica because most people have maids or relatives who do their laundry for them. Many hotels have laundry services. Most cheaper hotels have large sinks (*pilas*), where you can wash your own clothes, or they can connect you with a woman who will wash for you for about $1 an hour. There are many *lavanderías* (non-self-service laundries) in San José, but they are quite expensive. Recently, some self-service laundromats have opened up—**Lava Más** (25-1645) in Los Yoses, next to Spoon, **Beta-matic** (34-0993) behind Burger King, and **Lava y Seca** (24-5908) in San Pedro—where it costs about $3.50 to wash and dry one load of clothes.

LOCAL TRANSPORTATION

FROM THE AIRPORT

Taxi service into San José is about $8 per taxi. A bus (25 cents) goes into San José, but you can't take much baggage on it.

TAXIS

Taxis are relatively inexpensive by northern standards. Drivers are supposed to use computerized meters, called *marías*, in the San José metropolitan area or for trips of 12 kilometers or less. As soon as you get in the cab they should press a button and "60" should appear on the meter. If they don't put the *maría* on, ask them how much they will charge you to get to your destination. Prepare yourself by asking beforehand at your hotel how much it should cost to get to where you're going. Also check the official rates, because they might have changed. Official rates in October 1992 are ¢60 for the first kilometer and ¢25 for each additional kilometer, with a 20 percent increase after 11 p.m. Each hour that a *taxista* waits for you costs ¢400.

Many taxi drivers do not use their meters or claim that they are broken. Legally, they must have a letter from the Ministerio de Obras Públicas y Transporte certifying that their *maría* does not work. Passengers can take down their license plate number (*número de placa*) and report it to the MOPT if they refuse to use their meters in a 12-kilometer radius of San José. If you are going more than 12 kilometers, agree on a rate with the driver before you get into a taxi.

There are many honest taxi drivers and many dishonest ones. Even if they overcharge you, their rates are very reasonable compared to other places but it's good to know your rights. If you are on a budget, watch out for taxis that are called for you by hotels. They charge more because the hotel gets a cut. It is not customary to tip taxi drivers here.

Taxis can come in handy if you want to visit hard-to-get-to places but do not want the expense of renting a car. You can take an inexpensive bus trip to the town nearest your destination and hire a jeep-taxi to take you the rest of the way. Usually taxis hang out around the main square of any small town. It's best to ask several drivers how much they charge to make sure you are getting the going rate.

CARS FOR HIRE

As an alternative to a taxi, your hotel can probably recommend a bilingual driver you can hire to show you around.

HITCHHIKING

Because bus service is widely available, most people prefer to take buses. Hitchhiking is rare. In the countryside, where bus service is infrequent or nonexistent, cars often stop to offer rides to people on foot.

BUSES

Since most Costa Ricans don't have cars, buses go almost everywhere. Most buses that travel between San José and the provinces are quite comfortable, and fares rarely run more than $2-$6 to go anywhere in the country. Some provincial buses are a bit rickety, but all buses are fairly punctual. Buses from San José to the provinces are crowded on Friday and Saturday and the day preceding a holiday or three-day weekend. Likewise, it is difficult to get buses back to San José on Sunday, Monday, and the day following a holiday. This is especially true when trying to make connections in Liberia, Puntarenas, Quepos, and Limón.

Some buses don't have buzzers or bells to tell the driver when you want to get off. When the bus gets close to your stop, shout "*¡La parada!*" or whistle loudly. If you are traveling cheaply by bus, it's a good idea to bring as little with you as possible and leave most of your luggage at your hotel. Big suitcases are very inconvenient for bus travel.

The second half of this book gives detailed information on transportation, including locations of bus stops and numbers to call to check schedules. English is usually not spoken.

The **ICT** (Tourism Institute) (underneath the Plaza de la Cultura, Calle 5, Avenidas Central/2; 22-1090) keeps an updated, computerized list of bus stops and related information.

SAN JOSÉ AND SUBURBAN BUSES   The *Sabana–Cementerio* bus will take you through the area between downtown and the Sabana. Downtown, it stops at Parque Central (Calle 7, Avenida Central), Parque Morazán, and the Post Office. The San Pedro buses (Avenida 2, Calles 5/7) cover the eastern side of the city, through Los Yoses to San Pedro. The northern and southern boundaries of downtown are only an eight- or nine-block walk from Avenida Central. Most urban buses cost about 10 cents. Suburban buses cost 15 to 20 cents and run from 5 a.m. to 10 or 11 p.m.

If you are returning to San José by bus from the north or west, and want to get all the way downtown, get off early on Paseo Colón and hop on the *Sabana–Cementerio*. That way you avoid going to the Coca Cola or some other bad neighborhood terminal. (**The Coca Cola** is a large bus terminal on Calle 16 between Avenidas 1/3.) Following is a list of *paradas* (bus stops) for buses to the suburbs:

> Coronado: Avenida 3, Calles 3/5
> Curridabat: Calle 3, Avenidas 2/4
> Escazú: Avenida 6, Calles 12/14 (minibus); Avenida 1, Calles 16/18 (big bus)
> Guadalupe: Avenida 3, Calles 1/3
> La Uruca: Calle 6, Avenidas 3/5
> Moravia: Avenida 3, Calles 3/5
> Pavas: Avenida 1, Calles 16/18
> Sabanilla: Calle 7, Avenidas 2/4
> San Ramón de Tres Ríos: Calle 7, Avenida 2
> Santa Ana: The Coca Cola
> Villa Colón: The Coca Cola

BUSES TO PANAMÁ AND NICARAGUA   Since both Panamá and Nicaragua are somewhat unstable, it is essential to talk to people who have been there recently before going. Be sure to get an exit visa if you have been in Costa Rica more than 90 days (see Chapter Three).

People who have only read about Nicaragua in the headlines are usually surprised by the friendliness of the Nicaraguan people and their willingness to talk about their lives. You do have to watch out for contaminated water carrying amoebas or hepatitis. Because of the desperate economic situation there, it is good to bring simple things that people might need, like toilet paper, pens, toothpaste, clothes, and canned or dried food. U.S. citizens don't need a visa to enter, but Canadians do. For the latest rules, check with the Nicaraguan Consulate (33-8747). Most car rental agencies will not allow you to rent a car to go to Nicaragua. Airfare from Costa Rica costs about $98 one way. See the Guanacaste chapter for travel tips on Rivas, San Juan del Sur, Granada, and Isla de Ometepe.

The SIRCA bus leaves San José (Calle 11, Avenida 2; 22-5541; $9 one way) for Managua at 6 a.m. Sunday, Wednesday, and Friday. **Tica Bus** (Calle 9, Avenida 4; 21-9229, 21-8954; $9.30 one way) has better buses than SIRCA and goes to Managua daily at 7:30 a.m., arriving around 5 p.m. Make reservations several days in advance; Tica buses continue all the way to Guatemala.

People used to go to Panamá to change dollars and buy film before continuing to South America, but the economic situation is very precarious there now. Between the police and the robbers, personal safety is not assured. U.S. citizens and Canadians can get a 30-day tourist card for entry by land or air from **Copa** (Calle 1, Avenida 5; 23-7033, 21-5596), the Panamanian airline. Other nationalities should check with the Panamanian Consulate (open 8 a.m. to 12 noon; 25-0667) about visa requirements. Tica Bus (Calle 9, Avenida 4; 21-9229, 21-8954; $17 one way) leaves for Panama City daily at 10 p.m., arriving at 5 p.m. TRACOPA buses (Avenida 18, Calle 4; 21-4214, 23-7685; $7.50) leave San José daily at 7:30 a.m. and 12 noon, and arrive in David, Panamá, at 4:30 p.m. and 9 p.m. From David, you can get hourly buses to Panamá City (seven hours), or an express bus at 12 noon or 12 midnight (five and one-half hours). You can avoid at least seven hours on the bus by flying with SANSA to Coto 47 (Monday through Saturday, 10:30 a.m., $23 one way, see below) and taking a taxi to Paso Canoas on the border, then catching a bus from there. The border closes for lunch from 12 noon to 2 p.m. It's very hot and muggy in Paso Canoas. Airfare from San José to Panama City is $124 one way. See the Atlantic Coast section for travel tips on Bocas del Toro on the Caribbean in northern Panamá, crossing the border from Sixaola in Costa Rica.

TRAINS

Train service to Limón, the famed "Jungle Train," has been discontinued. A large landslide and an even larger operational deficit caused the demise of the old railroad, which would have completed its hundredth year of service on December 7, 1990. The only train service in the country now is between San Pedro (the university district east of San José) and Heredia. It leaves Heredia at 6:15 a.m., 1 p.m., and 6 p.m., returning from San Pedro at 12 noon and 5 p.m. The trip takes 45 minutes (26-0011).

PLANES

Because of Costa Rica's mountainous terrain, small aircraft are frequently used. A 20-minute flight can get you to Quepos and Manuel Antonio on the Pacific Coast, instead of spending three and one-half hours on a bus. SANSA, a local government-subsidized airline, flies very inexpensively to all corners of the country. Their flights are often delayed because of mechanical or weather problems. This has led to the creation of a new, unsubsidized local airline, **Travelair.** Although their flights cost two or three times as much as SANSA's, it's worth it for their increased reliability. For instance, SANSA flights to Guanacaste run $25 one way, while Travelair costs $50-$57. SANSA costs $11 to Quepos, Travelair, $30. Schedules and prices for SANSA and Travelair are included in the sections on: Barra del Colorado (near Tortuguero), Limón (near Cahuita and Puerto Viejo de Talamanca), Golfito (near Corcovado), Palmar Sur (near Drake Bay), Quepos (near Manuel Antonio), and Nosara, Carrillo, Sámara, and Tamarindo in Guanacaste.

Check current timetables before making plans. Make reservations at least two weeks in advance during the dry season, but note: *Your SANSA reservation means nothing until you have bought your ticket.* A microbus will take you to the Juan Santamaría Airport from the SANSA office on Calle 24, north of Paseo Colón. SANSA planes leave from the smaller terminal west of the main air terminal. In some places, like Quepos, SANSA buses will pick you up at your hotel for the return trip. SANSA (tours: 23-4179, 33-2714; reservations: 33-0397, 33-3258, fax: 55-2176) also offers some of the cheapest tour packages around to the areas they serve. In some places, like Manuel Antonio, there are buses to take you from your hotel to the airstrip for the return trip.

Travelair (32-7883, fax: 20-0413) planes leave from the Tobías Bolaños airport in Pavas, a suburb to the west of San José. Another advantage over SANSA is that they have Sunday flights to and from Quepos, Golfito, Palmar Sur, Carrillo, and Tamarindo.

Small, five-passenger planes can be rented for $220/hour (one motor), $290/hour (two motors). Seven-passenger planes cost around $400/hour. Most of the smaller planes leave from the Tobías Bolaños smallcraft airport near Pavas ($2 by taxi from San José). Look for them under *"Aviación"* in the phone book (*directorio telefónico*).

DRIVING IN COSTA RICA

CAR RENTALS

Car rental costs $52/day, including insurance and mileage (four-wheel-drive vehicles cost $80/day). All major rent-a-car agencies have branches in Costa Rica. You're more likely to get a special rate if you book a rental car in your country of origin. Local companies are fairly uniform in their rates, although you can often get a 10 percent discount during the off-season. If you don't have an American Express, Visa, Diners Club, or MasterCard, you must leave a deposit of $600 to $1000, depending on the company. Valid foreign drivers licenses are good in Costa Rica for three months. **Toyota** rents tents and coolers. If you are already here, reserve a car as far in advance as possible. Look under "*alquiler de automoviles*" in the phone book.

Note that all repairs must be okayed first with the main office, or you will not be reimbursed. According to Jim Corven's excellent Consumer Almanac column in *The Tico Times*, "Since most rental cars are compacts with small engines and the terrain is rarely level, stickshift is the norm. Coupled with the lethal potholes and winding roads, these cars must endure conditions unseen elsewhere. Breakdowns are major inconveniences at best; at worst they're complete trip-spoilers. Reduce your chances of a breakdown by checking the car out thoroughly before heading out. Do not assume the agency did it for you. Check the oil, water, brake fluid, tire pressure, air conditioner, lights, belts, and hoses while still in San José. Make certain there is a spare tire and jack. Also report any small nicks or dents on the surface. If you have any concern, whatsoever, contact the agency for service. You will have far less chance of getting their understanding after you've driven the car for a couple of days and develop problems." He also points out that the insurance you pay covers damage to vehicles, but not to your possessions within the vehicle. **Adobe, Budget,** and **National Rentacar** agencies are the only ones that allow customers to decline the regular insurance coverage and use their limited American Express card auto rental insurance (*The Tico Times*, February 14, 1992).

Renting a car makes exploring easier and is less time-consuming than taking the bus. However, renting a car just to get around San José is more hassle than it's worth. The cars must be left in parking lots at all times. Traffic is crazy. Left turns from right lanes are not uncommon. Taxis or buses are much cheaper and easier for city travel.

If you do rent a car, do not leave anything in it, even for a minute, unless it is in a well-guarded place. Rent-a-car plates are an open invitation to thieves.

Rental cars are also becoming an open invitation to certain policemen who stop tourists for "speeding," tell them they must appear in court at an inconvenient time in an inconvenient place, then offer to let them "pay on the spot" to avoid ruining their vacation. Law-abiding tourists fall for this ploy, and the cop supplements his meager salary (often under $200/month) by one or two thousand *colones*. You are not required to pay any policeman anything at any time. Just take the ticket and drive away. The car rental agency will make sure that your payment gets into the right hands upon your return. Officers are legally required to show their *carné* (ID card) on request, so if you feel you are being harassed or unduly pressured, get the ID number or at least the license plate number and report the officer to the Ministerio de Transporte (27-2188, ext. 546).

MOTORCYCLES

Heat Rentamoto (21-6671, fax: 21-3786) leases motorcycles for $20-$25/day, $5-$7/hour in San José. They also have offices in Montezuma, Limón, and Quepos.

MAPS

Small yellow posts mark the distance in kilometers from San José on Costa Rica's highways, but these aren't enough to find your way around. If you're going to be traveling on your own by car or by bus, *The Essential Road Guide for Costa Rica* is a must. Written by Bill Baker, the book breaks any trip down into maps accompanied by charts showing landmarks along the way, mileage, travel time, and notes on photo opportunities. Spiral-bound so that it can lay flat on your car seat, the 125-page guide is full of handy information about bus routes, driving customs and hazards, and regional notes. It can be used to plan a customized itinerary and lets you evaluate your progress en route. Available for $9.95 at bookstores and car rental agencies in San José. For more information, call 800-881-8607 in the U.S. and Canada.

The ICT (Tourism Institute) has put out a new road map that includes the locations of most national parks, reserves, and wildlife refuges. Order it through the ICT offices, or pick one up at the ICT office under the Plaza de la Cultura. ITMB Publishing also puts out an excellent map (736A Granville Street, Vancouver, BC, V6Z 1G3 Canada; fax: 604-687-5925; $7.95/copy). The maps that we've found to be the most helpful are in the *Guia Roja de Costa Rica*, which contains regional maps, maps of the major cities and suburbs, and great area maps of the Central Valley. Available in San José bookstores.

Even with a map, it's best to call a hotel at or near your destination and ask about current road conditions and travel times. A heavy afternoon rain can cause landslides, changing road conditions in a short time. Because of the unreliability of many roads, try to limit your driving to daylight hours. Hotels will also have current bus schedules.

Topographical maps can be purchased at **Librería Lehmann** (Calle 3, Avenidas Central/1), **Librería Universal** (Avenida Central, Calles Central/1), or the **Instituto Geográfico Nacional** (Avenida 20, Calles 5/7). Ask for *mapas cartográficos*. You'll be shown a little map of Costa Rica divided up into 20 x 30 kilometer sections. Indicate which sections you want. Maps show roads, trails, water sources including rapids, and contours at every 20 meters. They cost about $1.50 a section.

GAS

Fill up before leaving San José going west—there are no gas stations on the highway between San José and the airport. There are several gas stations on Avenida Central going east from downtown. Gas costs about $1.50/gallon, but is sold here by the liter, roughly equivalent to a quart. There are no self-service stations in Costa Rica.

ACCIDENTS

Call 27-7150 or 27-8030 for a traffic official if one doesn't immediately appear. Do not move vehicles until you are authorized to do so by an official. Offer paper and pencils to witnesses to write their names and *cédula* numbers (legal identification).

Do not remove badly injured people from the scene. Wait for the Red Cross ambulance (21-5818). Make no statements on the cause of the accident except to the official or a representative of the National Insurance Institute (INS).

A tow truck is likely to appear on the scene, even if you haven't called for one, as towing services routinely monitor the police radio. You may even have more than one to choose from.

Make a sketch of the area and the positions of the vehicles before and after the accident. Make note of the principal characteristics of the other vehicles involved, as well as the damage to your car and others. Avoid further damage by staying with your car. You must report the accident to the local municipality or Tribunal de Tránsito within eight days. A copy of this report must be presented to the INS (Avenida 7, Calles 9/11; 23-5800, 23-3446), along with your driver's license, insurance policy, police report, and information about injuries and witnesses.

Foreign insurance policies are not effective in court and only the INS can provide local service for defense or adjustment of claims. Insurance is included in car rental fees.

ROAD TROUBLE

If you have a rented car, call the rental agency first in all cases, and they will tell you what to do.

If you are driving your own car, by law you should have fluorescent triangles to place on the road in case of road trouble as a warning to other vehicles. Probably the best service to call in case of trouble with your own car in San José is **Coopetaxi Garage** (35-9966). Some operators understand English.

Do not abandon your car, if you can possibly avoid it. If you don't speak Spanish well, have someone explain your location in Spanish when you make the phone call. If a wrecker is needed, it can be called by Coopetaxi radios.

SAFETY AND THEFT

Take precautions to avoid theft. So far, San José is much safer than most other cities, except for theft. The whole downtown area of San José has become a mecca for pickpockets. Other places to watch out for are Limón and Quepos. The zippered compartments of backpacks are excellent targets. It's best not to wear them on your back downtown. Don't carry a lot of packages at once. Purses should be zippered and have short shoulder straps so that you can protect them with your upper arm. Wallets and passports should not be carried in your back pocket, and expensive watches, chains, and jewelry should not be worn. If, while on a bus or in a crowd, you feel yourself being jostled or pinched between several people at once, don't just be polite. Protect your purse or wallet and elbow your way out of the situation immediately. Don't leave tents or cars unguarded anywhere. Don't leave cameras or binoculars in sight of an open window, even a louvered one. A pole can be stuck in and they can be fished out. If you follow these precautions, you probably won't have any trouble. We have never been robbed on the street in ten years of living in Costa Rica.

NOTES FOR WOMEN

Even if you consider yourself a little on the chunky side in other cultures, you'll have plenty of admirers here. Ticos like to *piropear* (make flirtatious compliments) to women, especially unaccompanied ones. As you walk down the street, they will direct little comments at you, like *guapa* (pretty), *machita* (if you are blond), or *mi amor* (my love), or will just lean toward you with a meaningful *adiós*. If they are farther away from you, they hiss as you pass. This can be quite tiresome, but they mean no harm and there's not much you can do about it. Complete obliviousness is the best policy.

Ticos can be very compelling in their professions of eternal devotion. Whether they're married or not doesn't seem to have much to do with it. Real romantic relationships and friendships usually take a long time to develop in Costa Rica, so take anything that is too rash with a large grain of salt. Foreign women are regarded as loose and easy game (*conquistas*) by Latin men, but their hearts belong to *la Virgen Purísima*. Don't become another notch on a *gringa*-chaser's gun. If you act like a lady, most Tico men will respect you.

NOTES FOR MEN

Costa Rican women are sought out by foreign men because of their loveliness and their reputation for being *chineadoras*, i.e., able and willing to take care of men as if they were babies. Many men, frustrated from trying to "deal with" more assertive women back home, dream of a pretty Tica wife who won't give them any problems. These dreams may come true for a while, until deeply ingrained cultural differences arise, causing major communication problems, which can lead to gringos being taken to the cleaners in divorce courts. Of course, there are many successful intercultural marriages. This is just a warning that, as in any aspect of life, you cannot leave an unresolved problem behind and expect it not to resurface in another form elsewhere.

Prostitution is legal in Costa Rica, and prostitutes are given medical tests on a regular basis. Some prostitutes, however, have been found to be carrying AIDS. Others have been known to gang up on men in the street and rob them. Recently, there have been various cases of men being drugged and robbed after having invited women to their apartment or room. Be careful, guys.

BOMBETAS

If you hear two very loud explosions in rapid succession, don't run for cover—that's just the Tico way of celebrating momentous occasions. Usually the fireworks are from the neighborhood church, which is celebrating a Saint's Day, or are to announce events at a *turno* (town fiesta). In the case of a *turno*, the *bombetas* often begin at dawn and are fired off at regular intervals during the day, usually ending around 9 or 10 p.m. Sounding all the sirens in town is another way of expressing joy, as when the Pope or Tico astronaut Franklin Chang Diaz arrived in San José.

EMBASSIES AND CONSULATES

Many consulates are only open in the mornings. Following is a list of phone numbers for embassies and consulates in San José:

> Austrian Consulate: Avenida 4, Calles 36/38; 55-3007
>
> British Embassy: Centro Colón; 21-5566
>
> Canadian Embassy: Calle 3, Avenida 1; 55-3522
>
> Dutch Embassy: Los Yoses; 34-0949
>
> German Embassy: Rohrmoser; 32-5533
>
> Guatemalan Consulate: Guadalupe; 33-5283
>
> Japanese Embassy: Rohrmoser; 32-1255
>
> Mexican Consulate: Calle 5, Avenida 5; 33-8874
>
> Nicaraguan Consulate: La California; 33-8747
>
> Norwegian Embassy: Centro Colón; 57-1414
>
> Panamanian Consulate: San Pedro; 25-0667
>
> Swedish Consulate: La Uruca; 32-8549
>
> Swiss Embassy: Centro Colón; 33-0052
>
> United States Embassy: Pavas; 20-3939

HEALTH CARE

The following hospitals have emergency medical, x-ray, laboratory, and pharmacy services available to foreigners: **Clínica Bíblica** (Avenida 14, Calles Central/1; 23-6422), **Clínica Católica** (Guadalupe; 25-9095), **Clínica Santa Rita** (specializes in maternity care, Avenida 8, Calles 15/17; 21-6433).

According to a United Nations' study, Costa Rica holds first place in Latin America for development of preventive and curative medicine. It is ranked near the United States and Canada among the 20 best health systems in the world. Many Costa Rican doctors have been trained in Europe and the United States, and the University of Costa Rica Medical School is considered one of the best in Latin America.

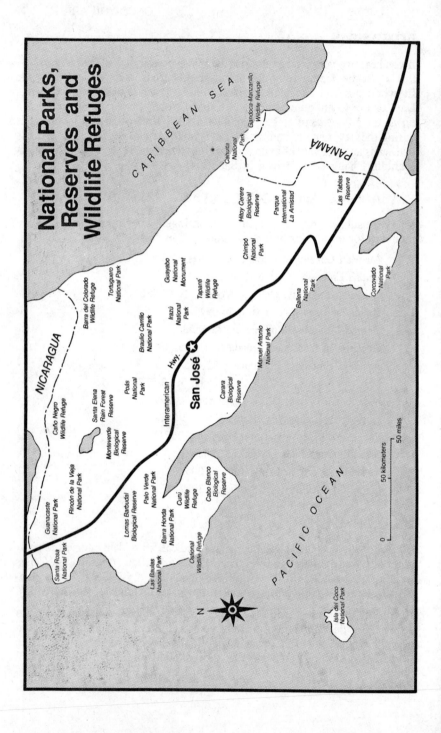

National Parks, Reserves and Wildlife Refuges

CARIBBEAN SEA

NICARAGUA

PANAMA

Santa Rosa National Park

Guanacaste National Park

Caño Negro Wildlife Refuge

Rincón de la Vieja National Park

Santa Elena Rain Forest Reserve

Monteverde Biological Reserve

Barra del Colorado Wildlife Refuge

Tortuguero National Park

Lomas Barbudal Biological Reserve

Palo Verde National Park

Poás National Park

Braulio Carrillo National Park

Irazú National Park

Guayabo National Monument

Tapantí Wildlife Refuge

Hitoy Cerere Biological Reserve

Gandoca-Manzanillo Wildlife Refuge

Cahuita National Park

Barra Honda National Park

Curú Wildlife Refuge

Chirripó National Park

Parque International La Amistad

Las Tablas Reserve

Ostional Wildlife Refuge

Cabo Blanco Biological Reserve

Carara Biological Reserve

San José

Interamerican Hwy.

Manuel Antonio National Park

Ballena National Park

Corcovado National Park

Las Baulas National Park

PACIFIC OCEAN

Isla del Coco National Park

N

0   50 kilometers

0   50 miles

FIVE

The Outdoors

Costa Rica is an outdoor adventurer's paradise. From volcanoes and cloud forests to pristine beaches, this tropical wonder boasts breathtaking beauty. Here you'll find every imaginable activity—from birdwatching to bungee jumping. This is definitely the place to come to take that walk on the "wild side."

NATIONAL PARKS, RESERVES, AND WILDLIFE REFUGES

Costa Rica's 46 national parks, reserves, and wildlife refuges occupy approximately 12 percent of national territory and protect jewels of the country's rich but diminishing wilderness. Most national parks have camping facilities. Most reserves and wildlife refuges do not. Nominal fees are charged for entering the parks, as well as for camping and anchorage.

If you want general information, call **Parques Nacionales** (57-0922, fax: 23-6963). All national parks, reserves, and refuges are indicated on the National Parks map of Costa Rica, and are described in the sections on the various regions. Specific regional park service telephone numbers are listed along with the descriptions of parks. Call those numbers to get an idea of current weather and road conditions, and to make reservations for camping or staying at park facilities. If you need specialized information on scientific aspects of the parks, call the **Conservation Data Center** (36-7690) at the Instituto Nacional de Biodiversidad, located in Santo Domingo de Heredia, just outside San José. Ask for Rita Alfaro.

As an introduction to Costa Rica's national parks, **Dr. Humberto Jiménez** gives a 45-minute video/slide show, followed by a question-and-answer period, several times a week at the **Cine Variedades** (31-1236, 55-3518; admission is $3) in San José. Call for current schedules.

The Association of Volunteers for Service to Protected Areas helps visitors donate support services to the severely understaffed parks and reserves. Volunteers must adapt themselves to work in all kinds of weather and should be willing to do everything that a normal park ranger would do. The commitment is for a minimum of two-and-a-half months, with a day off once every ten days. Volunteers receive free lodging but have to chip in on food and transportation. They should understand basic Spanish, and provide two letters of reference from organizations abroad or from individuals in Costa Rica, a photograph, and a copy of their passport. Volunteers will be given a personal interview and must sign a work contract before being formally accepted. Contact Stanley Arguedas at Parques Nacionales (57-0922, fax: 23-6963).

Note: Although Costa Rica has been described as a Disneyland of ecological wonders, you must be aware that here you are dealing with Mother Nature in all her harsh reality. Five foreigners were reported missing in 1989, and only three were found.

Three German hikers were lost in unseasonal fog and rain for 11 days on Barva Volcano on the west side of Braulio Carrillo National Park. Their goal was a simple day hike around the crater lake, but landslides blocking the trails threw them off course. Costa Rica's famous parks are victims of the country's budget deficit, and trails are not maintained with the same rigor foreigners are used to. Tropical weather itself makes trail maintenance a full-time job. The three hikers managed to keep each other warm and encouraged, and survived their ordeal well, but two older tourists disappeared without a trace, one on Coco Island National Park, the other in Cahuita National Park. Both were hiking or swimming alone when they disappeared.

CAMPING

Don't expect to find many well-organized campgrounds in Costa Rica. It's possible to camp in many places, but you often have to carry in your own water or make arrangements with local people to use their facilities. The national parks that allow camping are mentioned throughout the book. The main problems with camping are rain (it's better to come during the dry season if you plan to camp) and not being able to leave things in your tent unless there is someone around to watch it.

In San José, you can buy or rent **camping, snorkeling,** and **kayaking equipment** at several stores. Probably the best-equipped is the Centro de Aventuras on Paseo Colón between Calles 22/24. They also buy and sell used camping, rafting, and kayaking gear. Other camping stores are Aro (Avenida 8, Calles 11/13) and El Palacio del Deporte (Calle 2, Avenidas 2/4).

BEACH SAFETY

Each year, hundreds of ocean bathers suffer serious near-drownings or death due to their ignorance about rip currents, a phenomenon found on wave-swept beaches all over the world—including Costa Rica. Ironically, these currents can be fun if properly understood—yet they are responsible for 80 percent of ocean drownings, or four out of five.

A rip current is a surplus of water, put ashore by waves, that finds a channel to drain and reach equilibrium. All rip currents have three parts: the feeder current, the neck, and the head. The feeder current is made up of water moving parallel to the beach. You know you're in one when, after a few minutes, you notice that your friends on the beach have moved down 30 to 50 yards, yet you thought you were standing still.

At a depression in the ocean floor, the current turns out to sea. This can occur in knee- to waist-deep water, and is where the "neck" begins. The current in the neck is very swift, like being in a river. It can carry a swimmer out to sea at three to six miles per hour, faster than a strong swimmer's rate of two to four miles per hour, and can move a person 100 yards in just a moment. It's typical for an inexperienced swimmer to panic when caught in the neck, and it is here that most drownings occur.

Once you are no longer touching bottom and are in a rip, you should not fight against the current in a vain effort to get back to shore, for this is like "swimming up a river" and will sap your strength.

The rip current loses its strength just beyond the breakers, dissipating its energy and eventually delivering you to relatively calm waters. This area, known as the "head," may appear to have a mushroom shape when seen from the air, as debris picked up by the current is dispersed.

Here, the water is deep, but calm. You can get back to shore by moving parallel to the beach in the direction of the bend of the current, and then heading toward shore at a 45-degree angle rather than straight in, to avoid getting caught in the feeder current again.

There are four different types of rip currents: permanent, fixed, flash, and traveling:

Permanent rips occur at river mouths, estuaries, or by small streams, and can be quite wide. They also occur at finger jetties designed to prevent beach erosion, where the water's lateral drift is forced to turn seaward. Fixed, flash, and traveling rips are caused by wind-generated waves.

Fixed currents, which appear only on long, sandy, surf-swept beaches, can move up or down the beach depending on shifts in the ocean floor, but they are generally stable, staying in one spot for hours to a day.

Flash, or *temporary*, *rips* are created when an increased volume of water is brought to shore from sudden wave build-ups. These currents can occur on a warm, sunny day, generated by distant storms whose waves do not lose their energy until they crash on a shore. The excess water build-up has no opportunity to drain and reach equilibrium while the unusually large and fast waves are coming in; a flash rip current therefore forms during a lull in wave action.

A *traveling rip current* is just what the name implies. You'll see it in front of you; then, five minutes later, it may have moved 15 yards up or down the beach. Traveling rips can move 30 yards in a minute. They occur on long, sandy beaches where there are no fixed depressions on the ocean floor.

Some beaches, such as **Espadilla** at Manuel Antonio, or **Jacó**, are known to have rip currents and must be approached with caution at all times. The currents can be spotted by the trained eye by a brownish discoloration on the surface of the water, caused by sand and debris; or there can be a flattening effect as the water rushes out to sea, making the surface appear deceptively smooth.

As a safety precaution, before you enter the ocean, throw a buoyant object like a coconut or a stick into the water and watch where the current carries it, for this is the direction you will have to go in before you can get back to shore. There is definitely one direction that is better than the other.

If you're a weak swimmer, you should call for help as soon as you notice that a current is moving you and making it difficult to walk in toward land. Most drowning victims are caught in water just above waist level.

If you realize that you can't walk directly in, you should turn and walk sideways, leaping toward the beach with every wave, to let the water "push" you toward shore.

A crashing surf can throw you off balance, so it's dangerous to turn your back to it. Once off balance, a swimmer is unable to get traction on the ocean floor and can be dragged out four or five feet into deeper water with each swell. After a few swells you may be in over your head, and it becomes extremely important to float—by arching your back, head back, nose pointing in the air.

Floating conserves energy. The human body is buoyant, even more so in saltwater. Everyone should learn to float, because every minute that you can salvage gives someone the opportunity to make a rescue.

Rip currents are not dangerous to people who understand them. The more you know about the ocean, the more fun it can be. Surfers use rip currents as an energy saver, since they provide "a free ride" out to sea just beyond the breakers.

Good swimmers are encouraged to seek out rip currents under controlled conditions—and with experienced trainers. As long as you swim in the ocean, you might get caught in a rip current, so it's critical that you know how to get out of one.

Following are some rip current rules of thumb:

> Weak swimmers should avoid surf-swept beaches and swim instead at safer beaches like the third beach at Manuel Antonio or Punta Uva in Talamanca.

Inexperienced swimmers should never swim alone.

Always be prepared to signal for help at the earliest sign of trouble.

For more information, contact the Costa Rican Lifesaving Association (77-0345) in Quepos.

FISHING

With two oceans, beautiful freshwater lakes, and endless miles of magnificent rivers—all only a few hours' drive or minutes by air from the capital city of San José—Costa Rica offers fishing enthusiasts some of the most fantastic and diverse sportfishing in the world.

For the freshwater angler, **Lake Arenal** and many of the rivers provide outstanding action on rainbow bass (*guapote*), beautiful, fine-eating fish that may run eight pounds or more and are fished just as you would largemouth bass.

There are rainbow trout in the mountain rivers, and a range of such exotic species as the *machaca*, *bobo*, *mojarra*, and *vieja* to be found in lower elevation waters.

But Costa Rica's greatest claim to fame is the incredible deep-sea fishing for billfish and other gamesters on the Pacific Coast, and what is without doubt the world's finest tarpon and snook angling on the Caribbean.

Interest in Costa Rican sportfishing has increased dramatically in recent years, resulting in a tremendous expansion of the sportfishing industry, with new areas opening, improved and expanded facilities, and the introduction of world-class boats and equipment.

PACIFIC COAST Anglers routinely catch and release 500 or more marlin during the peak season from January through August. **The Costa Rican Amateur Fishing Club**'s annual International Sailfish Tournament posts the highest catch-per-angler record of any billfish competition in the world. Raising 10 to 20 sails a day is considered pretty ho-hum fishing in Costa Rica, and 20 to 30 a day isn't at all unusual. While both marlin and sails are around all year, heavy winds in Guanacaste hamper fishing in January and February, and sometimes well into April. During the windy months, the action centers farther south, where the shoreline configuration offers protection. That's when boats out of Quepos post their best scores.

Billfish are certainly the major attraction on the Pacific Coast, but there is also world-class angling for wahoo, jack crevalle, mackerel, roosterfish, *corvina*, Pacific dogtooth snapper, rainbow and blue runners, and a host of other species. It's a rare day when anglers on the Pacific side don't tie into dorado in the 30-pound-and-up class, and tuna are nearly always abundant.

Quepos-based **Sportfishing Costa Rica** offers year-round trips out of all three primary west coast fishing areas: Flamingo in Guanacaste, Quepos on the central coast, Drake Bay and Caño Island to the south. **Costa Rican Dreams** fishes out of the latter two ports, while **Tom Bradwell** operates out of Flamingo and Quepos. The major center of west coast fishing, however, is still the northern province of Guanacaste, where **Bahía Pez Vela, Flamingo Bay Pacific Charters, Ocotal,** and **Papagayo Excursions** all have added new, modern boats to their fleets. **Pesca Bahía Garza** and **Guanamar** are based at luxury hotels on the isolated Pacific side of the Nicoya Peninsula, where they enjoy better fishing during the winter months because they are protected from the fierce winds on the Bahía Papagayo. Additional boats operate at **Tango Mar,** just inside the Gulf of Nicoya, and **Oasis del Pacífico** further north near the Puntarenas ferry landing.

For information, reservations, or free brochures, contact the following operators on the Pacific Coast (arranged according to location):

Sportfishing Costa Rica—At Quepos; 33-9135, fax: 23-6728

Costa Rican Dreams—Out of Quepos; 39-3387, 77-0593, fax: 39-3383

Skip's Sportfishing—Quepos; 77-0275

Pisces Pacific Boat Tours—Playa Dominical; 21-2053

El Caballito del Mar—Drake Bay; 33-9135, fax: 23-6728

Drake Bay Wilderness Camp—Phone/fax: 71-2436

Río Sierpe Lodge—Near Drake Bay; 20-2121, fax: 32-3321

Golfito Sailfish Rancho—800-531-7232

Leomar—Golfito, 75-0230; fax: 75-0373

Sanbar Marina—Golfito; 75-0874

Zancudo Pacific Charters—Near Golfito; 75-0268, fax: 75-0105

Oasis del Pacífico—Across the Gulf of Nicoya via ferry from Puntarenas; phone/fax: 61-1555

Tango Mar—Near Tambor on the Nicoya Peninsula; 61-2798, 23-1864, fax: 55-2697

Hotel Flor de Itabo—Near Playa del Coco; 67-0111, 67-0292, fax: 67-0003

Hotel Ocotal—Near Playa del Coco; 22-4259, 67-0230; Apdo. 1013, San José 1002

Bahía Pez Vela—Gulf of Papagayo and Quepos; 21-1586

Flamingo Bay Pacific Charters—In the U.S. at Flamingo Beach, Florida, 305-765-1995, 305-467-0532; in Costa Rica, 25-4780

Tom Bradwell—Based at Flamingo Beach and Quepos; 68-0942, fax: 68-0928

Papagayo Excursions—At Tamarindo Beach; phone/fax 68-0859, phone/fax: 25-3648

Pesca Bahía Garza—At Punta Guiones de Garza, near Nosara; 68-0784

Guanamar—Playa Carrillo, Guanacaste; 20-0722, 20-0733, fax: 20-2095

CARIBBEAN COAST   If you have never battled a tarpon, you have a surprise and perhaps a shock in store. When those silver rockets, weighing an average of 80 pounds each, take to the air, jumping and twisting and turning and tumbling, and then running halfway to hell and back, only to start jumping again. . . .Well, all I can say is, "Try it."

You fish the tarpon from 16-foot outboards, and much of the action is in quiet jungle rivers and lagoons, where you're likely to see bands of monkeys in the trees overhead, alligators basking along the shoreline, and a host of brilliantly plumed birds flitting through orchid-draped tropical growth.

While I have caught tarpon every month of the year in Costa Rica, the peak season is considered to be from January through May. However, June through October frequently produces outstanding action as well, and it just doesn't get much better than it was one recent August and September.

Like tarpon, snook can be taken year-round, with 17 to 25 pounders common and a generous share of big fish (including the IGFA all-tackle world record) coming from the area. Peak season for big fish is usually late August into November. From late November through January, the area enjoys a run of smaller snook (known locally as *calba*) that average about five pounds and pour into the river in huge numbers. Catches of 20 or 30 a day are not unusual.

In addition to the tarpon and snook, Caribbean coastal waters abound in mackerel, jack crevalle, saltwater catfish, sharks, grouper, snapper, and more, while exotic freshwater species provide great light tackle action upriver and in the lagoons.

Five lodges provide accommodations, boats, and guides for visiting anglers. For information and free brochures, contact:

Casamar—43-8834, fax: 43-9287

Río Colorado—32-4063, U.S. phone: 800-243-9777

Parismina Tarpon Rancho—phone/fax: 35-7766

Tortuga Lodge—57-0766, fax: 57-1665

Isla de Pesca—23-4560, fax: 55-2533

Freshwater fishing permits can be obtained in San José from the Information Department at the Banco Nacional de Costa Rica, located behind the Central Post Office (Open 9 a.m. to 3 p.m. Monday through Friday; Avenida 1, Calles 2/4). Permits cost about $10 and must be presented with your passport if you encounter wildlife rangers at your fishing site. The same permits are good for fishing from the beach or at river mouths. Deep-sea fishing permits will be taken care of by your fishing guide.

Fishing equipment and tide tables are sold at La Casa del Pescador (Calle 2, Avenidas 18/20) and Deportes Keko (Calle 20, Avenidas 4/6) in San José. They can also direct you to the latest hot fishing spots, and even set you up with a private guide.

OTHER OUTDOOR SPORTS

SURFING

Costa Rica has become famous for its great waves. The Pacific, with its long point breaks, river mouths, and beach breaks, keeps surfers busy from late March to late November. If they want to get serious, they go to the Atlantic from December through March, where waves from deep water break over the shallow reef, creating the perfect imitation of Hawaiian surf.

The nearest surfing beach to San José is **Boca Barranca**, between Puntarenas and Puerto Caldera, known for long waves. About a half-hour to the south are **Playa Jacó** (good for beginners) and **Playa Hermosa** (not to be confused with Playa Hermosa in Guanacaste), where an international surfing contest is held each year. The whole area between Jacó and **Playa Dominical** to the south has many excellent surfing spots. **Playa Pavones**, south of Golfito on the Golfo Dulce is said to have a left wave "so long you can take a nap on it." **Playas Nosara, Junquillal,** and **Tamarindo** in Guanacaste have areas for surfing, as well as swimming and snorkeling spots. **Playa Naranjo,** in Santa Rosa National Park, is known for **Witch Rock,** which creates tubular waves. If you don't have four-wheel drive you have to hike 13 kilometers with your surfboard on your back, and camp out. On the Atlantic Coast, **Playa Bonita,** just north of Limón, offers waves that are very thick, powerful, and dangerous. There is an international competition there each year. **Puerto Viejo,** south of Limón, is famous for "La Salsa," a challenging ride responsible for many a broken surfboard. Most surfers say they can't decide which coast they like best.

The **Mango Surf Shop,** 25 meters west of the Banco Popular in San Pedro, buys and sells surfboards and accessories, as does **Tsunami** in Los Yoses. Marco Pacheco, of **Keola Surf and Ding Shop** (Apdo. 6280, San José; 25-6041), 100 meters east, 100 meters south of the Banco Popular in San Pedro, makes and repairs surfboards, guides surfing tours, and has up-to-date wave information. There are surfboard rental shops in Puntarenas, Jacó, Manuel Antonio, Limón, and Cahuita. Many car rental agencies and hotels give discounts to surfers, especially May through November.

SCUBA DIVING

Scuba diving excursions are available through:

Centro de Buceo Joaquín—International certification, 17 different courses. In Tárcoles, on the highway to Jacó.

Diving Safaris—Dive trips, rentals, and instruction at **Hotel Ocotal** in Guanacaste, 67-0230.

El Caballito del Mar—Diving in Drake Bay; 33-9135, 33-3892, fax: 23-6728.

Hotel Playa Cocalito—In Drake Bay; fax in CR 75-6291; in Canada: 519-782-4592

Okeanos Cruises—They take scuba divers to Isla de Coco and national parks on the Pacific Coast in a luxurious cruiser; in the U.S. phone: 800-348-2628

Temptress Cruises—They also take scuba divers to Isla de Coco and national parks on the Pacific Coast in a luxurious cruiser; 20-1679, U.S. phone: 800-336-8423

WHITEWATER SPORTS

Rafters, canoers, and kayakers are beginning to flock to Costa Rica because of its exciting rivers. The Río Pacuare, considered world-class by sportspeople, is threatened with being dammed for a huge hydroelectric project. **Ríos Tropicales** (33-6455), **Costa Rica Expeditions** (22-0333, 57-0766), and **Aventuras Naturales** (25-3939) will take you on one- to three-day rafting trips, with challenges graded to your level of skill and experience. The one-day trip is $69-$89, including transportation, breakfast, lunch, and expert guides. Ríos Tropicales also offers sea-kayaking trips. **Rancho Leona** (71-6312) takes beginners on river kayaking trips down the Río Puerto Viejo in Sarapiquí.

GOLF

The **Costa Rica Country Club** in Escazú and the **Los Reyes Country Club** in La Guácima, Alajuela, each have nine holes and professionals to teach the game. The only 18-hole golf course in the country is located near Juan Santamaría Airport at the **Cariari Country Club.** Cariari hosts the Friendship Golf Tourney and the American Professional Golf Tourney, which attract PGA professionals. Cariari rents equipment and provides pros for golf

lessons. **Tango Mar Surf and Saddle Club,** on the Gulf of Nicoya near Tambor, also has a nine-hole golf course.

TENNIS

Among the most important international tennis matches here is the World Friendship Tournament at the **Cariari Country Club** in March and April. In the Central Valley, the **Costa Rica Country Club** in Escazú hosts the Coffee Cup Tournament. **Los Reyes Country Club** (La Guácima), the **Costa Rica Tennis Club** (Sabana Sur), Cariari and **La Sabana** courts offer programs for learning and practicing tennis. Most beach and mountain hotels have tennis courts.

HORSEBACK RIDING

The **Portón del Tajo** at Hotel Cariari, near Juan Santamaría Airport, offers riding and jumping lessons, dressage, and trail riding (39-2248). International horse riding competitions are held each year at **Club Hípico La Caraña** in Río Oro de Santa Ana, west of San José (28-6106, 28-6754). Most beach and mountain resorts rent horses. Make sure that the horses you rent are not tired and do not have sores or swollen places. Give them plenty of opportunity to drink water during the trip and don't leave them standing in the sun. If you feel horses or any other animals are being mistreated, you can report it to the WSPA (39-7158, fax: 39-7323) in San Rafael de Heredia.

SOCCER

Costa Ricans are very sports-minded. There isn't a district, town, or city where *fútbol* (soccer) isn't played. It's said that Costa Ricans learn to kick a ball before they learn to walk! There are teams all over the country in every imaginable category, including all ages and both sexes, although only men play on the major teams. In June 1990, a Costa Rican team competed in the World Cup for the first time. All government employees were given time off to watch the games, and the streets of San José became a huge fiesta when they won.

RUNNING

There are many marathons throughout the year, including the one sponsored each April by the **University for Peace.** The **Hash House Harriers,** a worldwide organization devoted to running and beer-drinking, also meets here once a week. Call Bill Barbee (28-0769) for information. Also see Chapter Six for places to jog in San José.

BUNGEE JUMPING

Bungee jumping has come to Costa Rica. Thrill-seekers jump from a 235-foot abandoned bridge near the Grecia exit on the highway to Puntarenas. **Tropical Bungee** (33-6455, 32-4743) and **Saragundi Specialty Tours** (55-0011) are two companies that offer this ultimate endorphine rush.

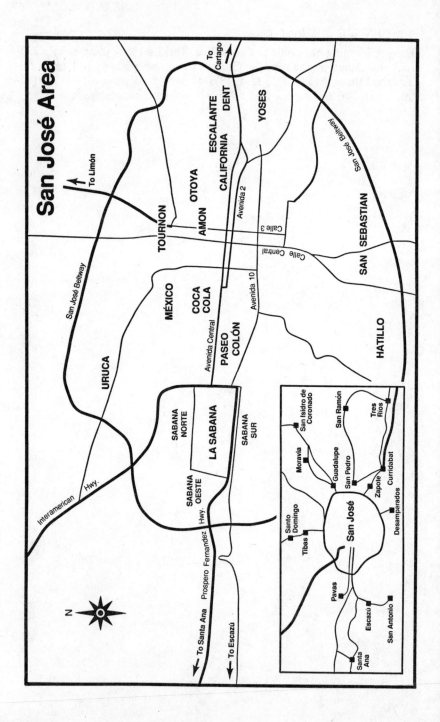

San José Area

SIX

Getting to Know San José

In 1821, after learning that Guatemala had declared its independence from Spain, Costa Rica began creating its own form of self-government. During this process, General Agustín de Iturbide, self-proclaimed emperor of México, sent word urging immediate annexation to his empire. The citizens of the older cities of Heredia and Cartago were in favor of annexation, but the more liberal residents of Alajuela and San José saw de Iturbide's demand as imperialist and chose independence. A short civil war ensued, which was won in 1823 by the *independistas*, who moved the capital city from Cartago to San José. In the same year, de Iturbide's government fell and Costa Rica joined the newly created Federation of Central America, from which it withdrew in 1838.

Today San José is a noisy, bustling city—the economic, political, and cultural center of the country. If you have come to Costa Rica to get close to nature, you will probably want to get out of San José as fast as possible. Set in the middle of the Central Valley, surrounded by high mountains, it is battling the demons of its rapid growth: congested one-way streets filled with too many cars, buses, and taxies belching black diesel smoke into the mountain air; a lack of jobs for all the country people who have given up on working the land and are trying their luck in the city; increasing petty theft.

On the upside, San José still ranks as one of the safest cities in the Western Hemisphere and has much less violent crime than most U.S. cities. Foreigners enjoy the city's springlike climate, the availability of high-quality cultural events like National Symphony concerts and international music, dance, theater, and film festivals, and the relaxed life in suburban areas like balmy Rohrmoser, Escazú, and Santa Ana to the west, and Moravia, Curridabat, and brisk San Ramón de Trés Ríos to the east. Great places to dine are also plentiful in San José, as you'll see in this chapter. Modern supermarkets and shopping malls have largely taken the place of the Mercado Central, but Saturday morning farmers markets held in the streets of different neighborhoods still provide a folksy tone and a fairlike atmosphere.

89

And Costa Ricans are almost always friendly and polite, ready to take a moment off for a joke or to help you find where you're going.

Here are some tips for while you're in the city:

> When crossing streets in downtown San José, always look over your shoulder at the cars coming from behind you. In practice, the pedestrian does not have the right of way. Drivers love to whip around corners whether or not people are trying to cross.

> When a traffic light for oncoming cars changes from green to yellow or red, do not take it to mean that the cars will stop. Look at the cars, not the light. When you see that the cars have stopped, run across real quick. This habit is easily developed because another characteristic of San José is that traffic lights are hung so that pedestrians cannot see them. *Buena suerte.*

> Street numbers are attached to the sides of buildings near intersections. Not all corners have them, but keep looking and you're bound to find one.

> To ask directions, you don't have to use a lot of fancy Spanish. It is acceptable to say "¿Para (name of your destination)?", like "¿Para Heredia?" or "¿Para la Coca Cola?", and the person you ask will point you in the general direction. We've found it's best to ask people who look like they drive, and it's best not to ask people standing in front of bars.

WALKING TOUR

The following tour can take several hours to a full day, depending on how involved you get.

We will start out at the **Correo Central**, or Central Post Office (open Monday through Friday, 8 a.m. to 12 midnight; Saturday, 8 a.m. to 12 noon) on Calle 2 between Avenidas 1 and 3. The entrance is in the middle of the block. The stamp windows are directly in front of you as you enter. Slots for mailing letters abroad are directly to your left. Philatelists will be interested in the commemorative stamp department on the second floor.

Walk two blocks west on Avenida 1, and you're at the **Mercado Central**, entering through the flower section. The market is a crowded, bustling maze of shops, restaurants, and produce stands covering the whole block between Avenidas Central/1 and Calles 6/8. Although there are quite a few more sedate places to buy souvenirs, at the Central Market you can get a glimpse of the lives of everyday Costa Ricans. Everything from hammocks to leather goods to fresh fish to mangoes is sold there. Of special interest are the stands where herbs are sold, labeled with their medicinal uses. It's easy to get quite disoriented in the market, but try to come out at the southeast entrance on Avenida Central and start walking east again. (If you don't like crowds, skip the market.)

Between Calles 6 and 4 on Avenida Central, you'll pass **La Gloria**, Costa Rica's largest department store. Across from that is the huge black marble **Banco de Costa Rica**. You can take an elevator there to the eighth floor to get a bird's-eye view of the city. Turn left at the corner and you'll pass a branch of **Pop's**, Costa Rica's excellent chain of ice cream stores.

At Calle 4, Avenida 1, turn right, heading for the post office again. You'll pass the **Banco Nacional** on your left. It often has art exhibits. Continuing on Avenida 1, a block and a half past the post office, you'll pass the **Librería Universal**, where you can buy anything from electronic appliances to art supplies, as well as books and stationery. It sells large-scale maps, which are helpful for hiking.

Look to your left at the intersection of Calle 1 and Avenida 1. Two blocks north is **Radiográfica**, where you can make long-distance phone calls, send telegrams, or send and receive faxes. **LACSA** (the Costa Rican airline) ticket offices face Radiográfica.

You are still on Avenida 1. In the next block after Calle 1 is **The Bookshop**, which sells newspapers, cards, and books in English. In the next block, **Book Traders** sells used books in English in the Edificio Omni. Continue east to Calle 5. Turn left. You'll pass three upscale crafts stores: **Atmósfera**, on the corner to your right, **Magia**, on your right in the middle of the block, and **Suraja**, on your left at the corner of Avenida 3. They feature excellent wood carvings, ceramics, and art, as well as furniture, bowls, and boxes made of tropical hardwoods. All merit a browse.

Parque Morazán is on your right. Its **Music Temple** is patterned after Le Trianon in Paris. On the northwest corner of the park is the **Hotel Aurola Holiday Inn**, with mirrored panels reflecting San José's changing skies. One block south of the Music Temple is the popular **Hotel Amstel**, which has a quiet bar and an excellent, reasonably priced restaurant.

Three blocks north of the Music Temple is the entrance to **Parque Bolívar**, the location of San José's **zoo** (open Tuesday through Friday, 8 a.m. to 4 p.m.; weekends, 9 a.m. to 5 p.m.; admission 20 cents). If you are idealistic about Costa Rica's commitment to wildlife, you will be disappointed in the zoo, which has received widespread criticism for its inadequate facilities.

East of the Music Temple is the green **Escuela Metálica**, a turn-of-the-century school building built with parts shipped from France. Next comes **Parque España**, which is filled with venerable and beautiful trees. Continue to Avenida 7 and the tall **National Insurance Institute** (INS), which houses a fine exhibit of jade, ceramics, and art in the **Jade Museum** on the 11th floor (open Monday through Friday, 9 a.m. to 3 p.m.; free admission). This museum rivals the National Museum in its extensive exhibits of pre-Columbian jade, gold, and ceramics. Modern art is also displayed in the outer gallery, and the 11th-floor location provides a good view of San José and the mountains beyond. It should be high on your list of places to visit.

Continuing east on Avenida 7, you will pass the **Casa Amarilla** with its wide stairways. It houses the country's Department of Foreign Relations. This building and the park in front of it were donated by Andrew Carnegie. On the east side of the park is the **National Liquor Factory**, founded by President Juan Rafael Mora in 1856. It is presently being converted into the headquarters of the Ministry of Culture.

Now you're going east again on Avenida 7, up a gentle hill, passing the Mexican Embassy on the north and arriving at the intersection of Avenida 7 and Calle 15. Turn right toward the **Biblioteca Nacional** (National Library). On its western side you'll come to the **Galería Nacional de Arte Contemporáneo** (open Monday through Saturday, 10 a.m. to 1 p.m., 2 p.m. to 5 p.m.; free admission), which often has good exhibits.

The library faces **Parque Nacional**. To the east of the park are the bus stations from which you can take the scenic trip to Limón. In the center of the park is the massive **Monumento Nacional**, which depicts the spirits of the Central American nations driving out the despicable William Walker. The statue was made in the Rodin studios in France and shipped to Costa Rica. Across the street from the park you will see a statue of **Juan Santamaría,** holding aloft his torch in front of the **Legislative Assembly** building, the Costa Rican Congress. Inside is a small library and an exhibit recounting momentous decisions in Costa Rica's legal history.

Two blocks south of the Parque Nacional, on Calle 17, is the **Museo Nacional** (open Tuesday through Sunday, 8:30 a.m. to 4:30 p.m.; admission 75 cents), housed in the former Buenavista Fortress. There are bullet holes in the turrets from the 1948 civil war. Inside are a lovely courtyard and large exhibits of indigenous gold and ceramics, religious objects, colonial furniture, and art. Definitely worth a visit.

The museum overlooks the **Plaza de la Democrácia**, built by the Arias Administration to receive visiting presidents during the historic Hemispheric Summit in October 1989. Return to Avenida Central, which borders the northern side of the plaza. Heading west, you'll pass the popular **Más x Menos** (pronounced "Más por Menos") supermarket. One and a half blocks to the left from the corner of Calle 11 is the **Mercado Nacional de Artesanía,** a good and inexpensive place to shop for souvenirs. One block to the right from the same corner is **CANAPI,** another souvenir cooperative.

Continue west on Avenida Central. You might be ready for a bite to eat at the **Balcon de Europa** (Calle 9, Avenidas Central/1), or coffee and cake at **Spoon** (Avenida Central, Calles 5/7). **ANDA** (Avenida Central, Calles 5/7) features weaving, ceramics, and wood carvings by Costa Rican Indians.

Now you're coming to the **Plaza de la Cultura** on Avenida Central, Calles 5/3. Down the grassy steps on Calle 5 is the information center of the **Instituto Costarricense de Turismo** (ICT), or Tourism Institute, to the left. There, too, is the entrance to the plaza's excellent underground exhibition rooms, which feature changing shows, and the famous **Gold Museum** (open Friday, Saturday, and Sunday, 10 a.m. to 4 p.m.; admission 75 cents).

The eastern half of the plaza is full of children chasing pigeons and feeding them popcorn, and the center is often the stage for street comedians, concerts, and fairs. The western end, bordered by the Gran Hotel Costa Rica with its outdoor café, is full of street vendors selling jewelry, crafts, Guatemalan clothing and purses, and a variety of Costa Rican crafts including hammocks, carved gourds, clothing, and imitation pre-Columbian ocarinas (a ceramic flute in the stylized form of an animal). It's also a good place to buy maps. Since this is a prime tourist area, beware of pickpockets.

Cross the plaza to the famous **Teatro Nacional** (National Theatre). In 1890 the world-renowned prima donna, Adelina Patti, appeared with a traveling opera company in Guatemala, but could not perform in Costa Rica because there was no appropriate theater. In response, newly rich coffee merchants financed the construction of a theater with a tax on every bag of coffee exported from the country. Belgian architects were called in to design and supervise the building, and the metal structure was ordered from Belgian mills. Painters and decorators were brought from Italy, along with that country's famous marble. The Teatro Nacional was inaugurated in 1894 with Gounod's *Faust* and an opening-night cast that included singers from the Paris Opéra. A source of cultural pride, the theater was made into a national monument in 1965. Extensive restoration work has recently renewed its beautiful ceiling paintings and sumptuous decor, but tropical weather and recent earthquakes have taken their toll on the old building. Its auditorium is closed until at least 1993, so there are no tours. Tourists can make donations in the lobby to help fund the theater's preservation. The **Café del Teatro Nacional**, to the left as you enter the building, has changing art exhibits and specializes in exotic coffee combinations and desserts. Sit down there to end the walking tour—you deserve a rest.

CREATIVE ARTS

Costa Ricans are well known for their interest in culture and the arts. The Ministry of Culture stimulates activity by sponsoring theater, choral music, opera, dance, literature, poetry, art, sculpture, and film.

MUSIC

Costa Rica's National Youth Symphony was inaugurated in 1972 by ex-President Figueres's famous quote: "We need to concern ourselves not only with the standard of living but the quality of life as well. Why have tractors without violins?"

Many of the young musicians trained in the Youth Symphony have graduated to participate in the National Symphony, which performs in the **Teatro Melico Salazar** (Thursday and Friday nights, 8 p.m.; Sunday, 10:30

a.m.; Avenida 2, Calle Central; 22-2653) across from Parque Central. Internationally famous guest directors and soloists are often featured. Entrance fees are kept low so that people at all economic levels may enjoy the concerts. The least expensive seats are in the *galería* section, which is up three flights of stairs through an entrance on the east side of the theater. The *butacas* are in the first tier of boxes above the *luneta* (orchestra) section. The *palcos* (box seats) are on the second tier. The symphony season starts in April and ends in December. Call to check show times.

Retired musicians, amateurs, and some symphony members play together for fun on Monday nights in Heredia. Foreigners are welcome to join. Call German Alvarado (21-1185) for information.

Radio Universidad (870 AM and 96.7 and 101.9 FM) plays classical music interspersed with educational programs. **FM 96** also broadcasts classical music. **Radio Estereo Azul** (99 FM) plays a lot of New Age music and jazz. **Radio for Peace International** is a worldwide shortwave radio station that provides provocative informational programming on a wide range of topics important to world peace and justice. It provides daily news from the United Nations in English, Spanish, German, and French (and in other languages soon). Its studios are on the campus of the University for Peace in Villa Colón (49-1821, fax: 49-1929; U.S. phone: 503-741-1794).

PEÑAS AND LA NUEVA TROVA

The *peña*, literally "circle or group of friends," is a tradition brought to Costa Rica by Chilean and Argentinean exiles. People of all nationalities come together at a favorite café and sing the moving and inspiring songs that have become the themes of today's Latin America: *La Nueva Trova*. Luis Angel Castro, Rubén Pagura, and Juan Carlos Ureña are some of the favorite leaders of *peñas* these days. **El Tablado** (next to Toruma Youth Hostel in Los Yoses), **Baleares** (25 meters east of La Nueva China in San Pedro), **Contravía** (75 meters south of La Nueva China in San Pedro), and **Los Balcones** (in El Pueblo on the north side of San José—see "Nightlife," below) often have *peñas*. Also keep your ears open for concerts by **Cantares, Canto America,** and **Adrián Goizueta** and his **Grupo Experimental**.

THEATER

Ticos are great actors. Even if you don't understand Spanish, it might be worth it to go to the theater, just to see the creativity that these people bring to the stage. The English-speaking community also puts a lot of energy into its **Little Theater Group** (31-0813), which presents musicals and comedies several times a year. Call for information.

The Tico Times and the *"Viva"* section of *La Nación* will tell you what is playing in local theaters. Admission is usually about $1.50. Theater addresses are listed below:

Sala de la Calle 15: Avenida 2, Calle 15

Teatro de la Aduana: Calle 25, Avenidas 3/5

Teatro del Angel: Avenida Central, Calles 13/15; 22-8258

Teatro Bellas Artes: East side of University of Costa Rica campus

Teatro Carpa: Avenida Central, Calle 29; 34-2866

Teatro Laurence Olivier: Avenida 2, Calle 28; 23-1960, 22-1034

Teatro La Mascara: Calle 13, Avenidas 2/4

Teatro Melico Salazar: Avenida 2, Calles Central/2; 21-4952

Teatro Tiempo: Calle 13, Avenidas Central/2; 22-0792

Teatro Vargas Calvo: Calles 3/5, Avenida 2; 22-1875

FILMS

North American movies dominate the film scene here, and are usually shown three to six months after they appear in the United States, with Spanish subtitles. All movie theaters charge about $1.50. Check schedules in *The Tico Times* or *La Nación*.

The **Sala Garbo** (Avenida 2, Calle 28) features excellent international films with Spanish subtitles. Next door, the **Teatro Laurence Olivier** offers films, plays, and concerts as well as a gallery and coffee house. Recently, local jazz groups have been playing in its Shakespeare Gallery. Take the *Sabana–Cementerio* bus (Calle 7, Avenidas Central/2) and get off at the Pizza Hut on Paseo Colón. The two theaters are one block south. You can walk to them from downtown in 25 minutes.

ART

The Ticos converted their former air terminal into the **Museum of Costa Rican Art** (open Tuesday through Sunday, 10 a.m. to 5:45 p.m.; closed Monday; admission 30 cents, free Sunday). This tastefully done museum displays the work of the country's finest painters and sculptors, as well as international exhibits. Located in La Sabana at the end of Paseo Colón.

The **Center for Creative Arts** (82-8769) combines art classes with yoga and relaxation to help people release their creative energy. It is located in Santa Ana, to the west of San José.

Check *La Nación* and *The Tico Times* for exhibits at the many galleries downtown. The Centro Cultural Costarricense-Norteamericano, the Alianza Francesa, and the Instituto Goethe (see below) have monthly art exhibits. Their openings are a good place to meet people and to fill up on free wine and *bocas*.

NIGHTLIFE

The area bordered by Calle 4 on the west, Avenida 9 on the north, Calle 23 on the east, and Avenida 2 on the south is the heart of downtown nightlife in San José and is usually quite safe.

These are some of our favorite nightspots. Most of them serve the traditional *bocas*, little plates of food that accompany each drink. Ceviche (raw fish "cooked" in lemon juice), fried fish, pork and beans, and *mondongo* (tripe) are common *bocas*. Usually they are free. As for beer, we recommend Bavaria, Imperial, or the more expensive Heineken.

Amstel Hotel Bar (open daily, 11 a.m. to 2 a.m.; Calle 7, Avenidas 1/3): A simple, elegant, and quiet bar.

Antojitos (open daily, 11 a.m. to 11 p.m.): Features good Mexican food and great mariachis. On Paseo Colón near the Pizza Hut, and in Los Yoses.

Baleares (open Monday through Saturday, 7 p.m. to 2 a.m.; closed Sunday; 53-4577): Has live jazz and Latin rhythms and a late-night restaurant featuring paella. In San Pedro, 150 meters west of the Más x Menos.

Charleston (open Monday through Saturday, 5 p.m. to 4 a.m.; closed Sunday; Calle 9, Avenidas 2/4; 55-3993): Has a nice 1920s decor and often plays good vintage jazz tapes.

Chelles (open every day, 24 hours): As far as atmosphere goes, there's not much, but if you're a people watcher, you'll enjoy hanging out at Chelles. Probably because it remains open all the time, Chelles has become a landmark. You'll see actors, musicians, and dancers from the National Theater there having a midnight snack. You'll see middle-aged Costa Rican men amusing each other with toothpick tricks. You'll be asked to buy wilted roses from intriguing old ladies and persistent young boys. There are free *bocas* with every drink. For those who tire of the glare of Chelles's bare lightbulbs, there is **Chelles Taberna** around the corner, where you can hide in booths. The Taberna has better *bocas*, too. Chelles Lite is at Avenida Central, Calle 9; Chelles Dark is at Calle 9, Avenidas Central/2. *Overpriced.*

Contravía (open 11 a.m. to 2 p.m., 6 p.m. to 1 a.m.; 53-6989): Contravía features good live music and is favored by the university crowd. It's in San Pedro, 75 meters south of Restaurante La Nueva China.

Crocodile Club (open Monday through Thursday, 5 p.m. to 2 a.m.; Friday through Sunday, 5 p.m. to 3:30 a.m.; 25-3277): This is a friendly bar featuring gringo-style hamburgers, a huge video screen, and a dance floor. Located in San Pedro, across from Banco Anglo.

El Cuartel de la Boca del Monte (open Monday through Friday, 12 noon to 2:30 a.m.; Saturday and Sunday, 7 p.m. to 2 a.m.; Avenida 1, Calles 21/23; 21-0327): By day a quiet, artistically decorated restaurant featuring Costa

Rican dishes. By night, the bar in the back becomes one of the most popular in San José. The *bocas* aren't free, but they're good. Most surprising are their fantastic cocktails, extravagantly decorated with tropical fruit and sometimes even sparklers. Reasonably priced.

La Esmeralda (open Monday through Saturday, 11 a.m. to 5 a.m.; closed Sunday; Avenida 2, Calles 5/7) is lots of fun. It's the home of the Mariachi Union. Groups of musicians stroll between the tables while their vans wait outside to transport them to emergency serenade sites. I'll never forget the best party I ever went to in Costa Rica—my landlady's 80th birthday. After eating, drinking, and dancing until one in the morning, I was ready to retire, but that's not the way Ticos celebrate birthdays. At 2 a.m. the mariachis arrived to serenade her with guitars, harps, trumpets, and violins. But I digress. La Esmeralda offers good, reasonably priced food as well as an enjoyable time, but don't expect much from their "Mexican" dishes.

Bar México (open Monday through Saturday, 3 p.m. to 12 midnight; closed Sunday; 22-7600): Bar México is one of San José's most revered traditional nightspots, where *boca*-making has been elevated to an art. It has live mariachi bands. To get there from downtown you have to walk through a bad neighborhood, so it's better to take the Barrio México bus at Calle 7, Avenida Central. A cab will take you there for about $1. It's kitty-corner from the Barrio México church.

El Pueblo, in Barrio Tournón near the entrance to the Guápiles Highway, is a huge maze of Spanish colonial-style alleyways and tiled roofs. You can spend hours wandering around there, getting lost and spending money. **Babaloo** (open Monday through Thursday, 5 p.m. to 2 a.m.; Saturday and Sunday, 5 p.m. to 4 a.m.; 22-5746) and **Los Balcones** (open Monday through Thursday, 5 p.m. to 2 a.m.; Saturday and Sunday, 5 p.m. to 4 a.m.; 23-3704) feature live music, from Latin fusion to Andean to *nueva trova* to jazz. There is a small bar where you can hear authentic Argentinean tango. A skating rink and three discotheques also await you at El Pueblo. **Lukas** (open Sunday and Monday, 11:30 a.m. to 12 midnight; Tuesday through Saturday, 11:30 a.m. to 5 a.m.; 33-8145) is a popular place to go for a moderately priced late dinner or snack. **Rias Bajas** (open Monday through Saturday, 12 noon to 3 p.m., 6 to 11:30 p.m.; closed Sunday; 33-3214), one of San José's most elegant seafood restaurants, is also there. At the **Cocina de Leña** (open daily, 11:30 a.m. to 3 p.m., 6 to 11:30 p.m.; 55-1360) you can eat native Costa Rican dishes in an authentic *campesino* atmosphere, for twice the price of the Mercado Central. The rest of El Pueblo is full of additional restaurants and nightclubs, as well as boutiques, galleries, and offices. Most nightspots have a cover charge, especially on weekends and holidays, but it's diverting to go and wander there, even if you don't go in any of them. El Pueblo is located north of downtown, across from the Hotel Bougainvillea. Walk, or take a Calle Blancos bus from Calle 1, Avenida 5.

Soda La Perla and **Soda Palace** (open all night; Avenida 2, Calles Central/2): Like Chelles, these two restaurants are not special in themselves. They are mentioned as places where budding novelists can go to polish their powers of character description. Apparently the 1948 insurrection was planned over fried fish *bocas* and beer at the Soda Palace. Roving calypso bands come in, take a table, and play for everyone just for the joy of it. The restaurants are on either side of the Teatro Melico Salazar. (Be careful in the Soda Palace neighborhood—Parque Central can be dangerous at night.)

Tonite (Calle 7, Avenidas Central/1): One of several gay discos in town, for both women and men. Located across from Casino Español.

RESTAURANTS

COFFEE SHOPS

Below are some of the best places we've found to eat a quick meal or have a cup of coffee. The traditional Tico way to serve coffee is in two separate pitchers, one filled with strong black coffee and the other with steaming hot milk. You can mix them to suit your taste. Many establishments have stopped this practice for economic reasons, but Manolo's, Spoon, and Giacomín have retained the tradition. Decaffeinated coffee is available only in those restaurants that serve Café Britt, Costa Rica's excellent export-quality coffee. Most places do not offer herbal teas, although some excellent ones are manufactured here. You can always bring your own and ask for a pot of hot water at restaurants. Incidentally, the concept of smoking and nonsmoking areas in restaurants is unheard of. If it matters to you, stick to vegetarian restaurants.

Abacus (open Tuesday through Saturday, 11:30 a.m. to 11 p.m.; Sunday, 11:30 a.m. to 6 p.m.; closed Monday; 28-9616): Serves crepes, salads, and yummy desserts. It is located next to Tega on the road to Escazú. *Moderate.*

Azafrán (open daily, 10 a.m. to 6 p.m.; 25-5230): They make delicious sandwiches, lasagna, canneloni, and desserts. The food can be ordered to go, and they offer an excellent catering service. Their *torta Azafrán* has to be one of the best cakes of all time. Located in Los Yoses, next to Dr. Starke. *Moderate.*

Giacomín (open Monday through Saturday, 8 a.m. to 12 noon, 2 p.m. to 7 p.m.): The upstairs tea room is a nice place to enjoy coffee and pastries or homemade bonbons. It is next to the Los Yoses Automercado. *Moderate.*

Café Ruiseñor (open Monday through Saturday, 11:30 a.m. to 7 p.m.; 25-2562): This is a lovely place that serves delicious pastries and light meals made with pure, healthful ingredients. It has some outdoor tables. Located in Los Yoses, 150 meters east of Automercado—a 20-minute walk from downtown toward San Pedro. *Moderate.*

Downtown San José

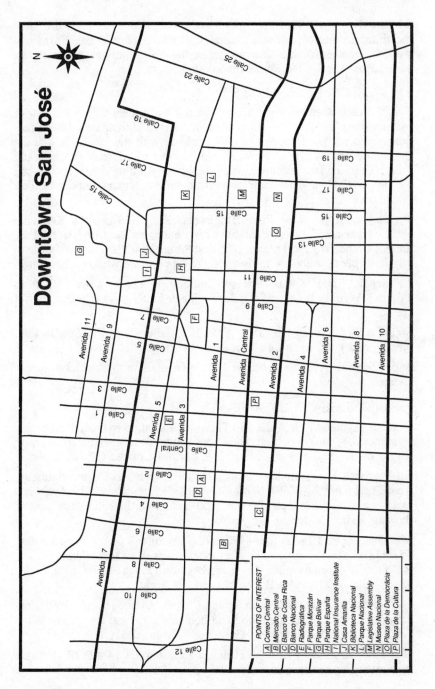

POINTS OF INTEREST

A	Correo Central
B	Mercado Central
C	Banco de Costa Rica
D	Banco Nacional
E	Radiografica
F	Parque Morazán
G	Parque Bolívar
H	Parque España
I	National Insurance Institute
J	Casa Amarilla
K	Biblioteca Nacional
L	Parque Nacional
M	Legislative Assembly
N	Museo Nacional
O	Plaza de la Democracia
P	Plaza de la Cultura

Spoon: Here you'll find light meals and outrageous desserts. It has three locations: downtown, Avenida Central, Calles 5/7; in Los Yoses, 100 meters west, 100 meters south of Cancún, before the three fountains; and in Pavas, across from the United States Embassy. *Moderate.*

INEXPENSIVE EATERIES

The **Mercado Central** (Avenidas Central/1 and Calles 6/8) is filled with inexpensive places to eat—many of them, like the Marisquería Ribera, recommended for good food. The only problem with the market is that the restaurants are usually so crowded, you don't feel you can sit down and relax. Go in the late afternoon when things are winding down, so you can eat inexpensively and not compete with hundreds of hungry workers on their lunch hour.

By the way, if you must, Pizza Hut, Burger King, McDonald's, Kentucky Fried Chicken, and Taco Bell all have branches here. They are fast, but they are not as cheap as local places. The best thing about them is that they usually have clean, easy-to-find bathrooms, a boon in downtown San José.

El Escorial (open Monday through Saturday, 11 a.m. to 2 p.m., 5 p.m. to 11 p.m.; Avenida 1, Calles 5/7): Serves lunch for $1 and has a good buffet for $3.

Soda La Casita (open weekdays; Avenida 1, Calles Central/1): Small, clean, homey, and good for a quick breakfast or lunch.

Soda Central (Avenida 1, Calles 3/5): Specializes in thick chicken empanadas.

VEGETARIAN RESTAURANTS

Don Sol (Avenida 7 bis, Calle 15): This is a pleasant, inexpensive vegetarian restaurant. Try the *energético*, a delicious natural fruit salad; the *plato fuerte* (lunch of the day) is very filling. It is northeast of the Casa Amarilla.

La Mazorca (open Monday through Friday, 9 a.m. to 8 p.m.; Saturday, 9 a.m. to 2 p.m.; 24-8069): Serves macrobiotic fare, whole-wheat pastries, and natural food products. Located 100 meters north, 200 meters east of the San Pedro Church in San Pedro.

Mordisco (open Monday through Saturday, 9 a.m. to 9 p.m.; closed Sunday; 55-2448): Offers elegant vegetarian meals, as well as fish and chicken. It is a bit more expensive than the others, but worth it. On Paseo Colón, Calles 22/24, next to Mercedes Benz.

La Nutrisoda (open 11 a.m. to 6 p.m.; Calle 3, Avenida 2; 55-3959): Features wholesome vegetarian food and homemade natural ice cream. In the Edificio Las Arcadas, next to Gran Hotel Costa Rica.

Shakti (open Monday through Friday, 7 a.m. to 4 p.m.; Calle 13, Avenida 8): Serves vegetarian goodies.

Vishnu: Gives inexpensive, generous servings. It's crowded at lunch—get there early. There are three locations: Avenida 1, Calles 1/3; Calle 14, Avenidas Central/2; and Calle 1, Avenida 4.

MODERATE TO EXPENSIVE RESTAURANTS

San José has many excellent restaurants. In the following list you will find many French, Italian, and Chinese places, but don't overlook those that specialize in Lebanese, Peruvian, Spanish, Hungarian, Korean, Japanese, or Swiss cuisines. See Chapter Seven for excellent restaurants in a mountain setting less than an hour's drive from the city.

Moderate means that most entrées are under $7.50. *Expensive* indicates that entrées are $7.50 to $15. Wine can really increase the total price of a dinner, since wines in Costa Rica are imported and expensive. All restaurant bills include a 10 percent tip and a 12 percent tax. Tipping is not customary but is certainly appreciated, especially when the service is good.

L'Ambiance (open Monday through Saturday, 7 to 10 a.m., 12 noon to 2 p.m., and 6:30 to 10 p.m.; Sunday, 7 to 10 a.m. and 12 noon to 12 midnight; Calle 13, Avenidas 9/11; 22-6702, 23-1598): Features elegant cuisine at reasonable prices. In Hotel L'Ambiance. *Moderate.*

Ambrosia (open Monday through Friday, 11:30 a.m. to 3 p.m., 6 to 10:30 p.m.; Saturday, 11:30 a.m. to 3 p.m.; Sunday, 11:30 a.m. to 10:30 p.m.; 53-8012): A quiet, cozy place for lunch, tea, or dinner, serving both vegetarian and nonvegetarian fare. All specialties are named after Greek deities. Located in the Centro Comercial de la Calle Real in San Pedro. *Moderate.*

Hotel Amstel (open daily, 6:30 a.m. to 10:45 p.m.; Calle 7, Avenidas 1/3; 22-4622): Well known for its reasonably priced, excellent meals and good service. *Moderate.*

Arirang (open Monday through Friday, 11:30 a.m. to 2:30 p.m., 5:30 to 9:30 p.m.; Saturday, 5:30 to 9:30 p.m.; 23-2838): Offers Korean specialties. Located in the Edificio Colón (Paseo Colon, Calles 38/40). *Moderate.*

Arlene (open Monday through Saturday, 12 noon to 2 p.m., 6:30 to 11 p.m., Sundays 1-5 p.m.; 28-0370): Arlene is the Julia Child of Costa Rica, a graduate of the Cordon Bleu. Her restaurant offers an elegant atmosphere and an unusual and creative menu offering everything from exquisitely prepared tamales to barbecued ribs to tournedos al Tarragon. The Sunday buffet features the cuisine of a different country each week. Rather pricey, but unique. Located across from the Escazú Country Club. *Expensive.*

Ave Fénix (open Monday through Saturday, 11 a.m. to 11 p.m.; 25-3362): Serves authentic Chinese cuisine featuring Szechuan specials. Located 200 meters west of the San Pedro Church. *Moderate.*

Balcón de Europa (open Sunday through Friday, 12 noon to 10 p.m.; closed Saturday; Calle 9, Avenidas Central/1; 21-4841): Chef Franco Piatti does his best to make you feel at home and serves homemade fettucine and delicious cheeses. *Moderate.*

Beijing City (open Tuesday through Friday, 12 noon to 2:30 p.m., 5:30 to 11 p.m.; Saturday, 12 noon to 11 p.m.; Sunday, 12 noon to 9 p.m.; closed Monday; 28-6939): Offers especially delicious and authentic Hunan and Szechuan specialties, including Peking duck (must be ordered 48 hours in advance). Located in Escazú, about 1 kilometer west of the United States Embassy residence. *Moderate.*

Beirut (open Tuesday through Saturday, 11:30 a.m. to 3 p.m., 6 to 11 p.m.; Sunday, 12 noon to 5 p.m.; Avenida 1, Calle 32; 57-1808): Features Middle Eastern specialties. Located one block north of the Paseo Colón branch of Pollos Kentucky. *Moderate.*

Le Bistrot (open Tuesday through Sunday, 11 a.m. to 10:30 p.m.; 53-8062): This is one of our favorite places, very small, with a relaxed French savoir faire. It is 100 meters east, 20 meters north of the San Pedro Church. *Moderate.*

Hotel Bougainvillea: The Barrio Tournón and new Santo Domingo Bougainvilleas, well known as fine hotels, have excellent restaurants as well. Try their breakfast buffets. Barrio Tournón: 33-6622; Santo Domingo: 40-8822. There is shuttle-bus service between the two hotels. *Moderate.*

Bromelias (open daily, 11:30 a.m. to 11:30 p.m.; Calle 23, Avenida 3; 21-3848): Serves superb and original European cuisine. Try the Hojaladre St. Jacques, or select the ingredients for your personalized grilled brochette. A bit pricey but worth it. Next to the Fercori building east of the old Atlantic railroad depot. *Expensive.*

Le Chandelier (open Monday through Friday, 11:30 a.m. to 2 p.m., 6:30 to 11 p.m.; 25-3980): Fancy French cuisine. From Spoon in Los Yoses, 100 meters south, 100 meters east, and 100 meters south. *Expensive.*

Flor del Loto (open Monday through Saturday, 11 a.m. to 3 p.m., 6 to 11:30 p.m.; Sunday, 11:30 a.m. to 9:30 p.m.; 32-4652): Offers delicious Hunan and Szechuan Chinese specialties. On the east side of the ICE (pronounced "ee-say") building, Sabana Norte. *Moderate.*

Fuji (open Monday through Friday, 12 noon to 2:30 p.m., 6:30 to 10:30 p.m.; Saturday, 6:30 to 10:30 p.m.; 32-8122): This is the Hotel Corobicí's Japanese restaurant, with tatami-covered, private dining rooms for six. The Corobici is near the northeast corner of La Sabana. *Expensive.*

La Galería (open Monday through Friday, 12 noon to 12 midnight; Saturday, 7 to 11 p.m.; 34-0850): This is one of San José's best restaurants, featuring excellent European cuisine. Call ahead for reservations. Located in Los Yoses, 50 meters west of Spoon. *Moderate.*

Goya (open Monday through Saturday, 11 a.m. to 2:30 p.m., 5:30 to 11 p.m.; Avenida 1, Calles 5/7; 21-3887): Noted for good food and pleasant service. *Moderate.*

L'Ile de France (open Monday through Friday, 11:45 a.m. to 2 p.m., 6:30 to 10 p.m.; Saturday, 6:30 to 10 p.m.; Calle 7, Avenidas Central/2; 22-4241): Offers excellent French cuisine and superb service. It's pricey, but you don't have to order a whole meal. *Expensive.*

Lai Yuin (open Monday through Saturday, 11 a.m. to 3 p.m., 6 to 11 p.m.; Sunday, 11 a.m. to 10 p.m.; 53-5055): Specializes in Chinese seafood. In Curridabat, across from the Indoor Club. *Moderate.*

Machu Pichu (open Monday through Friday, 11:30 a.m. to 3 p.m., 6:30 to 10 p.m.; Saturday, 6:30 to 10 p.m.; 22-7384): Features authentic Peruvian ceviche, pisco sours, and *anticuchos*. Located on Calle 32, Avenida 1, 125 meters north of Paseo Colón. *Moderate.*

Marcois (open daily, 12 noon to 10 p.m.; 24-9838): Has good food and service. The portions are small, but the ingredients are of excellent quality. Located 100 meters south of Pops in Curridabat. *Expensive.*

María Alexandra (open Monday through Saturday, 11:30 a.m. to 2:30 p.m., 5:30 to 11:30 p.m.; closed Sunday; 28-4876): Located in the aparthotel of the same name in Escazú, this small restaurant is quiet and intimate, with dependably good food and service. *Moderate.*

La Masía de Triquell (open Tuesday through Saturday, 11:30 a.m. to 2 p.m., 6 to 10 p.m.; Sunday 11:30 a.m. to 3:30 p.m.; 21-5073): Spanish cuisine in a lovely colonial atmosphere. Elegant. Calle 40, Avenida 2. *Expensive.*

Miro's Bistro (open Monday through Saturday, 12 noon to 10 p.m.; 53-4242): Features good Italian food and brick-walled bohemian decor. It is a pleasant walk from downtown in Barrio Escalante, 300 meters north and 20 meters east of the *pulpería* La Luz, along the train tracks. *Moderate.*

La Nueva China (open Monday through Friday, 11 a.m. to 2:30 p.m., 5:30 to 11:30 p.m.; Saturday and Sunday, 11:30 a.m. to 11:30 p.m.; 24-4478): This is one of San José's best Chinese restaurants. Located in San Pedro, across from the Banco Popular. *Moderate.*

Paprika (open Monday through Friday, 11:30 a.m. to 2:15 p.m., 6 to 10:15 p.m.; Saturday, 6 to 10:15 p.m.; Avenida Central, Calles 29/33; 25-8971): Serves delicious soups, salads, omelettes, main dishes, and desserts—all made with fresh ingredients—in a quiet, comfortable atmosphere. *Moderate.*

Rincón Europeo (open Tuesday through Saturday, 11 a.m. to 2 p.m., 6 to 10 p.m.; Sunday, 11:30 a.m. to 3 p.m.; 35-8678): Features great Hungarian food. Located near the souvenir shops in Moravia. *Moderate.*

Valerio's (open Sunday through Thursday, 11:30 a.m. to 11:30 p.m.; Friday and Saturday, 11:30 a.m. to 1 a.m.; 25-0838): Offers delicious pizza and lasagna and great desserts at reasonable prices. Located in Los Yoses, in the shopping center next to Cancún. *Moderate.*

Vía Veneto (open daily, 7:30 a.m. to 11:30 p.m.; 34-2898): Excellent Italian food, elegant atmosphere, delicious pastries. In Curridabat, across from the Indoor Club. *Moderate.*

Zermatt (open Sunday through Friday, 12 noon to 2 p.m., 7 to 11 p.m.; Saturday, 7 to 11 p.m.; 22-0604): Swiss specialties, including fondue. Located 100 meters north, 25 meters east of Santa Teresita Church (Calle 23, Avenida 11 bis). *Expensive.*

LODGING

In addition to the accommodations below, you may want to check the listings in the following chapter, which covers the Central Valley area. The towns of Alajuela and Heredia are closer to the airport than San José and may be good places to stay on your way in and out of Costa Rica.

LARGE DELUXE HOTELS

All have elegant restaurants, bars, casinos, and convention facilities and rooms with bathtubs, phones, and views. Prices are $100-$140, double occupancy.

Aurola Holiday Inn (cable TV, indoor pool; $120-$140; Avenida 5, Calle 5; 33-7233, 33-7036, fax: 55-1036): Has a sauna, a gym, and a nonsmoking floor and is firesafe and earthquake-proof. Located downtown, across from Parque Morazán.

Corobicí (cable TV, pool; $100-$120; 32-8122, fax: 31-5834): Has tennis courts and a sauna. On the northeast corner of La Sabana.

San José Palacio (cable TV, pool; $100-$140; 20-2034, fax: 20-2036). This is a very luxurious, Spanish-owned hotel, with a gym, sauna, and steam room, but we deplore the overuse of native endangered hardwoods such as *cristobal* in the ceilings, walls, and doors. Located on General Cañas Highway between La Sabana and La Uruca.

SMALL DELUXE HOTELS

L'Ambiance (cable TV; $90-$100; Calle 13, Avenidas 9/11; 22-6702, fax: 23-0481): This is a small, exclusive, and very quiet hotel in an old Spanish-style home with a courtyard and fountain. It is filled with antiques and features a gourmet restaurant and complete concierge service.

Tara Resort (pool; $140-$180; 28-6992, fax: 28-9651): This hotel is in an elegant antebellum-style mansion high in the hills above Escazú, a western suburb of San José. It has a restaurant. Breakfast and airport pickup are included in rates.

MODERATE HOTELS

These are in the $50-$90 range, double occupancy. Most are downtown, so ask for a quieter room off the street.

Ambassador (small refrigerator, cable TV; $50-$80; no charge for children under 12; 21-8155, fax: 55-3396): This hotel has rather dark, narrow hallways, but staying here gets you a 10 percent discount at discos, jewelry stores, and boutiques. It is a 20-minute walk from downtown on Paseo Colón, Calles 26/28.

Amstel ($50-$60; Calle 7, Avenidas 1/3; 22-4622, fax: 33-3329): This centrally located hotel is best known for its excellent restaurant. There are quieter rooms on the east side of the building.

Balmoral (cable TV; $80-$90; Avenida Central, Calles 7/9; 21-1919, 21-5022, fax: 21-7826): A centrally located hotel for business travelers. It has a sauna.

Bougainvillea: Features quiet, well-appointed rooms, an excellent restaurant, and superb service. Recommended. Make reservations far in advance. Two locations: Barrio Tournón ($60-$80; 33-6622, fax: 22-5211), north of downtown, and Santo Domingo de Heredia ($60-$80; 40-8822, fax: 40-8484), 9 kilometers from San José.

Don Carlos (cable TV; $50-$80; Calle 9, Avenida 9, No. 779; 21-6707, fax: 55-0828): Located in a pleasant historical neighborhood, this hotel has charming decor, a gym, tour videos, and a great souvenir shop. Very strict reservation and deposit policy.

Don Paco (cable TV; $50-$60 including breakfast; Calle 33, Avenida 9; 34-9088, fax: 34-9588): A very clean, nicely decorated small hotel in a refurbished colonial-style house in a quiet neighborhood near theaters and good restaurants. A good value. Recommended. Located 700 meters north of *pulpería* La Luz.

Dunn Inn (hot water, private bath, fans, cable TV, phone; $60-$80 including breakfast; Calle 5, Avenida 11; 22-3232, 22-3426, fax: 21-4596): A corner building in an old neighborhood, with a plant-filled patio/bar. Second-floor rooms are less noisy.

Europa (cable TV, indoor pool; $60-$70; Calle Central, Avenidas 3/5; 22-1222, fax: 21-3976): A distinctive European-style hotel with a light and airy atmosphere. Central, streetside rooms are discounted because of noise and fumes.

Gran Hotel Costa Rica (cable TV; $70-$80; Avenidas Central/2, Calle 3; 21-4000, fax: 21-3501): Located across from the National Theater; its outdoor café is popular with tourists.

Gran Hotel Doña Inez ($60-$80; Calle 11, Avenidas 2/6; 22-7443, fax: 23-5426): This hotel is small and fancy, with nice baths. Most rooms are off the street. Near the National Museum.

Grano de Oro (parking; $60-$80; Calle 30, Avenidas 2/4, No. 251; 55-3322, fax: 21-2782): In an elegant restored mansion located in a quiet neighborhood, yet near to restaurants, theaters, and shops. It has comfortable furnishings, deluxe baths, a good restaurant, no-smoking rooms, and a sunny patio. If you have to stay in San José, this is the way to go. Highly recommended.

La Gran Vía ($50-$60; Avenida Central, Calles 1/3; 22-7737, fax: 22-7205): Streetside rooms have balconies; back rooms are quieter. It is centrally located and clean.

Irazú (cable TV, pool; $60-$70; better rooms, $100-$110; 32-4811, fax: 32-45490): A large hotel with a convention center, casino, tennis courts, sauna, and bus service. Located 15 minutes west from downtown on the airport highway.

Napoleon (cable TV, pool; $60-$80 including breakfast; off-season discounts; Calle 40, Avenida 5; 23-3252, 23-3282, fax: 22-9487): Recently remodeled, attractive rooms in a clean, quiet neighborhood near La Sabana. A good value in this category. Recommended.

Rey (heated water, private bath, cable TV; $50-$60 including breakfast; Avenida 7, Calle 9; 33-3819, fax: 33-1769): A small, new, and very clean hotel. The streetside rooms have traffic noise. Free airport pickup with advance notice.

Royal Gardens ($50-$60; Calle Central, Avenida Central; 57-0022, 57-0023, fax: 57-1517): A centrally located hotel featuring a casino and a restaurant that serves authentic Chinese food.

Plaza ($60-$80; Avenida Central, Calles 2/4; 22-5533, fax: 22-2641): Clean, centrally located, and well run, with small rooms and a newly remodeled restaurant (open 6 a.m. to 10 p.m.).

Presidente (cable TV; $60-$70; Avenida Central, Calles 7/9; 22-3022, fax: 21-1205): Has a casino, a discotheque, glitzy decor, good service, and a central location.

Tennis Club (pool; $50-$60; 32-1266, fax: 32-3867): Complete with tennis courts, a gym, a sauna, and playgrounds. Located on the south side of La Sabana.

Torremolinos (cable TV, pool; $60-$70; Calle 40, Avenida 5 bis; 22-5266, 22-9129, fax: 55-3167): A quiet hotel, with sauna and a shuttle bus to downtown. Located two blocks east of La Sabana.

BED-AND-BREAKFASTS

These are a growing trend in Costa Rica and can be found both in the city and the country. Most of them offer a much more pleasant atmosphere than a regular hotel, and many are cheaper as well. Even though there are other hotels that include breakfast in their rates, the distinguishing characteristic of bed-and-breakfasts is that they are small and have a homelike atmosphere, usually with the owner in residence. All of the establishments listed below pride themselves on the personalized service they give to their guests in tour planning, car rentals, etc. Most provide lunch and dinner on request and offer kitchen privileges. The **Bed-and-Breakfast Association** has a "one call does it all" service to connect guests with the bed-and-breakfast that is right for them. Call Pat (28-9200) or Debbie (23-4168).

Ara Macao ($50-$60; phone/fax: 33-2742): Very clean, with pleasant, sunny upstairs rooms, a nice eating area, and free airport pickup. Near the National Museum in Barrio California, 50 meters south of the Pizza Hut.

Bello Monte (with shared bath, $40-$50; with private bath and balcony, $50-$60; phone/fax: 34-3879): Comfortable rooms with beautiful views in the cool, fresh climate of San Ramón de Trés Ríos, in the hills east of San José. Half an hour by bus to downtown.

Casa de Finca 1926 ($60-$80; phone/fax: 25-6169): Very quiet, in a beautiful old home elegantly decorated by the German owner. It has lovely gardens with a fountain and offers easy access to buses. Located east of San José, near the town of Trés Ríos.

Casa de las Tías (some private, some shared baths; $50-$60; phone/fax: 28-5517): An ample wood-paneled house at the end of a quiet street in Escazú. Each room is decorated with mementos of the owners' sojourns in various Latin American countries as part of the foreign service.

Casa 429 El Paso (no children; with shared bath, $50-$60; with private bath, $60-$80; Calle 3, Avenidas 4/6; 22-1708, fax: 33-5785): Tastefully refurbished old home in the heart of San José offering large comfortable rooms with wicker furniture and lots of plants. Most rooms are away from the street. There is a covered patio and jacuzzi in the back. Airport pickup ($10) is available. Located 150 meters south of the National Theater.

Casa María (some private, some shared baths; cable TV, pool; $40-$80; 28-2270, fax: 28-0015): Offers kitchen privileges. Located in a residential neighborhood in Escazú, 1 kilometer east of the church.

Casa Verde (with shared bath, $50-$60; suites with cable TV, $60-$80; Calle 7, Avenida 9; phone/fax: 23-0969): In a lovingly restored old home in San José's historic Barrio Amón. It has a sauna.

Center for Creative Arts ($20-$30; 82-8769, fax: 82-6959): The cabina-type rooms are not much to get excited about, but the massages, chiropractic treatments, color healing, painting, and wood-carving, orchid-growing, music, dance, and Kirpalu yoga classes are, for those who would enjoy getting to know this aspect of Costa Rica's multinational New Age community. Airport pickup ($10) is available. Located on spacious grounds in sunny Santa Ana, west of San José.

Costa Verde (private bath; $50-$60; phone/fax: 28-4080): Owned by the author of the *Insight Guide to Costa Rica*, an amusing host. It has well-tended gardens, a spacious patio, an outdoor jacuzzi, tennis courts, and king-size beds. Airport pickup ($10) is available. It is in Escazú in a quiet, secluded, country setting.

D'Raya Vida (some private, some shared baths; $80-$90; Calle 15, Avenidas 11/13; 23-4168, fax: 23-4157): In a very elegant and delightfully quirky house at the end of a quiet street near downtown, D'Raya Vida has many unusual and artistic touches, a small patio with fountain, a mirrored reading room, and free airport pickup.

La Evasión (hot water; some private, some shared baths; pool; $12-$80, depending on amenities; 28-1141, fax: 21-9466): Run by a young French couple in a large, rather dark, modernistic suburban house, it has a hot tub, a sauna, and hammocks and is favored by a younger crowd. Available for groups. Located in Escazú.

Maripaz (hot water; some private, some shared baths; $30-$40; 53-8456): In a friendly Costa Rican home in San Pedro.

Park Place (shared bath; $30-$40; phone/fax: 28-9200): Has views; light, airy rooms; access to tennis courts; and an inexpensive restaurant nearby. Located on the San Antonio bus line, 1.5 kilometers above Escazú.

Located west of Parque Nacional, **Pensión de la Cuesta** (shared bath, refrigerator; $20-$30; Avenida 1, Calles 11/15, 55-2896, fax: 57-2272) has eight rather dark rooms in an interesting old building run by artists—the rooms are filled with paintings and creative touches. The fun will be in hanging around with other guests in the light-filled living/dining room. Near museums and galleries.

La Posada del Bosque (hot water, shared bath; $40-$50; 28-1164, fax: 28-6381): A quiet home-away-from-home on ample grounds in Escazú, this posada is run by friendly Costa Rican owners who are world travelers and give true hospitality *à la tica*. The wonderful home cooking is by Doña Clarita—homemade tortillas, the works. There is access to pool and tennis courts at nearby Bello Horizonte Country Club. Airport pickup ($12) is available. Recommended.

Roxana's (shared bath; no children, no smoking; $30-$40; 35-0178, fax: 35-4440): Located in a quiet neighborhood in Tibás, a northern suburb of San José.

Hotel Santo Tomás (hot water, private bath; $50-$80; group and off-season discounts; Avenida 7, Calles 3/5; 55-0448, fax: 22-3950; German, French, and English spoken): This is larger than most bed-and-breakfasts, but still worthy of the name because of the personalized service. Secure and centrally located, it is in a beautifully remodeled old home with many nice touches. The rooms are back off the street, a real boon in noisy downtown San José.

Tres Arcos (with shared bath, $30-$40; with private bath, $40-$50; Avenida 10, No. 3773; phone/fax: 25-0271): Offers simple rooms in a large, rambling house in Los Yoses, a 20-minute stroll from downtown.

El Verolis (with shared bath, $30-$40; with private bath, $40-$50; 36-0662): Sunny rooms in an upscale section of Moravia, a northeastern suburb of San José.

Victoria Inn (some private, some shared baths; $30-$40; 40-2320, fax: 21-1514): Quiet rooms in a homey Spanish-style house in Moravia, near good souvenir shops.

Villa Escazú (hot water, shared bath; $30-$40; phone/fax: 28-9566): This attractive wood-paneled chalet-style house is on beautiful grounds and offers lots of peace and quiet. The upstairs rooms are more attractive. Recommended. In Escazú, west of San José.

APARTHOTELS

As the word implies, these are a cross between an apartment and a hotel. All have kitchens, phones, and TVs, but they tend to lack atmosphere. Discounts for weekly or monthly rental. It is best to make reservations by fax. If there is no fax, we have listed the mailing address.

Castilla ($40-$50; Calle 24, Avenidas 2/4; 22-2113, fax: 21-2080): Near Paseo Colon.

D'Galah ($50-$60; 34-1743, 53-7539; Apdo. 208, 2350 San José): Quiet, friendly, with music room and sauna. Rooms with or without kitchens. Across from the University of Costa Rica campus in San Pedro.

Don Carlos (color cable TV; $50-$60; weekly rates only; Calle 29, Avenidas Central/8; 21-6707, fax: 55-0828): Has views.

Lamm ($40-$50; Calle 15, Avenida 1; 21-4920, fax: 21-4720): These attractive older apartments are near parks and museums, but have traffic noise.

Llama del Bosque (cable TV, kitchenette, small pool; $40-$80 including breakfast; 24-0681, 25-5350): Situated on a clean, quiet street in Curridabat, east of San José, near buses and shopping. Rooms are around a plant-filled covered patio with the swimming pool. It tops all other aparthotels for atmosphere. Recommended. Located 100 meters south and 50 meters west of the Plaza de Sol shopping center.

María Alexandra (air-conditioning, cable TV, pool; $70-$80; 28-1507, fax: 28-5192): Quiet and very clean, with washing machines, a sauna, and an excellent restaurant. Located in Escazú, west of San José.

La Perla (color TV; $30-$40; 32-6153, fax: 20-0103): Has a friendly staff and is close to shopping. A good value. Located in La Uruca, 15 minutes by bus from downtown.

Ramgo ($50-$60; 32-3823, fax: 32-3111): Near La Sabana, 200 meters west, 100 meters south of the Tennis Club.

San José ($50-$60; Avenida 2, Calles 17/19; 21-6684, fax: 21-2443). Very convenient location near the National Museum.

Los Yoses (pool, parking; $50-$60 including breakfast; 25-0033, fax: 25-5595): Very clean. In Los Yoses, on the main thoroughfare.

MID-RANGE HOTELS

Alameda ($30-$40; Avenida Central, Calles 12/14; 21-3045, 21-6333, fax: 22-9673): Simple and friendly accommodations, located near the Coca Cola and other bus stops.

La Amistad (hot water, private bath, cable TV; $40-$50 including breakfast; Avenida 11, Calle 15; 21-1597, fax: 21-1409): Bills itself as a bed-and-breakfast, but its atmosphere is more hotel-like. It's clean. Located on a rather noisy corner in Barrio Otoya, east of downtown.

Bellavista (hot water, private bath; $20-$30; Avenida Central, Calles 19/21; 23-0095): Has chintzy charm but not a lot of fresh air. Most windows open onto a corridor. Fanciful *afro-caribeño* murals decorate the walls, and the baths are very clean. Near the Limón bus stop and the National Museum.

Cacts ($20-$30 including breakfast and airport pickup; Avenida 3 bis, No. 2845, Calles 28/30; 21-2928, fax: 21-8616): Quiet, very friendly, and helpful with travel arrangements. A 50 percent deposit is requested when making reservations. Located in a neighborhood west of the Coca Cola.

Costa Rica Inn ($20-$30; Calle 9, Avenidas 1/3; 22-5203, fax: 23-8385): Centrally located, with small rooms. Some have windows that open onto a corridor.

Diplomat ($30-$40; Calle 6, Avenidas Central/2; 21-8133, fax: 33-7474): This clean, well-run, centrally located hotel has a good restaurant and is a favorite with foreigners. A good value.

Doral (hot water, private bath, TV, phone; $30-$40; Avenida 4, Calle 8; 33-0665, 33-5069, fax: 33-4827): Offers clean, bright, sunny rooms with original art. The neighborhood is not great, but it's a good value.

Fortuna ($20-$30; Avenida 6, Calles 2/4; 23-5344, fax: 23-2743): Clean, but in a borderline neighborhood.

Galilea ($20-$30; 33-6925, fax: 23-1689): Clean, with light, airy rooms—the best are on the third floor—and an English-speaking staff. Near Plaza de la Democracia and the National Museum, Avenida Central, Calles 11/13.

La Gema (hot water, ceiling fans, TV; $30-$40 including breakfast; Avenida 12, Calles 9/11; phone/fax: 22-1074): A nice new hotel on a quiet street near downtown. The rooms in the back open onto a plant-filled courtyard, far from traffic noise, and there is a restaurant and bar. A good value.

Mansion Blanca Inn (heated water, private bath; $40-$50 including breakfast; Calle 9, Avenida 10; phone/fax: 28-9566): The second-floor rooms in this refurbished old home are bright and nicely decorated, with good beds. It is close to downtown, so there is some traffic noise.

Petit (some private, some shared baths; $20-$30; Calle 24, Avenidas Central/2; 33-0766, fax: 33-1938): The rooms are plain and a bit overpriced, but guests have kitchen privileges. Near La Sabana, in a good neighborhood yet close to buses.

Petit Victoria (heated water, private bath, cable TV, small refrigerator; $40-$50; Calle 24, Avenida 2; 33-1812, 33-1813, fax: 33-1938): A lovely old Victorian building in a nice neighborhood near La Sabana. There is some traffic noise. Guests have kitchen privileges. Located across from the Sala Garbo Theater.

Pico Blanco ($40-$50; 28-3197, 28-1908, fax: 28-5189): A mountain hotel with a great view, a friendly atmosphere, clean, charming rooms, and a restaurant. Recommended. In San Antonio de Escazú, 8 kilometers west of San José.

Posada Pegasus ($30-$40 including breakfast; weekly discounts; 28-4196, fax: 28-6381): "Dedicated to serenity, individuality, and natural beauty," this inn has views and a jacuzzi. It is in San Antonio de Escazú, next to Pico Blanco.

Ritz (heated water; with shared bath, $12-$20; with private bath, $20-$30; Calle Central, Avenidas 8/10; 22-4103, fax: 22-8849): This Swiss-owned hotel has a convivial atmosphere but is not in the best neighborhood.

San José Garden Court (hot water, private bath, air-conditioning, pool, parking; $40-$50 including full breakfast; Avenida 7, Calles 6/8; 22-3674, fax: 55-4613): This sparkling new 70-room hotel has a sauna and an exercise room. The north-facing rooms have a view of Irazú and Poás volcanos. A good value. It is in a centrally located but lousy neighborhood; hourly shuttle buses will whisk you away.

INEXPENSIVE HOTELS

These run $7-$20, double occupancy.

Astoria (with shared bath, under $7; with private bath, $7-$12; weekly discounts; Avenida 7, Calles 7/9; 21-2174): Quiet, with funky religious decor and small dark rooms.

Bienvenido (private bath; $12-$20; Calle 10, Avenidas 1/3; 21-1872): A large, clean, friendly, and well-run hotel one block from the Mercado Central. Most rooms are off the street, yet are light and fairly well ventilated. Recommended.

Boruca (heated water, shared bath; under $7; Calle 14, Avenidas 1/3; 23-0016): A clean, quiet, family-run hotel near buses. The small cubiclelike rooms don't have windows. It is secure, even though the neighborhood is not good. Very cheap—recommended for budget travelers.

Capital (hot water, private bath, ceiling fans, phone; $12-$20; Calle 4, Avenidas 3/5; phone/fax: 21-8497): Some rooms don't have windows. It's centrally located.

Centro Continental (hot water, shared bath; $12-$20; Calle Central, Avenidas 8/10; 33-1731, fax: 22-8849): A Swiss-owned hotel, next to Hotel Ritz.

Cocorí (hot water, private bath; $12-$20; Calle 16, Avenida 3; 33-0081): Has clean, light rooms and is close to bus stops, but is not in a good neighborhood. A good value.

Gran Hotel Centroamericano (private bath; $12-$20; Avenida 2, Calles 6/8; 21-3362): Has good wheelchair access and an inexpensive cafeteria.

Marlyn (heated water, both private and shared baths; $7-$12; Calle 4, Avenidas 7/9; 33-3212): This is an old house chopped up into dark rooms. It is fairly clean and is centrally located in a borderline neighborhood near the old penitentiary.

Morazán (under $7; Avenida 3, Calles 11/15; 21-9083): An old building with big, bare rooms and funky baths in a nice location near Parque Morazán and Parque Nacional.

Musoc (heated water; with shared bath, $7-$12; with private bath, $12-$20; Calle 16, Avenidas 1/3; 22-9437): Clean and well run, but the street noise is loud. It is a Peace Corps hangout. Located next to the Coca Cola bus station.

Otoya (heated water, both private and shared baths; $7-$12; Calle Central, Avenidas 5/7; 21-3925): Cheap, friendly, and centrally located, with large dark rooms.

Roma (cold water; under $7; Calle 14, Avenida 1; 23-2179): Noisy, but cheap and near buses.

HOSTELS

Toruma (under $7/person including breakfast; less with IYHF card; Avenida Central, Calles 31/33; 24-4085): This is the headquarters of the Costa Rica Youth Hostel Network. It has dormitory-style rooms, a washing machine, a kitchen, and an inexpensive *soda* (open 7:15 a.m. to 9 p.m.).

Casa Ridgway (heated water, shared bath; under $7; with private room, $7-$12/person; Avenida 6 bis, Calle 15; 33-6168; Apdo. 1507, 1000 San José): A small *pensión* that helps to support the Quaker Peace Center next door. It has a convivial atmosphere, kitchen and laundry privileges, and dormitory-style bunks in some rooms. Make reservations in advance—it is often full.

HOMESTAYS

Bell's Home Hospitality (with shared bath, $45; with private bath, $50; 25-4752, fax: 24-5884) matches you up with a compatible Costa Rican family. Breakfast is included in rates; dinner is $5 extra. Airport pickup ($10) is available. Free information service.

Renting a room with a Tico family: This is a good way to get to know the people and to practice your Spanish. To find a compatible family, call the language schools, look for signs at the University of Costa Rica, or contact Sra. Soledad Zamora (24-7937) or her sister Virginia (25-7344), women who specialize in connecting renters with rooms (Spanish only). The going rate for room, board, and laundry service is $180-$200 per person per month, less with fewer meals. Be prepared for a lot of hospitality. If noise bothers you, check first to see if your family leaves the TV or radio on all the time.

SOUVENIRS

Moderately priced souvenirs can be found at the government crafts cooperatives: CANAPI (Calle 11, Avenida 1) and the **Mercado Nacional de Artesanía** (Calle 11, Avenida 2 bis, behind the Soledad Church), as well as in the **Mercado Central** (Avenidas Central/1, Calles 6/8), and **La Casona** (Calle Central, Avenidas Central/1).

One of the most charming, complete, and inexpensive souvenir shops is in the converted home of one of Costa Rica's ex-presidents, now the **Hotel Don Carlos** (Calle 9, Avenida 9). **Arterica** (Avenida 2, Calles Central/2), a small shop next to the entrance of the Teatro Melico Salazar, is a showcase for artisans who are revitalizing Costa Rican native crafts, such a weaving, basket making, ceramics, and wood carving. It offers free courses in these through the University of Costa Rica, and gives workshops in the countryside to people wishing to develop their skills. You can also see indigenous crafts at ANDA (Avenida Central, Calles 5/7).

If you have a little more money to spend, visit **Atmósfera** (Calle 5, Avenida 1), **Magia** (Calle 5, Avenidas 1/3), **Suraska** (Calle 5, Avenida 3), or **La Galería** (Calle 1, Avenidas Central/1), where more artistic items are sold, including the innovative woodwork of two North Americans, Barry Biesanz and Jay Morrison. Biesanz specializes in exquisitely crafted bowls and boxes, as well as furniture, which can be seen at his workshop (28-1811) in Bello Horizonte, above Escazú. Morrison's creative hardwood furniture is displayed at Magia and also at his showroom, Tierra Extraña (82-6697), in Piedades de Santa Ana. Incidentally, the Audubon Society is not opposed to your buying souvenirs mad from tropical hardwoods.

The beautiful handicrafts of Guatemala and El Salvador can be found on the second floor of **La Casona** (Calle Central, Avenidas Central/1) and at **Sol Maya** (on Paseo Colón across from Hospital San Juan de Dios). Guatemalan textiles are also sold on Calle 3, Avenidas 3/5, next to the Automercado (closed weekends).

If you don't want to spend money, don't even think of visiting **Angie Theologos' gallery** (25-6565) of irresistible, one-of-a-kind jackets and vests. The individually designed, lined jackets are beautifully crafted from Guatemalan textiles. Each one is a work of art. By appointment only. The gallery is in La Granja de San Pedro, east of San José.

MISCELLANEOUS INFORMATION

NEWSPAPERS AND MAGAZINES

English-language newspapers and magazines are sold at the Candy Shop of the Gran Hotel Costa Rica (Calle 3, Avenidas Central/2), The Bookshop (Avenida 1, Calles 1/3), the Automercado (Calle 3, Avenidas 3/5), the Hotel Aurola (Calle 5, Avenida 5), Yaohan's (across from the Hotel Corobicí), the Hotel Bougainvillea (in Barrio Tournón on the north side of San José), and Librería Lehmann (Avenida Central, Calles 1/3). Most of them carry *The New York Times*, *The Wall Street Journal*, and the *Miami Herald*, as well as *Time* and *Newsweek*. You can also have the above periodicals delivered by calling **Agencia de Publicaciones de Costa Rica** (59-5555, 59-5658, 59-0812).

The **Mark Twain Library** of the Centro Cultural Costarricense-Norteamericano in Barrio Dent has the latest newspapers and a special room for watching CNN. German visitors can find a similar reading room at the **Instituto Goethe**, across from Pollos Kentucky on the road to San Pedro. Francophiles can visit the **Alianza Francesa** on the corner of Calle 5 and Avenida 7, behind the Hotel Aurola Holiday Inn in San José.

The best source of local news in English is *The Tico Times* (Apdo. 4632, San José; 22-8952; published Friday; 25 cents), which is available at the above places and at many hotels. Winner of the 1981 Interamerican Press Association award for distinguished service to the community, *The Tico Times* offers a well-researched synthesis of weekly events in Costa Rica and Central America as a whole. It is without comparison in its coverage of local environmental and political issues and gives an excellent rundown of cultural activities.

Casey's (Calle Central, Avenidas 7/9), Book Traders (in the Omni Building, Avenida 1, Calles 3/5), and Gambit (across from the bowling alley near the Centro Cultural) sell and trade used books in English.

MEETING PLACES

The **Friends' Peace Center** (Calle 15, Avenida 6 bis; 33-6168) in San José is a network for the various groups working for peace in Central America. It provides meeting space, activity coordination, a library, and educational programs, and hosts a weekly Quaker meeting. The staff of the center is made up of both Central and North Americans, most of them volunteers. They welcome donations of time or funding from interested people.

A variety of clubs meet regularly in San José, including The Women's Club, Bridge Club, Newcomer's Club, Republicans Abroad, Democrats Abroad, American Legion, Disabled American Veterans, Retired Officers Association, Masonic Lodge, Amnesty International, International Gay and Lesbian Association, La Leche League, Lions, Rotary, Women's Aglow Fellowship, Christian Women's Club, Amateur Fishing Club, Canada Club, Cricket Club, Coffee Pickin' Square Dancers, the Canoeing/Kayaking Club, Garden Club, AA, ACOA, and U.S. Citizens Concerned for Peace. Current hours and numbers are often listed in *The Tico Times*.

RELIGIOUS SERVICES

BAHA'I   There is a prayer breakfast Saturday at 8 a.m. in Escazú, 800 meters south of the first entrance to Bello Horizonte. The information center is on Calle 22, Avenida 4. (22-5335)

BAPTIST   English services are Sunday at 9 a.m., followed by fellowship and Sunday school. The church is in San Pedro, 125 meters south of Banco Anglo. (59-8743, 24-9424, 53-7911)

CATHOLIC   Saint Mary's Chapel, adjacent to the Sheraton Herradura Hotel, has an English mass Sunday at 4 p.m. The San Rafael de Escazú Church holds an English mass Saturday at 5 p.m. (39-0033)

EPISCOPAL   English services are Sunday at 8:30 a.m. at the Church of the Good Shepherd (Avenida 4, Calles 3/5; 22-1560).

ESCAZÚ CHRISTIAN FELLOWSHIP   Church and Sunday school are Sunday, 6 to 7 p.m., in the annex to the Country Day School. (28-2754)

HARE KRISHNA   Headquarters are at the Finca Nueva Goloka Vrindavana on the Cartago–Paraíso Road. (51-5422)

JEWISH   *Reform:* Bilingual services are held Friday at 8 p.m. at Congregation B'Nei Israel (32-9626, 57-1785, 31-6708). It also has Hebrew school, preschool, teen studies, and social programs. Call for information. *Conservative:* Synagogue Shaare Zion (Calle 22 bis, Avenida 1; 22-5449) has services Friday at 5:30 p.m.

METHODIST   Sunday services are at 9 a.m., Sunday school is at 9:30 in El Redentor. The Women's Aglow Fellowship (Avenida Central, Calles 9/11; 22-0360) meets on Wednesday.

MORMON   Sacrament meetings are on Sunday at 9 a.m.; adult Sunday school in English is at 9:30 a.m. The temple is in Barrio Los Yoses, 100 meters south of *pulpería* La Luz. (25-0208).

QUAKER   Bilingual worship services are Sunday at 11 a.m. at the Friends Peace Center (Avenida 6 bis, Calle 15; 33-6168, 24-4376).

THEOSOPHICAL SOCIETY   There are nightly lodges. (Avenida 1, Calles 11/15; 21-7246)

UNION CHURCH   The church offers free bus service, nursery and children's church, and neighborhood Bible-study groups. Sunday school is at 9 a.m., fellowship is at 10 a.m., and services at 10:25 a.m. It is located in Moravia. (26-3670)

UNITY   Prayer group is held Sunday at 9:30 a.m.; services are at 10:30 in Los Anonos in Escazú. (28-6805)

VICTORY CHRISTIAN CENTER   Sunday services are at 10 a.m. in La Uruca, 200 meters east and 75 meters north of Pozuelo. (82-7720)

YOGA   Gran Fraternidad Universal (Avenida 7 bis, Calle 15; 57-0928). *Kirpalu yoga:* eastside, 40-7325; westside, 82-8769.

SUPERMARKETS

Name-brand products from the United States are flooding Costa Rican supermarkets. Because they are imported, they are very expensive. Right next to them on the shelf will be a comparable locally made product for half the price.

Stores are often closed between 12 noon and 2 p.m. during the week. The **Más x Menos** supermarkets are open 8 a.m. to 8 p.m. and do not close for lunch or on Sunday. Ask at your hotel for the nearest one. The **Automercado,** less crowded, cleaner, and more expensive than the Más x Menos, is also open all day, but is closed Sunday. **Yaohan's,** a large Japanese-owned supermarket across from the Hotel Corobicí, Sabana East, is open on Sunday. It has a good produce section. On the east side, **Munoz y Nanne** in San Pedro is also famous for its produce.

ORCHIDS AND BUTTERFLIES

Orchid lovers should plan to visit during March or September when the **National Orchid Shows** are held. For more information, write the **Orchid Association of Costa Rica** (Apdo. 6351, 1000 San José). Butterfly enthusiasts will enjoy the **Museum of Entomology** at the University of Costa Rica's Facultad de Agronomía (open Wednesday and Thursday, 1 to 6 p.m.; free admission). It is located on the University of Costa Rica campus in San Pedro. (See Chapter Seven for information on the Butterfly Farm in La Guácima, and Chapter Eleven regarding the Butterfly Garden in Monteverde.)

PLACES TO WALK OR RUN IN SAN JOSÉ

LA SABANA   We know of no other city that has converted its outgrown international airport into a metropolitan park with sports facilities. The National Gymnasium was built on the southeast corner of the former airfield, the National Stadium on the northwest corner. A small lake, which had been filled in, is now restored, and the Air Terminal Building has become the

National Art Museum. Residential districts have been built on three sides of La Sabana (which means "the savannah").

With an Olympic swimming pool; jogging and walking paths; tennis, volleyball, and basketball courts; and soccer and baseball fields, La Sabana is a favorite recreation area on weekends and a training ground for runners and joggers during lunch hours (showers are provided). There's a hill for kite flying and lots of trees for relaxing in the shade. People fly-cast in the lake. To get there, take the *Sabana–Cementerio* bus (Calle 7, Avenida Central or Calle 2, Avenida 3).

BEHIND THE ZOO   Walk through Parque Morazán and Parque de España to the Casa Amarilla. Go north on Calle 11, which becomes a winding, quiet, tree-lined street along the upper border of Parque Bolívar. Keep winding around until you come to the railroad tracks and a rural guard station. Climb the steps and you're in Barrio Aranjuez, a nice, older neighborhood. You'll be walking east on Avenida 11. Go to your left two blocks after the tracks and soon you'll be at the edge of a cliff with cement stairs going down it. There, you'll find basketball courts, a soccer field, and a track, free from San José's diesel fumes.

THE BACK WAY TO SAN PEDRO   Walk through Parque Nacional to the Limón train station. Follow the tracks going east, across Calle 23 and on past some graceful old houses with lovely flower gardens. Follow the tracks one block past the *pulpería* Ambos Mares until you see a sign that says *Final del Patio*. After this, there is no sidewalk, so keep jogging to your left and head east at the next block. You'll only have to zigzag once; then, after the Colegium Fidelitas (notice the Centro Cultural Costarricense-Norteamericano to your right), it's a short zigzag, and you'll be heading east again. This street ends across from an entrance to the University of Costa Rica campus. A circular drive a mile long goes around the campus and is pleasantly shaded by beautiful trees. If you go early in the morning you'll see runners, walkers, and a lot of birds.

PARQUE DEL ESTE   This rather deteriorated park about 5 kilometers above San Pedro in San Rafael de Montes de Oca is a great place to escape from pollution for a few hours. It's an expansive green area cleared out of a lush canyon. There's a Vita Course jogging and exercise trail with little signs that invite you to do all sorts of strenuous things along the way. There's also a pool, basketball courts, a soccer field, picnic tables, playgrounds, a lookout point with a sign that identifies the mountains on the horizon, and a zigzagging nature trail. Get there on the San Ramón de Trés Ríos bus (Calle 7, Avenida 2) that and passes through San Pedro. The park is pretty crowded on weekends and holidays. (Open until 4 p.m.; closed Monday.)

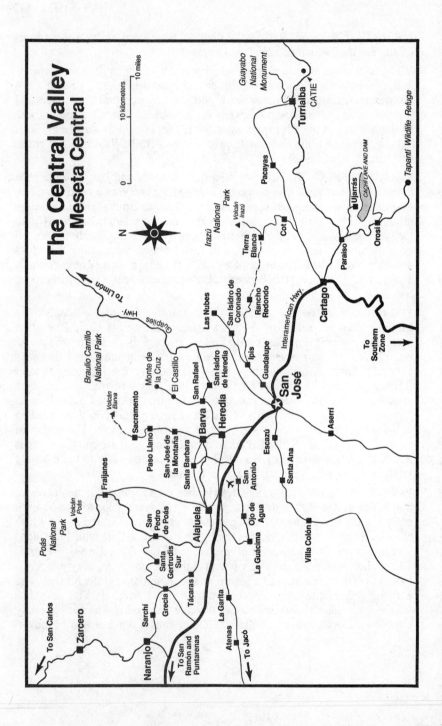

The Central Valley
Meseta Central

SEVEN

Central Valley and Surroundings

Costa Rica's Central Valley, or Meseta Central, is a large, fertile plateau surrounded by high mountains. Seventy percent of the country's population lives in this region, which centers around the towns of Alajuela, Heredia, and Cartago, as well as the city of San José. As you leave the more densely populated areas and drive toward the valley's western edge at San Ramón, or wind down through spectacular scenery to its eastern edge at Turrialba, you'll see large fields of sugarcane and corn.

Exploring the highlands leading to the volcanoes Poás, Barva, and Irazú, you'll see hills full of coffee bushes, flower plantations, and dairy farms. People enjoy the varying climates of the Central Valley, ranging from year-round summer in the lower, western towns of Alajuela, Santa Ana, and Villa Colón, to year-round spring at higher elevations.

A few years back, it was impossible to find lodging anywhere but in San José, but pleasant accommodations are now springing up all over the Central Valley. Since the Juan Santamaría International Airport is much closer to Alajuela and Heredia than to San José, it's possible to stay in or near these towns, avoiding the noise and pollution of the capital city.

Although only 20 kilometers from San José, **Alajuela** is 200 meters lower and considerably warmer. It is full of shady parks. On Sundays, old-timers sit in the Parque Central and entertain each other by thinking up nicknames for passersby. The **Juan Santamaría Museum** (open Tuesday through Sunday, 10 a.m. to 6 p.m.; free admission), housed in the former jail one block north of Parque Central, features relics of the 1856 rout of William Walker, including his incursion order and defense plea in English.

There are a variety of accommodations in or near Alajuela. The **Hotel Alajuela** (hot water, private bath; $20-$30; 41-1241, fax: 41-7912) is a good value, clean, with pleasant rooms and some very reasonable apartments in the older part of the building. It is on the southwest corner of Alajuela's Parque Central.

Two kilometers from the airport in Alajuela, the new **El Erizo** (cable TV; one or two bedrooms; $60-$80; phone/fax: 41-2840) has clean, fully equipped apartments and babysitting service. The owners are friendly, and the hotel's protected, motel-like setting makes it a good place for kids to run around. Recommended for families.

The resort hotel **Cariari** (cable TV, pool; $120-$140; 39-0022, fax: 39-2803) offers a golf course, tennis courts, an Olympic-size swimming pool, exercise classes, a sauna, riding horses, a casino, bars, restaurants, a convention center, and bus service to downtown San José. The **Villas de Cariari** ($80-$150; 39-1003, fax 39-2803) are apartments in the Cariari Hotel complex, which is located on the highway to the airport 20 minutes from San José.

The **Herradura** (cable TV, pool; $120-$140; 39-0033, fax: 39-2292; 800-245-8420) has access to the Cariari's recreational facilities, but is slightly more elegant. One of its restaurants, the **Sakura**, serves authentic Japanese cuisine, and includes a sushi bar. There are two other restaurants (one offers a dinner show, the other a more informal atmosphere) as well as a 24-hour coffee shop. The Herradura is also on the highway to the airport roughly 20 minutes from San José.

Near Parque San José, just west of Alajuela, the **Villa Raquel** (pool; $60-$80; 43-8926) has quiet, tastefully decorated rooms, a landscaped garden, and tennis courts. Breakfast included.

The American-owned **Las Orquideas Inn** (pool; with shared bath, $40-$50; newer rooms with private bath, $60-$80; no children; 43-9346, phone/fax: 43-9740) is on the road to San Pedro de Poás, about 3 kilometers northwest of Alajuela (ten minutes from the airport). The newer rooms are nicely decorated, with Guatemalan bedspreads. The Marilyn Monroe Bar serves buffalo wings every night. Breakfast is included in rates.

GETTING THERE: In San José, buses leave continuously for Alajuela (Avenida 2, Calles 12/14). By car, take the General Cañas Highway and watch for the Alajuela signs that are before the airport. The trip takes about 20 minutes.

Ojo de Agua is a recreational complex about half an hour outside of San José. Cold, clear water gushes up from an *ojo de agua* (spring) and is pumped down an artificial waterfall into large swimming pools. There's a manmade lake where you can rent rowboats; big, grassy fields for soccer, volleyball, sunbathing, and picnics; and a big *soda*. The complex is very crowded on weekends, but is relatively empty during the week. Unfortunately, the lowering of the water table due to deforestation is starting to affect the amount of water at Ojo de Agua at the end of the dry season, in April. Buses leave San José at least once an hour for Ojo de Agua from Calles 18/20, Avenida 1, a half block west of the Coca Cola. By car, take the General Cañas Highway west, turn left after the Cariari and Herradura hotels to San Antonio de Belén, and continue on to Ojo de Agua.

The Butterfly Farm (open daily, 9:30 a.m. to 4:30 p.m.; last tour begins at 3:30 p.m.; admission $7/adult, $2/child under 12; discount for residents) is a good example of what eco-tourism is all about. The largest such farm in the Western Hemisphere and the second largest in the world, it is devoted to the raising of live butterflies for exhibit in Europe. On the entertaining guided tours, you learn about the relationships between the beautiful winged insects, their host plants, and their predators, as well as the amazing transformations that take place within their life cycle. The farm owners have made it possible for all visitors to observe a butterfly emerging from its chrysalis by presenting an informative video during each tour. You can stay as long as you want to photograph the butterflies.

The Butterfly Farm is located southwest of the airport in La Guácima. To get there by bus, take the La Guácima bus at 11 a.m. from the stop marked San Antonio/Ojo de Agua (Avenida 1, Calles 20/22). The bus doesn't run on Sunday. Get off at the last stop, by a school. It's a one-hour trip. From the school, follow signs for 300 meters to the farm. There is a return bus at 3:15 p.m. For information about routes from Alajuela or Santa Ana, call 48-0115. Coming from San José by car, turn left at the large intersection after the Hotel Herradura to San Antonio de Belén. Once past the church in San Antonio, turn right for one block and then left. From there you'll see unobtrusive little butterfly signs directing you to the farm.

If you go to **La Garita**, you may want to stop at **La Fiesta del Maíz** (open Friday, Saturday, and Sunday), a restaurant where you can sample the wide variety of foods that Costa Ricans make from corn. Everything is delicious and homemade. The waitress will bring you little samples of the dishes if you ask.

The **Zoo Ave** (open daily, 9 a.m. to 5 p.m.; admission $3) in La Garita features 60 species of Costa Rican birds as well as monkeys, deer, crocodiles, turtles, and giant tortoises. By visiting it, you will support its efforts to breed and reintroduce native species—such as scarlet macaws, guans, and different kinds of parrots—to the wild. You also might want to stop at some of the *viveros* (greenhouses) near the Zoo Ave.

Chatelle (hot water, phone, pool; with cable TV and kitchenette, $60-$70, without, $50-$60; off-season discounts; 48-7781, 48-7271, fax: 48-7095) is a country inn located about 1 kilometer to the left of La Fiesta del Maíz. It consists of spacious, hexagonal cabinas and a restaurant on landscaped grounds and offers free airport pickup.

A large country home on spacious grounds, **La Piña Dorada** (hot water, private bath, pool; $50-$80; phone/fax: 48-7220) offers lovely, light-filled rooms and a large-screen TV room. The congenial Texans who own it are also good cooks. Breakfast included. An excellent value. Recommended. A converted *quinta* next to a river, the **Rio Real** (hot water, private bath, air-conditioning, phone, pool; $50-$60; 48-7022, fax: 42-1233) is clean and has a so-so restaurant and a conference room. Both the Rio Real and La Piña Dorado are on the road that goes left (south) from the school in La Garita. The Piña is 2.8 kilometers on the left and Rio Real is a few hundred meters beyond that, also on the left.

Villa Tranquilidad (hot water, private bath, small pool; $30-$40; 46-5470; weekly, monthly, and off-season discounts; Apdo. 28, 4013 Alajuela) is a bed-and-breakfast on a secluded organic coffee farm in Atenas, 15 minutes west of La Garita. The large rooms are part of the main house. Owners Frans and Kwin Lamers can arrange private sightseeing tours. Call or write the owners for information and reservations.

GETTING THERE: To get to the zoo by bus, go to Alajuela first from Avenida 2, Calles 12/14, then take a La Garita bus from there. By car, the bird zoo is 3.5 kilometers to the right at the Atenas exit, on a back road to Alajuela. The Atenas bus leaves hourly from the Coca Cola in San José and passes La Fiesta del Maíz. By car, take the Atenas turnoff about half an hour from San José on the General Cañas Highway to Puntarenas. The Fiesta del Maíz is 2.5 kilometers to the left.

San Ramón de Alajuela is a large agricultural center off the road to Puntarenas. Their *feria del agricultor* (farmer's market) on Saturdays is huge and worth going to for inexpensive fresh fruits and vegetables. Farmers markets are held on Saturday all over Costa Rica, even in San José.

The **San Ramón Museum** (open weekday afternoons), next to the plaza in the old Municipal Palace, features a replica of a *campesino* home from the turn of the century and recounts local history, from pre-Columbian times through local efforts to fight William Walker to the rise of famous native sons like former President José Figueres.

GETTING THERE: San Ramón is about one hour west of San José on the main road between San José and Puntarenas.

North of San Ramón is the beautiful **Los Angeles Cloud Forest** (admission $14, guides another $7), a private reserve owned by ex-President Rodrigo Carazo. The 2000-acre sanctuary rivals Monteverde in its beauty and is easily accessible for a day trip from San José—a good alternative for those who don't want to make the long, arduous trip to Monteverde. The 1.9-kilometer trail is paved with wood covered with chicken wire, a simple and practical way to prevent slipping. The entrance fee goes, among other things, to pay the salaries of a professional biologist to manage the reserve and guards to make sure that hunters do not bother the wildlife.

Hotel Villablanca (hot water, bathtub; $60-$80; 28-4603, fax: 28-4004), next to the reserve, consists of 20 *casitas*, charmingly decorated in the style of traditional *campesino* houses, each with its own fireplace, and a large central lodge where meals are served ($25/day). Budget dormitory-style accommodations with cooking facilities are almost complete; call for current information.

GETTING THERE: Once in San Ramón, take the road to La Tigra, 200 meters west of the hospital north of town, and follow the signs for the Los Angeles Cloud Forest and Villablanca (15 minutes on paved road, then about half an hour on gravel road). As you leave San Ramón, a winding road branches off to the right from the La Tigra road and takes you to Zarcero.

Zarcero is one of the most charming Costa Rican towns. It is perched on the hills that divide the Central Valley from the San Carlos plain, and its climate is fresh and invigorating. Its ruddy-cheeked inhabitants are famous for their peach preserves and homemade white cheese, but Zarcero's real claim to fame are the fancifully sculpted bushes in front of its picturesque little church: gigantic green rabbits, horses, ox carts, and elephants. When we were there, a huge rainbow guided us down the country roads above Zarcero to the town plaza, then remained in a perfect arc directly over the church. There are no real hotels in Zarcero, but if you ask around, you can probably find a family who will put you up for a modest fee.

Just before you reach Zarcero, there is a group of restaurants and stands selling cheese, candied fruit, and flowers. **Restaurant La Montaña** on the right specializes in hearty Italian dishes. If you want to stop for something to eat, any restaurant in that area is better than what is offered in Zarcero itself.

GETTING THERE: The Zarcero bus leaves from the corner of Calle 16 and Avenida 3 near the Coca Cola at 9:15 every morning, or you can take any of the hourly San Carlos buses in the Coca Cola. The trip lasts two hours. It's easy to catch a bus back to San José, or on to Volcán Arenal and the hot springs at Tabacón. By car, Zarcero is an hour and a half from San José. Take the Naranjo–Ciudad Quesada exit off the highway to Puntarenas.

The **Grecia** area offers many possibilities for day trips, by itself or including La Garita and Volcán Poás. Grecia was voted the cleanest town in Latin America, and its citizens take pride in maintaining that reputation. From its airy red metal church with delicate wooden filigree altars to the well-kept homes of its farmers, it still exudes the goodness and simplicity that many other parts of the country have lost.

Northwest of Grecia is the small town of **Sarchí,** home of Costa Rica's traditional brightly painted ox carts. You can watch artisans creating beautiful wooden bowls, plates, furniture, and walking sticks decorated with animals and birds. Although you can buy the same things in San José and Moravia, it's nice to go to the source. The most inexpensive place to buy crafts is at the cooperative, which is on the right at the end of town.

GETTING THERE: Take the hourly Grecia bus from the Coca Cola. In Grecia, connect with the *Alajuela–Sarchí* bus. You can catch the latter bus in Alajuela, but it takes a long, roundabout route to Grecia. To get there by car, take the Grecia exit off the Puntarenas Highway, 30 minutes west of San José. When you get to Grecia, turn left behind the church, left again (circling the church), then right for three blocks. The road going diagonally to your left is the road to Sarchí.

Sugarcane and coffee are the main crops in the Grecia area. A winding road through the hills to the northwest takes you to **Los Trapiches** (44-6656), where you can see how *tapa dulce*, the flavorful hard brown sugar of Central America, is made. A waterwheel activates the huge gears of a venerable Victorian cane press, imported 110 years ago from Aberdeen, Scotland. The cane juice is collected in enormous *pailas* (cauldrons) set into a brick vault in which a fire is built. As the liquid boils, it reaches different stages of consistency until it is ready to be poured into the flower-pot-shaped molds. At one point the sugar can be whipped into different forms, called *sobado*. It is quite an interesting process to see, and you can spend the day there, picnicking or eating *comida típica* in the restaurant. There are swimming pools and a small lake for boating. Nothing is very fancy—Ticos love to go there on weekends. Call before you go to make sure the *trapiche* is operating. To get there drive three blocks past the church in Grecia and turn left onto Route 13, winding through the hills to Santa Gertrudis Sur, following the Los Trapiches signs.

Los Chorros are two beautiful waterfalls, about 75 feet high, protected by the national park system. The area is not very developed, which is nice. Bring good hiking shoes because the trail to the waterfall is steep and muddy at the beginning and at the end. Take the little trail that goes up to the left, not the easier looking one to the right. It's only a ten-minute hike to the falls. Halfway down the trail, a sign indicates another branch to a *mirador* (lookout point) across from the top of one of the cascades.

The main trail takes you to the bottom of a second magnificent waterfall. The many little jets of water that look like they are pouring from the rocks give the place its name. There is a covered camping area and a rickety bridge, which takes you to the other side of the river. If you want to enjoy the waterfalls in peace, go during the week, as Los Chorros is crowded on weekends.

The journey to Los Chorros is an adventure. Take the road going west from Alajuela about 15 kilometers to Tácares. Turn right at the Tácares church and bear left for about 2 kilometers, until the road dead-ends near a cyclone fence on the right. There is a sign prohibiting you from entering. Just ignore it like the Ticos do and walk downhill about ten minutes until you come to a quarry. Walk to the left into the quarry and you'll see a path to the right. Follow the muddy footprints and soon you'll see the national park signs.

On the way back, you might want to stop at **Las Tinajitas**, a clean, nicely decorated restaurant with good food located a few minutes outside Alajuela on the road to Tácares and Grecia.

POÁS NATIONAL PARK

Poás is one of the few active volcanoes on the continent that is accessible by a good road. The 37-kilometer trip from San José is marked by beautiful scenery, with lookouts over the Central Valley. It is the most developed of the national parks, with a visitors center (which has a small *soda* and a good souvenir shop) and well-maintained nature trails.

The main crater of Poás is 1.5 kilometers wide and 300 meters deep. There was a hot, sulfurous lake at the bottom, but it recently evaporated due to increased volcanic activity. Geysers and active fumaroles are visible from the lookout point above the crater. A 20-minute uphill hike takes you to another lookout over jewel-like Botos Lake, which fills an ancient crater.

Volcán Poás is just coming out of an active phase, apparently part of a 40- to 45-year cycle. The volcano spewed a 4000-meter column of water and mud in 1910, sending ash as far as Puntarenas. Lava flow increased also in 1953. In May 1989, Poás shot ash a mile into the air, but still it is quiet compared to other volcanoes, such as Arenal and Irazú.

Scientists believe that Poás has a relatively open passage from its magma chamber to its huge crater, so it lets off steam more easily than other volcanoes and doesn't build up the pressure that causes large eruptions. Nevertheless, it is under close observation these days, and the park is sometimes closed to visitors because of sulfur gas emissions from the crater, which combine with steam to make sulfuric acid. It's difficult to predict when Poás will be emitting gases, just as it's difficult to predict when it will be clear enough to see the craters. Basically, you just have to take your chances.

Poás National Park (call Parques Nacional for information, 57-0922, fax: 23-6963) protects the headwaters of several rivers, which feed the Río Tárcoles to the southwest and the Río Sarapiquí to the north. While the active crater is full of subtle, moonscape colors, the rest of Poás is intensely green, with a great variety of wildflowers, bromeliads, ferns, mosses, and lichen. One of the most interesting plants there is the *sombrilla del pobre* (poor man's umbrella) which has thick, fuzzy leaves up to two meters in width. Hummingbirds are among the 26 species of birds most easily seen along the road or on the trails. Quetzales, the famed sacred birds of the Mayans, also frequent Poás. As you approach the park, you will pass a cyclone-fence gate. *Aguacatillo* trees, favored by quetzales, grow in the pastureland along the dirt road to the left of the gate, so you may be able to spot some of the birds.

The average temperature on misty Poás is 50 degrees, dropping as low as 22 and climbing as high as 70, so it is important to dress in layers. Bring rain gear. If you get there too late in the day, clouds will be covering the crater, so the earlier you go the better. When it's clear, you can see Poás on the horizon to the northwest of San José. If you can't see it, it's probably too late to go.

If you do go to Poás, be sure to stop at **Chubascos,** one of the nicest places we know for native Costa Rican food. It is set in a hillside garden with covered outdoor tables. Their large *casado* can't be beat, especially accompanied by *refrescos* made from local strawberries and blackberries and followed by homemade cheesecake. It's about 16 kilometers above Alajuela.

Another highly recommended eatery is **Las Fresas** (open every day; 61-2397), owned by an Italian family, where the pizzas are baked in a wood-heated brick oven. The steak at this elegantly cozy restaurant received an "excellent" rating from my husband. This was one of the only times I have heard him utter that word, so I took a bite myself, and it was truly tender and delicious. Coming down from the volcano, you'll see signs for Las Fresas on the road to San Pedro de Poás before you get to Sabana Redonda. You have to call ahead for the pizza or let them know on the way up.

Los Jaules, El Recreo, and **Restaurant Volcán Poás,** farther up toward the volcano, are also nice places to stop for a snack. **Churrascos Steak House** is in Poasito, about 10 kilometers from the park entrance. There is a little supermarket there also. **Lo Que Tú Quieras** (heated water, private bath; $7-$12; 48-5213) is 5 kilometers from the park entrance. It consists of a mediocre restaurant along with several cramped cabinas, but it has an incredible view.

About 14 kilometers east of the park, near **Vara Blanca,** is **Poás Volcano Lodge** (heated water; with private bath, $60-$70; with shared bath, $30-$40; phone/fax: 41-9102), a bed-and-breakfast especially suited for hikers and birders who like to get out and roam around the countryside. For generous servings and friendly service, nearby **Restaurant Vara Blanca** is recommended. Vara Blanca is at the junction of the Heredia–Sarapiquí road and the road approaching Poás from the east.

GETTING THERE: A bus to Volcán Poás leaves on Sunday from Parque de la Merced in San José (Avenida 2, Calle 12) at 8:30 a.m. Buses leave from Alajuela's Parque Central (41-0631, $3.30 round-trip) on Sunday, continuously between 8 a.m. and 9 a.m. Get there early to reserve yourself a seat. The bus arrives at the volcano around 11 a.m. Check with the driver for departure time. Many tour companies offer day trips to Poás for between $15 and $25.

To get there by car, take the Alajuela turnoff from the General Cañas Highway, about 15 minutes from San José. It goes past Alajuela's Central Park and the

Juan Santamaría Museum. Stay on the same road until you get to Fraijanes Lake and Chubascos. About 1.5 kilometers beyond the restaurant, you will connect with the road from San Pedro de Poás, which leads to the volcano. If you are near Heredia, take the Barva–Birrí road to Vara Blanca and turn left for 6 kilometers, then right at Poasito. If you are in Grecia, take the back road to Alajuela through Tácares, turn left at Hotel Las Orquideas to get to San Pedro de Poás, and continue on to the volcano. You can make a nice circular route, entering through Alajuela, and returning through Vara Blanca and Heredia. On the way down, take forks to the left, following the little signs to El Pórtico. Ignore the third El Pórtico sign and keep to the right.

Founded in 1706, **Heredia** has retained a friendly, small-town atmosphere. Its colonial church, built in 1796, has a pretty facade and a peaceful garden. There are concerts Thursday nights in the music temple in Parque Central.

In the **Mercado Florense** (300 meters south and 50 meters west of the church) there's an inexpensive place to have a good seafood lunch. You'll also find some nice, clean restaurants behind the Mercado Central, across from the buses. Near the National University are popular student bars, such as **La Choza** and **El Bulevar. Fresas,** a restaurant one block from the university, is clean and spacious with some outdoor tables. Servings are generous and inexpensive.

About 750 meters north of Colegio Santa Cecilia in Heredia, **Aparotel Vargas** (parking; $50-$60; 37-8526, fax: 38-4698) offers clean, new, fully equipped apartments on a quiet street across from a coffee field. The upper rooms are lighter. Laundry facilities and airport pickup are available. Recommended.

A Canadian-owned home in a rather sterile housing development in Santa Lucia de Heredia, **Los Jardines** (hot water, $30-$40; 60-1904) is clean and near buses to Heredia. It has cable TV in the living room. Breakfast included. Airport pickup ($6) is available.

Hotel Verano (cold water, shared bath; under $7; 37-1616), up three flights of stairs on the west side of the market in Heredia, is clean, friendly, and very inexpensive. Recommended for budget travelers. **El Parqueo** (cold water, shared bath; under $7; 38-2882), run by friendly owners, is in the same block as the Verano. It is a little grungier, but even cheaper, and has good mattresses.

GETTING THERE: Buses to Heredia leave every five to ten minutes from Calle 1, Avenidas 7/9 in San José, 5:20 a.m. to 10:30 p.m. (through Tibás), and from Avenida 2, Calle 12 every 20 minutes (through La Uruca). Train service between Heredia and San Pedro, the university district east of San José, has just been reestablished. Trains leave Heredia at 6:15 a.m., 1 p.m., and 6 p.m., returning from San Pedro as 12 noon and 5 p.m. The trip lasts 45 minutes with no stops.

A town to the west of Heredia, **San Isidro de Heredia** is visible throughout the area because of its white Gothic church. San Isidro and San Joaquín de las Flores are both known for their colorful Easter-week processions.

Across the river behind the church is a little road that goes uphill to the **Cerámica Chavarría** (39-8455), where doña Frances turns out her sturdy, ovenproof stoneware and blends her own nonleaded glazes. A mug we bought from her fell out of the car on the way back, and, true to her claims, it didn't break. Call first. She will give pottery demonstrations to groups.

Farther up the road is **La Posada de la Montaña** (hot water; with shared bath, $30-$40; with private bath, $40-$50; with private kitchen and fireplace, $60-$80; phone/fax: 39-8096). Rooms in the main house are sunny and clean, and the newer cabins are surrounded by gardens. There is a common living room with a fireplace, cable TV, and VCR. A good value. Recommended. As you enter San Isidro from the east, you'll see signs for it pointing up the hill.

The mountains above Heredia are full of evergreen forests and pastureland. It's exhilaratingly chilly there all year round, and a bright, sunny day can turn into a rainy one in minutes, especially after noon. From these mountains you can see the sun glinting off the Gulf of Nicoya in the west. A hike to **Monte de la Cruz** gives you an incredible panorama of the entire Central Valley and beyond. Take a picnic lunch, an umbrella, and a sweater. After you turn right at a fork in the road to go to Monte de La Cruz, you'll see **Le Barbizon** (open Monday through Saturday, 11:30 a.m. to 10:30 p.m., Sunday 10:30 a.m. to 6:30 p.m.; 39-7449), a large and very elegant French restaurant. Entrées are between $8 and $10. (Going left at that fork will take you in about 1 kilometer to Hotel Chalet Tirol.)

The **Hotel Chalet Tirol** (hot water, bathtub, electric heating; $90-$100; 39-7070, 39-7050), at 1800 meters (5900 feet), is surrounded by a cloud forest reserve that borders Braulio Carrillo National Park. It has charming two-story, vine-covered cabins with handpainted Tyrolean designs and offers room service, airport pickup, and an elegant **French restaurant** (open Monday through Saturday, 8 a.m. to 10 p.m.; Sunday, 8 a.m. to 6 p.m.; 39-7371). The newer rooms have fireplaces.

Two hiking trails are accessible from the reserve, one of which leads to a moss-covered cliff where a dozen small waterfalls cascade into as many small pools before joining the river below. It's a beautiful place and amazing in that it's so close to San José. Another trail follows the Río Segundo into Braulio Carrillo amidst a carpet of ferns and ancient trees covered with orchids and bromeliads. It's a great place for a day hike or for a weekend trip, and you can warm up with a hot chocolate and pastry on the second floor of the Chalet's restaurant, or stay for its excellent, albeit expensive, nouvelle cuisine specialties.

El Castillo (admission $2.50/person), a posh country club, has a similar view to Monte de la Cruz, plus an ice-skating rink, pool, gym, barbecue pits, go-carts, and miniature train. The entrance fee lets you use all of the facilities and entitles you to a discount on lunch in the dining room, which overlooks the skating rink as well as the Central Valley. The small, wrought-iron sign at the entrance to El Castillo is hard to spot, but you'll see its well-manicured lawns on the right a few hundred meters after a large sign for Residencial El Castillo.

Before you get to El Castillo, there is a sign for **Bosque del Río de la Hoja**. Go left, down a beautiful wooded road, for 2 kilometers. The entrance says "Bar las Chorreras." Bosque de la Hoja protects the water supply for Heredia. It is not developed for tourism and the roads are terrible, so leave your car where a guard requests a minimal entrance fee. There are trails through cool, fresh forests of *ciprés* and lovely meadows for picnics. Camping is allowed.

After your hike you might want to stop for lunch or dinner at **Stein Biergarten** (open Friday evening and from noon onward on weekends; 39-7021), down the road to the left just before you get to Bosque de la Hoja. It offers tasty German food including meat, sausage, chicken, sauerkraut, and potato salad. Not the place for weight watching, but even if you're on a diet, you can sip a club soda and enjoy the beautiful view and classical music. Once a month there is a live Tico and German band.

Añoranzas (39-7406), down a road on your left from the main road 4 kilometers above San Rafael, specializes in *comida típica* and has play equipment for kids.

GETTING THERE: Buses leave San José (Calle 4, Avenida 7/9) for San Isidro de Heredia every half hour. By car, take the San Isidro de Heredia exit on the left about 14 kilometers down the Guápiles Highway.

An hourly bus that passes the turnoff to Bosque de la Hoja and El Castillo leaves from behind the Mercado Florense in Heredia from 8 a.m. to 8 p.m. The 9 a.m., 12 noon, and 4 p.m. buses go to a fork in the road 1 kilometer from the entrance to Monte de la Cruz. If you're going to Chalet Tirol, take the left fork for about 1 kilometer.

Monte de la Cruz, El Castillo, and Bosque de la Hoja are all about 35 minutes from San José by car. Take the San Isidro exit to the left about 14 kilometers down the Guápiles highway right after the Restaurant Las Orquídeas. When you reach San Isidro, turn right in front of the church and go 2 kilometers to Concepción (ignore any previous Concepción signs). Continue a few minutes more to San Rafael, and again turn right at the church, to reach Bosque de la Hoja (5 kilometers north of San Rafael), El Castillo (1 kilometers farther), and the fork to Chalet Tirol (left), and Monte de la Cruz (right) is 2 kilometers beyond El Castillo.

BARVA AND VOLCÁN BARVA

The town of **Barva**, 2 kilometers north of Heredia, is one of the oldest settlements in the country. Its historic church and the houses near it have been restored.

The **Instituto de Café** (open Monday through Friday, 7 a.m. to 3 p.m.) has its research station in San Pedro de Heredia, northwest of Barva. During the coffee harvest in December and January, you can see how the *grano de oro* (the golden bean) is dried and processed and take a look at the station's collection of antique coffee grinders. To get there by bus, take the *Santa Bárbara por Barrio Jesús* bus from Heredia. If you're traveling by car, turn left as you reach the square in front of the Barva church, then continue 2 kilometers to San Pedro, bearing to the right. The institute is 400 meters beyond the San Pedro church.

Maker of Costa Rica's excellent export-quality coffee, **Café Britt** (presentations daily except Thursday, 9 a.m.; Tuesday and Sunday, 3 p.m.; 37-5044) has an educational tour of its operations, including a lively skit about the history and cultivation of coffee and a demonstration of the art of professional coffee tasting. Company representatives will pick you up at your hotel if you're staying in San José; call for information.

La Rosa Blanca (hot water, private bath, concierge service; $120-$230 including breakfast; 39-9392, fax: 39-9555) is near Santa Barbara de Heredia. Each room has a theme, and the architecture and hand-crafted furnishings are full of fantasy and delightful, creative touches. The honeymoon suite features a tower room with a 360-degree view and a bathroom painted like a rainforest, with the water for the bathtub bubbling out of a rocky waterfall. The restaurant is for guests only. Recommended.

Hotel Cypresal (hot water, private bath, pool; $50-$60; 23-1717, 21-6455, fax: 21-6244) is in a beautiful mountain setting north of Barva, but the grounds have been paved and cemented so much that they have become an eyesore. There is a sauna, some rooms have terraces, some have fireplaces, and there are two conference rooms with fireplaces.

Up the road from the Hotel Cypresal, **Hotel El Portico** (pool; $50-$60; 37-6022, 38-2930, fax: 38-0629) is graciously designed, with a lovely lounge and an attractive restaurant. The rooms have large windows, and there is a sauna and a jacuzzi. The staff, however, is not as helpful with travel arrangements as they should be in this rather isolated mountain setting. Both the El Portico and the Cypresal are 4 kilometers north of Barva (keep left), then 4 kilometers to the right at Restaurante Las Delicias in Birrí.

Volcán Barva, at 2900 meters (9500 feet), is on the western edge of Braulio Carrillo National Park. It's a great place for a day trip. The views on the way up are fantastic, the hour's hike to the crater lake is not too strenuous, the vegetation is vibrantly beautiful, and the forest is full of birds. Bring rain gear, a compass, and waterproof shoes or boots even in the dry season.

Quetzales are sometimes visible there. They migrate to forests more than 3600 feet above sea level, where they nest in the hollows of the tallest and oldest trees. Males and females share the incubation of their eggs and the feeding of their hatchlings. The females sit on the eggs at night and at midday, and the male sits with his beautiful green tail hanging out of the nest during the rest of the day. They cannot live in captivity. Also heard on Volcán Barva is the black-faced solitaire, which has been compared to the nightingale for the sweetness and delicacy of its song. If you want to see birds, you might do well to take a tour. **Jungle Trails** (55-3486, fax: 55-2782), specializes in hiking and birding trips to Barva.

Camping is permitted in the pasture behind the administration building at the entrance to the park. There are two covered picnic areas with grills along the trail to the lake.

Restaurante La Campesina, located 3.5 kilometers above Paso Llano, serves tasty, wholesome country food at outdoor tables overlooking the valley. **Restaurante Sacramento**, 4 kilometers above Paso Llano, looks like a rather dingy bar when you enter, but has a lovely covered porch for dining on the left side. Its owner, Manuel, is a good person to talk to about the area. Both places offer basic accommodations. You might want to stop and admire the view from Sacramento's little church, just down the hill from the restaurant.

Quetzal

In the rainy season, the road beyond Restaurante La Campesina is difficult for regular cars, and the road between Sacramento and the park is only for four-wheel-drive vehicles with chains. Often during the dry season the road will be smoothed out, making it possible for regular cars to drive the remaining 4 kilometers to the park entrance. Call Parques Nacionales (57-0922) to find out the road conditions. Even if you can't make it to the park, the scenery around Sacramento is worth the trip.

GETTING THERE: To climb Volcán Barva you should catch the 6 a.m. *San José de la Montaña–Paso Llano* bus from behind the Mercado Central in Heredia. At Paso Llano (Porrosatí), you'll see signs for the park entrance 8 kilometers uphill to the left. The crater lake is 2.6 kilometers beyond the entrance. Be sure to make it back for the 5 p.m. Paso Llano bus to Heredia. On Sunday you have to catch the bus at 7:10 a.m. in San José de la Montaña (take an early bus from Heredia), and the last bus from Paso Llano is at 4 p.m.

By car, follow the road north of Heredia through Barva. Take the right fork north of Barva to lovely San José de la Montaña, with its peaceful church and charming country houses. Continue 5 kilometers beyond it and turn right at the signs for Braulio Carrillo. In a few hundred meters you'll arrive at Paso Llano. Turn left. If, instead of turning right at the Braulio Carrillo signs, you go straight about 1 kilometer, you'll reach the hotels Cypresal and El Portico. The road after San José de la Montaña has quite a few potholes but goes through less developed country than the Barva–Birrí road.

BRAULIO CARRILLO NATIONAL PARK

The founding of **Braulio Carrillo National Park** in 1978 represented a compromise between the ecology and development. Environmentalists were concerned that the opening of a highway between San José and Guápiles would result in the ecological disasters that accompanied the opening of roads in Costa Rica: indiscriminate colonization and deforestation. The government agreed to make 80,000 acres of virgin forest surrounding the highway into a national park.

The Guápiles highway, opened in May 1987, makes Braulio Carrillo the national park most accessible by car. The scenery is inspiring. Hopefully it is an education in itself for all the motorists who pass through it on their way to the Atlantic coast—mountains of untouched rainforest as far as the eye can see. And just 30 years ago, most of Costa Rica looked like that!

In order to hike the trails accessible from the highway, you must stop and pay a minimal entrance fee, either at the administration buildings (1.8 kilometers after the toll booth on the San José side or 700 meters after the Zurquí tunnel if you're coming from Limón). The trail before the tunnel is steep and strenuous; the La Botella trail 17 kilometers beyond the tunnel is easier. Parts of the trail are muddy, and snakes are a danger, so wear boots. Porcupines, margays, tapirs, monkeys, coatis, kinkajous, peccaries, pacas, ocelots, sloths, and raccoons live in Braulio Carrillo, though chances are you won't see any of them—more visible are the 500 species of birds.

GETTING THERE: Take the hourly Guápiles bus from Coopetragua (Calle 12, Avenidas 7/9; $1). The La Botella trail is 2.5 kilometers before the Quebrada Gonzales station at the far end of the park. By car, the trip from San José takes about 20 minutes on the Guápiles Highway.

Note: Avoid the *miradores*, the scenic lookout points along the highway—especially the ones that are out of view of the main road. Tourists have been robbed at these places, and the park does not have enough personnel to guard them.

Rancho Redondo is a beautiful place to go for a drive and a view of the Central Valley. Just follow the main road through San José's northeastern suburb of Guadalupe. Soon the houses start to thin out, and the crowded thoroughfare becomes one of Costa Rica's charming country roads, lined with the famous "living fenceposts." (The volcanic soil is so fertile that fenceposts sprout and turn into trees.) About 15 kilometers from San José, just before you reach Rancho Redondo, is a good place to stop and look at the view.

Another nice drive involves heading out the same Guadalupe road, but taking the left fork at Ipis, about 6 kilometers from San José, arriving in about 2 kilometers at San Isidro de Coronado. From there follow signs 7 kilometers east to Las Nubes, misty mountains full of dairy cattle and strawberry plantations, where you'll find **Cronopios** (open Friday, 5 to 11 p.m.; Saturday, 12 noon to 11 p.m.; Sunday, 12 noon to 6 p.m.; 29-0517), a cozy gathering place that serves moderately priced soups, salads, mini-pizzas, and main dishes, and makes desserts from the strawberries that grow in the area. It has a fireplace and a good collection of Latin American and North American music.

Though **Cartago** was the birthplace of Costa Rican culture and the capital for 300 years, many of its historic buildings were destroyed in the earthquakes of 1823 and 1910. The 1910 quake prevented the completion of a cathedral in the center of town. The ruins of that church have been made into a pleasant garden. On August 2 every year, thousands of Costa Ricans walk from San José to Cartago in honor of *La Negrita*, the Virgin of Los Angeles, who appeared to a peasant girl in 1635. She has become Costa Rica's patron saint, and her shrine is surrounded by offerings from grateful pilgrims whom she has miraculously cured. Tiny metal arms, legs, hearts, and other charms decorate the walls inside the **Basílica**, an imposing structure on the east side of town.

GETTING THERE: Buses to Cartago leave often from Calle 13, Avenidas Central/2 in San José, west of the Plaza de la Democracia. It's a half-hour trip. By car, just follow Avenida Central east of San José through the suburbs of San Pedro and Curridabat. That will put you onto the Autopista Florencio del Castillo (50 cents toll), part of the Interamerican Highway, which leads to Cartago.

Volcán Irazú is 32 kilometers north of Cartago. On a clear morning, the trip up its slope is full of breathtaking views of farmland, native oak forests, and the Central Valley below. The craters are bleak and majestic. On March 19, 1963, the day John F. Kennedy arrived in Costa Rica on a presidential visit, Irazú erupted, showering black ash over the Central Valley for the next two years. People carried umbrellas to keep the ash out of their hair, roofs caved in from the weight of piled-up ash, and everything was black. Since then the volcano has been dormant, but there were a few tremors in 1991. Gases and steam are emitted from fumaroles near the sulfurous lake that recently formed in the crater. It is said that you can see both the Atlantic and the Pacific from Irazú's chilly 3432-meter (11,260-foot) summit. This is true on occasion, but often the Atlantic side is obscured by clouds. You can get plenty of exercise there, hiking to the crater from the *mirador*, then hiking halfway around it and back.

As you get toward the top of Irazú, you'll see some magical old oak trees covered with lichen and bromeliads. The mossy pastureland there is a good place for a picnic. If you want to try to catch the view of both oceans, you must go early. Bring warm clothes and rain gear; there are no facilities at the volcano—only some poorly maintained latrines.

GETTING THERE: Buses to Irazú (51-9795, 72-0651; $3 round-trip) leave Wednesday, Saturday, Sunday, and holidays at 8 a.m. from Avenida 2 across from the

Gran Hotel Costa Rica. The bus leaves Irazú at 12:15 p.m., arriving in San José at 2:30 p.m. Other days you have to drive or take a tour. By car, take the Interamerican Highway east to the Taras Intersection, 4 kilometers from the entrance to Cartago. There's a nondescript three-pronged monument there. Go straight instead of turning right towards Cartago, then take the first left (there's no sign). The road signs after that are pretty good. After going about 2 kilometers, turn right onto Route 233, which will take you to Route 8 and Irazú.

Restaurant Linda Vista, the first place on your right as you come down from Irazú, is a good place to eat. The bus stops there, too. About a third of the way down the mountain is **Hotel Gestoria Irazú** (cold water, shared bath; $12-$20; 53-0827), a large, charmingly gloomy building that has seen better days. Call for reservations. The restaurant here is not recommended.

Another good place to go for a day hike is **Area Recreativa Jiménez Oreamuno,** a reforestation project started after the 1963 eruption. It's located about halfway up the west side of the volcano, near Prusia. The hike to the forest is very beautiful, through steep hills covered with oak and pine. Once there, you'll find trails and picnic tables. To get there, take Route 8 to Terra Blanca and ask for directions from there.

Developed by English botanist Charles Lankester, **Lankester Gardens** (open daily, 9:30 a.m. to 3:30 p.m.) display the hundreds of varieties of orchids and bromeliads for which Costa Rica is famous. The gardens are run by the biology department of the University of Costa Rica. To get there, take the Paraíso bus from the south side of the church ruins in Cartago. Ask the bus driver to let you off near the gardens. There is a sign on the highway. The entrance is about 100 meters down a road to your right, then right again.

Orosi Valley, south of Cartago, is one of Costa Rica's jewels. You can visit the peaceful ruins of Costa Rica's oldest church at **Ujarrás,** then walk about half an hour to **Charrarra** (Tuesday through Sunday, 8 a.m. to 5 p.m.; admission 75 cents), ICT's tourism complex on the banks of Cachí Dam. Charrarra offers lakeside trails, a swimming pool, basketball courts, picnic facilities, a pleasant restaurant, and access to boating and windsurfing on the lake. There is a boat tour of the lake (40 cents) every 40 minutes on weekends and around noon on weekdays. To get there, take the Cachí bus one block east of the ruins in Cartago. Ask to be let off at the entrance to Ujarrás. On Sunday the buses go all the way to Charrarra.

South of Cachí Dam is the town of **Orosi.** It has a colonial church whose beautiful wooden altar and shrines were carved with a special grace—one of the few places in Costa Rica that has survived enough earthquakes to preserve its original atmosphere. A small museum of colonial religious history (open Tuesday through Sunday, 9 a.m. to 12 noon, 1 to 5 p.m.) is next door.

From Orosi, nature lovers can hire a jeep-taxi, hike, or drive the 10 kilometers full of potholes to **Tapantí Wildlife Refuge**. Tapantí protects the rivers that supply San José with water and electricity. There's great bird-watching, trout fishing, and river swimming. There are some cabinas near the entrance—ask the guards about them.

Albergue Montaña Orosi (heated water, shared bath; $12-$20; 73-3028, fax: 28-1256) is a large house that has been converted into a hotel. Rooms are simple and clean, and kitchen facilities are available. The owners, who also run the **Restaurant Coto** on the square in Orosi, can arrange guided tours to Tapantí and other points of interest in the area.

Motel Río Palomo (heated water, kitchen, pools; $20-$30; 73-3128, 73-3057) has a restaurant (open daily, 8:30 a.m. to 5 p.m.) that is a famous, traditional place to go for a fresh fish lunch. The Orosi minibus goes all the way to the motel about once an hour on weekends, and at noon on weekdays. If you're driving, watch for signs indicating the turnoff to the left, about 3 kilometers beyond Orosi.

GETTING THERE: All Orosi buses are 100 meters east of the church ruins in Cartago and 300 meters south. By car, go through Cartago to Paraíso and turn right at the square. You can make your tour of the Orosi Valley in a circular route: head south of Paraíso to Orosi and on to Tapantí. On your way back, cross the river at Motel Río and follow the river road north. It will circle around Cachi Dam, take you to the entrance to Ujarrás and Charrara, and return you to Paraíso. There is a *mirador* on the way to Orosi with picnic and barbecue spots and a beautiful view.

TURRIALBA AND GUAYABO NATIONAL MONUMENT

Turrialba is becoming known worldwide as the perfect winter training ground for kayakers. The town, which used to be the main stopping place on the old San José–Limón road, suffered an economic depression with the opening of the Guápiles highway, which bypasses the area completely. Now, however, it is a haven for international whitewater fans who rent houses there or stay with local families. Young Turrialbans are becoming interested in kayaking, but most of them do not have the means to outfit themselves for the sport.

Definitely off the beaten track, Turrialba offers many possibilities for an interesting day or weekend trip, especially now that the road to Guayabo National Monument is paved. If you have a car, you can take a delightful, paved back road that starts slightly south of the town of Cot on the slopes of Volcán Irazú, and skirts Volcán Turrialba, passing through the towns of Pacayas and Santa Cruz before arriving in Turrialba itself. The trip takes less than two hours from San José.

Turrialba is the home of CATIE (Centro Agronómico Tropical de Investigación y Enseñanza) (56-6431). Established in the 1930s, it is one of the five major tropical research centers in the world. Its extensive library houses Latin America's largest collection of agricultural literature in English.

CATIE's 27,500-acre facilities include greenhouses, orchards, forest plantings, experimental agricultural projects, a dairy, an herbarium, seed conservation chambers, a nuclear reactor, and housing for students and teachers. Seeds of fruit and nut trees, tropical forest species suitable for lumber, ornament, erosion control, shade, and pulpwood are available by writing CATIE, Turrialba, Costa Rica. It also sells livestock well adapted to the tropics. CATIE publishes a monthly newsletter in English. You can request it or arrange a visit to the center by calling.

Birders will find the purple-crested gallinet and other rare waterfowl around the lagoon at CATIE. There is a trail from behind the administration building to the Río Reventazón for more birdwatching. You can catch a bus to CATIE where the main road crosses the tracks in Turrialba. Ask about schedules at the Almacén González.

Once in Turrialba, there are several restaurants worth visiting. The charming and folkloric **Turrialtico** (56-1111) is high on a hill about 8 kilometers east of town. As you drive up, you'll see wonderful gargoyles popping out of carved branches of coffee wood bordering the spacious open-air dining room, which has a magnificent view of the valley. Native food is its specialty. Above the restaurant are comfortable rooms (heated water, private bath, playground equipment; $12-$20) with the same great view.

Two kilometers farther down the road is ◎ **Albergue de Montaña Pochotel** (56-0111), on an even higher hill with an almost 360-degree view of the entire area, including Cerro de la Muerte and Chirripó to the south, and volcanoes Irazú and Turrialba to the north. You can climb up the observation tower and see even more. The restaurant, which offers Costa Rican dishes, will send your refreshments up to the tower on a mini-ski-lift contraption. It also rents cabinas (heated water, private bath, playground equipment; camping allowed; $12-$20).

Just outside Turrialba is **Restaurant Kingston**, whose Limonese owner and chef has made it famous.

If it's hot, you might just want to take a dip at **Balneario Las Américas** (admission 75 cents), two large pools for kids and adults that have a bar-restaurant. You'll see signs for it on the main road, a few blocks toward town from Restaurant Kingston. To the west of town, 600 meters from the church, is **Parque La Dominica**, a pleasant place to stop for a picnic. There are swings, basketball courts, and a river (unfortunately it is too polluted to swim in).

The **Hotel Wagelia** (heated water; with no fans, $30-$40; with air-conditioning, TV, and refrigerator, $40-$50; 56-1566, 56-1596), at the entrance to Turrialba, 150 meters west of the central park, has clean, small rooms and a restaurant that offers an elegant menu with reasonable prices.

Hotel Interamericano (cold water; with shared bath, under $7; with private bath, $7-$12; 56-0142) is near the railroad station. The mattresses are saggy but clean, the staff is friendly, and guests have kitchen privileges.

Casa Turire (private bath, balcony, cable TV, phone, pool; no children; $80-$150; 73-7111) is a unique plantation-style hotel located on a curve in the Reventazón River. The elegant lodge is surrounded by thousands of acres of working fields in which coffee, macadamia nuts, and sugarcane are the main products. There are rainforests nearby. Here you'll find a spring-fed pool, conference center, five-hole golf course, and riding horses. The hotel also offers local tours. It is 15 minutes southeast of Turrialba.

High in the hills above Tuís, **Rancho Naturalista** (39-7138; Apdo. 364, 1002 San José), east of Turrialba, offers nature trails through virgin rainforest, the habitat of four species of toucans, the snow-capped hummingbird, and many other bird and butterfly species. There is a comfortable lodge (hot water, good mattresses) there that overlooks the wide valley. The restaurant's creative cookery is a special attraction. A week's stay, including meals, lodging, transportation, and guided birding trips, is $500; the price drops to $400 from June to November.

Guayabo National Monument (open 8 a.m. to 3 p.m.) on the slopes of Volcán Turrialba is considered the most significant archaeological site in Costa Rica. It is a glimpse into the harmony between people and nature that existed in pre-Columbian times. Birds abound in the ruins, which are set in premontane rainforest and dotted with the guava trees that give the town its name. *Oropéndolas* (related to North American orioles) hang their sacklike nests from tree branches. Water sings its song in ancient aqueducts.

Archaeologists have excavated only the central part of a 10,000-inhabitant city that existed from 1000 B.C. to about 1400 A.D. The exposed area is composed of circular mounds, which were the floors of large buildings raised to keep them dry; paved sidewalks, some of whose stones are decorated with petroglyphs; a large stone carved with stylistic representations of two Indian gods: the jaguar, god of the forest, and the crocodile, god of the river; a system of covered and uncovered aqueducts which still functions well; and the oldest bridge in Costa Rica, a flat rock now broken in several places, which crosses one of the aqueducts. Several roads radiate from the center of the town. Spot excavations verify that some of them extend at least 8 kilometers. It's theorized that the most important people—the chief, his family, and priests—lived in the center of town, and that common people lived outside.

There are many mysteries about the civilization that inhabited Guayabo. No one knows why the people left (just before the *conquistadores* discovered Costa Rica), nor why Spanish explorers never found or never kept records of finding the site. Yet the peace and beauty that reign in Guayabo echo a wise and gentle people.

From the *mirador*, you can see the green grassy mounds and stone sidewalks nestled within the rainforest. Hawks and vultures swoop and sail in front of the striking four-layered backdrop of mountains. Across the road from the site, behind the campground, a steep trail leads down to the fast-flowing Guayabo River, where you can sit bathing your feet and looking for birds.

Oropéndolas

You can also walk up the road past coffee and sugarcane fields for views of the green Guayabo valley.

Park personnel orient visitors when they arrive, then give them a pamphlet to do a self-guided tour. Camping is allowed. Bring rain gear.

Hotel La Calzada (heated water, shared bath; $7-$12; 56-0465), which is 400 meters before the entrance to the monument, is a pleasant country inn, with comfortable, light-filled rooms overlooking a large pond, a homey common area, and good *campesino* food in an open-air restaurant. Whether you stop there during the rainy season to warm up with an *agua dulce* or decide to spend a few tranquil days birding and writing in your journal, it's a nice place to be. There is no phone there, so leave a message at 56-0465, and they will contact the hotel by radio, then call back to confirm your reservations. You can get discounts at La Calzada with a student ID card.

GETTING THERE: *San José–Turrialba* buses (Calle 13, Avenida 6; 75 cents) leave every hour for the two-hour trip. To get there by car, follow the signs from Cartago to Turrialba, or take the above-mentioned back road from Cot, heading at first toward Volcán Irazú. Both are scenic and about equal in distance. The main road has more curves.

To get to Guayabo, take the Santa Teresita bus from the main bus stop in Turrialba at 10:30 a.m. or 1:30 p.m. It leaves you 4 kilometers from the entrance to Guayabo. Most people hike downhill to the crossroads to catch the 12:45 p.m. Santa Teresita bus back to Turrialba. You can also hitch back with families returning by car. José Miguel, the friendly owner of Hotel La Calzada, runs a once-a-day taxi service to meet the 10:30 Santa Teresita bus at the crossroads. Call to let him know when you are coming. The 19-kilometer trip to Guayabo takes about 40 minutes by car from Turrialba, a bit longer by bus. The road is paved except for the last 4 kilometers.

On the way back to San José on the main road, there are a couple of curious little places to visit. **La Posada de la Luna,** west of the church in Cervantes, halfway between Turrialba and Cartago, serves *comida típica* and delicious homemade desserts. The dining room is surrounded by cases full of antique memorabilia: Spanish swords, pre-Columbian artifacts, Japanese *netsuke*— you name it, they've got it. At the entrance to Paraíso, on the right coming from Turrialba toward Cartago, is the **Autovivero del Río** (free admission), a combination greenhouse and mini-zoo of native animals, including quail, *tepiscuintles*, *guatuzos*, ducks, turtles, and a monkey. Besides plants, they sell rabbits and colored volcanic stones, and there is playground equipment for kids. Although there is no entrance fee, they ask for donations to support the animals.

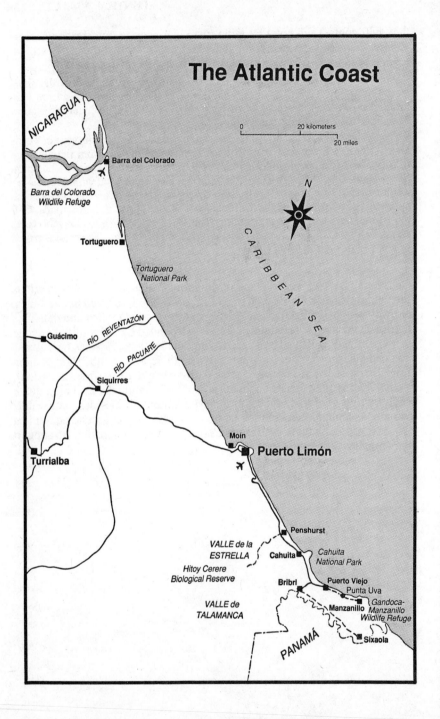

EIGHT

The Atlantic Coast

NICARAGUA

Barra del Colorado

Barra del Colorado
Wildlife Refuge

Tortuguero

Tortuguero
National Park

CARIBBEAN SEA

Guácimo

RÍO REVENTAZÓN

RÍO PACUARE

Siquirres

Moín

Puerto Limón

Turrialba

Penshurst

VALLE de la
ESTRELLA

Cahuita

Cahuita
National Park

Hitoy Cerere
Biological Reserve

Bribri

Puerto Viejo

Punta Uva

VALLE de
TALAMANCA

Manzanillo

Gandoca-
Manzanillo
Wildlife Refuge

PANAMÁ

Sixaola

0   20 kilometers

20 miles

The Atlantic Coast

A trip to the Atlantic coast in Limón Province offers a chance to enjoy this area's wild beauty and the distinct culture that characterizes it. Much of the region is a jungle-covered lowland, which is skirted by a coastline dotted with beautiful white- and black-sand beaches. Limón is the least-populated province in Costa Rica, and its slow-moving way of life makes it a good place to visit for people who want to avoid touristy atmospheres. Talamanca, south of Limón, is best if you want to relax and sunbathe or snorkel, although sometimes it is inundated by surfers. Naturalists will enjoy Tortuguero to the north, and anglers will gravitate to the lodges at Barra del Colorado, near the Nicaraguan border.

Limón Province is unique in its mix of ethnic groups. Afro-Caribbean peoples migrated to the Atlantic coast in the 19th century to fish, work on the railroad, and farm cacao and coconut, and they now comprise roughly a third of the province's population. A variety of English dialects are spoken here, including an elegant Jamaican English and the patois spoken by blacks. "What happen" (pronounced "whoppen") is the common greeting. Instead of saying "*adiós*" when they pass each other, people say "all right" or "okay." For a fascinating history of the region, read Paula Palmer's *What Happen*, in which elders of the black community tell their life stories.

Limón Province was hit very hard by the earthquake of April 22, 1991, a 7.4 on the Richter scale. Many bridges, roads, and buildings were destroyed by the quake, and the rocky shoreline was lifted to as much as five feet above its previous level in parts, exposing coral reefs along the shore. The bridges and roads have been repaired, but the damage to the water distribution system is still being worked on. There is no need to fear a major earthquake in this zone, because, historically, seismic activity has been less than in other parts of Costa Rica, following a 70-year cycle. That's good, because a visit to the Atlantic Coast is a unique experience that shouldn't be missed.

Note: Because of the damage to the water system, we recommend that while you're visiting the Atlantic coast area, you *avoid drinking tap water* (or any water not bottled or boiled), fresh juice made with water or ice, and raw fruits and vegetables that cannot be peeled. We always bring a large plastic bottle of San José water on our trips. You might want to bring your own fruits and vegetables, too (previously washed, of course), because it gets a bit expensive to eat three meals a day on the coast. Also the food in the region tends to be a bit greasy and salty, and lighter meals taste good in the hot weather.

PUERTO LIMÓN

Puerto Limón is Costa Rica's Atlantic port. Its main attraction is the annual carnival that coincides with *El Día de la Raza* on October 12. Brightly costumed *Limonenses* parade to the rhythm of drums, tambourines, pots and pans, maracas, and whistles. You're part of the parade, too, drawn in by the irresistible Afro-Caribbean beat. The drinking, dancing, and carousing last several days. Another annual event in Limón is the surfing championship that takes place on Playa Bonita, a tourist beach a few kilometers north of town. Limón is in transition from funky seaport to gateway to some of the country's most beautiful beaches. The streets are full of people, bicycles, dogs, and the occasional vulture.

A few kilometers to the north, in a more upscale and scenic area between Limón and the container port of Moín, is the **Hotel Matama** (heated water, air-conditioning, pool; $60-$70, off-season discounts; 58-1123, fax: 58-4499), which has shady gardens, a friendly staff, and a restaurant with international fare (Caribbean specialties are served on Sunday only). The rooms are clean and tastefully decorated. There is no cross-ventilation, so you have to use air-conditioning. The hotel also offers tours.

Directly across the street from the Hotel Matama are **Cabinas Cocorí** (ceiling fans, air-conditioning, kitchen, pool; $30-$40; 58-2930; Apdo. 1093), clean two-bedroom apartments. We have heard that the food is good at the big restaurant on Playa Bonita, next to Cabinas Cocorí.

Hotel Maribú Caribe (heated water, air-conditioning; $70-$80, off-season discounts; 58-4010, fax: 58-3541) is about 1 kilometer toward Limón from the Matama. Coming from the north you'll see its white, circular thatched cabinas sitting on a hill like a tribal fort. The rooms and pool are spotless, and the whole place has a sterility that makes it seem foreign to the Atlantic Coast. The parking lot guards carry small sidearms. Perched on the only cliff in the area, the breezy restaurant is a bit overpriced, but the view makes it a worthwhile place to stop after the long drive to Limón. The hotel also offers tours.

GETTING THERE: To get to the area north of Limón by bus take the Moín bus near Radio Casino in Limón. By car, you can avoid Limón altogether: Before you get to Limón, take the Moín exit that goes diagonally to the left from the main highway. The road signs marking the exit are confusingly placed, but you'll see signs advertising the hotels. Turn right just before the entrance to the port facility—you'll pass the beaches of Portete and Playa Bonita before you come to the hotels.

LIMÓN

Just as you enter Limón from the north, on the right, is **Restaurant Arrecife,** specializing in fresh seafood. A bit farther on is **Springfield,** a favorite with locals for Caribbean cooking.

In Limón, stop by the **Helenik Souvenir Shop and Tourist Information Center** (58-2086), two blocks north from the east corner of the *mercado.* They sell beachwear and local crafts and can connect you with low-cost **tours to Tortuguero.** They also have a same-day laundry service for about $2 per kilo.

You can stay just as cheaply in the more beautiful areas down the coast, so try not to get stuck in Limón for the night. If you do have to wait there, **Parque Vargas** is pleasant, with its huge palms, and you can take a refreshing walk along the sea wall. **Los Cuatro Mares** on the south side of the *mercado* is a nice, clean place to stop for a snack. Be careful in Limón after dark. Mugging is a danger. We were even stopped once by a uniformed person who seemed to be trying to trump up something about our identification in order to get a bribe. We just played dumb and walked away. If you do stay in Limón, here is a rundown of several hotels:

The **Hotel Acón** (heated water, air-conditioning; $20-$30; 58-1010, fax: 58-2924), 50 meters east of the market, has a restaurant and a big disco on the second floor. The best place to stay in its price range, the **Park** (cold water, no fans in some rooms; heated water, air-conditioning in others; $7-$20; 58-3476) has a certain aging charm. It's next to the sea wall, a block north of Parque Vargas. Ask for a room that faces the sea to take advantage of the ocean breezes.

Upstairs across from the Instituto Nacional de Seguros, the **Hotel Palace** (cold water, shared bath, fans; under $7; 58-0419) is fairly clean and not bad for the low-budget range in Limón. Next door, the **Hotel Cariari** (cold water, shared bath, no fans, thin mattresses; under $7; 58-1395) is very basic but has a lot of character. You can watch the street life from its balcony. The **Hotel Oriental** (cold water, shared bath, some fans; under $7; 58-0117), 75 meters north of the *mercado,* is clean but noisy. Ask for a room off the street. The **Lincoln** (cold water, private bath, ceiling fans; $12-$20; 58-0074), 200 meters north of the *mercado,* is pretty run-down.

The **Hotel Miami** (cold water, private bath; with fans, $7-$12; with airconditioning, $12-$20; 58-0490), 100 meters west of the *mercado,* is a good value and clean. The rooms on the street have more light but are noisier.

GETTING THERE: In San José, the buses for Limón, *San José–Limón* (23-7811, 21-5917; $1.90) stop is on Avenida 3, Calles 19/21, near the northeast corner of Parque Nacional. Buses leave almost every hour, but buy tickets in advance if it is a weekend or holiday.

By Car: Driving to the Atlantic Coast is fairly easy and enjoyable. The first part of the drive is through the beautiful mountains of Braulio Carrillo National Park. It's hard to believe that when it's raining cats and dogs in San José, it can be clear and hot on the other side of those mountains. It's true, though, especially in September and October, usually the heaviest months of the rainy season. Try to go early in the day to avoid fog and rain. And if it has been raining a lot, ask around about landslides in Braulio Carrillo before you set out.

Once you emerge from the park, there are numerous places to stop for a break. We can't recommend the food in one place over the other. The two restaurants on either side of the 24-hour gas station at the entrance to Guácimo are clean, and the **Centro Turístico Pacuare**, just south of Siquirres, is a good place to stop for a snack and a swim. To get to Talamanca, take a right at the first intersection you come to as you enter Limón.

We recommend going south to the **Talamanca** region rather than staying in the Limón area. When we first went to Talamanca in 1975, there was no road. We took a two-hour train ride from Limón to Penshurst on the Río Estrella, where we were met by a man in a dugout canoe who ferried us across the river to a rickety bus. Then it was another hour on a dirt road to Cahuita, a small village where horses grazed on the grassy paths between houses. That has all changed, now that there are roads. Cahuita's grassy paths have become dusty streets, and the people of Talamanca find themselves thrust uneasily into the 20th century. Independent farming and fishing are giving way to a tourism-based economy, with some related drug culture and theft. Tour buses lining the streets of this small town during the dry season make local people feel that their home is becoming lost to them. During the rest of the year, Talamanca reverts to its relaxed pace. The beaches are uncrowded, and the weather, in September and October especially, is beautiful in contrast to the afternoon rains in the rest of Costa Rica.

At the Pacific beaches, the local culture takes second place to a tourist milieu created by highland Ticos and foreigners of all nationalities. Talamanca, however, is still terra incognita for most Ticos. In 1975 a law was passed prohibiting construction within 50 meters of the shore. Then the point below Cahuita was declared a national park. Recently, the area south of Puerto Viejo has been made into a wildlife refuge. For these reasons the beaches retain their pristine beauty, and the people their unique way of life.

Life on the Atlantic coast is definitely laid back. Because of this, it is a great place to relax. There are a few places that offer air-conditioning and hot water, but service everywhere is generally very slow. When going to a restaurant, bring along some snacks to eat while you're waiting, or dance with your waiter or waitress. We hope that somehow the people of Talamanca can preserve their unique character without being run over by tourism.

CAHUITA AND CAHUITA NATIONAL PARK

The town of Cahuita is a 45-minute drive from Limón. There is one phone number for all of Cahuita: dial 58-1515 and ask for the extension you want.

Cahuita National Park protects a coral reef that extends 500 meters out from Cahuita point. One entrance to it is along the white-sand beach at the southern edge of town. *Note:* The first 400 meters of this beach are dangerous to swim in. The currents can be very strong and unpredictable.

The park **campsites** are at the **Puerto Vargas entrance** on the other side of the point, 4 kilometers south of Cahuita, and about 2 kilometers to the left. There is water available there, as well as showers and toilets. The park service charges a minimal fee to camp. Signs indicate the sections of Puerto Vargas Beach that are dangerous for swimmers. Take flippers and a mask to enjoy the underwater garden of 123 species of tropical fish, as well as crabs, lobsters, shrimp, sea anemones, sponges, black and red sea urchins, and sea cucumbers. In order to snorkel, you must enter from the beach on the Puerto Vargas side and swim out to the reef.

Biologists have observed that the coral in the reef has stopped growing. They attribute this to silt washed down by the river from the inland banana plantations, which inhibits the coral's ability to reproduce.

There is a shady 7-kilometer nature trail between the beach and the jungle. It's 4 kilometers by trail from Cahuita to the point, and another 3 kilometers to the Puerto Vargas camping area. You might see iguanas, sloths, and howler and white-faced monkeys along the trail. The freshwater rivers and estuaries are good places to spot caimans and herons. You can spend the day hiking and snorkeling, then come out on the highway at the Puerto Vargas entrance to the park and catch the 4 p.m. bus back to Cahuita.

Several local residents have begun to take tourists out to the better snorkeling spots by boat; ask around. **José McCloud** (ext. 256) has been recommended as an excellent guide to the flora and fauna of the Talamanca mountains and can tell you a lot about the community as well. **Cahuita Tours** (ext. 232) can take you to the reef in a boat with a glass window in the bottom (about $15). The trip takes an entire morning. (If it has been raining and the water is cloudy, it's not worth going out.) They also rent snorkeling equipment, bicycles, and binoculars; lead scuba-diving and sportfishing expeditions; run a taxi service; change travelers checks; and provide a public telephone. They're on Cahuita's main street, half a block from the Guardia Rural.

Moray's (ext. 216) offers snorkeling tours, boat tours of the beaches south of Cahuita, hiking and horseback tours, and tours to Tortuguero, as well as snorkeling and diving equipment rental. It also rents rooms. It's on the road to the black-sand beach next to the rural guard station.

At the entrance to the Cahuita National Park are several hotels and restaurants. (If you like peace and quiet, you won't enjoy this part of town.)

Hotel Cahuita has overpriced cabinas (private bath, table fans, pool; $20-$30; ext. 201), as well as cheaper rooms (shared bath, no fans; $7-$12) in the old hotel above the restaurant. Across the street, **Cabinas Vaz** (private bath, table fans; $7-$12; ext. 218) are similar and have a restaurant.

The **Sol y Mar Restaurant** next door offers local specialties and also has spacious, clean cabinas (cold water, private bath; upstairs rooms, $12-$20; downstairs, $7-$12; ext. 237). The upstairs rooms have balconies with views. The **Cahuita National Park Restaurant** (open daily, 8 a.m. to 9 p.m.) has a good view but slow service. Across the street, the **Vista del Mar** (open daily, 7 a.m. to 11 p.m.) specializes in seafood.

Around the corner from Cabinas Vaz, the **Defi Restaurant** (open daily, 6 a.m. to 11 p.m.) offers vegetarian specialties, as well as seafood and pizza. It has a "rasta" atmosphere, a reputation for good food, and live reggae on weekends.

You can have fresh coral crabs at **El Típico**, which is toward the main highway from the Defi. Make sure you ask them how much their seafood costs. The price on the menu is for the smallest size. Our large crab, though delicious, was almost twice as expensive ($7.50) as the menu price.

Near El Típico is a place to rent surfboards and snorkels. Across from El Típico are **Cabinas Corre Oso** (private bath, table fans; $7-$12).

Cabinas Palmer (table fans; with shared refrigerator, $7-$12; with kitchen, $12-$20; ext. 243) are located a half block from the bus stop. Down the street from Palmer's are **Cabinas Jenny** (cold water, private bath; $20-$30; ext. 256), a nice place to stay in a new two-story building overlooking the sea. Handpainted clothing by local artists is on sale at the boutique.

Run by friendly owners, **Surfside Cabinas** (private bath, table fans; $7-$12; ext. 246, 203), located behind the school, are a good value. They also have four rooms on the water and a restaurant (open daily, 7 a.m. to 9 p.m.). The local dish of rice and beans, made with coconut milk, is served on weekends only.

Near the sea, the **Cabinas Brisas del Mar** (cold water, private bath; $12-$20; ext. 267) across from the school, are clean.

One block to the right from the Guardia Rural, **Miss Edith** (breakfast served 7 a.m. to 9 a.m., closed Tuesday; only open for supper on Sunday) cooks up a storm, ladling out tasty, down-home Caribbean food. In response to the requests of her customers, she also includes vegetarian fare in her menu, as well as native medicinal teas such as bay rum, *guanabana* leaves, *sorosi*, and lemongrass, which are good for what ails you. If you want her to make *rondon*, a native stew, let her know early in the day so she can get it started. You can also buy fresh lobster on the beach and bring it to her to cook. Miss Edith's sister is starting a laundry service; ask about it.

North of Cahuita is a long, beautiful, black-sand beach. As you walk along the road toward Black Beach, you'll come to the **Tienda de Artesanía**, featuring locally made clothes and jewelry. A road to the left connects with the main highway. On this road is the **Cafetería Vishnu**, which offers breakfast all day and an "emergency" campground, which has a toilet but no showers. The campground is surrounded by coconut trees—don't get bonked. Across the street is the Swiss-owned **El Cactus** (open from 4 p.m., closed Monday), which specializes in pizza and pastas.

Back on the road to Black Beach, **Cabinas Tito** (cold water, table fans; $12-$20; ext. 286), 250 meters north of the Guardia Rural, are nice, new, and very clean little houses with porches and cooking facilities, run by friendly owners. Recommended. Next down the road is **The Pastry Shop**, with delicious take-out cinnamon rolls, cakes, breads, and other baked goods. Try the banana cream pie. It also has one cute Caribbean-style cabina. Next to that is the entrance to **Cabinas Colibrí** (heated water, private bath, ceiling fans; $30-$40; ext. 263), artistically designed and furnished accommodations, complete with kitchens and hammocks. Recommended. They are set back about 200 meters from the road; you can also enter from the main highway.

Atlántida Lodge (heated water, private bath, ceiling fans, screens; $30-$40 including breakfast; ext. 213) is diagonally across the ballfield near the beginning of the black-sand beach. It is clean and tranquil, with well-kept grounds and safe parking, and you can rent bicycles, boogieboards, and snorkels. Just north of the Atlántida Lodge a path takes you 250 meters back to **Cabinas Iguana** (cold water, ceiling fans; $20-$30; no phone), two nicely designed houses that have kitchens, porches, and hammocks. Recommended.

Continuing north, **Cabinas Black Beach** (private bath, protected parking; $12-$20; ext. 251) are charmingly designed two-story stone-and-wood structures. One of the owners is Italian, so you'll find Italian dishes in their restaurant.

Next door, **Cabinas Brigitte** (shared bath, no fans; under $7) has rooms with mosquito nets for budget travelers. The owner is Swiss, but cooks native- and European-style food, and her restaurant (open 7 a.m. to 9 p.m.) is popular with locals as well as visitors. Her menu features daily specials and includes good inexpensive soup, six kinds of salads, and home-baked bread. She also offers a four-hour jungle tour by horseback for $20.

Directly behind Brigitte's are **Topo's Cabinas** (heated water, private bath, ceiling fans; $30-$40; no phone), which are run by a European reptile specialist. There are frogs in the backyard, fluorescent green Thai snakes in a cage, and other such creatures, and the owner loves to tell you all about them. The cabins are little works of art.

Cabinas El Ancla (private bath; $7-$12) are next door. They are basic cabinas, with a friendly "rasta" atmosphere. A lot of surfers hang out at the restaurant because it's near the best waves in Cahuita.

Hotel Jaguar (cold water, no fans, screens; $40-$50 including breakfast and dinner; ext. 238), 1 kilometer north of the national park, is still partly under construction. It has large rooms with natural ventilation that sometimes doesn't work. Rooms with a view of the ocean are also right on the street. The restaurant has an international menu.

The European-owned **Chalet Hibiscus** (Apdo. 943, Limón) is very beautiful, with two two-story beach houses (heated water, no fans, kitchen; $60-$80) that have ocean views, two bedrooms, a garage, a porch, and a patio, as well as three cabinas (heated water, no fans; $30-$40;) that are right on the beach. Recommended.

Cabinas Algebra (cold water, private bath, table fans; $7-$12; 58-2623 for messages), whose restaurant **Bananas** serves some of the best Caribbean food we've had in Cahuita, is just down the road. The cabinas are a bit run-down, but the owners are friendly.

The Canadian-owned **Margaritaville Restaurant** (open daily for dinner at 6 p.m.) is at the north end of Black Beach. Its specialties are home cooking and baking with lots of organic fruits and vegetables, as well as seafood and meat dishes.

Club Campestre Cahuita (private bath; with cold water, $12-$20; newer cabinas with heated water, $20-$30; 58-2861) is not in Cahuita, but halfway back to Limón. It has pools and dark rooms with heavy-duty ceiling fans. Its generous but greasy restaurant is open all day, every day. **Camping** ($3) is allowed on the beach across the road from the hotel. Rooms are only open to nonmembers during the off-season, May through November.

Hitoy Cerere Biological Reserve is definitely off the beaten track and has hardly been developed for visitors. Trails are overgrown and unmarked and there are no camping facilities. Park guards spend most of their time cutting down marijuana that people plant within the reserve. But for hardy explorers, there are beautiful views, clear streams, waterfalls, and lots of birds to see. You have to take a Valle de la Estrella bus from Limón to get to

A lovely waterfall in Monteverde. This privately operated park offers numerous trails that hug the Continental Divide. On a clear day you can see both the Atlantic and the Pacific from the summit lookout. Monteverde includes extensive high altitude rainforest, home to hummingbirds, quetzals, and other birds.

Above: The steaming caldera of Poás Volcano, centerpiece of Parque Nacional Volcan Poás, about two hours from San José.

Below: Clouds often cover the upper peaks of the Continental Divide. These mountains are seen from the summit of Irazú volcano, about 75 minutes northeast of San José and historic Cartago.

San José spreads out in a huge valley surrounded by lushly forested volcanic mountains.

Above: The Saturday street market in San José is a colorful way to mingle with locals.

Right: Coffee plantations dot the mountainous landscape. The harvest provides Costa Rica with one of its major export crops.

Left: The annual rodeo and festival in Liberia draws cowboys from neighboring ranches in Guanacaste and the Nicoya Peninsula.

Below: A young woman prepares food in a restaurant in Tamarindo.

Above: A vibrant rainbow colors the landscape near Lake Arenal (Laguna de Arenal).

Right: Interesting churches grace Costa Rica's villages.

Above: Lowlying clouds filter the late afternoon sun, bathing the rural landscape near Lake Arenal in dramatic light.

Below: The beach at Playa Grande, one of dozens of beaches along the Pacific coast of San José Province.

Top: Iguanas are commonly found along the dry Pacific coast.

Middle left: Crabs are part of the food supply for the numerous birds that live and nest along Costa Rica's Pacific and Atlantic coasts.

Middle right: A leatherback turtle makes its way back to the Pacific after digging a nest and depositing up to 25 eggs.

Right: Hummingbirds are abundant in Costa Rica's mountainous rainforests.

Hitoy Cerere, which winds its way into the banana plantations. Get off at Finca Seis, the end of the line. Jeep-taxis there will take you 10 kilometers farther for around $4 and leave you within 1 kilometer of the entrance. They will return to pick you up at an agreed-upon time and can take you back to Cahuita if you want (one and a half hours, $25).

GETTING THERE: *By Bus*: *Limón–Sixaola*: The Sixaola bus leaves for Cahuita at 5 a.m., 10 a.m., 1 p.m., and 4 p.m. The stop is one block north and half a block west of the Mercado Central in Limón. Get there early to buy a ticket. If you catch the 7 a.m. bus from San José, you should be able to make the 10 a.m. bus down the Talamanca coast (one hour to Cahuita). *San José–Sixaola*: There is a direct bus (21-0524, 58-1572; $4) that leaves from Avenida 11, Calles 1/Central each day at 6 a.m., 2:30 p.m., and 4:30 p.m. It is a three-and-a-half-hour trip. It reaches the same Bribri–Puerto Viejo *cruce* around 6:30 a.m., 9:30 a.m., 11:30 a.m., and 4 p.m. on its way back to San José from Sixaola and Bribri. If you are staying near Black Beach in Cahuita, you will need to walk at least a kilometer to get to your hotel, whichever bus you take, so travel light. *By Car*: From Limón it is pretty much a straight shot down the coast: 45 minutes to Cahuita.

PUERTO VIEJO

Puerto Viejo is 19 kilometers south of Cahuita, on paved road except for the last 6 kilometers after the turnoff to Bribri. The town is smaller and less developed than Cahuita, and the beaches to the south are some of the most beautiful in the country.

The area outside the reef in Puerto Viejo has become famous in surfing lore as "La Salsa Brava." The waves are world-class from December to April. Another season opens up in June and July. During the high season, surfers on their way out often sell their boards to new arrivals. This avoids the tremendous hassle of taking surfboards on the bus. Some surfers hire a taxi or truck to haul their gear from Limón ($25-$30). This is cheaper than renting a car in San José, and most of the good waves are an easy walk from Puerto Viejo. La Salsa Brava is definitely not for neophytes. We have heard that at least one surfboard per day breaks on the reef.

In September and October the sea is calmer and better for snorkeling and swimming. Nonsurfers will be able to enjoy Puerto Viejo a lot more in those months. Everything is less crowded, and the weather is generally beautiful. Swimming is best at **Punta Uva**, a gorgeous beach 7 kilometers south of Puerto Viejo.

The Puerto Viejo area is home to at least three different cultures: the English-speaking black farmers who grew cacao and coconut until a blight in the early 1980s ruined the cacao harvest, the indigenous people of the Bribri and Cabécar tribes who live in the foothills, and the Spanish-speaking immigrants who came to the area in search of land. The Talamancan Ecotourism and Conservation Association publishes an excellent pamphlet,

Welcome to Coastal Talamanca, which describes the cultural heritage of the zone and provides visitor information. Also look for *Taking Care of Sibo's Gifts*, in which the people of the KékoLdi reserve explain their way of life and their commitment to conserving nature.

Because the Talamanca region was until recently so isolated from the rest of Costa Rica, many of its cultural traditions are still alive. Miss Dolly can prepare you a traditional Caribbean meal (ask her a day in advance) or take you for a walk to learn to identify medicinal plants and herbs. Mauricio Salazar of Cabinas Chimuri takes visitors on horseback through the KékoLdi Indian reserve to observe flora and fauna and learn about customs of the Bribri and Cabécar people.

Ask local fishermen to take you ocean fishing. Daniel Brown at the **Soda Aquario** and "Papi" Hudson in Puerto Viejo arrange snorkeling trips. You can rent bikes and horses in Puerto Viejo, or walk the 9.5-kilometer **beach trail** from Barra Cocles to Manzanillo.

Note for drivers and bicyclists: Do as the locals do and get off your bike to cross the small wooden bridges along the beach road. It's very easy to lose your balance on the uneven wooden surface, and there are no railings to keep you from falling into the rocky river below. If you are in a car, drive slowly, because the bridges are unmarked, and you can be on them before you know it.

Insects: Just to be on the safe side, we recommend that you invest in some mosquito coils (about $1 at the local *pulpería*) or bring mosquito nets. Whether you will be bothered or not depends on the climatic conditions and the location and design of your hotel. If there are mosquitos, they will only bother you at night. Worse than mosquitos are no-see-ums in the sand, which bite your ankles around dusk. And watch out for mean biting ants in the grass.

RESTAURANTS   Definitely the best breakfast in Puerto Viejo is at the **Coral** (breakfast, 7 a.m. to 12 noon; dinner, 6 p.m.; closed Monday). Hot home-made whole-wheat and French bread accompany the eggs and omelettes. The rest of the menu ranges from yogurt and granola to *gallo pinto* to hearty whole-wheat buttermilk pancakes. The dinner menu features Margarita's famous delicious pizzas and pastas. The Coral is located 200 meters south of Manuel León's *pulpería*.

The **Soda Bela** (open daily, 6 a.m. to 4 p.m.), near the Hotel Puerto Viejo, is also a clean, pleasant breakfast or lunch spot, offering homemade bread, jam, cakes, good coffee, and local herbal teas. It also rents sturdy, reliable one-speed bikes (about $1/hour).

The **Garden** (open 11 to 3 p.m.; 5:30 to 9:30 p.m.; closed Wednesday) is another outstanding restaurant. It specializes in Asian, Caribbean, and Creole cuisines featuring vegetarian dishes and seafood. All breads and desserts are homemade. It is near the soccer field.

The **Soda Támara** (open 6:30 a.m. to 9 p.m.; closed Tuesday) is a popular place to eat, as is the **Parquecito** (open all day), which is right on the beach. **Salsa de Talamanca** is a surfboard repair shop and open-air restaurant with a nice view of the sea. In addition to lunch, it has locally made baked goods and stamps, runs a book exchange, and rents boogieboards. It sometimes sells little rounds of unsweetened cacao—just the thing to take back for hot chocolate in town, which you can sip while you recall the misty beaches and reggae rhythms of the Talamanca coast. The above three places are about one block down the beach from the Rural Guard.

The **Mexitico Restaurant** (open daily, 6 a.m. to 9:30 p.m.) at the Hotel Puerto Viejo serves good homemade chips and salsa. **Johnnie's Place** serves hefty, inexpensive portions of greasy, salty "Chinese" food and is also a disco. It is next to the Rural Guard.

Stanford's Restaurant El Caribe is famous for fresh seafood, although it is often overcooked. His disco is jumping Thursday through Sunday. You can cash traveler's checks there, but the exchange rate may be less favorable than in San José.

Fresh fruits and vegetables are delivered to Puerto Viejo on Wednesday. You can buy them from the delivery truck as it makes its rounds or at the vegetable stands near the bus stop and at the Parquecito. Miss Dolly makes bread with coconut milk, which is good with her homemade guava jam. You can buy ginger biscuits, pineapple rolls, plantain tarts, and *pan bon* from local women, such as Miss Sam and Miss Daisy. To locate these ladies, ask any resident.

LODGING ☺ **Cabinas Chimuri** (shared bath; $20-$30; message, 58-3844) are typical Bribri constructions of thatch over bamboo set on a hill in a cool, shady forest. A large, open-walled *palenque* serves as a common cooking area. Near the cabins are waterfalls with pools for a refreshing swim. The owners are Colocha, from Austria, and her husband, Mauricio, a Bribri from Talamanca. Mauricio's nature tours ($25/person) on horseback are a favorite with visitors. Longer treks through the Atlantic side of Parque International La Amistad are possible if you come prepared with good shoes, sleeping bags, and other camping gear. These three-day camping trips require advance notice and payment so that supplies can be bought and preparations for the boat trip out can be made. Mauricio also sells traditional Indian crafts. Cabinas Chimuri is a great place to stay for those who like simplicity: doing their own cooking, living in nature, and getting to know the Bribri way of life. Recommended. To get to the cabinas, go down a road to the right 300 meters before you get to the black-sand beach that leads to Puerto Viejo.

Cabinas Black Sands (cold water, shared bath; $7-$12) are right on the beach and are private and tranquil. The Indian-style thatch-roofed structure has three rooms and a shared kitchen. Recommended for budget travelers. It is located just before the road turns to go along the black-sand beach that leads to Puerto Viejo. Turn left at *pulpería* La Violeta and follow the road when it veers to the right (about 400 meters). It is about a 20-minute walk to Puerto Viejo.

Cabinas Las Brisas (cold water, shared bath, table fans; $7-$12) are right next to the Pulpería Violeta. The accommodations are basic but nice, although there is usually loud music playing nearby.

Cabinas Playa Negra (cold water, no fans; $20-$30; 56-1132, 56-6396) have breezy, second-story sleeping spaces for six with a kitchen below. They are about 300 meters back from the beach as you approach Puerto Viejo. Their *soda* offers fresh fish and *comida típica*.

Preserving the natural wood style of most coastal cabinas, **El Pizote Surf Lodge** (with shared bath, $30-$40; individual bungalows with private bath, $50-$60; 29-1428, 58-1938) offers many amenities: storage space, reading lamps by the beds, large comfortable mattresses, mirrors you can actually see yourself in, and ceiling fans. Rates include breakfast and dinner. The lodge offers bicycles, diving gear, and horses for rent, and there are nature trails into the forest from its quiet grounds, which also contain guanabana and Hawaiian papaya plantations. El Pizote is set back from the road, about halfway down the black-sand beach as you approach Puerto Viejo.

Pensión Agaricia (cold water, shared bath, table fans; $12-$20) is a small family-style hostel run by a Costa Rican artist and his European wife, who like to maintain a quiet, private atmosphere. The small second-floor rooms are clean and sunny. The pension rents bikes, has a souvenir shop, and is a good place for groups. Breakfast ($3-$6) is served for guests only. The pension is located right at the entrance to Puerto Viejo, across the street from the beach.

One block farther down are **Cabinas Grant** (cold water, private bath, table fans, wheelchair accessible, locked parking lot; $20-$30; 58-2845).

Hotel Maritza (heated water, private bath, ceiling fans; $12-$20; 58-3844), one block to the left of Cabinas Grant, used to be the only place you could stay in Puerto Viejo. Its small, ramshackle second-story rooms have been supplemented by newer, modern cabinas set around a parking lot.

A block down, near the bus stop, are **Cabinas Ritz** (cold water, private bath; $7-$12), which have no fans and are rather stuffy. A couple of blocks down and to the right are **Cabinas Manuel León** (cold water, private bath; $7-$12; 58-0854, or ask at Manuel León's *pulpería*), which are run-down but are right across from the beach.

Catering to surfers, the **Hotel Puerto Viejo** (shared bath, no fans, mosquito nets; $7-$12) offers good budget accommodations. It has basic second-story rooms, most of which are well ventilated. Bicycles are for rent behind the hotel.

Next door are **Cabinas Stanford** (private bath, table fans; $12-$20), which are rather dark but fairly secure. Make arrangements at Stanford's Restaurant. Farther down the same street are **Cabinas Támara**, (cold water, private bath, ceiling fans; $7-$12; with stove, $12-$20; with kitchen, $20-$30), clean rooms that have shady, furnished porches. Recommended. Make arrangements through the Soda Támara. The above three lodgings are about a block from the beach.

Nicely furnished and decorated, the ○ **Cabinas Jacaranda** (shared bath, no fans, mosquito nets; $7-$12) share a building with the Garden Restaurant, one block inland from Cabinas Támara. Recommended for budget travelers.

Hotel Pura Vida (hot water, shared bath, ceiling fans; $12-$20), across from the soccer field, is a good value. Built by the Swiss owner himself, it is tastefully designed with hardwood floors and large screened windows, and each room has a sink with hot and cold water, although baths are shared. Bicycles are available for rent. Recommended.

The **Kiskadee** (outhouses, no fans; under $7) is a real treat. I'm a lousy birdwatcher, but even I couldn't help spotting scarlet tanagers and the yellow and black kiskadee for whom the lodge is named, flitting through the heliconias by the side of the trail. There are two second-story rooms—one with double beds, one with bunks—and ample communal kitchen space below. The dormitory-style accommodations are clean, nicely decorated, and run by a friendly retired American woman who charges relatively little for them. Recommended for budget travelers. Bring a flashlight, and boots if it's rainy. To get there, go to the right at the end of the block the Garden Restaurant is on, where you'll find the *cancha de fútbol* (soccer field). Go to the far goalpost and you'll see the Kiskadee sign. It is five minutes up a path through the jungle beyond the soccer field.

Out on the beach past Stanford's are the basic **Cabinas La Salsa Brava** (cold water, private bath; $7-$12). About 450 meters down the road to Punta Uva, you'll find the **Escape Caribeño** (cold water, private bath, ceiling fans, refrigerators; $20-$30), tidy cabinas with porches and hammocks and a communal cooking area (bring your own utensils). It's a good value. Recommended. The office is on the left, cabinas on the right.

Cabinas Garibaldi (cold water, private bath, no fans; $7-$12), next on the left, have a beautiful ocean view. They're basic but built in the traditional Caribbean style and painted green and yellow.

There are new hotels and cabinas all along the road to Punta Uva. With balconies overlooking the beach, the **Villas del Caribe** (hot water, private bath, ceiling fans; $100-$120; 33-2200, fax: 21-2801) are luxury apartments with room for two to five people.

Cabinas Dasa (cold water, boiled drinking water, shared bath, no fans; $12-$20) rents three cabinas at Playa Chiquita, just past Villas del Caribe. About

200 meters beyond them is **Maracú** (cold water, shared bath, no fans; under $7), primitive Indian-style cabins with cooking areas.

Next on the right is the entrance to **Hotel Punta Cocles** (heated water, private bath, ceiling fans, air-conditioning, pool; $60-$80; with kitchens, $80-$100; 34-0306, fax: 34-0014), one of the largest projects in the area. The well-designed bungalows have private porches facing the jungle. There is also a snack bar. A nature trail identifies the local trees and plants and offers a chance to birdwatch. Guests can swim at Playa Chiquita, about 300 meters from the hotel. Bikes, snorkeling equipment, binoculars, surfboards, and horses are available for rent. Since the hotel is about 4.5 kilometers south of Puerto Viejo, you can end up spending a lot of money if you leave the driving to them. For instance, it costs $13 for hotel transportation to Puerto Viejo, $8 to Punta Uva, and $18 to Manzanillo. There is absolutely no problem with tourists taking the local buses, which are much cheaper (see below for schedules).

A few meters beyond the Punta Cocles is **Miraflores Lodge** (heated water, table fans; with shared bath, $30-$40; with private bath, $50-$60; 33-5127, fax: 33-5390), a tastefully decorated bed-and-breakfast surrounded by a tropical flower plantation. Recommended.

Nearby are **Cabinas Aquario** (cold water, kitchens, outhouse; $200-$300/month), rent snorkeling equipment, and arrange boat trips. The *soda* is open daily for breakfast, and for dinner with reservations only.

Playa Chiquita Lodge (cold water, private bath, ceiling fans; $50-$60 including breakfast) is 6 kilometers south of Puerto Viejo. The cabins are nicely designed and blend in with the environment, but are a bit overpriced for the area. It has a restaurant.

About 1 kilometer farther down the road on the left are **Selvyn's Cabinas** (cold water, shared bath, no fans; under $7; larger separate cabin, $12-$20). Selvyn's restaurant (closed Monday) specializes in fish and lobster dinners and serves the local dish of rice and beans on weekends. The basic cabins are a boon for budget travelers since they are a short walk from the most beautiful part of the beach at Punta Uva.

Soda and Restaurant Naturales (open for breakfast, lunch, and dinner; closed Wednesday) is across the road from Selvyn's. It's clean and airy, with a nice view of the sea and the jungle. Reasonably priced meals include homemade breads and cakes. The restaurant also rents bicycles and provides information for tourists.

Cabina Punta Uva (cold water, private bath, kitchen; $20-$30) is at the next entrance to the beach, about 1 kilometer from Selvyn's. A road on the left another kilometer down takes you to the other side of Punta Uva, which is not as spectacular.

There are a couple of bar-restaurants on the beach: **Cabinas Dasa** (cold water, private bath, no fans; $30-$40, weekly rates only), two two-story cabinas with furnished kitchens, and **Hotel Las Palmas** (hot water, private bath, air-conditioning or ceiling fans; $60-$70; 55-3939, fax: 55-3737), solidly built cabinas.

RESERVATIONS Communicating with Puerto Viejo in order to make reservations is not easy. You can leave messages for the hotel of your choice at the Hotel Maritza (58-3844) or Manuel León's (58-0854), but having your call confirmed is another story. The phones are often out of order or are constantly busy because they are the only phones that residents and visitors can call out on. You may just have to take your chances. Do not go without reservations during Christmas or Easter, and try to go on weekdays in the high season.

Seven kilometers beyond Punta Uva is the small fishing village of **Manzanillo**. The **Gandoca-Manzanillo Wildlife Refuge** protects a 9-kilometer beach where four species of turtles lay their eggs, including the giant *baula* (leatherback). The turtles' main nesting season is January through April. Villagers are given a certain number of their eggs to sell, then the rest are raised in incubators to protect them from human and animal predators, after which they are reintroduced to the wild. The refuge also includes two swamps important as wildlife habitats, a 300-hectare forest, and coral reefs. The Gandoca River estuary is a nursery for tarpon, and manatees, crocodiles, and caimans are also seen there. Talk to Florentino Grenald, the enthusiastic refuge administrator in Manzanillo, about hiring local guides. He can also provide you with a list of the 358 bird species that have been identified in the area.

Maxi's Cabinas (shared bath, no fans; under $7) are basic, but the only place to stay in Manzanillo; locals gather to play dominos in the bar/disco.

In Manzanillo, sightseeing or snorkeling tours of the coast in motorized dugout canoes can be arranged through Willie Burton. Miss Marva, Miss Alfonsina, Miss Edith, and Doña Cipriana will prepare meals for you in their homes, if you make arrangements with them in advance. Miss Alfonsina will also share her knowledge of local medicinal plants with you. To find any of these local people, just ask around.

GETTING THERE: *By Bus:* There are two ways to get to the Talamanca region by bus. The first is to take the *San José–Limón* bus, then either the *Limón–Sixaola* or the *Limón–Manzanillo* bus. Both enter Puerto Viejo, making it the bus of choice if you are staying there. If you want to stay south of Puerto Viejo on the road to Punta Uva, you should take the *Limón–Manzanillo* bus.

The second way is the direct bus from San José that goes all the way to Sixaola on the Panamanian border, passing the entrance to Cahuita and the Bribri turnoff 6 kilometers from Puerto Viejo. Some hotels, like the Maritza, will meet the

San José–Sixaloa bus at the turnoff to Puerto Viejo if you arrange it with them beforehand, charging $2-$3 for the ride.

Limón–Sixaola: The Sixaola bus leaves for Cahuita, Puerto Vargas, and Puerto Viejo at 5 a.m., 10 a.m., 1 p.m., and 4 p.m. The stop is one block north and half a block west of the Mercado Central in Limón. Get there early to buy a ticket. If you catch the 7 a.m. bus from San José, you should be able to make the 10 a.m. bus down the Talamanca coast (one and a half hours to Puerto Viejo). Buses leave Puerto Viejo for Limón at 6 a.m., 1 p.m., and 4 p.m. (there is no 1 p.m. bus on Sunday).

Limón–Manzanillo: There is also a bus from Limón all the way past Punta Uva to Manzanillo. It leaves Limón at 6 a.m. and 2 p.m., and returns from Manzanillo at 9 a.m. and 4:30 p.m.

San José–Sixaola: The direct bus (21-0524, 58-1572; $4) leaves from Avenida 11, Calles 1/Central each day at 6 a.m., 2:30 p.m., and 4:30 p.m. The three-and-a-half-hour trip leaves you at the Bribri turnoff 6 kilometers from Puerto Viejo. It reaches the same Bribri–Puerto Viejo *cruce* around 6:30 a.m., 9:30 a.m., 11:30 a.m., and 4 p.m. on its way back to San José from Sixaola and Bribri.

(There's not much to see in the town of Bribri. It is an administrative center more than anything. If you want to experience Indian culture, talk to Mauricio Salazar at Cabinas Chimuri.)

By Car: From Limón it is pretty much a straight shot down the coast: 45 minutes to Cahuita, another 20 minutes to the place where the paved road curves to the right toward Bribri and a gravel road forks off straight ahead of you, which goes 6 kilometers to Puerto Viejo. *Note:* Cars are often stopped by police and checked for Panamanian contraband as they leave Talamanca.

PANAMÁ COAST

If your visa has run out and you want to leave Costa Rica for 72 hours in order to become a legal tourist again, **Bocas del Toro** on the Caribbean coast of Panama is a nice place to go. Christopher Columbus reached Bocas del Toro on October 5, 1502, on his fourth and last trip to the New World. The town is on Isla Colón at the northernmost part of the archipelago of the same name. The road that circles the island next to the sea is great for biking or peaceful walks. Snorkeling is also good there. The island is pretty and almost deserted. You can rent a boat with a guide ($5/hour, plus gas). There's a light turquoise speck in the bay—an island that sank during the April 1991 earthquake. You can go out and stand on it.

Botel Thomas (private bath, air-conditioning or ceiling fans; $12-$20; 507-78-9248, 507-78-9309) is a 50-year-old wooden hotel built on stilts over the water. From the terrace of the building you have a view of a small fishing island, a peninsula of Isla Colón, and the distant breakers of the open sea. There is a restaurant, and the hotel rents bicycles, native canoes, and snorkeling equipment.

The former headquarters of United Fruit, **Hotel Bahía** (some with cold, some with heated water; private bath, air-conditioning or ceiling fans; $12-$20; 507-78-9341, 507-78-9211) is located right on the bay. It has a restaurant.

Pensión Peck (cold water, shared bath, table fans; under $7; 507-78-9252) is next to the market. The owner, Xenia Peck, knows the history of the area and is a storehouse of information on nearly every topic imaginable.

GETTING THERE: You can get a tourist card for Panamá from any travel agency that deals with Copa, the Panamanian airline. Take the Sixaola buses from San José or Limón or catch them in Cahuita or at the *cruce* outside Puerto Viejo. At Sixaola, walk across the border to Guabito and take a bus to Changuinola. From there take a bus or a train to Almirante. (*Note:* Be careful of what you eat and drink on this part of the trip.) The train goes slowly through banana plantations and passes some of the traditional grass huts of the Guaymi people. A water taxi from Almirante to Bocas costs $3. There is also the big Chiquita ferry, which takes cars, but it only goes every ten days or so. It costs $10 for two people to make the entire trip from Puerto Viejo to Bocas by bus. It's important to start your trip as early as possible so you won't get stuck in Almirante for the night.

TORTUGUERO NATIONAL PARK

Tortuguero National Park protects a unique series of natural inland waterways that are home to freshwater turtles; crocodiles; sloths; howler, spider, and colorado monkeys; toucans; *oropéndolas*; parrots; morpho butterflies; and many other species. In addition, it is known as one of the world's richest fishing grounds for tarpon and snook.

Tortuguero is the largest nesting area in the Caribbean for the green sea turtle. They return to Tortuguero every two to four years to mate offshore and dig their nests. Although their feeding grounds can be as far away as Florida and Venezuela, none of the 26,000 turtles tagged in Tortuguero has ever been found to mate at any other beach. Green turtle nesting season is from July through September. The leatherbacks usually nest in May and June. But you can usually see nesting turtles at any time of year. Their flipper marks look like tractor treads, showing up as wide black lines on the beach at night.

Tortuguero has been famous for its turtles—and as a source of their shells, meat, and eggs—since the 1600s, when the Spanish set up cacao plantations on the Atlantic coast. Turtles were valued as a meat source on early ships, because they would stay alive if they were kept out of the sun and sprinkled with water. Turtle soup became a delicacy in England around the end of the 1800s. Large-scale turtle export from Tortuguero started in 1912, and by the 1950s, the green turtle faced extinction.

Long-term biological research on the green turtle, started by the Caribbean Conservation Corp. (CCC) in 1954, has helped greatly in understanding and preservating this species. Dr. Archie Carr, the founder of CCC, wrote an entertaining and informative book, *The Windward Road* (see "Recommended Reading" in Chapter Thirteen), about his wanderings in search of the green turtles' nesting ground, which finally led him to Tortuguero. Thanks to international interest in Carr's work, Tortuguero was declared a national park in 1970 by the Costa Rican government.

Recognizing that no conservation effort can succeed without full support from the human community, the CCC has begun an outreach program to Tortuguero village. Besides employing several townspeople in their research station (locally called Casa Verde, about 2 kilometers north of the town), the CCC in partnership with the National Parks Service has trained local people as turtle guides. Young men who in earlier times might have become expert turtle hunters are learning a new way to make their living from the town's unique natural resource. They have formed a cooperative and take small groups (10 to 15 people) onto the beach to see the turtles during nesting season. (Tickets sold daily, 4 to 6 p.m., in the information kiosk; $2/2 people, plus $1 admission; less per person for parties of four) The guides instruct you when to take flash pictures and how to approach the turtles and share other information about the area.

The CCC training program is one of a handful across Costa Rica that are striving to involve local residents in tourism in a productive, autonomous way. CCC is also training naturalist guides who can show people around when it's not nesting season.

When we were in Tortuguero in March, we saw two huge *baúl* (leatherback) females laboriously digging holes in the soft brown sand by the light of the full moon. Witnessing this age-old ritual left me with a deep respect for the primordial instincts of all creatures, including humans. The turtles lay about 100 eggs at each of several nestings per season. The eggs incubate for approximately 60 days, then the baby turtles bite through the rubbery

Green sea turtle

shells and clamber out of the nest, heading straight for the ocean, which they try to reach before dawn. Once they hit the water, their instinctive navigational powers direct them to the open sea.

The area north of Limón, like most of the Atlantic Coast of Nicaragua, is a water-based society. All travel is by boat. In 1974, a series of canals was built to connect the natural inland waterways between Limón and Barra del Colorado, thus allowing coastal residents to get to Limón without the hazards of sea travel. In 1979 the government established a twice-weekly launch service up the inland waterway. Tortuguero got its first electric generator in 1982. (Roads are planned for the future, but are meeting opposition from residents and tour operators, who recognize the importance of keeping Tortuguero isolated and car-free.) In the information kiosk near the center of Tortuguero village, there is a fascinating exhibit on the cultural history of the area, illustrated by Deirdre Hyde.

The best way to enjoy the exuberant vegetation and abundant wildlife of Tortuguero's canals is to rent a **cayuca**, or dugout canoe (about $1 per person per hour, slightly more with guide; no charge for children). Miss Eva, Rubén Aragón ("Bananero"), Mr. Dama, Alberto Taylor, and Juan José Artencio ("Mille," who owns a friendly bar, **Bayby Doll 2**, on the water 100 meters south of the dock) are some of the villagers who currently rent out *cayucas*. There is also a dugout rental and guide service just before the National Park Office on the riverbank. *Cayucas* are quite stable and easy to paddle. Paddle around for awhile to see if your dugout is the right size for you and make sure it is of solid, one-piece construction and not caulked together. Check also that it has a plastic bailer.

You have to pay $1 admission to the park at the administration office (300 meters south of the information kiosk) before you set off in a *cayuca*. The main waterway of the park is inland from the canal that comes from Moín. Paddle south. You will see smaller waterways branching off that you can explore. If you go out without a guide, ask where the currents are most gentle. The current in the Río Tortuguero can be quite strong. If you would like to hire a **guide**, try Mr. Dama, Bananero, or Jim.

Motorboats to tour the canals of Tortuguero National Park are also available in town and from the lodges. These are okay for going fast, but the noise disturbs the quiet beauty of the jungle streams, and you might scare away any wildlife before you can see it.

To make your boat trip more comfortable, make sure to bring the following:

    Thick-soled athletic shoes
    Socks
    Insect repellent
    Sunblock
    Broad-rimmed hat or visored cap
    Umbrella for sun or rain

Lightweight plastic poncho or picnic cloth for rain
Lightweight long-sleeved and short-sleeved shirts
Towels
Lunch in waterproof bags
Drinking water
Swiss army knife
Flashlight (don't ask why, just take it)

Camping is allowed in the park, but remember that Tortuguero has one of the highest annual rainfalls in the world: more than 200 inches a year. *Terciopelo* (fer-de-lance) snakes are not uncommon on land, especially at night. There is a nature trail on the narrow piece of land between the large canal and the sea. It is a bit less swampy in the dry season.

Note: If you want to go swimming, Tortuguero is not the ideal place. The beach offers little shade, has rough, unfriendly surf, and is frequented by sharks.

LODGING   If you make arrangements to get to Tortuguero with the boatmen from Limón or Barra del Colorado, you can stay at the less expensive places in the village listed below. Many people prefer to splurge on a tour to Tortuguero because the logistics are easier, or because they can be flown directly in and out. The boat trip up the canals from Limón is time consuming and boring for some. If you go on a tour you'll stay at one of the hotels in the "Tour Package hotels" listed on the next page.

It's a good idea to make reservations ahead of time at the hotel of your choice, as all of them work with tour groups and can be crowded. Call 71-6716—the number of a pay phone at the *pulpería*—and leave a message for your hotel with Olger Rivera. The hotel owner should call you back to confirm your reservation.

There are several inexpensive hotels in the village. **Brisas del Mar** (cold water, shared bath, no fans; under $7), known as *El Bochinche* (The Commotion) in honor of a memorable fight that took place there once, has cheap, dark cabinas right on the beach. It doesn't serve food, but it has a bar and holds dances there Wednesday and Saturday nights.

Next door, where most foreign tourists go, is **Sabina's** (cold water; with shared bath, no fans, under $7 to $12; with private bath, table fans, $30-$40). She is often grumpy with tourists, but her cabinas are clean and some have good ocean views. She can give you boat-rental information.

The **Meryscar** (cold water, shared bath, screens, some table fans; under $7; with three meals, $12-$20), 200 meters south of the information kiosk, has a friendly family atmosphere.

More remote and pleasant is **Tatané** (cold water, shared bath; $7-$12), which has individual mini-A-frame cabins. It is five minutes by boat from town, on the canal to Barra. Owner Marcos Zamora is an authorized turtle guide; he can also take visitors on trips through the canals and will take you to and from town free of charge. When you arrive in the village, ask around for him, or hire a boat to take you there.

Cabinas Miss Junie (58-3880, 58-2917), north of town, might be finished by the time you read this. Call for more information. Next door, the **Paraíso Tropical** souvenir shop has canoe-rental information, but is a bit overpriced.

Don't miss eating at the **Pancana Restaurante** (open all day), famous for its homemade cinnamon buns, gringo-style sandwiches, and hearty dinners. It shows natural history videos at night and is a good source of information on what's happening locally. The Pancana is located 200 meters south of the information kiosk.

TOUR PACKAGE HOTELS   All of these lodges offer two- and/or three-day packages that include transportation from San José, food, lodging, and some or all of the following: day or night tours of the canals via motorboat or *cayuca* (some charge extra for this), ascent of Cerro (Mount) Tortuguero, and night-time turtle-nesting tours. Most tours include bus and boat transportation between San José and Tortuguero, and all offer an air transport upgrade.

We recommend **Mawamba Lodge** (cold water, private bath, ceiling fans; $40-$50; 23-2421, fax: 22-4932), which has pleasant cabinas and a large, airy dining room that serves very good food. It is 1 kilometer north of Tortuguero village on the ocean side of the canal. Because it is in walking distance of the village, you can visit it or go to the beach without hiring a boat. Packages: two days, one night, $155; three days, two nights, $180; bus and boat transportation included.

Costa Rica Expeditions flies five-passenger planes directly to and from the comfortable **Tortuga Lodge** (heated water, private bath, ceiling fans; $60-$70; 57-0766, 22-0333, fax: 57-1665). The lodge is on 50 hectares of the forested spit, 2 kilometers from the village across the canal from the Casa Verde. Packages: one day, one night with air transportation, $239; one day, one night with six hours of canal or ocean fishing, $350; three days, two nights with bus and boat transportation, $365.

Cotur takes you by bus to Moín (two and a half hours) and up the canals in launches. You'll stay at the shady **Jungle Lodge** (cold water, private bath, ceiling fans; package only; 33-0155, 33-6579, fax: 33-0778), across the canal from Mawamba. Package: three days, two nights, $198. Daytime *cayuca* tours on the canals are $10; at night, $15.

Agencia Mitur takes people via bus and boat to **Ilan Ilan** (cold water, private bath, table fans; 55-2031, 55-2262, fax: 55-1946), 1.5 kilometers north of Tortuguero across the canal. Rooms are basic though comfortable, and each has an ice cooler. Package: three days, two nights, $198.

GETTING THERE: The old, flat-bottomed boat the **Gran Delta** used to be the main means of transportation for the people who live along the canals. It was crowded and noisy, and the trip took at least seven hours. Because of frequent mechanical problems, the Gran Delta is not running anymore, which creates difficulties for canal dwellers and budget travelers.

Various boatmen, however, take people from Moín to Tortuguero ($50/person round-trip). Modesto and Fran Watson offer a flexible tour aboard their canopied **Riverboat Francesca** (26-0986), stopping to see animals along the way and providing beverages and snacks. **Alfred Brown** (58-0824) also takes people up the canals. They will connect you with other available boatmen if they cannot take you. Otherwise, you can usually find a boat by going to the Moín dock around 8 a.m. You'll be much more comfortable if the $50 fee includes a canopy and refreshments.

Helenik Souvenir Shop (58-2086) also provides current information about getting to Tortuguero. **Laura's Tropical Tours** in Limón (58-2410; $65 including lunch) will take you up and back the same day. The boat leaves daily at 9:30 a.m., arrives in Tortuguero at 12:30 p.m., and returns at 2 p.m. The trip is a little too quick for sightseeing along the smaller canals in the park.

You can also take the SANSA flight to Barra del Colorado and leave a message at the SANSA office for Alphonso, who charges about $50 a boatload to Tortuguero. A ride can also be arranged through the Tarponland Hotel in Barra (see below).

Barra del Colorado, at the northeast end of Costa Rica is a sleepy, rainy, car-free town occupying opposite banks near the mouth of the Río Colorado. There is excellent fishing in the river, nearby canals, and the Caribbean sea. All of the hotels here specialize in fishing.

Tarponland (cold water, both private and shared baths, ceiling fans; $20-$30; 71-6917) is the most modestly priced hotel. Owner Guillermo Cunningham will take guests fishing ($55/day) or to Tortuguero ($65-$70/day). He will also arrange group tours of the area. The rooms are clean, but don't stay there during lobster season (December and January), because the lobstermen drink and fight in the bar all night. Tarponland is located right next to the airstrip.

Archie Fields' **Río Colorado Fishing Lodge** (heated water, private bath, ceiling fans; $60-$80/person including three meals and free drinks at happy hour; 32-4063, U.S. phone: 800-243-9777) has become an institution. The maze of hallways and rooms winds around courtyards full of caged animals (monkeys, a deer, a tapir, pheasants, parrots, scarlet macaws). There is a bar with a dart board serving daiquiris and piña coladas, a TV with U.S. channels thanks to an 18-foot satellite dish, and a dining room overlooking the town and the rest of the hotel, with the best-equipped kitchen north of Limón. The lodge's fishing fleet is outfitted with sonar fish finders, radios, and skilled guides. Now that there is no Contra activity on the Río San Juan, Costa Rica's northeastern border with Nicaragua, the lodge is again offering its famous San Juan tour, which ends in the town of Puerto Viejo on the

Río Sarapiquí (see the following chapter on the Northern Zone). Package: $225-$245/day/person, including all-day fishing trips.

Several A-frame cabins with thatched roofs that share a grassy palm-filled court make up **Isla de Pesca** (heated water, private bath, ceiling fans; 23-4560, fax: 21-5148). It is five minutes from Barra by motorboat. Packages: $225 for three-day Tortuguero tour; $999 for three-day fishing tour.

A few minutes farther down the waterway is the homey **Casamar** (43-8834, fax: 43-9287), with well-designed, comfortable duplex cabinas. Mango trees shade the grounds; howler monkeys provide the sound effects. Casamar is open only during peak fishing seasons—September through October and January through March. Package: $900 for three days of fishing, plus airfare to Barra.

GETTING THERE: See the next chapter for more information on boat trips down the Río San Juan to Barra. SANSA (21-9414, 33-0397, 33-3258, $45 round trip) has half-hour flights to Barra from San José Tuesday, Thursday, and Saturday at 6 a.m., returning at 7 a.m. Travelair (32-7883, fax: 20-0413, $88 round-trip) goes daily at 6:30 a.m., returning at 7:05 a.m.

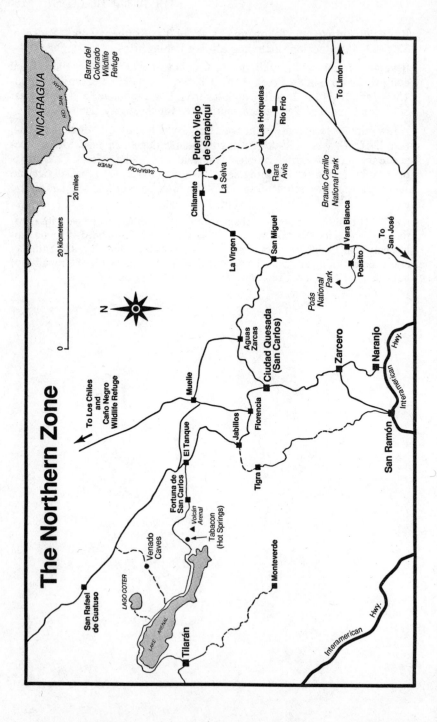

The Northern Zone

NINE

The Northern Zone

The Sarapiquí region to the north of Poás and Barva volcanoes is a large fertile plain that extends to the Atlantic Coast in the east, the Nicaraguan border in the north, and Lake Arenal and the Guanacaste and Tilarán mountain ranges in the west. Mostly jungle until a few decades ago, the area was first deforested for cattle ranches, and through government land-reform projects that gave small farms to *campesinos*. The remaining forests that are not protected by Braulio Carrillo National Park are now falling to banana plantations.

Recently, tourism and the banana industry have been fighting neck-and-neck for first place in Costa Rica's economy, and the Sarapiquí region is one of the major battle zones. Some of the country's best eco-tourism experiences, like Rara Avis, Selva Verde, and La Selva, are seeing the importance of their decision to preserve rainforests through tourism and scientific research as they become islands in a sea of banana plantations with the attendant heavy use of fertilizers and pesticides.

RARA AVIS

Many people are appalled at the destruction of vital rainforests in Costa Rica, but few are doing anything about it. Amos Bien, an ecologist and former manager of La Selva, the biological reserve of the Organization for Tropical Studies near Puerto Viejo de Sarapiquí, decided that the best way to convince people not to cut down rainforests is to demonstrate that it is economically sound to conserve them through tourism and ecologically concerned land management. The result of Amos Bien's efforts is ✪ **Rara Avis** (53-0844, fax: 21-2314), a 1500-acre forest reserve near the small village of Las Horquetas, southeast of La Selva. Through its excellent tours, visitors get a short course in how the rainforest works, why it is being cut down, and how it can be restored—without feeling that they've been in school. Rara Avis is the site of biologist Don Perry's research on the rainforest canopy, which he writes about in his fascinating book, *Life Above the Jungle Floor* (see "Recommended Reading" in Chapter Thirteen).

Rara Avis offers two places to stay. The comfortable, new, eight-room **Waterfall Lodge** (hot water, private bath, no electricity; $70/per person, double occupancy) is 500 feet from a gorgeous three-tiered waterfall. **El Plástico Lodge** (hot water, shared bath; $40-$50/person, double occupancy; more for single occupancy) is more rustic but comfortable as well. Prices for both include three hearty meals, guided tours, and transportation from Horquetas. Discounts for children, residents, students, and researchers are available.

GETTING THERE: Because transportation to Rara Avis is difficult, you need to make reservations in advance. They will help you arrange transportation from San José. If you want to handle it on your own, know that in order to get there, you must arrive by 8:30 a.m. in Las Horquetas. At 9 a.m. a tractor-pulled *charabanc* leaves Las Horquetas for Waterfall Lodge, 15 kilometers away. (Don't attempt this adventure if you have a bad back.) The trip takes four hours. It is impossible to get to Rara Avis any other way, except by horse (available through Rara Avis), which takes longer and involves walking the last 3 kilometers, because the road is paved with logs. *By Car:* Take the Guápiles Highway from San José. A few kilometers after you emerge from Braulio Carrillo National Park, take the Rio Frío-Puerto Viejo turnoff to the left. Horquetas and the Rara Avis office are 15 kilometers north on that road.

LA SELVA

La Selva, a 3500-acre research station and biological reserve of the Organization for Tropical Studies (OTS), has brought fame to Sarapiquí because of its enormous variety of tropical plants and animals. Recently, in an effort to secure the large hunting territories needed by jaguars and pumas, it was made part of a "protected zone," which adjoins Braulio Carrillo National Park to the south. Over 450 species of trees have been identified there so far, as well as 113 species of mammals, 81 species of reptiles, and 48 species of amphibians. More than 400 species of birds either live in or migrate to La Selva from the highlands, including toucans, *oropéndolas* (golden orioles), tinamous, and umbrella birds. More than 300 different species were observed in a single day in the Birdathon, an annual event in which people pledge money for each species observed by Audubon Society birdwatchers. The money goes to an endowment fund that will protect Braulio Carrillo on a permanent basis and, it is hoped, will serve as a model for conservation-project funding worldwide.

One of the many courses offered at La Selva is not for biologists, but for the world's decision makers: government and business leaders who need to understand tropical ecology in order to guide their countries along the soundest environmental paths.

At La Selva, tourists can roam freely on 50 kilometers of well-kept nature trails, but the scientists there want people to understand that research and education are the reserve's top priorities. All visitors must make reservations through the OTS office in San José (40-6783), whether they will be there for a few hours or a few days. La Selva is expensive to visit, so it is primarily an attraction for those with an interest in natural history. A day on the trails, three meals at the reserve's cafeteria, and a night in rustic but comfortable lodgings is around $75. There are special rates for card-carrying graduate students in tropical sciences. A less expensive way to visit is by spending just a day there ($15 including lunch). A bus ($10) leaves the OTS office for La Selva three times a week.

Puerto Viejo de Sarapiquí was Costa Rica's main port in colonial times. Boats embarked down the wide Sarapiquí River, north to the Río San Juan, which forms Costa Rica's border with Nicaragua, and from there to the Atlantic. During the years of Contra activity in northern Costa Rica, the area was closed to tourists, but now the rivers are opening up again.

Today Puerto Viejo is nothing special. When we were there, it was crowded with banana workers, because the banana companies, in their haste to plant, had not had time to construct housing for the thousands of workers they had brought into the area.

A few kilometers to the east of Puerto Viejo is MUSA, a cooperative of local women who grow and sell native medicinal herbs. They will give you a tour of their farm and explain the uses of the different plants. They also offer excellent *romero* (rosemary) and *manzanilla* (chamomile) shampoos, and natural clay preparations. The farm is in El Tigre, on the road to Horquetas.

The nicest place to stay in town is **Mi Lindo Sarapiquí** (heated water, private bath, ceiling fans; $20-$30; 71-6101, ext. 246), next to the soccer field. When making reservations, ask for Tony, who speaks English. It is a new building with bright, sunny rooms upstairs and good food and service in the restaurant below. Otherwise there's **Hospedaje Santa Marta** (cold water, no fans; under $7; ext. 295), which has only a couple of shared baths for 20 rather dark rooms. The friendly owners don't sell liquor—a plus in this town, which has one too many rowdy bars.

Close to the dock, the **Hotel Gonar** (cold water, shared bath, ceiling fans, polyester sheets; under $7; ext. 196), is not too clean and has a bar next door, but is acceptable. **Cabinas Monteverde** (cold water, private bath, table fans; under $7; 71-6901) are okay but noisy. The owners are building a 20-room hotel nearby that looks nicer.

Oro Verde Station (cold water, both private and shared baths, natural ventilation; $50-$60; $195 for three-day package including transportation from San José; 33-6613, phone/fax: 23-7479), 40 kilometers north of Puerto Viejo, is the only lodging on the Río Sarapiquí. Although the accommodations are rustic, they are quite aesthetic. The food is overpriced, however, and the six-hour package boat ride to get there offers no lunch stop and hard, uncomfortable seats. There are bunk rooms ($7-$12) for students, which make Oro Verde Station a reasonable place to stay if you want to take the **public boat** ($2) up the Sarapiquí. It leaves from the dock in Puerto Viejo every morning between 10 a.m. and 12 noon. The boat goes as far as the Río San Juan and returns at 5 a.m. the next day. You can find boatmen around the dock who might be willing to take you all the way to Barra or Tortuguero, but you have to negotiate a price (usually per boat, rather than per person).

The family-run **Ecolodge Sarapiquí** (shared bath, ceiling fans; $7-$12/person; 53-2533, fax: 53-8645), just east of La Selva, provides clean bunk-bed accommodations. The restaurant serves native food cooked on a wood stove. It is located on a curve in the Río Puerto Viejo, where the current slows down enough for a good swim.

Also to the east of Puerto Viejo is ✪ **El Gavilán Lodge** (heated water, both private and shared baths; $20-$30/person including breakfast; 34-9507, 23-7479, fax: 53-6556), on a former cattle ranch that converted its remaining forest into a reserve. An outdoor jacuzzi and tours of rainforest by horseback and nearby rivers by boat are offered. The lodge menu includes fresh fruits, salads, and tropical fruit drinks.

Note: If you want to enter Nicaragua by this route (at San Juan del Norte on the Atlantic coast), you must first obtain permission from the Costa Rica Immigration Department in San José.

Hotel La Selva Verde ($60-$70/two people, including meals; 20-1712, 71-6459, fax: 32-3321) in Chilamate, five minutes by car west of Puerto Viejo, has one of the most beautifully designed lodges we've seen, a good library, and a forest reserve along the river that is great for birdwatching. The hotel will arrange trips down the Sarapiquí, nature walks, and tours by horseback. Make reservations in advance. William Rojas, who works at the hotel, can connect you with **boat trips** (71-6901, ext. 260; $75 round-trip) down the Río San Juan to Barra del Colorado (see Chapter Eight).

Islas del Río (heated water, bathtub, both private and shared baths, no fans, screens; $40-$50/person including three meals; 33-0366, fax: 33-9671) is 6 kilometers west of Puerto Viejo. It is frequently used for seminars and meetings of the banana companies, so it is often crowded. There is also a restaurant.

In the village of La Virgen, **Rancho Leona** (solar-heated water; phone/fax: 71-6312, English spoken), 12 kilometers southwest of Puerto Viejo has a restaurant that offers a varied menu including eggplant parmesan, BLTs, vegetarian dishes, and homemade whole-wheat bread. The rancho offers a family environment, with good music, games, and a library. Leona and Ken, the owners, have an art studio where they design and make beautiful T-shirts, stained glass, and jewelry out of native seeds. They can advise you about hiking, camping, and swimming in the area.

Rancho Leona runs **Kayak Jungle Tours**, which offer several adventures: a one-day kayak trip for beginners ($75; no experience necessary) on the Sarapiquí, and one-day trips on local rivers for more advanced kayakers ($75), separated according to skill level. They now have double kayaks so that children can come along. Groups of six or more can kayak in seven days from Puerto Viejo to Tortuguero, or take a five-day trip to Caño Negro (see below). (Both trips are $125/day, including lodging and motorboats back to La Virgen.) All trips include two nights' bunk-bed lodging at Rancho Leona.

GETTING THERE: *By Bus:* Buses to Puerto Viejo de Sarapiquí are called *Río Frío* buses. They leave six times a day from San José (Avenida 11, Calles Central/1). The 6:30 a.m., 12 noon, and 3 p.m. buses go on the scenic route above Heredia. The bus trip takes four hours. The 9 a.m. bus goes on the Guápiles Highway through Braulio Carrillo and turns north to Horquetas, La Selva, and Puerto Viejo, where it ends, so you will have to change buses or get a taxi to go to Chilamate or La Virgen. The 1 p.m. bus makes a full Guápiles–Heredia circuit back to San José. The 4 p.m. bus takes the same route but stops about 8 p.m. in La Virgen.

If you come to Las Horquetas from San José on the 6:30 a.m. Río Frío bus (Avenida 11, Calles Central/1), Rara Avis will arrange for a taxi to meet you at the *cruce para Horquetas* and take you to the office for a small fee. If you are coming from Monteverde or Guanacaste and want to explore the Northern Zone without going back to San José, you can take buses from Cañas to Tilarán and Tilarán to San Carlos. To do this, you will have to spend the night in San Carlos or La Fortuna (see below). The *San Carlos–Río Frío* bus leaves at 6 a.m., 9 a.m., and 3 p.m. and takes about two hours to reach Puerto Viejo.

By Car: There is a scenic route above Heredia that winds around the northeast side of Poás Volcano to the northern plain and passes through La Virgen, Chilamate, and Puerto Viejo before reaching La Selva. (Don't go this route if you tend to get carsick.) It is one of the most beautiful rides you can take, passing by the powerful **La Paz waterfall** on a hairpin turn, with vistas of the forests of Braulio Carrillo to the east. This route is two and a half hours, all on paved road. The trip from Cañas to La Fortuna takes about two hours, including 45 minutes on bad road on the northeast side of Lake Arenal. You can get from Volcán Arenal to Puerto Viejo in under two hours, avoiding San Carlos, if you turn left at El Tanque, a few kilometers out of Fortuna, then take the turnoff to Muelle (Route 4), following signs to Aguas Zarcas and turning right at each turn. At Aguas Zarcas, 23 kilometers west of San Carlos, turn left to San Miguel, and left again to La Virgen, Chilamate, and Puerto Viejo, all on good roads.

SAN CARLOS

Ciudad Quesada, more commonly known as San Carlos, is located in the San Carlos plain of central Alajuela province, one of Costa Rica's most agriculturally productive zones. As is true in many areas, its forested hills and family farms have been bought up by large-scale cattle farmers, some of them expatriate North Americans. Although increasing the country's export capacity, cattle farming contributes to Costa Rica's serious deforestation problem.

Ciudad Quesada is a midpoint for trips north to Volcán Arenal, Tabacón thermal spa, Caño Negro Wildlife Refuge, and the Venado Caves. You can also go east to connect with Highway 9 to La Virgen and Puerto Viejo de Sarapiquí.

Hotel La Central (hot water, private bath, no fans; $20-$30; 46-0766, 46-0301, fax: 46-0301) and **Hotel El Retiro** (private bath, some with heated water, no fans; $12-$20; 46-0275) are both clean and comfortable and located on Parque Central in San Carlos. There is a crafts cooperative on the northwest corner of the park.

Balneario San Carlos (hot water, no fans, refrigerator; $12-$20; 46-0747) has a large swimming pool, kids' pools, a Tico-style restaurant, roller-skating twice a week, dances on Sunday, a small lake for boating and fishing, and somewhat rundown cabinas. You'll see signs for the Balneario five blocks northwest of Parque Central.

GETTING THERE: *San José–San Carlos* buses ($1.50) leave almost every hour, 5 a.m. through 6 p.m., from the Coca Cola. It's a three-hour trip. Try to get a Directo bus—it makes less stops. By car, take the Naranjo exit, about an hour down the General Cañas Highway from San José, and continue north through Zarcero to San Carlos.

There are several nice places to stay outside of San Carlos, most of which arrange tours to points of interest in the area:

El Tucano (heated water, private bath, bathtub, pools; $70-$80; 46-1822, 21-8321, fax: 46-1692), which is set back from the road in a shady forest, offers mini-golf, tennis courts, horses, and tours. The beautifully kept grounds are complete with swimming pools, a sauna, and a jacuzzi fed partially by a thermal spring. (Use of pools and sauna costs about $2 for nonguests.) The elegant restaurant offers an international menu including seafood and Italian specialties. El Tucano is 20 minutes (8 kilometers) northeast of Ciudad Quesada on the road to Puerto Viejo. You can take a Río Frío, San Miguel, Aguas Zarcas, Pital, or Venecia bus from the terminal in San Carlos.

You can continue east from El Tucano 32 kilometers to San Miguel at the junction of Highway 9. Go left to Puerto Viejo and La Selva, or right to San José via Heredia, one of the most beautiful drives in Costa Rica. The return trip takes about three hours by car.

La Quinta Lodge (hot water, private bath, ceiling fans, pool; $7-$12; 39-4689), 15 kilometers north of San Carlos, has two chalet-style cabinas with bunk beds sleeping up to ten people, and some double and triple rooms. There is a restaurant, and the friendly owners speak English.

Tilajari Resort Hotel (hot water, private bath, air-conditioning, ceiling fans, pools; $80-$90; 46-0979, phone/fax: 46-1083), in Muelle de San Carlos, 22 kilometers north of Ciudad Quesada, is also a country club. It offers tennis, racquetball and basketball courts, a sauna, a game room, a conference room, a bar, a restaurant, and a disco. The well-groomed lawns are interspersed with stands of bamboo and other tropical plants; rooms overlook the Río San Carlos. The Tilajari offers horseback riding and guided walking tours through its private forest reserve (one of the few remaining in San Carlos), as well as tours of the surrounding area.

Río San Carlos Lodge (hot water, private bath, ceiling fans, pool; $50-$60; 46-0766, 46-0301, fax: 46-0391), 9 kilometers north of Muelle, also offers a nice view from high on the river bluffs. It has tranquil, beautiful gardens, a bar, and a restaurant.

From Muelle, it's a straight shot 84 kilometers north to **Los Chiles**, near the Nicaraguan border, where you can rent a boat to visit the **Caño Negro Wildlife Refuge**. Boatmen at the Los Chiles dock will rent their canopied, motorized dugouts with themselves as guides ($60-$75) for the five-hour trip down the Río Frío to the refuge and back. As in Tortuguero, you are sure to see crocodiles, iguanas, monkeys, turtles, and many species of birds. Bring water, food, and rain gear during the wet season. During the dry season the boats only go to the edge of the refuge and the trip is shortened to three hours, but you can still see plenty of animals and birds along the river.

There is only one fairly run-down hotel in Los Chiles, the **Río Frío** (cold water, shared bath, no fans; under $7; 47-1127), located just past the municipal building. It's not really necessary to stay there, as you can return to Muelle, San Carlos, or La Fortuna the same day. Several buses leave daily for Los Chiles from Ciudad Quesada. By car the trip takes a little over an hour from Muelle. (The road is paved the entire way.)

VOLCÁN ARENAL

Volcán Arenal is the quintessential volcano. Its perfectly conical shape emerges from Alajuela's gentle green hills. From time to time, loud explosions are heard, a mushroom cloud of grey, brown, orange, or blue smoke billows out of the top, and you can see the smoky trails of ejected boulders as they bounce down the slopes. Although the volcano is capable of inspiring intense fright and awe in visitors, inhabitants of nearby **Fortuna de San Carlos** and the dairy farms at the volcano's base seem to live with relative peace of mind. If you ask, they will tell you with a surprising tranquillity about the last time it erupted.

Since Arenal was dormant until the late 1960s, the only people who suspected that it was a volcano were those who had scaled it and found a crater and steam vents at the top. But few listened to them, until an earthquake shook the area on July 29, 1968. Twelve hours later, Arenal blew, sending out shock waves that were recorded as far away as Boulder, Colorado. All damage occurred roughly 5 kilometers west of the volcano, where people were knocked down by shock waves, poisoned by volcanic gases, and struck by falling rocks. Lava flows eradicated the town of Pueblo Nuevo, and by the end, 78 people had died. Three new craters formed during the eruption. Since then Arenal hasn't erupted; it just rumbles and explodes, shooting out rocks, soot, and smoke.

Arenal is most impressive at night—in the dark, bursts of fire and red-hot rocks shoot hundreds of feet into the sky. Incandescent material cascades down the sides, especially on the north side. In the day you only see smoke and hear the volcano's terrible roar. There are explosions every few hours during Arenal's active phases, but it can go for months without activity.

Note: Although the volcano is not dangerous at a distance, it is very perilous to climb. One tourist was killed and another burned in July 1988, when they hiked too near the crater, foolishly trusting the Arenal's placid appearance between explosions. If they had seen it explode before climbing, they probably would never have begun. They also unwittingly risked the lives of 15 Costa Rican Rural Guards and Red Cross workers who heroically searched the volcano to retrieve the body of its victim. *Please do not climb this volcano.*

The **Catarata La Fortuna** is a beautiful waterfall 5.5 kilometers from the town of La Fortuna. You'll see a sign pointing south on a road at the back of the church. Go 1 kilometer and turn right down a country lane. There is one hill, roughly paved with rocks, about halfway there that you can drive up if your engine is powerful enough and you don't mind a few dents in your chassis. If you have the time, it's a nice walk from La Fortuna; if you drive you'll have to abandon your car at a series of muddy hills about 20 minutes by foot from the waterfall (don't get your rear wheels stuck in the rut on the left when you're parking). There's a fork about 100 meters before you get there. Take the left fork and soon you'll see the sign pointing to the *mirador*, where you can see the falls cascading on the other side of the ravine. If you want to walk down to the bottom of the falls (about ten minutes), keep to the right on the ravine trail. At one point a fork goes sharply down to the left, but it is treacherous and only takes you to the river. The force of the waterfall is such that swimming is not possible.

Los Lagos (admission about 75 cents) is a lovely park and camping area on the lower slopes of Arenal, a few kilometers northwest of La Fortuna. Depending on how much it's been raining, you can drive all or most of the 3 kilometers from the entrance to the first lake, which has emerald-green water for swimming and paddleboating. A 2-kilometer walk through a beautiful forest brings you to the second lake. The restaurant and camping area are farther along the main road, just before you get to Tabacón.

At **Tabacón** (open daily, morning to evening; admission $1.50), thermal waters spring out of the volcano and are channeled down a tiled slide into a pool. A more natural pool with some shade trees over it is in the back, as well as an amazing warm waterfall that will give you the massage of your life. I'm not sure if it was designed to massage you or only to be looked at, but I recommend that if you have stiff shoulders or a tense back you maneuver yourself over the rocks into a relatively comfortable position and hang on tight—the water comes down with a lot of force. Tabacón also has a restaurant. The whole complex is surrounded by the area's brilliant vegetation, and, of course, smoking Arenal serves as a stunning backdrop. It is most crowded on weekends.

Beyond Tabacón is **Lake Arenal**, a large reservoir. The original Laguna Arenal was the source of a river whose waters flowed east to the Atlantic. But dams built for a hydroelectric energy plant enlarged the lake and diverted the waters. Now they flow from the northwest side of the reservoir to irrigate Costa Rica's dry Pacific Coast. Many people enjoy boating, fishing, and windsurfing on the lake. The east side, near Tabacón, retains its original lush greenery, but as you travel west, you will see the devastating effect of cattle ranching, as the exuberant vegetation gives way to grassy pastureland.

The **Cavernas de Venado** (admission $3) are large caves located an hour's drive north of Lake Arenal. They are more accessible than the caves of Barra Honda (see the Guanacaste chapter), but are not for the fainthearted. To explore them, you must wade through a rushing underground river and, at some points, crawl on your hands and knees. There are thousands of bats. Bring a change of clothes.

Four kilometers northeast of the caves, **Cabinas Las Brisas** (cold water, shared bath, no fans; under $7) are a clean, cheap place to stay in the nice little town of **Venado**. You can also rent rubber boots and flashlights there. A bus leaves San Carlos at 2 p.m. for Venado, arriving at 4:30 p.m.

La Fortuna, several kilometers east of the volcano, offers a few places to eat and several comfortable, inexpensive places to stay.

El Jardín (open 6 a.m. to 11 p.m.), across from the gas station, has good Tico-style food, reasonable prices, friendly service, and playground equipment for kids. **La Vaca Muca**, 3 kilometers west of La Fortuna, on the road to the volcano, offers generous *casados* and other local dishes. **El Coquito**, two-thirds of the way to Ciudad Quesada, is a good place to stop for a *refresco* and ceviche.

The nicest accommodations in La Fortuna are: **Hotel Las Colinas** (heated water, private bath, table fans; $20-$30; 47-9107), clean, located 100 meters west and 50 meters south of the gas station; **Hotel San Bosco** (private bath, ceiling fans; $7-$12; $12-$20 for newer rooms with heated water; 47-9050), also clean, 200 meters north of the gas station; and the ☻ **Burío Inn** (heated water, private bath, table fans; $30-$40 including breakfast; $20-$30 in off-season; 28-0267, phone/fax: 47-9076), on the main street. The Burío has lots of maps and original art on the walls. Its rooms are small but aesthetically pleasing.

Located 100 meters beyond the gas station, **Hotel La Central** (shared bath, no fans; under $7; 47-9004, fax: 47-9045) is basic, fairly clean, and friendly. On the main road near the church are the new **Cabinas La Amistad** (cold water, no fans; with shared bath, $7-$12; with private bath, $12-$20; 47-9035).

The more expensive accommodations are located nearer to Lake Arenal: the ✪ **Arenal Volcano Observatory** (heated water, private bath; $40-$50/person including meals), sometimes used by Smithsonian investigators in their volcanological research, has recently been conditioned for guests. Visitors must make reservations through Costa Rica Sun Tours (55-3518, 55-3418, fax: 55-4410), although you do not have to be part of a tour to go there. Located on a private macadamia farm, the observatory offers a close-up view of the south side of the volcano and part of Lake Arenal. Accommodations are simple, with three bunk beds per room and a common dining area serving hearty *campesino* food. The climate at the observatory is cool and fresh, in contrast to that of La Fortuna, which can get a little muggy. To get there, you have to ford two rivers on the road up the mountain, but bridges are in the process of being built, so check with Sun Tours for exact directions.

Arenal Lodge (heated water, shared bath; $60-$80/person; 28-2588, 46-1881, fax: 28-2798) is a large, comfortable house with a library, billiard table, and lovely view of Arenal in the distance. Fishing packages are available. The lodge is 4 kilometers up a gravel road near the northeastern tip of the lake.

✪ **Lago Coter Ecoadventure Lodge** ($60-$80/person including meals; 69-5711, fax: 69-5579; or Tikal Tours: 23-2811, fax: 23-1916, for tour packages) offers hiking, horseback riding, mountain biking, water sports, windsurfing, and volcano trips with all equipment provided (even such things as backpacks and binoculars). The entrance, near heart-shaped Lake Coter, a few kilometers west and 4 kilometers north of the town of Nuevo Arenal, is well marked. Attention to detail, quality, and comfort are evident in everything there, but baths are shared, dormitory-style, which fits in with the outdoor emphasis of the place. The lodge's rainforest nature trail is completely lined with wooden planks, so you won't slip and slide. Large, well-padded armchairs in front of a fireplace await those who want to relax with a drink and a book. In short, it's a place for those who want to experience nature but enjoy their creature comforts, too. You can get to Lago Coter either from the Interamerican Highway via Cañas and Tilarán (paved except for the entrance road to the lodge) or from La Fortuna, going over the 9 kilometers of unpaved road on the northeast side of Lake Arenal.

A few kilometers to the west of the entrance to Lago Coter is **Mirador Los Lagos** (heated water, private bath; $40-$50; 69-5484), simple cabinas and a restaurant (open 8 a.m. to 8 p.m.) high on a hill overlooking Lake Arenal.

Another option is **Magil Forest Lodge** (heated water, private bath, table fans; $80-$90 including meals; 21-2825, 33-5991, fax: 33-6837), located on the lower slopes of Volcán Tenorio, about 20 kilometers west of the town of San Rafael Guatuso. It is not really close to anything else, and must be taken as an experience in itself. Although the lodge is in pastureland, guests can ride horses to nearby protected virgin rainforest. The rooms are comfortable, and the food is very good. Access is the only problem, because the lodge is at the end of 20 kilometers of dirt road, the last three kilometers passable only with four-wheel drive or on horseback.

TOURS   **The Burío Inn** offers tours of Arenal, Caño Negro, and the Venado Caves, as well as fishing and other types of tours. Prices are divided by the number of people in the group, so it can work out to be quite reasonable. **Aventuras Arenal,** a locally owned company across from the plaza in Fortuna de San Carlos, also has reasonably priced tours. We recommend their three-hour sunset boat tour on Lake Arenal (47-9133; $15). At one point we saw thousands of snowy egrets coming to roost for the night, and at the same moment lava flowing out of the volcano—quite a sight. **Natanael Murrillo** (47-9087) offers low-cost fishing trips on the lake. You can rent mountain bikes from **Repuestos y Acesorios** (about $1/hour) in the center of La Fortuna.

GETTING THERE: *By Bus:* The 5:45 a.m. *San José–San Carlos* bus (which leaves from the Coca Cola) continues on to Fortuna every day, returning at 2 p.m. You can also catch a Fortuna bus in San Carlos at 6 a.m., 9 a.m., 1 p.m., and 4:30 p.m. From Fortuna, it's 13 kilometers to Tabacón. Buses leave San Carlos at 6 a.m. and 3 p.m. for Tilarán, passing through Fortuna and Tabacón around 8 a.m. and 4 p.m.

By Car: You can take a circular route, turning north at San Ramón de Alajuela, 55 minutes west of San José on the highway to Puntarenas. There, ask directions for the road to La Tigra, which is paved except for a 12-kilometer stretch in the middle. It borders a reserve that protects a beautiful rainforest southeast of Monteverde and conserves the water supply for the town of San Ramón. A few kilometers beyond La Tigra, turn right at a large gas station, then go 4 kilometers on bumpy gravel road to Jabillos, where you connect with the San Carlos-La Fortuna road. You can return to San José via San Carlos, Zarcero, and Naranjo, all on paved road. The San Ramón–La Tigra road winds less than the Naranjo–Zarcero route. Both are picturesque and are about three hours from San José.

Zarcero is the midpoint on the trip between San Carlos and San José. You will probably want to stop and see the famous gardens in front of the church, where bushes are pruned as elephants, airplanes, a bullfight, and other shapes. If you want to eat, you should stop five minutes south of Zarcero, where there are a few nice restaurants and kiosks selling preserves, sour cream, cheese, and the like. The food is better there than in Zarcero itself.

You can also come from the west, combining a trip to Guanacaste or Monteverde with a visit to Arenal by taking a half-hour bus ride from Cañas to Tilarán, and catching the *Tilarán–San Carlos* bus at noon, which reaches Tabacón around 3:30 p.m. It takes a lovely route around the north side of Lake Arenal, paved except for a 9-kilometer strip. By car, it's one and a half hours from Tilarán to La Fortuna.

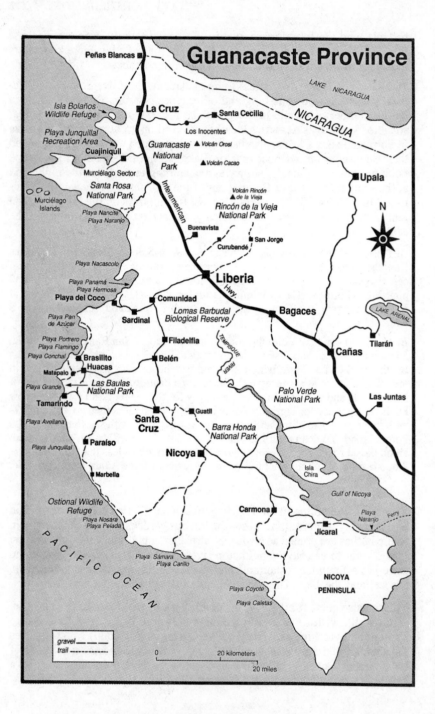

Guanacaste Province

Peñas Blancas ■

LAKE NICARAGUA

■ La Cruz
■ Santa Cecilia

NICARAGUA

Isla Bolaños
Wildlife Refuge
Los Inocentes •

Playa Junquillal
Recreation Area
Cuajiniquil ■

*Guanacaste
National
Park*
▲ *Volcán Orosi*

▲ *Volcán Cacao*

Murciélago Sector

■ Upala

*Santa Rosa
National Park*

Volcán Rincón
▲ de la Vieja

N

Murciélago
Islands

Playa Nancite
Playa Naranjo

*Rincón de la Vieja
National Park*

Interamerican

Buenavista •

Playa Nacascolo

• San Jorge
Curubandé •

Playa Panamá
Playa Hermosa
Playa del Coco

Liberia ■

Hwy.

■ Comunidad
*Lomas Barbudal
Biological Reserve*

Playa Pan
de Azúcar

Sardinal ■

Bagaces ■

LAKE ARENAL

Playa Portrero
Playa Flamingo
Playa Conchal

■ Filadelfia

Tilarán ■

Brasilito ■
Huacas

■ Belén

TEMPISQUE RIVER

Cañas ■

Matapalo •
*Las Baulas
National Park*

Playa Grande ◄

Tamarindo ■

Playa Avellana

*Palo Verde
National Park*

Las Juntas ■

■ Guatil
**Santa
Cruz**

Playa Junquillal

Paraíso ■

*Barra Honda
National Park*

Nicoya ■

Isla
Chira

Marbella •

Gulf of Nicoya

*Ostional Wildlife
Refuge*
Playa Nosara
Playa Pelada

Carmona ■

Playa
Naranjo
Ferry

Jicaral ■

PACIFIC OCEAN

Playa Sámara
Playa Carillo

NICOYA
PENINSULA

Playa Coyote

Playa Caletas

gravel ———
trail ············

0   20 kilometers
         20 miles

TEN

Guanacaste Province

Guanacaste was a separate province of Spain's Central American empire until 1787, when it was given to Nicaragua. In 1812, Spain gave Guanacaste to Costa Rica so that Costa Rica would be large enough to be represented in the colonial government, which ruled from Guatemala. After independence, both Costa Rica and Nicaragua claimed Guanacaste. *Guanacastecos* were divided, too. Liberians, whose founders were Nicaraguan cattle farmers, wanted to join Nicaragua. Nicoyans were in favor of joining Costa Rica. Nicoya won in a vote, and an 1858 treaty declared Guanacaste part of Costa Rica.

Its long period of autonomy, sizeable indigenous population, and geographic isolation from the Meseta Central have contributed to make Guanacaste a unique part of Costa Rica. Many "Costa Rican" traditions originated here. The people, dark-skinned descendants of the Chorotega Indians, are possibly closer to their cultural and historical roots than other Costa Ricans, and there is a special *campesino* richness in their friendly manner.

Most of Guanacaste has been converted into pastureland for beef production. The deforestation of the region has altered its climate and ecosystems, causing occasional droughts. But Guanacaste is beautiful, nonetheless. Brahma bulls lounge under the graceful, spreading shade trees that gave the province its name. The brilliant yellow blossoms of the *corteza amarilla* dot the plains in February, and in March the light red blossoms of the *carao* (carob tree) brighten the landscape. The clear, gentle waters of Guanacaste's beaches attract Ticos and foreigners alike. The dry climate helps keep mosquitos to a minimum.

LAS JUNTAS DE ABANGARES

Las Juntas de Abangares, the old gold-mining capital, is a historic part of Costa Rica that is just beginning to open up to tourism. From 1884 to 1931, its mines attracted workers and gold seekers from all over the world, including North and South Americans, Europeans, Chinese, Russians, Lebanese, and Jamaicans. The multiracial background of the residents of Las Juntas distinguishes it from the rest of Guanacaste. Also unlike the rest of Guanacaste, it is mountainous, with a cool climate.

The **Eco Museo** has trails through tropical dry forest to the top of an old gold mine built into the beautiful Río Abangares. The old mine structure bears a striking resemblance to a Mayan ruin rising out of the forest. To get there, turn right at the historic **Caballo Blanco Cantina** in Las Juntas, which has a good collection of turn-of-the-century artifacts, and go 4 kilometers to a fork where there is a sign. When we were there, at the end of the rainy season, the last kilometer of road to the museum building was in pretty bad shape, so we left the car at the fork. The road might have been improved by now. It is also a nice, shady walk from town, and you can stop at La Sierra, the original basecamp of the gold-boom years, for a *refresco*. Taxies and horses can also be found in Las Juntas.

Another nice day hike is to walk the road to **Los Angeles,** a small community with a tiny church at the foot of a huge hill.

If you have four-wheel drive or a horse, a longer trip can be taken to **Boston,** where independent gold miners are working cooperatively. They will show you the whole mining process and take you into their candlelit tunnels. Like most mining operations, this one uses mercury to separate the ore, and dumps it straight into the river. **Geoaventuras** (21-2053, 82-8950, fax: 82-3333) has tours of the mining area from San José. The road to Boston connects to the back road to Monteverde and Tilarán through Turín. Both roads are in very poor condition, but the views are great.

There is only one place to stay in Las Juntas, the somewhat run-down **Cabinas Las Juntas** (cold water, private bath, table fan; under $7; 62-0069). Their restaurant is pretty good, as are **La Familiar** on the plaza and **Las Gemelas.**

GETTING THERE: Las Juntas is about three hours (145 kilometers) from San José. Direct buses leave from the Puntarenas bus station (Calle 12, Avenida 9; 22-1867) in San José at 11 a.m. and 5 p.m. If you're going by car, the turnoff is clearly marked on the Interamerican Highway. Las Juntas is only an hour from Puntarenas and 30 minutes from Cañas, so you could make one of those your base for exploring this area.

Half an hour northeast of Cañas is the clean, pleasant mountain town of **Tilarán,** the western gateway to Lake Arenal and the Northern Zone of Costa Rica. For the adventurous, it's also on the way to Monteverde through Cabeceras, although the road from Tilarán to Cabeceras is paved only as far as Quebrada Grande, a few kilometers south of Tilarán. The rest of the journey is on steep, unpaved, weather-beaten roads, in worse condition than the regular road to Monteverde through Lagarto (see the following chapter on the Central Pacific Zone).

Cabinas El Sueño (heated water, private bath; $12-$20; 69-5347) or **The Spot** (heated water, private bath, no fans; $40-$50; 69-5711, fax: 69-5579), with its excellent **Restaurante Catalá**, are nice places to stay in Tilarán. **Cabinas Mary** (heated water, both private and shared baths; under $7; 69-5479), upstairs from the restaurant of the same name on the south side of the central park, are clean and a good bargain for budget travelers.

Aventuras Tilarán, across from the Cámara de Ganaderos, arranges inner-tubing, biking, canoeing, and windsurfing trips as does The Spot. It also owns the **Albergue Tilarán** (heated water, shared bath, ceiling fans; $20-$30; under $7 for International Youth Hostel members; 69-5008).

GETTING THERE: There are frequent buses from Cañas to Tilarán, and buses from Tilarán also go to San José and San Carlos (Ciudad Quesada). The roads are well paved all the way from Cañas to Lake Arenal.

About 4 kilometers north of Cañas on the Interamerican Highway is **Safaris Corobicí** (phone/fax: 69-0303), which offers three- and five-hour raft trips ($33 and $50, respectively, children half price) down the Río Corobicí. These are scenic floats where the guide does all the work and are good for breaking up the monotony of a long trip to the coast. In order to promote reforestation in Guanacaste, native hardwood trees are available for rafters to plant along the river. Safaris Corobicí also has bikes for rent and moun-tain-bike tours, including a 20-mile descent from the shores of Lake Arenal. Make reservations in advance.

Centro Ecológico La Pacífica (heated water, ceiling fans, pool; $60-$70; 69-0050, fax: 69-0555) is a shady, green oasis in the midst of Guanacaste's heat. More than 200 different bird species have been observed in its woods and near the Río Corobicí, which flows through the ranch. Lists of the birds are available to guests, and trees are labeled with their scientific and com-mon names. The center has tastefully designed cabinas, a lovely pool, and a restaurant with an international menu. It is located just after Safaris Coro-bicí, 4 kilometers north of Cañas on the Interamerican Highway.

Right on the river just after the entrance to La Pacífica, **Rincón Corobicí** is also a cool, pleasant place to stop—for a few hours or the whole day. Its Swiss-owned restaurant specializes in beef and seafood, and there is a souvenir shop, a playground, clean bathrooms, a small campground, and a trail along the riverside.

PALO VERDE NATIONAL PARK

Palo Verde National Park (67-1062) is one of Central America's last natural refuges for the thousands of birds that pass through this region during their annual migrations, including North American ducks and egrets and birds from the Guanacaste plains. In addition to being a resting spot for 260 species of birds, Palo Verde is a habitat for mammals, amphibians, and reptiles, many of which can be observed relatively easily. During the dry season, animals stay near the few permanent springs in the area, one of which is only a hundred meters from the park's administration building and campsite. The best observation spot for birds is about 1 kilometer before the administration building, in the swamp. The best months to go to Palo Verde are January and February.

Camping is allowed in the park. If you notify the administration beforehand, Palo Verde might also be able to offer you meals, transportation, and/or lodging, for a fee. Bring your own water.

The **Organization for Tropical Studies** has a research station in the northern part of the park, where visitors can stay. Arrangements must be made in advance through OTS in San José ($40-$50/person; 40-9938). Bring your own food and water.

Note: The number listed above (67-1062) is often busy. It is for the **Tempisque Conservation Area** (open 9 a.m. to 5 p.m.) office in Bagaces, which directs all the parks and reserves in the region. It's worth stopping there personally before visiting Palo Verde, Lomas Barbudal, or Barra Honda. It is located right on the Interamerican Highway, next to the Bagaces gas station.

Palo Verde is on the east side of the mouth of the **Tempisque**, Guanacaste's major river. Stretching along the banks of the river is a plain that floods during the rainy season and dries to a brown crisp in the dry season. Farther from the river rise bluffs dotted with limestone cliff outcrops. The park administration is set in an old hacienda at the base of the bluffs; there are a couple of trails that begin there and go up to lookout points.

If you call the park director beforehand, you may be able to join the park rangers on their weekly patrols to the **Isla de Pájaros** ($25 for the boat ride), a bird-filled island in the Tempisque. **Guanacaste Tours** (66-0306; $70) also visits the island. Be aware that tour boats should remain 50 yards from the island and no one should try to startle the birds into flight, because that endangers their nestlings. If your tour does not obey these rules, notify the park director or the Audubon Society.

GETTING THERE: Turn left at the gas station in Bagaces, north of Cañas. The park administration is 35 kilometers from there. Signs mark the way. A taxi from Bagaces costs about $25, round-trip. There is a small building at the entrance to the park, but don't get off there, because it's about 8 more hot, dry kilometers to the administration building. **Transporte Palo Verde** offers trips in a motorized catamaran-type launch down the Río Bebedero to the park. There also is a three-hour Bird Watchers' Special ($33) and a half-day trip all the way to the Tempisque estuary ($50 including lunch, $25 for children). Transporte Palo Verde is located in the lobby of the **Hotel El Corral** (69-1091, fax: 69-0544) in Cañas.

During the dry season you can enter the area from the Nicoya Peninsula. Take a bus from Nicoya to Puerto Moreno. Local boatmen there will take you across for a minimal fee and indicate which way to hike to get to the park station. Don't try this route in the rainy season—the whole plain is swamped.

Many *campesinos* feel that environmental concerns interfere with their livelihood rather than support it. This has made enemies of ecology and community development, creating an impossible situation for both. By involving the community in the formation of its reserve, **Lomas Barbudal Biological Reserve** (67-1062, 67-1029; admission $1) is actively trying to bridge this gap. Local schoolchildren, for example, are helping to plan the visitors center and clear trails. The reserve's main attractions are birds, monkeys, waterfalls you can hike to, and rivers with pools you can swim in shaded by graceful trees. Friends of Lomas Barbudal has a visitors center and exhibit about the reserve in **Bagaces**, where you can stop before heading out. Once you get to the reserve entrance, the guardhouse is across a little stream on the far side of the road. In the dry season, refreshments are sold to the right about 200 meters down the road. The swimming hole is about 200 meters to the left. Camping is allowed. Bring your own food and water, plus insect repellent during the rainy season. Call for more information.

In Bagaces, the best place to eat is **Soda Fuentes**, two blocks to the left of the plaza. The best place to stay is **Cabinas Eduardo Vargas** (cold water, private bath, table fans; $7-12; no phone), several blocks to the left of the main square beyond Cabinas Miravalles. There is no sign, so ask around for the location.

GETTING THERE: The dirt road to Lomas Barbudal is on the left, 20 minutes north of Cañas, soon after Bagaces. After 6 kilometers on the dirt road, you'll come to the entrance. A taxi to the reserve from the bus station in Bagaces costs $20-$25, round-trip. They will wait for you for a couple of hours.

LIBERIA

Liberia is known as the "White City," because many of the buildings along its wide, clean streets are painted white. It is the historic capital of Guanacaste's beef industry. You'll notice that some of the corner houses have a door on each side of the corner. This is known as the *puerta del sol*. The door on the east side lets in the morning sun, while the door on the south side lets in the afternoon sun. Liberia is bright and hot, so bring a hat or use your umbrella to shade yourself.

The **Casa de Cultura** (open Tuesday through Saturday, 9 a.m. to 12 noon, 1 to 6 p.m.; Sunday, 9 a.m. to 1 p.m.; closed Monday; 66-1606), three blocks south of the church, is a very helpful tourist information center and a museum dedicated to the *sabaneros*, Guanacaste's cowboys. There you can find topographical maps of the region, directions to some of Liberia's historical homes, and anything else you want to know about the region.

Galería Fulvia shows the work of local artisans and sells U.S. newspapers and magazines, including *The New York Times*. It is one block north of the church, in the Centro Comercial Bambú.

RESTAURANTS   **Las Tinajas**, on the west side of Liberia's Parque Central, serves pizza, tender deep-fried fish, and chicken at outdoor tables and offers live music on weekends. **Restaurante Do**, 100 meters north of the church, serves good, inexpensive food 24 hours a day. The **Jardín de Azúcar**, one block north of the park, specializes in the native food of Guanacaste. The elegant **Pókopí**, across from Hotel El Sitio, has a varied menu that will be familiar to North Americans, including a delicious pizza and homemade cookies. It also makes boxed lunches and breakfasts for birders and hikers—order them the day before. The discotheque **Kurú** next door has a gigantic TV screen with a satellite dish and will show United States sports events on request.

LODGING   About 2 kilometers before you get to Liberia, on the right, is **Hotel Las Espuelas** (heated water, air-conditioning, pool; $60-$70; 66-0144), which has a restaurant and is the most pleasant and well-maintained hotel in that area.

There are three gas stations where the main road to Liberia intersects the Interamerican Highway. (They are the surest places to get gas on holidays.) At this intersection are **Hotel Boyeros** (heated water, air-conditioning, phone, pool; $30-$40; 66-0722), with a restaurant, and **Hotel Bramadero** (pool; with fans, $12-$20; with air-conditioning, $20-$30; 66-0371), which has quieter rooms in the back away from the pool, good dinners, and overpriced breakfasts. **Hotel El Sitio** (heated water, pool; with fans, $30-$40; with air-conditioning, $40-$50; 57-0744, 66-1211) is about 100 meters to the west, with spacious grounds and a restaurant.

The clean, quiet **Hotel La Siesta** (air-conditioning, small pool; $20-$30; 66-0678), which has a restaurant, is five blocks into Liberia and two and a half blocks to the right from the Farmacia Lux. **Hotel Daysita** (heated water, private bath, ceiling fans, pool; $20-$30; 66-0197, fax: 66-6927), next to the stadium, has a lot of nice touches and a family atmosphere.

For budget-priced accommodations, **Hotel Oriental** (private bath, air-conditioning, parking; $7-$12; 66-0085) is a good value. It is 200 meters south of the new bus station at the entrance to town. **Hotel Liberia** (cold water, both private and shared baths, no fan; under $7; 66-0161) offers basic, dark, but clean rooms. It is 75 meters south of the park. **Pensión Margarita** (cold water, shared bath, no fan, polyester sheets; under $7; 66-0468) is in a nice old wood building with a balcony. It is run-down, but clean, and run by friendly people. It is located 300 meters beyond the park.

Note: You need to make reservations for all Liberia hotels during the dry season.

GETTING THERE: Most bus transportation to Guanacaste is by way of Liberia, 45 minutes north of Cañas on the Interamerican Highway. Even though it looks farther away on the map, a trip to Liberia from San José (four hours) takes less time than a trip to Nicoya by way of the Tempisque ferry. You can take a circular route through Liberia, Santa Cruz, and Nicoya, the gateways to the Guanacaste beaches, and come back on the ferry. Roads are paved along that circular route, making it a two-hour trip by car from Liberia to the Tempisque.

BEACHES NEAR LIBERIA

Playa del Coco is the most centrally located of the beaches near Liberia and has some of the least expensive cabinas in the area and most of the dance halls. Its waters are full of small craft. It is not the place to go if you want solitude and relaxation, but it is the only place to stay relatively cheaply in this area, which tends to be overpriced.

Pizzeria Pronto (open 11:30 a.m. to 10 p.m., closed Tuesday), 300 meters before the central plaza, has good, reasonably priced Italian food, a nice outdoor patio, and good music.

Next door to the pizzeria, **Cabinas Las Brisas** (cold water, private bath, ceiling fans; $12-$20; 67-0155), are basic and clean. **Cabinas Catarino** (cold water, private bath, table fans; under $7; 67-0156), a block before the central park on the main street, are basic, with laundry and cooking facilities—good for budget travelers. A good value are the **Cabinas Chale** (cold water, private bath, ceiling fans, refrigerators; $12-$20; 67-0036), which have a huge swimming pool and basketball courts. They are 700 meters north of the park, half a block from the beach.

With breezy second-floor rooms, **Hotel Anexo Luna Tica** (cold water, private bath, table fans; $12-$20; 67-0279) and **Cabinas Luna Tica** (cold water, private bath, ceiling fans; $12-$20 including breakfast; 67-0127) are both a block to the left as you near the beach. **Pirates Cove Hotel** (heated water, private bath, ceiling fans; $20-$30; 67-0367, fax: 67-0117), which offers tours and has a restaurant with international cuisine, is on the west side of the soccer field.

The relatively clean **Cabinas El Coco** (cold water; with fans, $7-$12; with air-conditioning, $12-$20; 67-0276, fax: 67-0167) are right on the beach and have a restaurant. The sound of the waves muffles the noise from the neighboring discotheque somewhat, but not completely. The less expensive, less breezy, and noisier rooms are in back—it's best to get a front room on the second floor.

In a very quiet area, the **Flor de Itabo** (hot water, air-conditioning, pool; $60-$70; apartments, $80-$150; 33-1109, 67-0011, fax: 67-0003) is about 1 kilometer from the beach as you enter town. It is a well-designed hotel with a lot of nice touches, a restaurant, tours, and sportfishing.

Perched high on a hill, 4 kilometers south of Coco, **El Ocotal** ($100-$120; 67-0230, 22-4259) is the most elegant hotel in the area. Even if you can't afford its sportfishing, tennis, and swimming facilities, you can visit its restaurant for breakfast or lunch and enjoy the beautiful view. A dirt road to lovely, shady **Playa Ocotal**, a small cove, is to the right of the hotel gate, a 40-minute walk from Coco.

On the way to Playa Ocotal, you'll see signs for the very pleasant **Villa Casa Blanca** (heated water, private bath, ceiling fans; $40-$50; phone/fax: 67-0448), a new Canadian-owned bed-and-breakfast. **Bahía Pez Vela** ($60-$80; 21-1586), right after Playa Ocotal, has a small black-sand beach and comfortable cabinas for dedicated sportfishers.

GETTING THERE: A bus leaves San José (Calle 14, Avenidas 1/3) every day at 10 a.m. and returns at 9:15 a.m. Buses leave Liberia for Playa del Coco (30-minute trip) at 5:30, 6:30, and 11:30 a.m., and 12:30, 5:30, and 6:30 p.m., returning one hour later.

With gentle waves and clear water, **Playa Hermosa**, 9 kilometers to the north, is quiet and clean. The turnoff is to the right before you get to Playa del Coco. Follow the signs to Condovac La Costa.

Cabinas Playa Hermosa (heated water, private bath, ceiling fans; $30-$40; phone/fax: 67-0136) are quiet, fairly comfortable, and right on the beach, with a good Italian restaurant. Right next door are three *campesino* restaurants that offer a whole fish for $2. **Cabinas Vallejo** (cold water, both private and shared baths, table fans; $20-$30; $7-$12 in off-season; 67-0050) are basic; they also rent boats ($15/hour).

Halfway down the beach is **Aquasport** (67-0158), where you can rent snorkeling equipment, kayaks, windsurfing boards, and sailboats, or have an excellent seafood dinner (paella is their specialty). Aquasport will not rent windsurfing boards during the dry season, because heavy winds on that beach make the sport dangerous. They also rent a single cabina and have a well-organized grocery store where you can get bottled water, cash travelers checks, make phone calls, and mail letters.

Los Corales (air-conditioning, kitchen, pool; $100-$120; 57-0259, 55-4978, fax: 55-4978) are cabinas with a jacuzzi and a conference room. The posh **Condovac La Costa** (heated water, air-conditioning, cable TV, kitchen, pool; $90-$100; 21-8949, 33-1862, fax: 22-5637) overlooks Playa Hermosa from the north. If your beach experience requires a discotheque, you'll get it there, plus a restaurant; sportfishing facilities; windsurfing, waterskiing, and snorkeling rentals; tennis courts; and little golfcartlike vehicles to transport you up and down the hill. It has a direct bus (21-8949) from San José for guests.

Best for camping is **Playa Panamá**, 3 kilometers north of Hermosa. The wide bay makes for very gentle water, especially at low tide, when tidepools form near the north end of the beach. Watch out for sea urchins! **Jardín del Mar** ($3/person, children, $1.50; rental tents, $5; 31-7629) is a new campground with a restaurant, store, showers, toilets, electricity, and guard service. A large hotel is under construction there.

You can hire a fisherman at any of the beaches to take you across Bahía Culebra to **Playa Nacascolo**, where many Indian artifacts have been found. You can camp there, but there is no fresh water.

GETTING THERE: Buses leave Liberia for both beaches at 11:30 a.m., returning at 4 p.m. You can also take a bus from Coco to the turnoff and walk or hitch 5 kilometers to Hermosa or 8 kilometers to Panamá. A bus leaves San José (Calle 12, Avenidas 5/7) for Playas Hermosa and Panamá at 3:20 p.m. and returns at 6 a.m.

By car, Coco, Hermosa, and Panamá beaches are about a half hour from Liberia. There is a gas station on the road to Coco after the turnoff to the town of Sardinal.

RINCÓN DE LA VIEJA NATIONAL PARK

Rincón de la Vieja is one of Costa Rica's richest, most varied, and least known parks. Volcanologists say that Rincón de la Vieja volcano, although active, is unlikely to erupt because the geysers and mudpots in the area help it to let off steam. It is a compound volcano, made up of nine craters that melded together about a million years ago. Rincón's most recent violent activity was in 1966 and 1967, when it erupted frequently, destroying trees and pastureland. Some of the rivers that spring from the volcano's slopes were polluted by poisonous gases from the eruptions. There was a volcanic mud flow from the north side as recently as 1990, but all lodging and park attractions are on the south and west sides.

The park is a watershed for 32 rivers, many of which empty into the Tempisque. Three hundred species of birds have been identified there, as well as deer, collared peccaries, coatimundis, pacas, agoutis, raccoons, jaguars, two-toed sloths, and three species of monkeys.

Also in the park, **Las Pailas** (The Cauldrons) is a 50-hectare wonderland of pits of boiling hot water; vapor geysers that stain the rocks around them red, green, and yellow because of the iron, copper, and sulfur in the steam;

Coatimundi

a minivolcano that formed a couple of years ago; and seven bubbling pots of grey mud called the *Sala de Belleza* (Beauty Salon). You can dip a stick in the smooth glop, let it cool, and make yourself a rejuvenating face mask.

On the eastern side of the park are *Los Azufrales*, hot sulfur springs at a perfect bathtub temperature that are right next to a cold stream to splash in (don't let the sulfurous water get in your eyes, and don't stay in longer than five minutes without alternating with the cold water).

The park is great for hiking because it is largely untouched, and the trails are not too steep and are dry most of the year. Unlike the slippery, muddy cloud forests and rainforests, Rincón is a transitional area between dry forest and cloud forest. The trails get a bit muddy only at higher altitudes, right before the forest gives way to rocky, windblown volcanic terrain.

If you want to hike to the volcano's craters and **Laguna Jilgueros**, a scenic lake where tapirs and quetzales can sometimes be seen, it's best to camp overnight. March and April are the best months for this, but it is always wise to bring rainsuits, warm clothes, several changes of clothing wrapped in plastic, good hiking boots, a waterproof tent, and a compass. We saw a well-prepared group of campers in July who made the trip with no problem.

Note: It's a good idea to hire a guide from a local hotel or tour company if you are going to the volcano, because the paths are not clearly marked in the rocky terrain, and thick mists come up frequently. A guide would also be helpful in Las Pailas, because the dry, crusty earth around the mud-pots is brittle and thin in some places and the unsafe areas are not clearly marked. We know of two cases in which people were severely burned when the ground under them gave way and they fell into boiling water or mud.

LODGING   Near the official park entrance, **Albergue Rincón del Turista** (cold water, outhouses; $7-$12/person including meals) is in a cool valley in the village of San Jorge. It has rustic cabins near a river, surrounded by flowers and fruit trees. The owners, transplanted *josefinos*, rent horses and guides to visit the park. Arrange your visit through the Casa de Cultura (66-1606) in Liberia. Transportation from Liberia is $25, one way.

Albergue Rincón de la Vieja (cold water; both bunk and double beds; with shared bath, $30-$40/person; with private bath, $40-$50/person; student discounts; 23-5502, 33-4578, fax: 23-5502) is a rustic lodge that offers a private entrance to Rincón de la Vieja (see "Getting There" below). Meals are included in rates. Guides and horses ($30-$45/day/person) and one-day tours ($74-$86) are available. Packages: From $137 for one night to $304 for four nights.

Albergue Buenavista (both private and shared baths; $50-$60/person including meals; 69-5147, fax: 69-0090) is not as close to the park, but has beautifully designed rooms and many similar attractions on its property. There is a sauna constructed over steaming pools of water, with a cold river and mudpots next to them, a natural hot tub, and a waterfall with a crystal-clear blue pool for swimming. To get there, go 14 kilometers north of Liberia on the Interamerican and turn right at Cañas Dulces. Go 17 kilometers more on a rough road to the owners' ranch house (regular cars can make it). They will take you in a jeep the remaining 6 kilometers from there.

GETTING THERE: There are two entrances to Rincón de la Vieja. If you decide to go by the official access road be prepared for an ordeal. The road is in very bad condition, and you must have four-wheel drive. The park entrance is 25 kilometers north of Barrio Victoria in Liberia. Depending on time and space available, park guards might be able to help you with transportation, meals, and lodging. The park headquarters in Santa Rosa (69-5598) can make radio contact with them.

There is another, much easier entrance to the park, where a huge hotel, spa, and country club complex is being built. Access by this entrance is only allowed to guests of Albergue Rincón de la Vieja (see above), which is owned by the company that is building the hotel. To get to Albergue Rincón de la Vieja, go 4.5 kilometers north of Liberia on the Interamerican Highway until you see yellow bumps on the road, which indicate a school zone. Then turn right onto a road that leads in about 10 kilometers to the small town of Curubande. Continue 2 kilometers farther to the entrance to Hacienda Guachipelin, then follow signs to the left indicating the entrance to the Albergue, about 15 minutes from there. It takes just about as long to get to Rincón from San José by this route as it does to get to Monteverde, because even though the road is an hour farther north, it's in a lot better condition.

SANTA ROSA NATIONAL PARK

While most of Costa Rica's parks aim to preserve virgin forest, Santa Rosa National Park not only protects the little remaining tropical dry forest, but tries to promote its regeneration. This park encompasses almost every ecosystem that exists in Guanacaste. The most recent addition to the park is a large tract of pastureland, overgrazed and biologically bankrupt, where biologists are applying research findings about how forests propagate themselves. Seeds for forest regeneration are primarily carried by the wind, and by mammals and birds who eat seeds and then defecate in treeless pastures. By encouraging this kind of seed dispersal and burning fire lanes to control the spread of wildfires, the scientists are allowing the dry forest to renew itself. Instead of making the park off-limits to local *campesinos*, who formerly eked out an existence as ranch hands, the park hires them as caretakers, research assistants, and guides. In addition to receiving a salary, they live and farm within the park, so that their social framework, as well as the environment, is preserved. The new addition, by the way, includes the area where the clandestine airstrip, which figured in the Iran-Contra fiasco, was located.

The three times that Costa Rica has been militarily invaded, the invaders were defeated at the Hacienda Santa Rosa's **Casona** (big house). These days the Casona is a museum with historical and environmental education exhibits. Near the museum is a trail you can follow for a short natural history jaunt.

There is **camping** (for a minimal fee) in a central area of Santa Rosa, with water, toilets, showers, and nice big shade trees. The ranger will tell you which parts of the park are especially rich in wildlife at the moment. You can eat lunch with the park personnel if you give them three hours' notice.

A 13-kilometer trail will take you to **Playa Naranjo**, a long stretch of white sand that you can usually have all to yourself. At **Argelia**, right off the beach, there is a camping area, an outhouse, and a windmill-pumped well. There is another camping area at **Estero Real**, which you can reach by bearing right at a fork on the trail to Playa Naranjo. It is shady, close to the beach, and has water and outhouses. Off Playa Naranjo is **Witch Rock**, famous with surfers the world over for creating the perfect wave.

The trail to Estero Real is probably a creek in the rainy season, and is only open to vehicles from December 15 to April 1. We made it down to the beach in a huge four-wheel-drive jeep once, but the boulders made it a harrowing trip. A tank would be the appropriate vehicle. The walk to the beach takes three hours, and you must start early because of the heat.

Santa Rosa is home to a wide variety of easily observed animals. There are three types of monkeys. Howlers emit deafening growls through their enlarged voice boxes. Spider monkeys owe their remarkable agility to a long tail with something like a fingerprint on its end, which helps them grip tree branches. White-faced monkeys, whose varied diet allows them to live in several ecosystems, are the most inquisitive of the three. You'll also see vultures, falcons, and a blue-and-white jay, which has a feather on top of its head that looks like a curled ribbon on a birthday present. This bird's beauty is contradicted by its obnoxious squawk. Twenty-two species of bats inhabit the park, including two vampire varieties (they rarely attack humans—their victims are almost always livestock). Pelicans, gulls, herons, and sandpipers are the most common birds on the beach. Cicadas buzz from tree branches, so loud you sometimes have to shout to be heard.

There are collared and white-lipped peccaries whose reputation for ferocity is misleading, according to a Santa Rosa biologist we talked to. Peccaries are actually afraid of humans and flee when they are near. White-tailed deer wander in the savannah, coatimundis prowl around the forests, and caimans live in the estuaries of Playa Naranjo. As in most areas of the Pacific Coast, iguanas are everywhere.

One evening we came across a Pacific ridley turtle digging a hole to lay her eggs. Some 500,000 turtles nest on the Pacific coast of Costa Rica, of which 200,000 choose **Playa Nancite**, which is a two- or three-hour hike from Playa Naranjo. Their largest *arribada* (literally, arrival by sea) usually takes place in October. After an approximately 60-day incubation period,

Collared peccary

the baby turtles hatch and crawl into the sea. An estimated 2 percent survive all the hazards of turtlehood to become adults.

Playa Nancite is covered with turtle eggshell fragments and a few shells and skeletons of unfortunate mother turtles who didn't make it. You can't stay at Nancite overnight without a permit—it serves mainly as a biological research station. To hike there from Argelia, walk north along the beach. Go at low tide so that you can wade across the river. During high tide, you have to swim across, and the currents are strong. Find the trail behind the estuary and you'll arrive at the Estero Real picnic and camping areas. Inland from Estero Real, the trail turns off on the left and goes over a ridge to Nancite. Take drinking water on the hike.

The formerly inaccessible **Murciélago** sector of Santa Rosa has some lovely beaches that are easier to get to than those in the southern part of the park. There is also the **Playa Junquillal Recreation Area**, north of Murciélago, which protects a calm bay that is good for snorkeling, a tropical dry forest, and a mangrove swamp. Four species of turtles lay eggs there. Camping is allowed, but bring your own water.

About 15 minutes down the winding road to the park is the **Restaurant Cuajiniquil**, where you can have a good, fresh fish lunch (about $3).

Cabinas Santa Elena (cold water, shared bath, natural ventilation; under $7; leave message: 66-9112), located above a *pulpería* near the fishing village of Cuajiniquil, are very basic but clean. Two rooms are available for tourists. The rest are rented out to local fishermen, who can take you on inexpensive boat tours ($20-$40/boatload depending on length of trip) of the local estuary—which is rich in birds and wildlife—or nearby beaches and islands. The cabins are about 4 kilometers south of Playa Junquillal.

West of Cuajiniquil on the Santa Elena peninsula are peaceful **Bahía Santa Elena** and **Bahía Playa Blanca**, accessible by car only in the dry season. Fishermen will also take you around the peninsula to the **Murciélago Islands,** but the boat trip must be done during the rainy season to avoid the strong "summer" winds. There is a camping and picnic area with bathrooms at the Murciélago ranger station, just past Bahía Santa Elena.

GETTING THERE: A bus to Cuajiniquil leaves Liberia daily at 3 p.m., returning at 7 a.m. There is also a 12:30 p.m. bus from La Cruz (see below), which returns at 6 a.m. If you're going by car, keep on the Interamerican Highway five to ten minutes beyond the Santa Rosa turnoff, then turn left on the road to Cuajiniquil. Playa Junquillal is 4 kilometers to the north of Cuajiniquil on a very bad road, Bahía Santa Elena is about 12 kilometers southwest on a difficult road, and Playa Blanca is another 8 kilometers beyond that. This trip is best done in the dry season with four-wheel drive.

You can also explore this area and the rest of Guanacaste's Pacific coast with the **Temptress Cruise** (June to October only; 20-1679, fax: 20-2103; in U.S. 800-336-8423).

GUANACASTE NATIONAL PARK

Guanacaste National Park was created in 1989 to protect the migratory paths of animals that live in Santa Rosa, so it extends from the Interamerican Highway east to the Orosi and Cacao volcanoes. Many species of moths procreate in the high mountains during the dry season, then fly down to spend the rainy season at a lower, warmer altitude. The *jabalí*, a wild pig, retreats from the volcanoes to the dry forest in January to search for seeds of the *encino* (evergreen oak) tree. Scientists studying the wildlife in Santa Rosa have found that in order to protect these and other animals, the environments so necessary to their existence must also be protected.

Although Costa Rica has about .001 percent of the world's landmass, it has 5 percent of the world's biodiversity. For instance, an estimated 3800 species of moths live in Santa Rosa alone. Studying all of them would take years. However, in an exciting new project, local park employees are being trained in biological inventory techniques by some of the best scientists in the world. By all reports, the program is a tremendous success, due to the sharp powers of observation of the *campesinos*, their familiarity with the region and its wildlife, and their motivation to learn a new career that was not open to them until a few years ago. People are now being brought to Guanacaste from parks all over the country to be trained in the same techniques. All specimens will be turned over to the new **Biodiversity Institute** in Santo Domingo de Heredia, which hopes to identify every plant and animal species in Costa Rica.

Three different biological stations exist in the new park: one, on **Volcán Cacao**, is open to tourists. It has a rustic wooden lodge with a fantastic view in a cloud forest. The park administration might be able to provide food and transportation if you contact them in advance. To get there by car, take the Potrerillos turnoff from the Interamerican Highway. The road is paved to Quebrada Grande, where you turn left onto a dirt road. Go about 1 kilometer to the fork and bear left. From there the road is virtually impassible without four-wheel drive, so if you don't have it, you'll have to walk about an hour more to the station.

Note: Rincón de la Vieja, Santa Rosa, and Guanacaste parks are all administered from headquarters in Santa Rosa National Park (open 8 a.m. to 4 p.m.; 69-5598). Contact them for reservations and directions. The above phone line is often busy, so it's best just to go there in person.

GETTING THERE: *By Bus:* Buses that go to Peñas Blancas on the Nicaragua border pass the entrance to Santa Rosa. They leave San José (Calle 16, Avenida 3; 55-1932; $3.50) at 5 and 7:45 a.m. It's a four-hour trip and you have to buy tickets in advance. Because of the tremendous heat, it's better to take a *San José–Liberia* bus, stay overnight, then take a *La Cruz* (not *Santa Cruz*) bus from Liberia at 5:30 a.m. (check the bus schedule first). Ask to be let off at the "*entrada a Santa Rosa.*" You must walk or hitchhike 7.2 kilometers to the Casona and camping area before you start the 13-kilometer hike to Playa Naranjo. It's easy to hitchhike this distance in the dry season because there are many people going to and from the park.

By car: Santa Rosa is only 20 minutes north of Liberia on the Interamerican Highway, to the left. The entrance to the Murciélago sector, through Cuajiniquil, is about five minutes beyond Santa Rosa, also to the left.

LA CRUZ

The La Cruz area, near the Nicaraguan border, is still off the beaten track for tourists. There are spectacular views from the well-designed **Restaurante Ehecatl** at the *mirador* in La Cruz, situated on high bluffs overlooking Bahía Salinas. Try its excellent and inexpensive shrimp salad. *Ehecatl* means "god of wind" in Chorotega—there is always a strong breeze there. **Soda y Comedor Santa Marta** is a good place for breakfast.

Cabinas Santa Rita (cold water, private bath, natural ventilation; $7-$12; 66-9062) have well-kept, spacious rooms and are quiet at night. They are next to a machine shop, across from the Tribunales de Justicia.

Bahía Salinas is a tranquil bay surrounding the **Isla Bolaños Wildlife Refuge**. That rocky island is the nesting site for brown pelicans, American oyster-catchers, and magnificent frigate birds, who puff up their red throat pouches to attract mates. **Puerto Soley,** a few kilometers southwest of La Cruz, is the only village on the bay. It tends to be quite windy there in the dry season. You can drive from there to the Playa Junquillal Recreation Area (mentioned above).

One kilometer south, **Cabinas Las Salinas** (hot water, both private and shared baths, table fans; $12-$20) have big bright rooms, a shady camping area with bathrooms and picnic tables, and a restaurant.

Playa Jobo, on the tip of the Descartes Peninsula, which forms the southern rim of Bahía Salinas, is where the people of La Cruz go to play. We haven't been there, but we've heard that it's nice.

GETTING THERE: Buses to La Cruz leave at 5 a.m., 7:45 a.m., and 4:15 p.m. from San José (Calle 16, Avenida 3; 55-1058). The trip is four and a half hours.

Return buses are at 5:45 a.m., 8 a.m., 11 a.m., and 4 p.m. Check at the Liberia bus station for the *Liberia–La Cruz* timetable. It's a one-hour trip. By car, La Cruz is a straight shot up the Interamerican Highway from Liberia.

Buses leave the mirador in La Cruz for Playa Jobo, 13 kilometers away, at 5 a.m., 10:30 a.m., and 1:30 p.m., passing through Puerto Soley. A taxi to Puerto Soley costs about $2.50 for the 6-kilometer trip.

South of La Cruz is the turnoff for **Los Inocentes** (hot water, shared bath, pool; $100-$120 including meals; 39-5484, 66-9190), the large estate of the Víquez family near Volcán Orosi. They have converted their old family hacienda into a lodge from which visitors can ride horses to the forests surrounding the volcano to observe birds, monkeys, and other wildlife. Trips to nearby beaches and to Santa Rosa are also offered (one-day tour, $20). The food and service at Los Inocentes are excellent, and one comes away with a sense of the graceful way of life of traditional Costa Rica. To get there, turn right at the security post about five minutes north of the turnoff to Cuajiniquil (the sign points to Upala and Santa Cecilia). After 14.5 kilometers on paved road, you'll see a "Los Inocentes" sign and a store to the right. The hacienda is beyond the first gate after the store.

SIDE TRIPS TO SOUTHERN NICARAGUA

If your 30- or 90-day Costa Rican visa is about to expire, and you want to get legal again, you might want to take a quick trip to Nicaragua while you're in this part of the country. Tourists who leave the country for 72 hours can come back with a renewed tourist visa. If your visa has already expired, you must have an exit visa in order to leave Costa Rica ($40 if you leave by land, plus approximately $2.50 per month you've overstayed). You must get the exit visa in San José. If your tourist visa is still *vigente* (valid), you only have to pay about 60 cents to leave, and you don't need an exit visa.

U.S. citizens do not need visas to enter, but Canadians do. These visas take at least 24 hours to get in San José. Check with the Nicaraguan Consulate (open weekdays, 8 a.m. to 12 noon; 33-8747) regarding regulations for other nationalities.

Buses to La Cruz continue 14 kilometers to the Nicaraguan border. Change money on the Costa Rican side for the best exchange rate. Food is also cheaper on the Tico side. After you get your passport stamped, walk about 800 meters and wait for a minibus, which takes you 4 kilometers to the **Nicaraguan Migración** (Immigration Building). Entrance fees are $2 for nationalities that don't need a visa, $25 for those that do, or $14 for a three-day transit visa. There is a simple, clean, but overpriced cafeteria just past Migración with a great view of Lake Nicaragua and the Concepción Volcano.

The first town north of the border is **Rivas**, site of the battle where Juan Santamaría set fire to the stronghold of William Walker's troops, losing his life and becoming Costa Rica's national hero. Today it is a sleepy, friendly town—a good homebase for excursions to the beach. In Rivas, facing the cathedral, there is a good little open-air restaurant, the **Rinconcito Salvadoreño**, which serves *pupusas* and *comida típica*.

Hotel Nicarao (cold water, private bath, air-conditioning and table fans; $12-$20; 04-234-606), one block west of the central park behind the Banco Nacional, is a good value. It has a breezy, plant-filled restaurant with a pleasant atmosphere.

GETTING THERE: Buses leave the border every hour and a half or so for the 45-minute trip to Rivas; taxis cost $5.

Boats leave daily from San Jorge, Rivas's port on Lake Nicaragua, for the one-and-a-half-hour trip to **Isla de Ometepe**, a tranquil, picturesque island rarely visited by foreigners. Thirty-five thousand people share the island with the huge Volcán Concepción.

In Ometepe's port, **Moyogalpa**, you can stay at **Hospedaje Aly** (cold water, shared bath, no fan; $12-$20; no phone), which has clean, basic rooms, cot-like beds, and a restaurant with a pleasant, shady patio. It is 300 meters from the lake. There is also **Hospedaje Moyogalpa** (shared bath; $12-$20; no phone), which has a restaurant and is across from the dock.

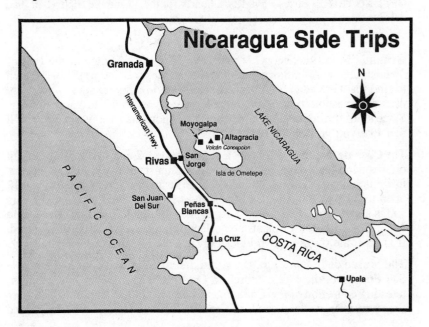

In the village of **Altagracia** on the northeast tip of the island, a line of pre-Columbian statues flanks the main square. The basic but friendly **Hospedaje Castillo** (cold water, outhouses, no fan; under $7; no phone) offers walking tours of the volcano and neighboring indigenous ruins.

Returning to Rivas, you can venture out again to **San Juan del Sur** on the Pacific coast. Sailboat and fishing trips are available there, as well as windsurfing board and bicycle rentals. You can swim in San Juan, but there are deserted, pristine swimming beaches a half hour south, near **La Flor**, a turtle-nesting area.

Restaurant Lago Azul, 100 meters past the estuary north of San Juan, offers fresh fish grilled over a wood fire ($5-$10) and a good sunset view.

In town, **Hotel La Estrella** (cold water, shared bathrooms outside, table fans; $12-$20; 04-66-210) is in a classic old building with balconies overlooking the beautiful bay. It's reminiscent of how Costa Rican beach hotels were ten to fifteen years ago. The rooms are basic, and there are no screens—bring mosquito nets. It has a restaurant.

The Norwegian-owned **Casa Internacional Joxi** (cold water; with shared bath and table fans, $20-$30; with private bath and air-conditioning, $30-$40; 04-66-348), one block east of Hotel La Estrella, is a comfortable place to stay. **Casa Quebec** (cold water, shared bath, ceiling fans; $30-$40; 04-66-307), one block south and three blocks east of Hotel La Estrella, is also nice.

GETTING THERE: Buses leave Rivas hourly for the 30-minute trip to San Juan del Sur.

Granada is full of history. If you have been disappointed at the lack of Spanish colonial buildings and churches in Costa Rica, you'll be pleased to find that Granada is full of them. Horse-and-buggy taxis ($20/hour) are used for transportation. Hiring one is a great way to get to know the city. Since all of the houses lining the streets are more than 100 years old, you'll feel like you've stepped back in time.

The **Casa de la Cultura** (open 8 a.m. to 12 noon, 2 to 5 p.m.), in a beautiful old mansion facing the central park, has a museum and a library. Posters in front announce current cultural events. Its restaurant, **El Otro** (open 12 noon to 11 p.m.), has high ceilings and beautiful wood tables and chairs and is a nice, cool, reasonably priced place for lunch or dinner. The **China Nica**, which has lots of plants and oriental decor, is also reasonably priced. It is on Calle Calzada, two blocks toward the lake from the central park.

The **Museo de la Isla Zapatera** (free admission) is next door to the Iglesia San Francisco, the oldest church in Granada. The museum houses an interesting collection of pre-Columbian Chorotega Indian statues, which were found on a large island south of Granada that was used as a burial ground and ceremonial center. The museum is now being restored with a grant from the government of Spain.

The beautifully designed **Centro Turístico** stretches for about a kilometer along the lake. Tile-roofed restaurants specializing in fresh fish are interspersed with playgrounds and benches. On weekends there is a lot of live music and dancing—*muy alegre*. On Sunday you can take a one-hour boat tour of **Las Isletas** ($4), the small islands in Lake Nicaragua; on other days of the week, you can rent launches.

One of the two best hotels in town is **Hotel Granada** (heated water, private bath, air-conditioning; $30-$40; 2974, fax: 4128), nicely furnished with gardens everywhere and a so-so formal restaurant, located across from the Guadalupe church. The other is **Hotel Alhambra** (cold water, with air-conditioning, $20-$30; cheaper with table fans; 4486), on the west side of the central park—ask for a balcony room facing the park.

Hospedaje Cabrera (cold water, shared bath, no fans; $7-$12; phone/fax: 2981), on Calle La Calzada six blocks before the lake, has a plant-filled patio with comfortable tables and chairs for guests. Rooms are basic but clean and are partitioned off from each other with walls that are open at the top. **Hospedaje Vargas** (cold water, shared bath, table fans; 2897), across the street, is pretty basic and run-down, but has a nice patio.

GETTING THERE: There are eight buses a day between Rivas and Granada.

SANTA CRUZ

Santa Cruz is the home of much of Costa Rica's folklore. The music department of the University of Costa Rica has a special branch there, devoted to investigating and celebrating traditional songs, dances, and instruments.

Coopetortillas (open 5 a.m. to 7 p.m.), 500 meters west of the church, has grown from a tortilla factory to a popular restaurant featuring typical Guanacaste food. The 16 women who run it share equally in the work, the expenses, and the profits. **La Taberna**, across from Plaza López, serves Chinese food, pizzas, and soda fountain specialties on the lower floor, and shows videos upstairs every night.

The **Diriá** ($30-$40; 68-0080) and the **Sharatoga** ($20-$30; 68-0011) both offer air-conditioning and swimming pools, almost necessities in the inland heat. Budget travelers will feel welcome at **Hospedaje Avellanas** (cold water, table and ceiling fans; with shared bath, under $7; with private bath, $7-$12; 68-0808), a family home with small rooms for rent and a restaurant. Kind of noisy, but very friendly—it could be a good homebase for exploring local beaches. It is 150 meters north of the Banco Anglo.

The old road to Nicoya goes to the left after you cross a bridge leaving Santa Cruz. It's an interesting drive through the hills that are the heartland of the province. You'll pass through **Guaitil**, where local artisans have been reviving the art of pottery making in the Chorotega style. With little or no use of a wheel, they recreate every known original style and design from native clay and natural paints and colors. The pottery is displayed at the local shop and in front of peoples' houses. Stop for a chat with them, and you'll feel the warmth and goodness of the Costa Rican *campesino*.

San Vicente, 2 kilometers southeast, also has a pottery shop in the center of town. The pieces range from $2 to $30. Cold drinks are available at the **Guaitil Artesanía Co-op.**

GETTING THERE: Buses leave Santa Cruz for Guaitil every two hours between 7 a.m. and 5 p.m. Daily Tralapa buses to Santa Cruz leave at 7:30 a.m., 10:30 a.m., 12 noon, 4 p.m., and 6 p.m. and return at 4:30 a.m., 6:30 a.m., 8:30 a.m., 11:30 a.m., and 1:30 p.m. Most *San José–Nicoya* buses (Calle 14, Avenida 5; 22-2750) also pass through Santa Cruz. By car it's 12 kilometers southeast of Santa Cruz and 19 kilometers northeast of Nicoya. The road is paved between Santa Cruz and Guaitil, unpaved between Guaitil and Nicoya.

BEACHES NEAR SANTA CRUZ

The beaches near Santa Cruz include some of the most famous and ritzy in the country. Flamingo is definitely the place to go if you or your yacht need luxurious accommodations, and the sand there is less volcanic (whiter) than at many other beaches. This area attracts sun worshippers, sportfishing enthusiasts, and surfers. Because the land is largely deforested, naturalists do not usually enjoy this part of Guanacaste, except for the turtle observation on Playa Grande. Tourists are allowed to get closer to the turtles in Tortuguero on the Atlantic Coast.

Brasilito is a small town on a grey-sand beach. Just before you reach the village, on the main road, are the new **Cabinas Conchal** (cold water, private bath, table fans; $30-$40; $20-$30 in off-season; no phone), which offer bicycle, horse, and boat rentals.

Rooms at **Mi Posada** (cold water, private bath, no fans; $7-$12; 68-0953) in the village were unclean and the people unfriendly last time we were there. To the left, on the beach, are shade trees to camp or park under. To the right are restaurants and bars. **El Rancho** (one of the restaurant/bars) has a spigot you can get water from. The beach at Brasilito is no great shakes. Half an hour south on foot is **Conchal**, a beach remarkable for its hill of shells.

Leaving Brasilito, you'll pass the entrance to **Villas Pacifica** (air-conditioning, cable TV, pool; $100-$120; 67-4139, fax: 67-4138; U.S. phone: 817-738-1636, fax: 817-738-9240), fancy condominiums on a hill with a restaurant and access to sportfishing facilities at nearby Flamingo Beach.

Five minutes down the road from Brasilito is the entrance to **Playa Flamingo**, one of Costa Rica's most exclusive beaches, which sports its own marina and landing strip. Windsurfing and scuba-diving equipment is available for rent there.

Flamingo Bay Pacific Charters offers well-equipped sportfishing trips. **Marie's Restaurant** nearby has good omelettes for breakfast.

Hotel Playa Flamingo (air-conditioning, cable TV, pool; $120-$140; 39-1584, fax: 39-0257) is huge, has a swim-up bar in its pool, boutiques, fancy restaurants, private terraces, and other amenities, and is right on the beach. The **Presidential Suites** (air-conditioning, cable TV, pool; $120-140; 39-1584, fax: 39-0257), up the hill, offer spacious, comfortable, nicely decorated apartments, with great views, breezy cross-ventilation on the top floor, private terraces, a restaurant, and maid and laundry service.

The nearby **Flamingo Marina Resort** (air-conditioning, cable TV; $100-$120; 57-1431, 67-4142, fax: 21-8093) offers suites that have their own terraces, with jacuzzis and bars, plus regular rooms and five-person apartments. The resort overlooks the marina and bay, is 300 meters away from the beach, and has a restaurant. It will arrange transportation from the airport in Tamarindo ($20 round-trip) or air charter service.

Across the bay from Flamingo, 6 kilometers from Brasilito, is **Playa Potrero**.

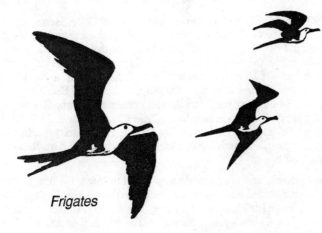

Frigates

Bahía Flamingo Beach Resort (hot water, private bath, ceiling fans, kitchenettes, small pool; $60-$70; 67-4014) offers large, simple rooms with good mattresses and a restaurant on a rather barren strip of beach. The quiet **Cabinas Cristina** (cold water, private bath, ceiling fans, kitchens, small pool; $20-$30; 67-4006) are 250 meters inland.

Rosalee's Beach Bar and Restaurant, just past the hotel, features friendly service and good homestyle meals including fresh-baked cinnamon rolls. She also rents a couple of rooms (heated water, shared bath, ceiling fans, pool; $20-$30 including breakfast; 67-4269).

Fifteen minutes by car, farther north of Playa Potrero on a gravel road, is **Playa Pan de Azúcar.** It's a pretty beach with some shade, a rocky area for snorkeling, and a sandy area for swimming. You can stay at **Hotel Sugar Beach** (heated water; $90-$100; 67-4242, fax: 21-8245, U.S. phone: 818-905-5605). There's a great view from the restaurant and bar (open every day). Pet monkeys, iguanas, and a scarlet macaw entertain the guests. A charter boat is available for fishing and snorkeling trips. The hotel is 15 kilometers from the turnoff at Huacas.

Note: If you are snorkeling anywhere in northern Guanacaste, beware of the *pelamys platurus,* a small, thin sea snake with yellow and black stripes whose venom is lethal in 15 to 30 minutes and has no antidote. Fortunately, they have a very small mouth in which their teeth are set far back and, like most animals, they won't bother you if you don't bother them. There have been no reports of fatal run-ins with this snake in Costa Rica, but it does live here, and I'd think twice about snorkeling with children in this area.

GETTING THERE: *By bus:* If you are at *playas* del Coco, Hermosa, or Panamá, and want to go to the beaches near Santa Cruz, take a returning bus from your beach and get off at Comunidad (also called Tamarindo Bar), where the road from Coco meets the road from Liberia. There you can intercept a Santa Cruz or Nicoya bus. In 15 minutes you'll be in Belén, where a bus passes around 10:30 a.m. and around 2:30 p.m. for *playas* Flamingo, Brasilito, and Potrero. Buses leave Santa Cruz for Brasilito and Potrero at 4 a.m., 10 a.m., and 2 p.m. A direct Tralapa bus leaves San José (Calle 20, Avenida 3; 21-7202; $3) every day at 8 a.m. A slower bus leaves San José at 10:30 a.m. reaching Santa Cruz around 2:30 p.m., and arriving in Flamingo around 5:30 p.m. Return buses are at 7 a.m. and 2 p.m.

The most reliable and comfortable way to get to Playa Flamingo is to take one of the air-conditioned buses from the Hotel Herradura near San José ($40 round-trip). They leave for Flamingo Monday, Wednesday, and Friday at 9 a.m. and return Tuesday, Thursday, and Saturday. The trip is four and a half hours. Car rental is available in Playa Flamingo.

The direct Flamingo bus from San José (see above) goes all the way to Potrero. There is no bus service beyond Potrero.

By car: If you're traveling by car, you'll see the turnoff for the beaches about a block after you pass the plaza of Belén. A winding road leads to the village of Huacas, where you turn off to the right. Turn right again after about 200 meters to go to Playas Flamingo, Brasilito, Potrero, and Pan de Azúcar. Go straight to get to Playa Conchal and Playa Grande (described below). The trip from Belén to Brasilito, the closest beach, takes about a half hour by car or an hour by bus, and is on paved road. The road is unpaved after Playa Flamingo, as is the road to Playa Grande. There are a couple of gas stations in Filadelfia, about halfway between Comunidad and Belén.

If you do not take the Brasilito turnoff on the road from Huacas, you will soon reach the village of Matapalo. The **Condor Club** (heated water, private bath, ceiling fans, air-conditioning, TV, pool; $80-$90; 31-7328, fax: 20-0670) is perched on a hill above the southern end of **Playa Conchal**. Each solidly built cabina is almost totally taken up by a huge, incredibly firm mattress with a heavy-duty fan right over it. The elegant but moderately priced restaurant, the disco, and the pool all have a stunning view of the coast. A beach shuttle, regional tours, and tennis, basketball, and volleyball courts are available for guests. Make reservations well in advance. To get there, follow signs from Matapalo for 5 kilometers.

LAS BAULAS NATIONAL PARK

The *baula* (leatherback) sea turtle is the largest reptile in the world, around five feet in length, some weighing over a ton. Around 80 leatherbacks come every night to nest on the beach at **Playa Grande** from October through March, making it one of the most important leatherback nesting sites in the world. Because turtles return to the same beach over and over again to nest, it is necessary to keep those beaches as clear as possible, or risk interfering with the turtles' reproductive cycle. Recent studies have shown that the presence of humans does indeed affect turtle reproduction, and peaceful Playa Grande is the scene of a battle to protect the venerable and voiceless turtles' right to nest where their instincts demand they must.

In the last few years, turtle watching has become a new source of quick and easy income for people in this area, whether it be fishermen from Tamarindo who take a load of tourists to Playa Grande in their boats, often without any life jackets, or luxury hotels who send people in by the busload. Excursion buses from the Central Valley have brought in fun-loving Ticos who ride on the mother turtles' backs. At times, more than 150 people have been gathered around a nesting turtle.

One hotel is operating on the beach, and several other development projects are under construction. The area between the point to the north of Playa

Olive ridley turtle

Grande, extending south through Tamarindo and Playa Langosta, has recently been declared Las Baulas National Park, which means that the already impoverished national park system will have to come up with money to make a settlement with the developers. **Turtle watching** (admission 75 cents, guide 75 cents) is now permitted only from platforms placed along the edge of the beach. Local guides regulate the number of tourists in the park and lead people to the platforms.

Before becoming a national park, Playa Grande had already established a reputation as a favorite spot for surfers, because of its long waves. As is true with most beaches that are good for surfing, Playa Grande is not good for swimming. Although surfers are usually respectful of the turtles, they and other beachgoers should avoid playing or lying down on the dunes or making holes in the sand that could slow down the turtle hatchlings' already hazardous journey to the sea. In other words, Playa Grande cannot be considered a recreational beach. Camping is not allowed.

According to national park representatives, even though there are various collection boxes in Playa Grande and Tamarindo for turtle preservation, the only donations that go directly to Las Baulas National Park are those made to the Fundación de Parques Nacionales, Fundación Neotrópica, or Fundación Chorotega (55-2122, 31-2608; Apdo. 189, Santa Cruz de Guanacaste), a group of local people dedicated to helping the turtles. (For phone numbers and addresses of Fundación de Parques Nacionales and Fundación Neotrópica, see Chapter Two.)

Hotel Las Tortugas (cold water, private bath, pool; $70-$80; 68-0765, 23-2811; Apdo. 164, Santa Cruz de Guanacaste), which is right on the beach, states in its brochure, "Our staff and guests are watchdogs for the wildlife area and always on the alert to sound the alarm at the first scent of ecological danger." The hotel is purposely designed with no ocean views toward the south, where the turtle-nesting beach is located. It has a jacuzzi and a good restaurant and bar; rents canoes; arranges fishing and scuba-diving tours; and can tell you about local tidepools and trails.

Half a kilometer before Playa Grande is **Centro Vacacional Playa Grande** (cold water, private bath, ceiling fans, kitchen; $20-$30; 37-2552), which has six-bed rooms and a restaurant. Someone from the hotel will meet your bus in Huacas, Matapalo, or Tamarindo if you give a day's notice of your arrival.

GETTING THERE: The 10 a.m. and 2 p.m. *Santa Cruz–Flamingo* buses stop in Matapalo first, as does the 10:30 a.m. *San José–Flamingo* bus. From there it's a few minutes by car or taxi to Playa Grande. By car, go straight on the road going west from Huacas instead of turning right (north) for Playa Brasilito. Turn left at the village of Matapalo.

Tamarindo is a wide white-sand beach with a large estuary—a favorite with surfers and windsurfers. The estuary has been made into a wildlife refuge. Leatherback turtles nest on the beach from October to March. Many baby turtles have been crushed as they scramble to the ocean by inadvertent tourists, because it is hard to see them in the dry, loose sand high up on the beach. Be sure to walk near the waterline, where it is easier to spot them.

Tamarindo is also an active fishing village, which is something to be valued since many Guanacaste beaches have lost such traditional occupations to tourism. You can watch the fishermen *zarpando* (sailing out to sea) at dawn, and you can eat their catch at the **Fiesta del Mar** and **Tercer Mundo** restaurants or at the hotels.

Johan's Bakery (open daily, from 6 a.m.) makes European bread, pastry, and pizza. You can also buy food at **Supermercado El Pelícano** (open 9 a.m. to 5 p.m.; closed Sunday). Next to it is a place where you can rent scooters, boogieboards, beach chairs, and umbrellas, and find out about houses and rooms for rent.

Across the street, **Coconuts** is an exceptional and somewhat expensive restaurant, with candlelight, good music, fresh flowers, and three chefs cooking on open air grills. **Restaurant El Milagro** also serves excellent food and has beautiful gardens with carved stone statues. It's expensive, but the daily specials are reasonably priced.

The **Tamarindo Information and Welcome Center**, at the end of the road, has topographical maps of the whole country as well as practical information about the zone. **Papagayo Excursions** (68-0859, 68-0652, 23-3648, fax: 68-0859, 25-3648), at the entrance to town, offers sportfishing, scuba diving, and nature safaris by boat or on horseback.

LODGING As you enter Tamarindo, you'll find **Cabinas Pozo Azul** (cold water, private bath, air-conditioning, pool; $20-$30; 68-0147), which have refrigerators but not much atmosphere. The **Pueblo Dorado** (heated water, air-conditioning, pool; $60-$80; $30-$40 in off-season; phone/fax: 22-5741) has small, clean, comfortably furnished rooms. **Pensión Doly** (both private and shared baths; $12-$20; 68-0174) is definitely basic, with small cement rooms, but it's clean and friendly and right on the beach. Don't go swimming there—that section of the beach is dangerous. Pozo Azul and Doly have been known to demand advance deposits and then not honor the reservations.

Cabinas Marielos (cold water, private bath, ceiling fans; $20-$30; $12-$20 in off-season; 41-4843) are new and clean with nice gardens. The large **Tamarindo Diriá** (heated water, fans, air-conditioning, cable TV, pools; $60-$80; 68-0652, 33-0530, fax: 22-0568) is a comfortable place to stay, with smallish rooms. It has shady grounds, tennis courts, a game room, and a restaurant, and can get crowded during tourist season. Local people sell jewelry and animals made out of shells at the entrance to the beach from the hotel.

Cabinas Zully Mar (private bath; with cold water and ceiling fans, $12-$20; with refrigerator, $20-$30; with heated water and air-conditioning, $30-$40; 26-4732) are in "downtown" Tamarindo, where the road ends in a clutch of bar-restaurants on the beach. The rooms are clean, and the management friendly. Recommended.

The American-owned **Tamarindo Resort** (heated water, private bath, ceiling fans, air-conditioning, kitchens, maid service, pool; $90-$100; 68-0883, 55-2263, fax: 55-3785) has a restaurant and dozens of cheaply built bungalows. It is at the south end of town in a shady area set back from the beach.

GETTING THERE: *By Bus:* Empresa Alfaro buses to Tamarindo (Calle 14, Avenida 5; 22-2750; $4) leave from San José at 3:30 p.m. and return at 5:30 a.m. Buy tickets in advance for weekends and holidays. Tralapa buses (Avenida 3, Calle 20; 21-7202; $4) leave at 4 p.m. and return at 8:30 a.m. Buy these tickets in advance also. Buses leave Santa Cruz for Tamarindo daily at 3 p.m., and on weekends at 10 a.m. and 3 p.m.

By Car: If you're going by car, the turnoff for Tamarindo is 13 kilometers south of Huacas on paved road, about an hour from Liberia. There are gas stations in Filadelfia, between Liberia and Belén. There's an outdoor tire repair shop on the left on the dirt road to Tamarindo, on a rise after a little bridge.

By Air: SANSA flies to Tamarindo from San José Monday, Wednesday, Friday, and Saturday at 8:45 a.m., returning at 9:35. Flights to Nosara on Monday, Wednesday, and Friday at 6 a.m. also include a stop at Tamarindo (33-0397, 33-3258, 21-9414; $25 one way). Check schedules. Travelair has daily flights to Tamarindo at 12:35 p.m. Its daily Nosara and Carrillo flights at 12 noon include a stop in Tamarindo (32-7883; $57 one way). Most hotels in the area arrange transportation for guests from the Tamarindo airport.

Playa Junquillal is a wide, almost deserted beach with high surf and strong rip currents. Just before you get there is the French-owned **Hotel Hibiscus** ($100-$120 including meals for two; phone/fax: 68-0737), which has beautifully designed and decorated bungalows. **Hotel Junquillal** ($12-$20), at the entrance to the beach, has a restaurant and the most economical cabinas in the area. You can also use its shady camping area ($4/night).

Right on the beach are two comfortably elegant hotels with nice pools, tennis courts, and spacious two-unit bungalows. The German-owned **Villa Serena** (hot water, private bath, ceiling fans; $100-$120; phone/fax: 68-0737) is smaller and more intimate and includes three excellent meals in its rates. Sauna and videos are also available there. **Hotel Antumalal** (heated water, private bath, air-conditioning; $80-$90; phone/fax: 68-0506) is farther down the beach.

The new, Canadian-owned **Iguana Azul** (hot water, private bath, ceiling fans, pool; $60-$70; $30-$40 in off-season; phone/fax: 68-0783, 32-1423) is 1 kilometer north of Playa Junquillal. It has good food, good music, and friendly people. It rents videos, snorkeling and surfing equipment, mountain bikes, and horses. Sportfishing and scuba-diving trips are also available. Iguana Azul runs a private bus service to and from San José three times a week ($20 one way). Otherwise, get off the Junquillal bus at the Iguana Azul sign and walk 1 kilometer to the right.

GETTING THERE: A direct *San José–Junquillal* bus (21-7202; $4) leaves from the Tralapa station (Avenida 3, Calle 20) at 2 p.m. daily, arriving around 8 p.m. and returning at 6:30 a.m.

To reach Junquillal from Tamarindo by car, continue south 18 kilometers to a crossing called "27 de Abril." Turn right onto an unpaved road and go another 12 kilometers. Turn left at Paraíso. The hotels are a short distance from there. If you are coming from Liberia, it is faster to take a turnoff to the right just before you reach Santa Cruz (follow the signs). From there it's 19 kilometers to "27 de Abril." Turn left, and proceed as above.

Playa Avellanas is popular with surfers for its beach break with both right and left waves. It's way off the beaten track, 4.5 kilometers north of Paraíso and 5 kilometers south of Tamarindo.

✪ **Lagartillo Beach Hotel** (cold water, private bath, ceiling fans, pool; $50-$60; 57-1420, fax: 21-5717), set about 200 meters back in the forest lining the pristine beach, is beautifully designed with much attention to detail and has a good restaurant.

Down the beach, **Freddy's Surf Camp** ($7-$12; no phone) has a beautiful location and a seafood restaurant, but its outhouses and garbage dump are right on the estuary.

GETTING THERE: There is no public transportation to Avellanas. If you drive there, go through Paraíso and plan to arrive at low tide so you can cross the river (just before the Lagartillo Beach Hotel).

NICOYA

While Liberia is the transportation and commercial capital of Guanacaste, Nicoya is the cultural capital. Its **church** (open 8 a.m. to 12 noon, 2 to 6 p.m.; closed Sunday and Wednesday), dedicated to San Blas, was built in 1644 and is presently undergoing restoration. Next to it is a lovely, shady **square** abloom with flowers.

Café Daniela, an open, airy restaurant on the main thoroughfare one block from the park, has freshly baked goods, pizzas, and ice-cold *refrescos*, plus a full Tico menu in an *agradable* atmosphere. For tasty Chinese food, try **Restaurante Jade,** 100 meters east and 75 meters north of the church.

Hotel Jenny (cold water, private bath, air-conditioning, TV; $12-$20; 68-5050), 100 meters south of the park, and **Las Tinajas** (cold water, private bath, table fans; $7-$12; 68-5081), 200 meters west of the park, are both pleasant places to stay in the center of town. The **Pensión Venecia** (cold water, both private and shared baths, table fans; under $7; 68-5325), across from the church, is clean and basic with a nice sitting area. **Hotel Curime** (heated water, private bath, pool; $40-$50; 68-5238), south of town on the road to Playa Sámara, has a restaurant, modern cabinas with refrigerators, and the world's noisiest air-conditioning.

GETTING THERE: Buses to Nicoya through Liberia leave San José from Empresa Alfaro (Calle 14, Avenida 5) at 6 a.m., 10 a.m., and 1:30, 3, 4:30, and 5:30 p.m. You must buy tickets in advance. Buses that go to Nicoya by way of the ferry (22-2750; $3.50) leave San José at 8 a.m., returning at 4 p.m. The ferry ride (10 cents) across the Tempisque River is a pleasant 20 minutes. The ferry crosses continuously, but if you get there when it is pulling away, you have to wait, so it can take as long to go to or from Nicoya by the ferry route as it does through Liberia—five hours. If you do not buy your ticket quickly and jump on the ferry when it is there, your bus will leave without you. By car, Nicoya is about 20 minutes from Santa Cruz on the paved road, an hour on the old road. The ferry takes 12 cars ($2.25) at a time.

BEACHES NEAR NICOYA

Playas de Nosara is an international community with many North American and European residents. About half the land in this 12-square-kilometer development has been set aside as a wildlife reserve and park. The maritime zone fronting 4 kilometers of beach is protected by the forest service. Because of these reserve areas, Nosara is generally much greener than the rest of Guanacaste. No hunting has been allowed there for decades, so birds and wildlife are plentiful. It is common to see coatimundis, armadillos, howler monkeys, and even the jaguarundi, a cat that looks black from a distance but actually has a grey diamond pattern on its fur. Parrots, toucans, cuckoos, trogons, and pelicans are also easily observed. Humpback and grey whales can be seen offshore during the winter months. The beaches have community-maintained shelters for picnicking and camping.

There are coral reefs and tidepools on **Playa Guiones** that are good for snorkeling. Surfing is best there and at the mouth of the **Nosara River**. A small restaurant on **Playa Pelada** offers fresh fish and provides water for campers.

The **Gilded Iguana** (68-0749) is famous for its Black Panther cocktail, named after the local jaguarundi. It serves soup and sandwiches Wednesday through Sunday and hosts a traditional bridge game on Saturday. It also rents furnished efficiency apartments ($60-$80).

Views from the very pleasant **Hotel Playa Nosara** (hot water, ceiling fans, pool; $60-$80; phone/fax: 68-0495) are magnificent. The hotel and restaurant are high on a point, so you can see the long Playa Guiones on one side and the beautiful Playa Pelada on the other.

The new **Condominio de las Flores** ($500/week, $1500/month during high season; 68-0696) offers completely equipped two-bedroom, two-bath apartments. The Swiss-owned **Rancho Suizo Lodge** (cold water, private bath, fans upon request; $30-$40; 53-4345, fax: 24-4392; Apdo. 14, Bocas de Nosara, 5233 Guanacaste), 800 meters north of the condominiums and a five-minute walk from the beach, has clean, new bungalows and an excellent restaurant. Videos are shown in the evenings and the staff will arrange tours.

The Swiss-owned **Cabinas La Estancia** (cold water, private bath, ceiling fans, kitchens, pool; $30-$40; no phone) have a tennis court and are five minutes from the beach, 4 kilometers south of Nosara.

The village of **Nosara** is 5 kilometers inland from Playas de Nosara. **La Lechuza** (open for lunch Monday through Saturday), 2 kilometers north of the beach on the road to the village, is a favorite gathering place for residents. There is a gas station and a *pulpería* in town. Next to the gas station, **Cabinas Chorotega** (cold water, both private and shared baths, ceiling fans; $7-$12; 68-0836) are very clean. **Cabinas Agnnel** (cold water, private bath, ceiling fans; under $7) also look well-kept.

A few kilometers south of Nosara at Punta Garza is the Italian-owned **Villaggio la Guaria Morada** (heated water, private bath, ceiling fans; $120-$140; 68-0784, 33-2476, fax: 22-4073), a very elegant beachside hotel. It is known for good food, but we've heard complaints about the service. A uniformed, armed guard meets you at the gate.

GETTING THERE: Regular buses leave Nicoya for Nosara at 12 noon and return at 6 a.m. The trip takes about two and a half hours by bus, and one and a half by car on dusty, bumpy, gravel roads that can become impassable in the rainy season.

Instead of going back to Nicoya, we explored the coastal road through Paraíso to Santa Cruz. The going was rough, with several riverbeds to cross, but it got a bit smoother after Marbella. The trip took two hours and wasn't very exciting.

SANSA flies to Nosara (21-9414, 33-0397, 33-3258, fax: 55-2176; $27) Monday, Wednesday, and Friday at 6 a.m., returning at 6:50 a.m. Check schedules. Travelair goes to Nosara daily at 12 noon (32-7883, fax: 20-0413; $50 one way). Hotel Playa Nosara will pick up guests from the plane.

Ostional Wildlife Refuge, just north of Nosara, protects the breeding grounds of *lora* (olive) ridley turtles, which arrive in great numbers between the third quarter and the new moon during the months of April to December, with peak activity in August and September. The people of Ostional are allowed to harvest turtle eggs during the first 36 hours of the *arribada*, since the eggs laid during that period are usually dug up and crushed by subsequent waves of mother turtles. The eggs are sold to bars across the country to be gulped raw as *bocas*. After the first 36 hours, community members guard the beach to make sure that the rest of the eggs are laid without disturbance. They will be glad to show you around and tell you about their cooperative.

You can stay in simple cabinas there (shared bath, no fan; under $7), which unfortunately have lots of insects, and buy meals from local families or from the bar next door. Call the village *pulpería* (68-0467) to reserve cabinas and to find out if the turtles are active.

GETTING THERE: A bus leaves Santa Cruz at 12 noon each day during the dry season and arrives at Ostional at 3:30 p.m. By car, during the dry season, you can ford the river between Nosara and Ostional. The road is smoother going southwest from Santa Cruz via Marbella, at least through July.

Playa Sámara, an hour south of Nosara, is a perfect, long, white-sand beach with shallow, gentle waters. It's a favorite with swimmers and windsurfers. Many Ticos have summer homes there.

The well-designed **Hotel Las Brisas del Pacífico** (heated water, ceiling fans, pool, jacuzzi; $50-$100; 68-0876, 55-2380, fax: 33-5503) is at the southern end of the beach. A number of inexpensive cabinas and *hospedajes* are at the north end of the beach. **Hotel Playa Samara** (cold water, private bath, table fans; $12-$20; 68-0724) is the best-looking one, but must be awfully loud on weekends because of its disco. Residents of the north end are good about letting visitors camp on their land and use their facilities. **El Acuario,** 100 meters south of the soccer field, rents camping space and use of its facilities ($1). It also offers a good fish dinner ($4). **Villas Playa Sámara** are timeshare condominiums south of Sámara that were just being completed when we were there.

GETTING THERE: A direct *San José–Sámara* bus leaves from Empresa Alfaro (Avenida 5, Calles 14/16; 22-2750, 23-8227, 23-8361; $4) daily at 12 noon. It's a six-hour trip. Buy tickets several days in advance for three-day weekends. Buses leave for Sámara from Nicoya during the dry season Monday through Friday at 3 p.m. and Saturday and Sunday at 8 a.m. and 3 p.m., returning from Sámara at 5:30 a.m. daily and again at 2 p.m. on weekends. During the rainy season, there is one bus only, at 12 noon.

To drive to Sámara from Nosara, you have to ford an ankle-deep river about halfway there. The trip from Nicoya by car is about an hour and a half on bumpy dirt roads that are dusty in the dry season and muddy in the rainy season.

There is a SANSA flight that stops in Tamarindo and Sámara (21-9414, 33-0397, 33-3258; $27) on its way to Nosara. It leaves Monday, Wednesday, and Friday at 6 a.m. Check with SANSA about schedule changes and buy your ticket two weeks in advance during the dry season. Travelair flies there (32-7883, fax: 20-0413; $50 one way) daily at 12 noon. The airport for Sámara is at Playa Carrillo (see below).

About five minutes south of Sámara by car is **Playa Carrillo**, another beautiful white-sand beach whose waters are kept calm by a reef at the entrance to the bay. Carrillo also boasts an ice factory.

There is a large bar and restaurant (good breakfasts for $1.50, fish for $3) with a great view at the entrance to the village, up on a cliff where it receives the sea breezes. Next door are some rather unattractive cabinas for up to 3 people (cold water, private bath, natural ventilation; $12-$20).

The exclusive Japanese-owned resort and sportfishing hotel **Guanamar** (hot water, air-conditioning, cable TV, phone, pool; $120-$140; 20-0722, fax: 20-2095, in United States and Canada: 800-245-8420) has an excellent restaurant and beautiful terraces overlooking the bay. The grounds are lush with palms and flowers. Some of the bungalows have kitchens, and all of them have tremendous views and private balconies.

If you travel south from Carrillo by car, you must ford the Río Ora at low tide. It's good to purchase a tide table if you are going to travel the unpaved coastal roads in Guanacaste.

About two hours south of Carrillo is **Playa Coyote**, which has primitive showers and a bar. The beach is long and deserted and was very windy when we were there. It is most easily reached by gravel road from Jicaral, which is an hour northwest of Playa Naranjo, where the Puntarenas ferry lands. The trip from Jicaral takes an hour and a half. We were told that **Playa Caletas,** one beach to the south, sometimes has 15-foot waves.

BARRA HONDA NATIONAL PARK

El Cerro Barra Honda is part of a flat-topped ridge that juts up out of the dry cattle-grazing land of the Nicoya Peninsula. People used to call the ridge a volcano because it's covered with large white limestone rocks piled around deep holes that look like craters. In the 1960s and 1970s speleologists discovered that the holes were entrances to an intricate series of interconnected caves, some as deep as 200 meters. The caves are so spectacular that the area was made into a national park.

When the region was under the sea millions of years ago, marine animals deposited calcium carbonate that hardened and became limestone. Later, when the land was pushed up out of the sea, rainfall combined with carbon dioxide and dissolved the limestone to hollow out the caves. In a process similar to how icicles grow, dripping water carrying calcium carbonate formed stalactites and stalagmites that look like curtains, pipe organs, fried eggs, and pearls.

Within the caves all sorts of creatures flourish: bats, insects, birds, blind salamanders, and fish. In the **Nicoa cave**, speleologists discovered human skeletons that were quite old—a stalagmite was growing on one skull. It is assumed that they were the remains of Indians from the region, since some Indian artifacts were found near them. Fortunately, the deep vertical drops at the entrances have discouraged all but the best-equipped from entering, so the caves have suffered almost no vandalism.

Park rangers can take you down into **Terciopelo**, the cave with the most beautiful formations of all. A visit requires a week's notice to the national park regional headquarters in Bagaces (67-1062). They won't take you down in the rainy season or during Holy Week.

Ríos Tropicales (33-6455) runs spelunking tours into the caves. It has better equipment than the park rangers and can go places they can't. **Turinsa** (21-9185) also runs tours to the caves. **Olman Cubillo** provides independent tours (Spanish only, 68-5580).

Even if you can't get down into the caves, a visit to Barra Honda is rewarding. You can explore the flat top of the ridge, where birds screech, iguanas stand motionless, and trees are full of howler monkeys. The lookout point reached by following the *Sendero al Ojoche, la Trampa, la Terciopelo* affords wide views of the peninsula and the Gulf of Nicoya. The *Sendero al Ceibo* leads to a waterfall decorated with lacy calcium carbonate formations. It's about 6 kilometers from the trailhead.

In the dry season it's very hot, so bring a canteen with you as you explore. The campsite is up the road to the right, on the left side of the trail. There are picnic tables and water.

GETTING THERE: You can take a bus at 12 noon from Nicoya to the village of Santa Ana (an hour-and-a-half trip) and walk 2 kilometers to the park. Buses leave Nicoya for Barra Honda village at 10:30 a.m. and 3 p.m., leaving you 6 kilometers from the park.

Barra Honda is a half hour from Nicoya by car. Take the main road east and make a left when you see signs for the village of Barra Honda. You can also come from the east via the Tempisque ferry and turn right at the Barra Honda turnoff. The road to the village is paved. Beyond that, the dirt road to the park gets narrower and bumpier, but national park signs clearly mark the way.

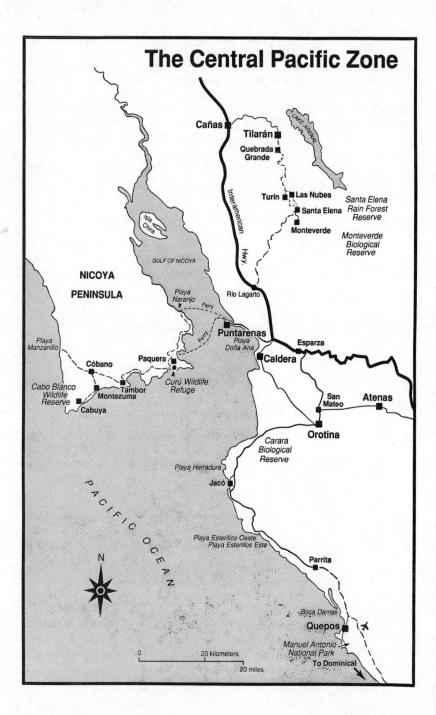

The Central Pacific Zone

Cañas

Tilarán

Quebrada
Grande

LAKE ARENAL

Interamerican Hwy.

Turín Las Nubes

Santa Elena

Santa Elena
Rain Forest
Reserve

Monteverde

Monteverde
Biological
Reserve

Isla
Chira

GULF OF NICOYA

NICOYA

PENINSULA

Playa
Naranjo

Ferry

Río Lagarto

Ferry

Puntarenas

Playa
Doña Ana

Esparza

Playa
Manzanillo

Cóbano

Paquera

Caldera

Cabo Blanco
Wildlife
Reserve

Tambor

Montezuma

Curú Wildlife
Refuge

San
Mateo

Atenas

Cabuya

Orotina

Carara
Biological
Reserve

Playa Herradura

Jacó

PACIFIC OCEAN

N

Playa Esterillos Oeste
Playa Esterillos Este

Parrita

Boca Damas

Quepos

0   20 kilometers

Manuel Antonio
National Park

20 miles

To Dominical

ELEVEN

The Central Pacific Zone

Puntarenas Province extends along the Pacific Coast from Guanacaste to the Panamanian border. The Central Pacific Zone roughly corresponds to the northern part of the province, from Monteverde, near the border with Guanacaste, to Quepos and Manuel Antonio National Park, about halfway down Costa Rica's Pacific Coast. Like Guanacaste, the Central Pacific is famous for its beaches from the rocky coves of Montezuma on the Nicoya Peninsula to the beautiful beaches of Manuel Antonio.

The climate of the Central Pacific is not as dry as that of Guanacaste, however. You'll feel the heat and the heaviness of the moist, tropical air, so be prepared to slow down and let your body adjust to the change. Bring sunblock, insect repellent, and an umbrella to use in the sun or in case of sudden showers.

Note: In general, sanitary conditions are very good on the Pacific Coast, but if you don't want to take chances with the water, it's wise to bring a large plastic container of tap water from San José so that you won't have to live on soft drinks or beer. Don't swim in estuaries or rivers, as inviting as they may seem. Most of them are polluted. The heavy surf and currents of the Pacific keep the beaches free of contamination. (Be sure to read the section on how to handle rip currents in Chapter Five.)

PUNTARENAS

The town of Puntarenas was Costa Rica's main port for most of the 1800s. The treacherous terrain between San José and the Atlantic Coast made an eastern port impossible, until the railway was completed in 1890. So ox carts laden with coffee rumbled down to Puntarenas, from which the precious beans were shipped to Chile, to be re-exported to Europe. In 1843, English Captain William Le Lacheur landed in Puntarenas on the way back from a business failure in Seattle, Washington. Worried about the danger of sailing with an empty ship, he traveled five days by mule to San José, hoping to find some cargo for ballast. It turned out that coffee had been over-produced that year, and growers were desperate for new markets. Even though he was a stranger and had no money to give them, the growers entrusted him with a weighty shipment. He came back two years later with the payment, and a thriving trade with England was established.

Since the inauguration of Puerto Caldera a few years ago, Puntarenas is no longer used for shipping but is still the center of Costa Rica's fishing industry. It is closest beach to San José, but unless you have a thing about funky seaports or are into sailing, you won't want to spend your vacation there. If you have to spend time there en route to somewhere else, it is pleasant to stroll along the Paseo de Turistas, feel the sea breezes, and watch the sun set behind the mountains of the Nicoya Peninsula.

The town is only four blocks wide for most of its length, because it is built on a narrow spit. Fishing boats and ferries dock on the estuary side; a beach runs along the Gulf of Nicoya side. The Ministry of Health warns against bathing in the estuary, but apparently the beaches have been cleaned up quite a bit in the last few years.

For visitors, Puntarenas has two distinct characters, determined by season: it is lively and full of people in the dry season, sleepy and tranquil in the rainy season. In summer, people watchers will enjoy the never-ending parade of tourists up and down the wide sidewalk next to the beach. Kiosks there serve snacks, *refrescos*, and ice cream. There's an entertaining, inexpensive series of concerts and plays at the Casa de la Cultura during the summer. We enjoy Puntarenas more in the rainy season, when it is uncrowded, breezy, and refreshed.

On the oceanfront, **La Caravelle** is recommended for good food. **Restaurante Miramare** specializes in Italian seafood.

The new 174-room **Hotel Fiesta** (hot water, air-conditioning, cable TV, pools; $100-$120; 63-0185, 63-0808, fax: 63-1516) in El Roble, a few kilometers to the west before Puntarenas, caters to the big-time tourist trade. It has restaurants, a casino, tennis and volleyball courts, a gym, conference rooms, access to fishing, and water sport equipment for rent.

The verdant residential San Isidro area, near the hospital, has many cabinas with kitchens that can be rented by the day or week. **Cabinas Los Chalets** (cold water, pool; $30-$40; 63-0150) are the nicest. Frequent buses connect San Isidro with Puntarenas.

The loveliest hotel in Puntarenas is the **Portobello** (hot water, air-conditioning, cross-ventilation, pools, $40-$50; 61-1322, fax: 61-0036), about 7 kilometers from downtown on the estuary. Its lush, colorful, beautifully tended gardens create a sense of privacy and tranquillity and attract many birds. It also has a good restaurant.

Next door, the **Hotel Colonial** (both heated and cold water, ceiling fans, air-conditioning, pools; $40-$50 including breakfast; 61-1833, fax: 61-2969), appeals to a younger crowd. It has swings, pingpong, and other diversions.

The **Yacht Club** (hot water, air-conditioning, pool; $12-$20; 23-4224, 61-0784), just before the Portobello, offers decent accommodations for a very good price, but rooms are usually taken up by Yacht Club members, especially on weekends. The above three hotels offer free mooring and use of their facilities to sailboats passing through.

Downtown, near the bus stop, are two hotels with restaurants: The **Chorotega** (with shared bath, $7-$12; with private bath, $20-$30; Calle 1, Avenida 3; 61-0998), favored by backpackers, and **Las Hamacas** (cold water, ceiling fans, air-conditioning, pool; $12-$20; Avenida 4, Calles 5/7; 61-0398).

The **Ayi Con** (cold water, both private and shared baths; with ceiling fans, $7-$12; with air-conditioning, $12-$20; Calle 2, Avenidas 1/3; 61-0164) is probably the cleanest of the inexpensive hotels near the market. The **Imperial** (cold water, both private and shared baths, ceiling fans; $12-$20; 61-0579) is in a nice old building right across from the beach near Calle Central. The upstairs rooms have more light. **Cabinas El Jorón** (hot water, air-conditioning; $12-$20; Calle 25, Avenida 2; 61-0467) are dark and noisy but have refrigerators and a restaurant known for its steaks.

A favorite with visitors, **Hotel Tioga** (hot water, air-conditioning, indoor pool; $30-$40 including breakfast; 61-0271, fax: 61-0127) was *the* place to stay 25 years ago and is still comfortable and well maintained, with a cafeteria. **Las Brisas** (cold water, air-conditioning, small pool; $30-$40; 61-2120) has large, clean rooms with no cross-ventilation. It is three blocks west of the ferry landing. **Hotel La Punta** (cold water, ceiling fans, pool; $20-$30; 61-0696, fax: 61-0440) is clean, has a restaurant, and is probably the most convenient for those who want to catch the ferry in the morning—it's just around the corner from the terminal. The fancy **Hotel Yadran** (hot water, bathtub, carpeting, air-conditioning, TV, pool; $40-$50; 61-2662, fax: 61-1944) is on the ocean side of the point. It also has a restaurant.

Calypso Tours ($70, including transportation to and from San José; discounts with OTEC card; 33-3617, fax: 33-0401) takes you around the gulf in its luxurious yacht. It offers fresh tropical fruit and ceviche to nibble on; serves a gourmet seafood buffet on Tortuga Island, where you can swim and snorkel; and provides fishing tackle for the trip back to Puntarenas. The boat passes the Islas Negritos Wildlife Refuge, one of the main nesting grounds for pelicans and frigate birds. You can combine the Calypso cruise with trips to Carara Reserve or Monteverde, or rafting down the Corobicí River. Calypso also offers a romantic two-hour sunset cocktail cruise every Saturday.

Bay Island Cruises (39-4951, 39-4403), **Costa Sol** (39-0033), and **Fantasy Yacht Tours** (22-4752, 55-0791, 61-0697) are recent clones of Calypso, which has been offering the cruise for 16 years. **Seaventures** (55-3022) has sailboat tours of the gulf and three-day excursions to Cabo Blanco Wildlife Reserve (see below).

Note: Camping on the beach at Puntarenas is not recommended.

GETTING THERE: *By Bus: San José–Puntarenas* buses (Calle 12, Avenida 9; 22-1867; $1.50) leave continuously from 6 a.m. to 7 p.m. Get there early on weekends and holidays. *Directo* buses take two hours.

NICOYA PENINSULA

The Nicoya Peninsula on Guanacaste's southern tip is part of Puntarenas Province. This is because ferries have traditionally connected the western side of the Gulf of Nicoya with the mainland through the port of Puntarenas. The fastest way to get there is by boat, although it's still a time-consuming adventure. Tourism in the area has centered around Playa Naranjo, where the car ferry from Puntarenas docks; Playa Tambor, located midway down the coast; the beaches of Montezuma to the south; and the Cabo Blanco Absolute Biological Reserve at the very tip of the Peninsula.

The Nicoya Peninsula is on the brink of a tremendous change because one of the largest hotels in the country is scheduled to open there soon. Part of the government's initial agreement with the hoteliers, Spain's famous Barceló family, involved promises to pave roads, improve ferry service, and install a much-needed infrastructure which area residents have been requesting for years. There is no telling when the government will make good on its promises, so check with the ICT before venturing out to this region.

For lodging near the Playa Naranjo ferry landing check out **Hotel Oasis del Pacífico** (ceiling fans, pools; $40-$50; phone/fax: 61-1555), on Playa Naranjo to the left of the ferry landing. It offers sportfishing, horses, and tennis courts. Its restaurant is a bit overpriced, but a stop at its swimming pools ($3/person) can make the difference between a pleasure trip and a hot, dusty ordeal. The hotel provides transportation to and from the ferry landing.

Hotel de Paso (cold water, pool; with shared bath, $12-$20; with private bath, $20-$30; with private bath and air-conditioning, $30-$40; 61-2610), inland and to the right from the ferry landing, is clean and pleasant. Its restaurant is open December through May.

Hotel Bahía Gigante (cold water, fans, pool; $20-$30; with kitchen and view, $40-$50; phone/fax: 61-2442), about 15 minutes south of Playa Naranjo on a gravel road, has condominiums on a hill overlooking the bay of the same name. Its restaurant, pool, and regular cabinas are behind the hill, making them rather landlocked and buggy.

GETTING THERE: *By Bus:* There is no bus service between Playa Naranjo and Paquera, to the south.

By Car: If you have a car, you can continue south from the ferry landing at Playa Naranjo to Paquera, Tambor, and Montezuma on the gulf side of the Nicoya Peninsula. There are several inexpensive and good *sodas* at the peninsula landing, as well as a gas station.

By Boat: A **ferryboat** (61-1069; 80 cents/adult, $5.50/car) leaves from the estuary at the far end of Puntarenas at 7 a.m., 11 a.m., and 4:30 p.m. every day. It returns daily at 9 a.m., 1 p.m., and 6 p.m. The hour-long ride takes you between verdant islands and makes you feel adventurous. Hungry seagulls follow the boat and catch food thrown at them in mid-air. Pelicans are plentiful, especially on the Puntarenas side. Snacks are sold on board. We arrived too late to get on the returning 1 p.m. ferry one Sunday, so parked our car in the line for the next ferry, locked it, and went swimming in the lovely pools of the Hotel Oasis (see below). We were then treated to a beautiful trip back across the gulf in the moonlight, which transformed the aging ferry into a romantic ocean liner. *Note:* If you have a car, be sure to get in line at least an hour and a half before the ferry leaves from either end, as only a limited number of cars can fit. Drivers only are allowed to enter the ferry in their cars. Passengers must walk on. For some reason, drivers have to give their passport or *cédula* number when buying a ticket, plus the license number of the car. A Nicoya bus meets the ferry, but it's a bumpy three-hour trip. It's better to take the Tempisque Ferry to Nicoya.

Paquera is a small town 45 minutes from Playa Naranjo by car. It has gas stations, food and clothing stores, and pharmacies. (See above for the ferry schedule to Paquera.)

In Paquera, **Cabinas Ginana** (cold water, private bath, ceiling fans; $7-$12; 61-1444, ext. 119) are clean and inexpensive and have a restaurant. Bring mosquito coils.

Curú Wildlife Refuge (61-2392, 26-4333) is located on a private farm 7 kilometers south of Paquera. Its beach is home to thousands of phantom crabs, one of which stole my watch while I was enjoying the warm, gentle waters of the picturesque, cup-shaped bay. Luckily we could see the watchband at the bottom of the nearest crab hole, and we fished it out with a stick. Snorkeling is supposed to be good there, but we didn't stay long enough to find out because no-see-ums and other nasty biting bugs were making mincemeat of us. Fortunately the effects of the bites were not long-lasting.

The farm has banana plantations that are specifically for wildlife, so it's not difficult to see howler and white-faced monkeys, *pizotes* (coatimundis), iguanas, and 115 species of birds from the five different hiking trails. (The trails are not well marked.) Three kinds of turtles nest on the beach. Because the reserve is on private land, it is necessary to call before arriving. Leave plenty of time to do this because the phone connections are very poor. There are primitive showers and toilets near the beach and very rustic accommodations for groups of students and researchers.

Bahía Ballena is a deep, round bay on the southeast end of the Nicoya Peninsula. Its waters are gentle and warm, but are not very clear near the shore. This bay is the site of a controversial large-scale beach hotel, being built by the Barceló family, owners of the San José Palacio in San José.

Hotel La Hacienda (cold water, ceiling fans, pool; $50-$60; 61-2980) is a peaceful resort. Its main claim to fame is its beautiful nonchlorinated freshwater pool, near shaded cabañas where you can relax and look out over the ocean (which is better to look at than to swim in). It also has horses for rent and a restaurant. Air transportation to the hotel's airstrip can be arranged. (Hotel La Hacienda, incidentally, is now owned by the Barceló family.)

In the village of **Tambor**, on the southern rim of the bay, is **Hotel Dos Lagartos** (cold water, some rooms with fans; with shared bath, $7-$12; with private bath, $12-$20; 61-1122, ext. 236), which is clean, friendly, low-key, and quiet (and has good mattresses). From the beach in front of the hotel you can see two points in the distance that resemble crocodiles or lizards, hence the name. The beach is nice for kids because the sand is spongy and the bay is shallow, with gentle waves. A river to the north fills the water with leaves, but beyond the breakers it's cleaner. The hotel is a great place for budget travelers, but there's no place to store or hang anything, and you should bring your own soap, towels, a universal plug for the sink, and a flashlight in case of power failure. There's a very annoying water pump that goes on and off every 30 seconds during the night, which you can hear from the rooms that face the ocean. We've never noticed any bugs there, however.

Down the beach from the hotel, **Pulpería Los Gitanos** is well stocked and friendly. Meals are plentiful, cheap, and good at **Cristina's,** across from the school.

The restaurant at the **Bahía Ballena Yacht Club,** on the marina at the southern end of the bay, features the world-class cuisine of Louisiana's Chef Bob, formerly of Tango Mar. Every night has a different theme: Creole, Cajun, Mexican, Country Cookin'. You can be sure the ingredients are fresh and the cuisine creative. The yacht club also arranges scuba diving, waterskiing, windsurfing, Hobie cat rentals, sightseeing tours, sunset cruises, and sea taxi services to such places as Herradura, Puntarenas, and Montezuma.

You can walk there along the beach or take the turnoff to the left as you leave Tambor. Half a kilometer beyond the restaurant the road dwindles to a trail. You can walk around the point 8 kilometers to Tango Mar, and see monkeys, iguanas, and seabirds along the way.

The marina at Bahía Ballena has a floating dock with fresh water, gas and diesel tanks to service boats, and 30 moorings. We were told that yacht books recommend going 250 miles out to sea to avoid the Papagayo winds off the northwestern coast of Costa Rica, then tacking in to the Gulf of Nicoya to refuel. This new marina eliminates the need to go all the way to Puntarenas.

Tango Mar (23-1864, 61-2798, fax: 55-2697) is a unique resort on a beautiful stretch of beach south of Bahía Ballena. Its one- or two-bedroom thatch-roofed cabinas (hot water, kitchen; $140-$160) are well designed and comfortable, and its new hotel rooms (hot water; $140-$160) are clean, well ventilated, and right on the beach. There are also standard villas (kitchens, two bedrooms, $200-$220, three bedrooms, $220-240) as well as two-bedroom beach villas (kitchens, $300-$320). Tango Mar boasts the only seaside golf course in Costa Rica and offers sportfishing, sailing, surfing, windsurfing, waterskiing, and beach volleyball. It also rents golfcarts, vans, and four-wheel motorcycles. Tango Mar will arrange to have you picked up in Paquera, or you can fly in from San José to its airstrip. By car, follow the signs south of Tambor. Reservations are required.

GETTING THERE: *By Bus:* Tambor is about an hour and a half from Paquera on the bus that meets the Puntarenas–Paquera boat daily, around 7:30 a.m. and 4:30 p.m. Tambor is an hour and a half south of Playa Naranjo by car. Tango Mar has signs out marking the road, so follow them to get to Tambor.

By Boat: A boat leaves the dock behind the market in Puntarenas at 6 a.m. and 3 p.m. for Paquera, across the gulf. It takes people only, no cars. A bus meets the boat and continues to Tambor and Cóbano, near Montezuma.

The 53-foot sailing yacht **Pegasus** has just inaugurated a passenger service (Monday and Friday only; $30 one way, $50 round-trip) between Playa Herradura, north of Jacó, and Tambor. The boat leaves from Tambor at 8 a.m., arriving at Herradura at 12 noon, and returns to Tambor at 1 p.m., arriving at 5 p.m. More trips will be added during high season. Call **Veleros del Sur** (61-1320) for more information.

Like other beautiful places in Costa Rica, **Montezuma** is having to adjust to its sudden fame as a tourist destination. Backpackers and campers have spread the word about its lovely rocky coves and waterfalls. Just to get there from San José is an adventure that can take a day or two. Because of the rocky coastline, it is not ideal for swimming, but the many tidepools lend themselves to a refreshing dip. There are shady places to camp at various beaches, but no toilets, so responsible campers should bring a foldable shovel and their own water and camp only in designated areas.

The first few rocky bays to the north of the village have very strong currents, especially during high tide. **Playa Grande**, about 30 minutes north by foot, is calm and shallow, the best and safest place for bathing. There's fresh water in a shower in the park behind Chico's Bar, and a few freshwater streams near pleasant campsites that you'll see as you walk along the beaches. Don't drink the water, and beware of hungry monkeys who will steal your food if you don't keep it in your tent. That ominous sound coming from under the dry leaves is probably just hermit crabs. There are some other nice places to camp south of the village, especially a few hundred meters south of Hotel Amor de Mar.

There is a **boatmen's cooperative** in Montezuma that arranges transportation across the gulf to Puntarenas, Jacó, Manuel Antonio, and Dominical, or around Cabo Blanco to Carrillo, Sámara, and Nosara (see the Guanacaste chapter). It also arranges tours to points of interest in the Montezuma area. Contact the cooperative through the information kiosk across from Hotel Moctezuma.

There's a gorgeous **waterfall** about 20 minutes south of town with a large pool that's nice for swimming. People like to cliff-dive there, but it's dangerous, so be very careful. A tourist slipped and fell to his death a few years ago. To get there, walk along the road to Cabo Blanco until you get to Restaurant La Cascada. At the bridge, head upstream over the rocks for half a kilometer or so.

If it's the dry season, call for lodging reservations beforehand. The number for the whole town is 61-1122; an operator will connect you with the extensions given below.

At the entrance to town, to the right, is **El Jardín** (cold water, private bath, fans; $12-$20; ext. 284). **Tútiles** (open for dinner only), on the corner, serves authentic Italian specialties including pizza.

As you turn toward the beach, you'll see **Cabinas Karen** (no fans; under $7; no phone), a white house with simple rooms and cooking facilities. Doña Karen, who, with her late husband, was responsible for founding the Cabo Blanco Reserve, also offers simple cabinas (under $7) with shared kitchens and baths set back in the forest on a beach north of town.

Next comes **El Sano Banano** (ext. 272), a pleasant vegetarian restaurant that shows videos on a large screen at night. It also prepares sack lunches and sells filtered water.

On the inland side of the church is **Hotel Montezuma Pacific** (both cold and heated water, private bath; with ceiling fans, $20-$30; with air-conditioning, $30-$40; ext. 200, or 22-7746), the only place in town with air-conditioning. The peaceful ◎ **Cabinas El Sano Banano** (cold water, private bath, ceiling fans; $30-$40; with refrigerator, $40-$50; with kitchen, $50-$60; off-season discounts; ext. 272) in the woods behind the second beach to the north, owned by the same people who own the Sano Banano.

Hotel Moctezuma (fans; with shared bath, $7-$12; with private bath, $12-$20; no phone) tends to be noisy because of Chico's bar next door, but has a good restaurant. In back of Chico's are **Cabinas Mar y Cielo** (private bath, fans; $12-$20; no phone), which are right on the beach. **El Pargo Feliz,** 50 meters north of Chico's, has good fish and lobster dinners.

El Caracol (under $7; no phone), 100 meters south of the village, serves seafood and *casados* and rents primitive thatched-roofed huts on stilts. **Cabinas Las Arenas** (shared bath, natural breeze or fan; under $7; no phone) on the beach to the south have small rooms that are okay if you have quiet neighbors. They provide a grill and firewood for guests. On the other side of the point to the south are **Casa de Huéspedes Alfaro** (cold water, private bath, fans; $12-$20; ext. 259), which has a *soda*, and **Hotel Lucy** (cold water, shared bath; under $7; ext. 273) has breezy rooms.

Hotel Amor de Mar (cold water, table fans; with shared bath, $20-$30; with private bath, $30-$40; with kitchen, $40-$50; ext. 262) features quiet rooms, spacious grounds, its own private tidepool, and hammocks hung under trees overlooking a stream that flows into the ocean. The restaurant (open for breakfast and lunch) serves homemade bread. It's located a few hundred meters south of Lucy's.

Fresh fruits and vegetables are delivered to Montezuma four times a week. The well-stocked *pulpería* **Manantial** will prepare fileted and seasoned fish for you to grill (be careful of gringo prices there).

GETTING THERE: *By Bus:* Take a bus to Puntarenas. From the dock behind the Mercado in Puntarenas take the *lancha* (boat) to Paquera ($1), which leaves at 6 a.m. and 3 p.m. Two public buses wait for the *lancha* at Paquera. Be sure to take the one marked *Directo* ($3), which makes the trip to Cóbano down a bumpy road, through beautiful country, in about an hour and a half. There is a private bus from Hotel Alfaro, which also meets the ferry but costs a bit more. During the dry season the bus goes all the way to Montezuma. Otherwise, take a jeep-taxi the remaining 7 kilometers from Cóbano. If you want to take the 6 a.m. boat, you'll have to spend the night in Puntarenas. The boat returns to Puntarenas from Paquera at 8 a.m. and 5 p.m. Buses leave Montezuma for Paquera at 5:30 a.m. and 2 p.m.

By Car: It is not really necessary to have a car to go to Montezuma, but if you do, take it on the big ferry from Puntarenas to Playa Naranjo and follow the road south to Paquera. Turn left about a kilometer beyond Paquera, at the Tango Mar sign. Continue one hour to Cóbano and turn left when you see the Cabo Blanco sign. The trip takes about two and a half hours, all on gravel roads. Montezuma is about 45 minutes south of Tambor.

Don't try to go in a regular car if it has been raining. You have to ford a couple of streams, and the hills become treacherous. The worst section is the last hill that goes down to Montezuma, which becomes a mountain of slippery mud. Regular cars will be okay if it hasn't rained for a few days. Only the beaches and campsites south of the village are accessible by car. You have to hike to the beaches north of town.

Howler monkey

We explored the road going west to Río Negro and Manzanillo from Cóbano on our way to Playa Sámara in Guanacaste. You have to ford several rivers, and sometimes the road fades into little more than a trail, but we made it through. Just keep asking people if you're going the right way—there are no signs. We would have made it to Sámara in about four hours by jeep if we hadn't hit the Río Ora at high tide.

A road continues south from Montezuma through Cabuya and on to **Cabo Blanco Wildlife Reserve.** You have to ford two streams, which cannot be crossed in a regular car at high tide; the 12-kilometer trip takes over an hour by four-wheel drive. Cabo Blanco was the first national reserve in Costa Rica—its founding in the late 1960s was the initial step in the development of the country's extensive national park system. Preserved with the encouragement of a Danish biologist who was concerned about the encroaching deforestation that was threatening the area's rich and varied wildlife, it is an "absolute reserve," which means that most of the area is accessible only to scientific researchers.

Stop at the ranger station to get an entrance permit. You can take a fairly strenuous two-hour hike up the *Sendero Sueco* and down to Playa Balsitas. (Bring food and plenty of water.) Hike left around the point to Playa Cabo Blanco for another two-hour hike back.

At high tide you won't be able to make it around the point, so ask the guards about tides before you leave. You'll see lots of howler monkeys. (Don't stand directly underneath them—they like to pee on sightseers.) There are pelican colonies on either side of the point, which has beautiful pinkish coral sand.

MONTEVERDE RESERVE

The road to the Monteverde Reserve from the turnoff on the Interamerican Highway is rough, steep, and dusty. It's a two-hour climb through sadly deforested country until you reach the green pastures that lead to the famous cloud forest reserve. Many Monteverdeans would like to keep the road that way: they not only want to preserve the cloud forest in its natural state, they also want to protect the simple, friendly lifestyle that has made their community such a special place. Many communities in Costa Rica have opened to tourism quickly over the last few years because they desperately need the business, but some things have been lost in the process.

The town of **Monteverde**, because it has always concerned itself with social issues, is perhaps more articulate about these problems than most rural villages being overwhelmed by tourism. A group of Alabama Quakers who felt that Costa Rica's disarmament policy was in line with their pacifist tradition started dairy farming in Monteverde in the early 1950s. Visiting biologists found the cloud forest above their community rich in flora and fauna, and the Quakers, along with the Tropical Science Center, had the foresight to make it a reserve.

Monteverde Reserve (field station open daily, 7 a.m. to 4 p.m.; closed October 6 and 7; admission $7.50, discount for students with ID and residents, no charge for children under 15) is not a place you can visit in one day. You need a day for travel and recovery each way, plus at least one day to visit the reserve. A self-guiding pamphlet is available at the field station for a few dollars, and guided four-hour nature walks ($12.50/person) are given by naturalists who have years of experience here. Meet the guides at the field station at 7:30 a.m. (Part of the park's fees for the tours go to environmental education programs.)

In order to protect the forest, only 100 people can be in the reserve at one time. If you'd like to miss the crowds, avoid the peak hours: 8 to 10 a.m. The least crowded months are sometime between May and December, although it is rainier during that time. You can buy your entrance ticket the day before, so that you can arrive at dawn (5 to 5:30 a.m.), which is the best time to observe the bird population.

The cloud forest stretches from the lush ferns and mosses that cover the ground to the dark canopy formed by the tallest trees. Vines and weblike moss hang down and swing slowly in the breeze. Some of the trees look top-heavy because their branches are so densely enveloped with epiphytes and moss.

Quetzales feed on the tiny, avocadolike fruits of *aguacatillo* trees. They are most visible in the early morning from January through September, especially during the mating season in April and May. Beautiful and strange frogs also live in the cloud forest, but they're very difficult for the inexperienced forest wanderer to spot. The golden toad, endemic to the Monteverde area, is remarkable for its color and the poison glands behind its ears, but it has not been observed for the last few years and is feared to be extinct.

The popularity of the Monteverde Reserve has given impetus to the preservation of several other similar areas nearby:

The **Reserva Sendero Tranquilo** is run by David Lowther on his family's farm in Monteverde. Only two to six people are allowed in each group, so that a maximum of 12 people will be in the 200-acre reserve at one time. Groups are for the most part silent when in the forest, and visitors are usually pleased with the amount of wildlife they see. Make reservations through the Sapo Dorado (61-2952).

The 900-acre **Santa Elena Rainforest**, 5 kilometers northeast of the nearby town of Santa Elena, has 4 kilometers of trails through rain- and cloud forest, a lookout point to Volcán Arenal, and local guides. Ask at your hotel for current information.

Cañitas, a few minutes north of Santa Elena on the road to Tilarán, has a *trapiche*, where sugarcane is pressed to remove the juice, which is then boiled down into *dulce*, a delicious and nutritious hard brown sugar. Nearby, in **Los Tornos**, is an abandoned gold mine with chalk and crystal deposits. Cañitas is definitely off the beaten track, but has lodging, restaurants, a craft store, horse rentals, and guides to take you to nearby forests. On the way to Cañitas, a fork to the right leads to **San Gerardo Abajo**, where the Quesada family has rustic cabins with an amazing view of Volcán Arenal and the lake. Call for reservations (61-2757) and horse rentals. The trip takes three hours on horseback—San Gerardo Abajo is accessible by car between February and May only.

The **Butterfly Garden** (open daily, 9:30 a.m. to 4 p.m.; admission $5) is a section of forest at a lower altitude than the Monteverde Reserve that has been covered with a fine screen. There you can see all the different species of butterflies that inhabit the zone, including the beautiful blue morpho. You're likely to see more there on a sunny day than a cloudy one. Guides give a fascinating explanation of the habits of each species, with ample botanical information as well. At the entrance is a free exhibit about the butterfly's life cycle. To get there, follow the small butterfly-shaped signs that start across from the Hotel Heliconia on the road to Monteverde. Take the dirt road to the right 600 meters, turn left, then go another 300 meters.

Children from all over the world have been inspired by the efforts of a group of Swedish fourth-graders who organized the first **Children's Rainforest** campaign in 1987, in response to a presentation at their school by a biologist from the **Monteverde Conservation League** (open daily, 8 a.m. to 12 noon; Monday through Friday, 1 to 5 p.m.; 61-2953, fax: 61-1104; Apdo. 10165, 1000 San José). Since then, schoolchildren from Costa Rica, Europe, Japan, and the United States have raised money to buy 23,000 acres of rainforest on the Atlantic slope behind the reserve and are negotiating the purchase of 23,000 more. Besides on-going programs in environmental education, reforestation, and protection, the league also has an ambitious plan to link up remnant patches of forest (especially near rivers) to make green corridors that will ensure the continued existence of habitats for migratory birds and butterflies. Donors of $25 or more receive the Conservation League's quarterly newsletter, *Tapir Tracks*. The league's office is across from the gas station as you enter Monteverde.

For arts and crafts, be sure to stop by **CASEM**, a cooperative of local women who make beautiful embroidered and hand-painted clothing and souvenirs portraying quetzales, golden toads, and other cloud forest flora and fauna. It's located on the right next to the food coop as you enter Monteverde. Across the street, above the stables, is the studio-gallery of Monteverde artists Stella Wallace and Meg Laval. You can also see their paintings at the Monteverde Lodge in Santa Elena. Watercolor paintings by resident artist Sarah Dowell are also exhibited in local hotels. Visitors are welcome to tour her studio, a short hike above the cheese factory.

The **Hummingbird Gallery** (61-1259), near the entrance to the reserve, exhibits Michael and Patricia Fogden's photographs from around the world. The Fogdens spend months at a time with sloths, frogs, snakes, insects, and birds, trying to get just the right shot. You'll never see better wildlife photographs. They also sell beautiful and inexpensive Guatemalan textiles, T-shirts, and high-energy snacks for the trail.

Don't miss the Fogdens' spellbinding slide show about Costa Rican rainforest wildlife, presented at the Hummingbird Gallery. The entrance fee goes to preserve and enlarge a quetzal habitat on the Pacific slope.

Monteverde is now the Tanglewood of Central America with the initiation of a series of **sunset concerts** presented by top members of Costa Rica's National Symphony Orchestra and international artists. It's a great opportunity to hear these fine musicians without having to go to San José. Visitors are bussed from their hotels to the concerts, which begin at 5 p.m. during the dry season.

Mount Cycle Adventures (61-1007, 61-0957) in Santa Elena offers tours by mountain bike. Almost all hotels arrange tours on horseback.

The famous **Monteverde cheese factory** (open Monday through Saturday, 7:30 a.m. to 12 noon, 1 to 3:30 p.m.; Sunday, 7:30 a.m. to 12:30 p.m.) gives tours daily, 9 to 11 a.m. and Monday through Saturday, 1:30 to 3 p.m. It sells delicious cheddar, jack, Gouda, and other cheeses for less than San José prices. You can also buy great homemade whole-wheat bread and rolls, fresh milk, and *cajeta* (scrumptious milk fudge) there.

LODGING AND RESTAURANTS   The huge, white **Monteverde Lodge** (hot water, bathtubs; $70-$80; meals $35/day; 57-0766, 61-1157, fax: 57-1665,

61-2651) glints from the hills near Santa Elena, a town 6 kilometers from Monteverde Reserve. The lodge, built especially to accommodate tour groups from Costa Rica Expeditions, is spacious and comfortable. It features an indoor atrium with a large jacuzzi in which guests can relax after their trek through the chilly cloud forest. A multimedia slide show incorporating sounds of the rainforest is shown several times a week. Bus service to San José from the lodge is $30, one way.

In Santa Elena you'll find some inexpensive and comfortable pensiones. **Pensión Santa Elena** ($7-$12/person including meals; 61-1151) is basic but fairly clean and features home cooking. The **Tucán** (heated water, private bath; $20-$30/person including meals; 61-1007), around the corner, has clean hillside cabinas with porches and other homey touches. It also rents rooms farther down the street (shared bath; $12-$20; 61-1007). The **Pensión Colibrí** (heated water, shared bath; under $7/person including two meals; 61-2757), across the street from the Tucán cabinas, has wooden balconies. At the end of the same street is the **Hotel Arco Iris** (heated water, both private and shared baths; $20-$30; 61-2757), which has a restaurant. The Arco Iris and the Tucán's new cabinas are the best places to stay in Santa Elena proper.

Hospedaje El Banco (heated water, shared bath; $7-$12; no phone), behind the Banco Nacional, is basic but friendly. The basic **Pensión El Sueño** (heated water; with shared bath, $7-$12/person; with private bath, $12-$20/person; no phone) consists of rooms connected to a family's house, next to the Salon Parroquial, around the corner from the church. Two meals are included in rates.

The cloud forest is a windy 6 kilometers from Santa Elena, but there is usually enough friendly traffic to try hitching, at least part of the way. Taxi service from Santa Elena to the reserve costs about $6.

✪ **El Sapo Dorado** (Golden Toad) is a friendly hotel/bar/restaurant between Santa Elena and Monteverde. It features spacious, comfortable, well-designed cabins (hot water, private bath; $60-$70; off-season discount; phone/fax: 61-2952) with fireplaces. The restaurant (open daily, 7 to 10 a.m., 12 noon to 3 p.m., and 6 to 9 p.m.) features healthful and tasty cuisine and always has a vegetarian selection on the menu. It serves elegant sunset suppers, accompanied by classical music, on a terrace overlooking the gulf. Occasionally at night they play a variety of taped music for dancing. You'll see the Sapo Dorado sign shortly after leaving Santa Elena. The hotel is about 300 meters up the hill on the left.

A few hundred meters past the Sapo Dorado is **Pensión Heliconia** (hot water, private bath; $40-$50; phone/fax: 61-1009), a wooden building with balconies, a restaurant, and a comfortable, homey atmosphere. Next door is **El Establo** (hot water, private bath; $50-$60 including breakfast; phone/fax: 61-2851, 25-0569), with good beds and carpeted rooms.

About 100 meters farther along the main road, you'll find a road to the right, which leads to **Pensión Manakín** (heated water, both private and shared baths; $7-$12 without meals; $12-$20 including two meals; 61-2854), one of the most basic and inexpensive hotels near Monteverde.

Hotel de Montaña Monteverde (hot water, private bath; $50-$60; 61-1846, fax: 22-6184) has a sauna and jacuzzi, a restaurant, views of the Gulf of Nicoya, and a private reserve with nature trails. It is overpriced compared to other lodging in the area.

On the left is the entrance to **Cabañas Los Pinos** (hot water, private bath, kitchen; $30-$40; 61-0905, 61-2952), separate cabins in a peaceful setting—a good value. The chalet-style **Belmar** (hot water, private bath; $50-$60; phone/fax: 61-1001) has beautiful views, comfortable rooms, and a good restaurant. Its entrance is uphill from the gas station on the left.

Where the main road turns right, you'll find the **Soda Manantial**, which has a view over the stream and is popular with students and volunteers. It also rents basic rooms (under $7; no phone). **Bar Restaurante La Cascada**, across the road, has a nice view, lots of wood and windows, and moderate prices.

At this point, you still have not arrived in the community of Monteverde, and when you do you might not realize it, because Monteverde is not really a town. Most houses are back in the woods where you don't see them, and are connected by footpaths.

On the right as you enter Monteverde, **Hotel and Restaurant El Bosque** (hot water, private bath; $20-$30; 61-1258, fax: 61-2559) is a bargain in its price range. A few meters down the road is a well-stocked food store and CASEM, the crafts cooperative.

The next entrance on the right is to **Pensión Quetzal** (with heated water and shared bath, $20-$30/person; with hot water and private bath, $30-$40/ person; 61-0955). The oldest lodge in Monteverde, it has cozy, wood-panelled rooms and some newer cabinas. Rates include three meals. The Conservation League's **Bajo Tigre Nature Trail** (admission $1, including self-guiding map) is about 100 meters from the Pensión Quetzal.

Out on the road again, you'll see the cheese plant up ahead. The **Pensión Flor-Mar** (heated water; with shared bath, $40-$50/person; with private bath, $50-$60/person; phone/fax: 61-0909) is about 200 meters beyond the bridge to the right, where the road turns left to go to the reserve. Rates include three meals.

A few hundred meters up the hill, toward the reserve, is the ✪ **Hotel Fonda Vela** (hot water, private bath; $40-$50; $50-$60 for suites; 57-1413, 61-2551, fax: 57-1416), which has a secluded camping area, a meeting room, and views of the gulf and the forest. Its restaurant (open 6:15 to 9 a.m., 12 noon to 2 p.m., and 6 to 8:30 p.m.) is excellent.

Across the road is the **Hospedaje Mariposa** (heated water, private bath; $12-$20; 61-1153). **Hotel Villa Verde** (heated water; with shared bath, $12-$20/person; with private bath, $20-$30/person; 61-1255) is on the road to the reserve after the Fonda Vela. Meals are included in rates.

All of the above hotels will bag breakfasts and lunches for birders and hikers, and prepare vegetarian meals on request. Laundry services, horse and boat rental, transportation to the reserve, and tours to nearby points of interest are also available through the hotels.

Monteverde Reserve is a 30-minute uphill walk from the Fonda Vela. The **Reserve Field Station** sometimes has room in its dormitories (heated water, shared bath, $20-$30/person including three meals; 61-2655) for students or researchers. You must make reservations with a 30 percent deposit 45 days in advance.

Note: Many Monteverde hotels are completely booked by tour companies from December through May, the best time to go. Most of the hotels require a deposit to secure a room, usually the cost of one night's stay. Your best bet would be to call or fax the hotels to confirm the availability of space, then send a deposit at least six weeks before you plan to arrive. Christmas and Easter are booked months in advance. Write all of the above hotels at Apdo. 10165, 1000 San José.

Bring rain gear, warm clothes, and good socks. Most hotels rent rubber boots. Be sure to dress in layers for the trip up and down. You forget when you are in cool, windy Monteverde how swelteringly hot you'll be by the time you get to the Interamerican Highway.

GETTING THERE: *By Bus:* There are three options by bus:

A bus leaves San José from the Tilarán terminal (Calle 12, Avenidas 9/11; 22-3854; $4) for Monteverde at 2:30 p.m. Monday through Thursday, and Saturday at 6:30 a.m. Buy tickets in advance. It returns to San José Tuesday through Thursday at 6:30 a.m. and Friday, Saturday, and Sunday at 3 p.m. Buy return tickets as soon as you get there through the Hotel El Bosque (61-1258, 61-1152). Don't wait until the last minute because these buses serve the entire community and are often very crowded. Seats are numbered. The return bus leaves from the cheese factory, but will pick up ticket holders along the way. For current schedules, check with your hotel when making reservations.

There is also a daily bus from Puntarenas to Santa Elena, 3 kilometers from Monteverde. It leaves Puntarenas at 2:15 p.m., turns off the Interamerican Highway at the Río Lagarto around 3:30 p.m., and arrives in Santa Elena around 5:30 p.m. You can leave San José on the 10 a.m. Puntarenas bus (Calle 12, Avenida 9), arrive in Puntarenas around 12:30 p.m., have a leisurely lunch (be careful of the water, natural fruit drinks, drinks served with ice, and raw fruits and vegetables) and catch the Santa Elena bus on the oceanfront, one block from the *San José–Puntarenas* bus station. If you are in Manuel Antonio, you can take an early *Quepos–Puntarenas* bus to connect with the 2:15 p.m. Santa Elena bus, which returns to Puntarenas daily at 6 a.m. Hotels in the Monteverde area will send a taxi to meet you in Santa Elena if you have made reservations. The 12:45 p.m. *San José–Tilarán* bus (Calle 12, Avenidas 9/11; 22-3854) connects with the *Puntarenas–Santa Elena* bus at the Lagarto turnoff around 3:15 p.m. Buy tickets a half hour in advance.

If you are coming from the north, any San José-bound bus will let you off at Lagarto, where you can intercept the Santa Elena bus.

During the school year (March through November) you can catch a **milk truck** from Santa Elena to Cabeceras, from which you can catch a bus to **Tilarán**, a clean, pleasant town a half hour uphill from Cañas where the weather is much cooler. The whole trip takes about three hours. Check at the Restaurant Imán (61-1255) in Santa Elena for current information. If you stay overnight in Tilarán, you can catch a bus to San Carlos that passes Volcán Arenal.

By Car: Turn off the Interamerican Highway at the Río Lagarto, about a half hour north of the Puntarenas turnoff. Go uphill from there for one and a half to two hours. Try not to be astounded by the bad condition of the road. (**Chino's**, on the left a few kilometers before you get to Lagarto is an inexpensive place to stop for a drink on your way up or down the mountain. It has clean, locked bathrooms. There is a *pulpería* and *soda* at Lagarto, but their facilities leave much to be desired.)

If you don't mind even worse roads, you can also travel by car from Tilarán to Monteverde by way of Quebrada Grande, Cabeceras, and Santa Elena. In Cabeceras you can choose to go straight, through Turín, or uphill to the left through Las Nubes. Both routes have beautiful scenery—the Las Nubes route is 2 kilometers longer and gorgeous—and are in equally terrible condition. The trip takes two and a half hours. Even though this route looks much shorter on the map, you don't save that much time because the roads are so difficult. From Tilarán to the Lagarto turnoff by way of Cañas and the Interamerican Highway is only an hour and a half. Paved roads make all the difference.

Playa Doña Ana is a small beach 2 kilometers south of Puntarenas that has been developed by the Tourism Institute. It has covered picnic tables, dressing rooms and showers, and a restaurant with blasting music that competes with the sound of the waves. Surfers say the waves at Doña Ana and Boca Barranca are great. **Hotel Río Mar** (private bath; $12-$20; 63-0158), which has a restaurant, is on the left just before Doña Ana. Buses from Puntarenas to Mata Limón, Jacó, Orotina, and Quepos pass by the entrance. The turnoff for Playa Doña Ana is right before the overpass on your way out of Puntarenas. The signs are not well placed.

Located near Orotina, **Carara Biological Reserve**, southeast of Puntarenas, is in a transitional area between the dry climate of Guanacaste and the humid climate of the southern coast. It has wildlife common to both regions, like macaws, toucans, trogons, waterfowl, monkeys, alligators, crocodiles, armadillos, sloths, and peccaries. Jaguars, pumas, ocelots, jaguarundis, and margays are also present, but rarely seen. No camping is allowed in the reserve. Tourists are only allowed on certain trails, but can go with professional guides into restricted areas. **Geotur** (34-1867) in San José specializes in guided nature tours to Carara. You can get to Carara Biological Reserve on any Jacó or Quepos bus.

PLAYAS HERRADURA AND JACÓ

Besides Puntarenas, *playas* Jacó and Herradura are the closest beaches to San José. **Playa Herradura** is right after the Río Caña Blanca, about 7 kilometers north of Jacó, and 3 kilometers down a gravel road from the main highway. It is smaller than Jacó, its waves are gentler, and it has more shade and good trees for hammocks. Fishing boats anchor in the bay, near the dock that was built for the filming of the movie *Columbus.*

Cabinas Herradura (cold water, private bath, table fans, kitchen; $20-$30; 64-3181), on the beach, are basic and some have room for up to ten people. **Cabañas del Río** (cold water, table fans, kitchen; $20-$30; 64-3029) are neat *casitas* with two bedrooms upstairs and a small porch. They are about 400 meters from the beach.

A few kilometers north of Herradura is **Punta Leona**, which until recently was a private club, but is now open to the public. **Hotel Punta Leona** (hot water, private bath, ceiling fans and air-conditioning, pool; $50-$60; with kitchens, $90-$100; 31-3131, fax: 32-0791) has access to several lovely beaches, restaurants, a disco, soccer fields, and basketball courts.

Playa Jacó is long and wide and much more developed than Herradura. As in most "civilized" areas, it's not wise to swim in the estuary or near river mouths. The rip currents there can be dangerous, so don't swim alone. In fact, it's best to consider Jacó a wading beach. In a country full of tropical paradises, Jacó certainly does not stand out, but if you like sun and fun, surfing and beer-drinking contests, and you want to get to the beach and back as fast as possible, Jacó is for you.

The Tourism Institute has created the **Núcleo Turístico BriBri** (40 cents/person) there, which offers parking, locked closets, bathrooms, and showers for those who visit for the day. Sometimes it's hard to rouse the administrator, and the bathrooms are not that clean. The pizza is good at the **Pizzería Bribri** (open evenings and for lunch on weekends), next door. It is to the right at the second entrance after Hotel Jacó Beach.

Surfers use Jacó as a base for trips to nearby beaches like **Boca Barranca** (very long left wave), *playas* **Tivives** and **Valor** (rights and lefts), **Escondida** (accessible by boat from Jacó), **Playa Hermosa** (very strong beach break 3 kilometers south of Jacó), the site of an annual surfing contest, and *playas* **Esterillos Este, Esterillos Oeste, Bejuco,** and **Boca Damas,** which are all on the way to Quepos. Many hotels give surfers discounts from May to December.

LODGING AND RESTAURANTS   There are plenty of hotels, cabinas, and campsites in Jacó. Many have kitchenettes complete with utensils. They give substantial discounts during the off-season, and Jacó is often sunny when it's raining in San José. All of the following establishments are off Jacó's main street, which runs parallel to the beach. We'll mention them in order of their appearance, north to south.

Centro Vacacional Bancosta (cold water, ceiling fans, screens; $30-$40; with kitchens, $40-$50; 64-3116) is right on the beach next to the estuary at the extreme north end of Jacó. It provides live calypso music on Thursday and Sunday. **Cabinas Gaby** (hot water, ceiling fans, $20-$30; with kitchen, $30-$40; 41-9926, 64-3080, fax: 41-5922), is 100 meters south and right on the beach. The nearby German-owned **Hotel Pochote Grande** (both hot and heated water, private bath, table fans, small pool; $40-$50; 64-3236) has a restaurant, shady grounds, and good-sized rooms with lots of windows, making it one of the best hotels at this end of the beach.

Cabinas Antonio (cold water, private bath, ceiling fans; $7-$12; 64-3043) and its shady **Restaurant Fragatas** are clean, relatively quiet, and a good bargain for this area. They are next to the main bus stop. **Cabinas Las Palmas** (both heated and cold water, private bath, ceiling fans, screens; $20-$30 in older, darker cabinas; with kitchen, $30-$40; 64-3005; English, Ukrainian, German, Spanish, and Russian spoken) are between the main boulevard and the beach on a dead-end road, west and north of Cabinas Antonic. They feature quiet, pretty gardens and enclosed parking.

The Belgian-owned **Hotel El Jardín** (hot water, private bath, ceiling fans, pool; $30-$40; $12-$20 in off-season; 64-3050), on the beach 100 meters from the bus stop, is clean, comfortable, and quiet. Rates include breakfast. Its rather pricey restaurant is one of the best dinner spots in Jacó, featuring flame-cooked brochettes, a salad bar, and live jazz every other weekend.

Directly north of the Hotel El Jardín, **Cabinas y Restaurante Clarita** (cold water, private bath, ceiling fans; $7-$12; 64-3013) have a very Costa Rican feeling and seem off the beaten track even though they're on such a popular beach. The rooms are dark and basic, but are right on the water. The clean restaurant has a beautiful view and a reasonably priced menu.

Next is **Hotel Jacó Beach** (hot water, air-conditioning; $70-$80; 20-1441, fax: 32-3159, in North America: 800-27-2664), which features a large, circular pool; a discotheque; and rentals of cars, bicycles, mopeds, surfboards, sailboats, kayaks, and tennis equipment. It works directly with travel agencies that charter flights from Canada, so it is very busy. Musak is piped into the main floor, so you feel like you're in a shopping mall, and CNN shows all day on lobby TVs. Rates include breakfast in the off-season.

The same owners have recently built the **Jacó Princess** across the street—28 villas with full kitchens. They will look better when the landscaping is in place.

Just down the beach, **Restaurante El Gran Palenque** offers good food and excellent service. It has a wide selection of wines and a pleasant atmosphere complete with Spanish guitar music. Entrées start at $4.

Cabinas García (cold water, private bath, table fans; $12-$20; 64-3191), on the boulevard 300 meters south of Hotel Jacó Beach, is clean but lacks atmosphere. Around the corner, **Hotel Lido** (cold water, private bath, table fans, no screens, kitchen without refrigerator; $20-$30; 64-3171) hasn't given much attention to decor or comfort.

Recommended for budget travelers, **Cabinas Emily** (cold water, ceiling fans, screens; with shared bath, $7-$12; with private bath, $12-$20; 64-3328) have the motto, "a friend in Costa Rica." They are basically a surfers' hostel, and provide surfing information and repairs. Located right on the main boulevard, Cabinas Emily will arrange transportation from San José.

Cabinas Las Sirenas (cold water, private bath, ceiling fans; $20-$30; 64-3193), located between the boulevard and the beach, are a good value for groups. The two-bedroom cabinas sleep six to eight. **Tangerí Chalets** have three bedrooms, kitchens, and pools for adults and children. They prefer to rent by the week. **Hotel Tangerí** (hot water, private bath, ceiling fans or air-conditioning, refrigerator; $70-$80; $50-$60 in off-season; 64-3001, fax: 42-1160) is next door.

Cabinas Pacific Sur (cold water, private bath, ceiling fans, screens; $20-$30; 64-3340) are halfway between the boulevard and the beach, to the right after the second small bridge. Owned by a native of Jacó, they are neat and clean but lack atmosphere and are slightly overpriced for the area.

Next door, the Texas-owned **Los Ranchos** (hot water, private bath, ceiling fans, screens, pool, laundry service; phone/fax: 64-3070) attracts young people and surfers. It has upstairs suites ($20-$30), rooms with kitchenettes ($30-$40), and two-story cabins ($40-$80) that sleep six to eight with kitchens. The owners are friendly and give good surfing information. Recommended. Be aware that the Papagayo disco next door can be rather loud at night.

Cabinas Cindy (cold water, private bath, table and ceiling fans, screens; $7-$12; no phone) are basic rooms behind the owner's house, down the next street to the right from the boulevard. They have a mean dog. **Hotel Bohio** has seven new apartments (cold water, ceiling fans, kitchen; $30-$40; 64-3017) and eight older and rather run-down cabinas (cold water, private bath, ceiling fans, murky pool; $12-$20) right on the beach.

The Belgian-owned **Villas Miramar** (hot water, ceiling fans, kitchen, pools; $30-$40; $50-$60 for the largest villas; 64-3003), in a garden setting, is one of the loveliest and most tranquil places in Jacó. It is located down the next road to your right after Hotel Bohio. **Apartotel Flamboyant** (hot water, private bath, ceiling fans, kitchen; $40-$50; 64-3146, fax: 64-3250), recently built by Jan Dankers, the original owner of the Miramar, is tastefully designed and located right on the beach. There are a coin-operated laundry and a public telephone just north of the Apartotel Flamboyant's driveway.

Cabinas Zabamar (private bath, screens; with cold water and ceiling fans, $30-$40; with hot water and air-conditioning, $50-$60; 64-3174) all have front patios built around one of the cleanest pools in Jacó. They also have two pools for children. **Camping El Hicaco** ($3; 64-3004) has campsites near the beach and a nice-looking restaurant. A block from the beach, **Cabinas Recreo** (cold water, private bath, ceiling fans, screens, pool; $12-$20; 64-3012) are next to the Banco Nacional. They are basic cement boxes owned by friendly local people. On the beach, **Hotel Cocal** (hot water, private bath, ceiling fans, pools; $30-$40; with kitchen, $40-$50; 64-3067, fax: 64-3082) is your standard beach hotel—clean, with pretty gardens and a restaurant.

Las Gaviotas (hot water, private bath, ceiling fans, pool; $50-$60; 64-3092, fax: 64-3054) is clean and pretty. Rooms have patios and kitchenettes. It's 250 meters from the beach, 100 meters north and 50 meters east of the Banco Nacional. **Cabinas Alice** (cold water, private bath, ceiling fans; older cabins, $20-$30; new cabins nearer the beach with kitchens and more light, $50-$60 or $270/week; 64-3061, 37-1412) are toward the beach from the Red Cross. Doña Alice serves good food at shady outdoor tables.

Casas de Playa Mar Sol (cold water, private bath, table fans, kitchen; $30-$40; 64-3008), 150 meters south of the Cruz Roja, have small, murky wading pools in front of each house. Half a block toward the beach, **Apartamentos El Mar** (hot water, private bath, ceiling fans, kitchen, pool; $50-$60; 64-3165, 78-1098) are secure, clean, and spacious. They are often full in the high season.

Hotel Jacofiesta (hot water, air-conditioning, cable TV, pools; $70-$80; 64-3147, fax: 64-3148) is one of the largest in Jacó. Unfortunately it is built next to the estuary. Cheerfully painted on the outside with a broad blue stripe at the base of white walls in the style of a *casa típica*, it has a restaurant and light and airy rooms with efficient kitchenettes. Across the street, **Chalets Santa Ana** (hot water, private bath, ceiling fans, screens; $20-$30 for up to five people; with kitchen, $30-$40; 64-3233) are not on the beach but are nice enough and a good deal for groups. **Restaurante y Cabinas El Naranjal** (hot water, private bath, ceiling fans, screens; with one bedroom, $30-$40; with two bedrooms, $40-$50; 64-3006), next to the Catholic church, are very clean.

The **Marparaíso** (cold water, private bath, ceiling fans, pools; $40-$50; 21-6544, 64-3025), which has a restaurant and a jacuzzi, is located toward the far end of the beach. It's very popular, but its design creates a crowded, closed-in feeling and it's rather run-down for a semiluxurious hotel. New rooms are being built that may be nicer.

Beyond it are **Cabinas Madrigal** (cold water, private bath, no fans; $7-$12; 64-3230), which has funky rooms, a greasy restaurant, and shady campsites ($1.50/night) with toilets, showers, makeshift tables, and barbecue pits.

About two blocks inland from Cabinas Madrigal, where the street connects with the main highway to Quepos, is **El Bosque**, a nice place for breakfast. On a quiet cove at the far end of the beach is ✪ **Hotel Club del Mar** (both hot and heated water; private bath, table fans, pool; $50-$60; 64-3194). Each of its tastefully designed and furnished apartments have a bedroom, kitchen, living room, dining area, and private balcony overlooking the bay. It has a restaurant and even has a good library. Highly recommended. Swimming is probably safer here than at any other part of the beach.

Hotel Hacienda Lilipoza (hot water, private bath, air-conditioning, phone, cable TV, pool; no children under 16; $180-$200 including breakfast; 64-3062, fax: 64-3158) is the most luxurious and aesthetically designed hotel in the area. Each room has a different color scheme and is furnished in wicker, bamboo, and wood. It has tennis courts and a restaurant (which is open to the public). The Swiss chef prepares international dishes, including Texas barbecue. Hotel Hacienda Lilipoza is located in the hills south of Jacó (not much view), 600 meters inland from the Quepos–Puntarenas highway.

GETTING THERE: *By Bus:* San José–Jacó buses (64-3074, $2) leave the Coca Cola at 7:30 a.m. and 3:30 p.m., returning at 5 a.m. and 3 p.m. The trip takes three and a half hours. Get to the bus stop early on weekends, because you'll be waiting with a big crowd of Joséfinos. A bus from Quepos to Puntarenas passes Jacó on the main road around 6 a.m. and again at 4:30 p.m. ($1.40 to Jacó, $2.25 all the way). All Quepos and Manuel Antonio buses pass Jacó ($4.70) on their way to and from San José. Look at the Quepos–Puntarenas schedule at the end of this chapter and add or subtract one and a half hours for arrival times. Get off at Restaurant El Bosque, two blocks from the beach at the southern end. You can get a taxi from there. Catch *Puntarenas–Quepos* buses to Jacó at 5 a.m. or 2:30 p.m. near the Puntarenas train station.

Hotel Irazú near San José, a sister of Hotel Jacó Beach, has a comfortable mini-bus to and from Jacó (32-4811; $11 one way) every day, which leaves Irazú at 9:30 a.m. and returns at 2 p.m. The trip takes two and a half hours. Make reservations in advance (priority is given to hotel guests). See the Manuel Antonio section below for information on luxury bus service to Jacó and Manuel Antonio.

By Car: Herradura and Jacó are a two-hour drive from San José on a winding road through beautiful countryside. Take the Atenas turnoff on the highway to Puntarenas. The road is in fairly good repair most of the way through the mountains and offers some magnificent views. Near Orotina you can buy watermelon, mangos, and sugarcane juice. After Orotina the road is excellent, with sea views on one side and green rice fields on the other. You'll pass the entrance to Carara

Biological Reserve (see above) about 20 minutes before Jacó. A new section of highway now connects Puntarenas and Jacó and can be driven in an hour. You can continue on to Quepos (70 kilometers farther), Dominical, and San Isidro de El General on the same road.

MANUEL ANTONIO

When you first glimpse the sea from the hills above Manuel Antonio, the word "paradise" might cross your mind. The lovely beaches were made into a national park before they could be turned into another Acapulco. So far, the hotels that have sprung up in the last few years have taken advantage of the beautiful views without calling too much attention to themselves. But as Manuel Antonio becomes better known, the influx of tourists is taking its toll on the delicate environment.

Manuel Antonio is one of the few remaining habitats of the *mono tití* (squirrel monkey). Howler and white-faced monkeys, two-toed sloths, coatimundis, and raccoons frequent the beaches, which are shaded by leafy trees. Iguanas pose like statues unless they are moving their heads up and down like pumps (a territorial signal made by males).

There is a trail that takes you through the jungle to the top of Cathedral Point, where you can look down the vertical cliffs to the blue ocean 300 feet below. You start from Playa Espadilla Sur (the second beach) and take a circular route, about an hour from start to finish. At low tide you can also begin or end on Playa Manuel Antonio, the third beach. The trail is very steep in some parts and muddy and slippery in the rainy season, so don't go alone, and wear hiking boots if possible.

The wedge-shaped piece of land that is now Cathedral Point used to be an island. As you can see from the illustration below, a neck of land connects

Manuel Antonio

it to the beach. This rare phenomenon is known as a tombolo: a deposit of sand that builds up over thousands of years and finally connects an island to the mainland. Northern-flowing currents pushed water and sand through the opening between the island and the beach, and then flowed on to Punta Quepos, farther north, which forced the water back. The sand-bridge was formed after about 100,000 years of this action. Grass and shrubs gained a foothold on it, followed by the present-day trees that keep the formation from returning to the sea. The Manuel Antonio tombolo is one of the most perfect in the world.

The Indians who lived in Manuel Antonio 1000 years ago observed that while female green turtles were laying their eggs in the sand at high tide, the male turtles were waiting for them in the water. The Indians fashioned balsawood models of female turtles to attract the males into an area surrounded by rocks. The males would stay with the decoy females and be trapped by the rocks when the tide went out. You can see these pre-Columbian turtle traps on either end of Manuel Antonio Beach at low tide.

Snorkeling is a rewarding adventure at Manuel Antonio. In the dry season, when the water is clear, you'll see iridescent peacock-colored fish, conservative pin-striped fish, and outrageous yellow fish with diaphanous capes, all going in and out between the coral rocks. Fins and a mask are all you need. *Note:* If you burn easily, watch out—you'll lose track of time staring at the fish while the sun is staring at your back. It's best to wear a T-shirt in addition to waterproof sunblock.

The entrance to the park is on the other side of a stream that changes width and depth with the tides. Try to go at low tide, because you have to wade across. Around high tide the water is waist-high.

Camping is no longer allowed within the park. Overcrowding was leading to pollution and destruction of the vegetation, threatening the wildlife.

Kayaking, biking, and horseback-riding tours in the area are available through **Ríos Tropicales** (33-6655) and **Unicorn Adventures** (77-0489). For tours by sailboat, call 77-0424.

Manuel Antonio is one of the most popular tourist destinations in Costa Rica, and deservedly so. However, the tourist explosion has outstripped the infrastructure of the area, so that waste disposal, both liquid and solid, has become a real problem. If you long to visit this beautiful area, try to go in the off-season (May through November). As we've stated elsewhere, you'll still have most of the day to play, you can relax with a book in your hammock if it rains, you can get a substantial discount on lodging in most hotels, and you'll be able to enjoy Manuel Antonio in its more pristine, uncrowded state, knowing that you are not overtaxing its carrying capacity.

Note: Do not leave your belongings unattended on the beach. If anyone offers to guide you through remote areas of the park, they should have an official ID card, or be in a park service uniform.

Near Manuel Antonio the most beautiful places to stay are in the hills between the former banana port of **Quepos** and the park. There you'll find small, elegant hotels owned by tropics-lovers of many nationalities. Nearer the park entrance on the beach are older, funkier cabinas. There are some nice rooms there, too. Low-cost lodging in the town of Quepos is cleaner and more comfortable than many of the cheapest rooms near the beach. Unfortunately, theft is becoming more and more common. We have heard three reports of hotel rooms being robbed while people were sleeping in them, two in Quepos and one in the plushest section of Manuel Antonio Hills. Due to the skill of Costa Rican sneak thieves, no one realized they were robbed until they woke up the next morning.

Make reservations three months in advance during Christmas or Easter, and at least one month in advance during the tourist season (December through May).

If you have more time to spend, you might want to rent a house by the week or month. For example: There are fully equipped houses (77-0345, 77-0292) with breathtaking views of Manuel Antonio that rent for $600/week (two bedrooms) and $400/week (one bedroom) during the high season. Call or look around for signs on the road.

If you're trying to save money, keep in mind that this area as a whole is not for budget travelers. Those who can afford $70-$150 per day will find some of the most beautiful accommodations in the country, but if you're looking for budget beachfront places, go south to Dominical or the Golfito area or east to the Caribbean coast.

La Buena Nota, a beachwear and gift shop, is the official information center for Manuel Antonio. It sells *The Tico Times* and publishes a useful pamphlet with a map of the area, current bus schedules, and tips on water safety. It's on the oceanfront after the bridge at the entrance to Quepos.

QUEPOS LODGING AND RESTAURANTS   Rooms in Quepos tend to be noisy, so bring your earplugs.

Hotel Ceciliano (cold water, ceiling fans; with shared bath, $12-$20; with private bath, $20-$30; 77-0192), about 50 meters west of the SANSA office in Quepos, is well kept, but don't pay in advance if you're not sure you're going to stay there. We've heard several complaints that people cannot get their money back. The **Hotel Quepos** (cold water, ceiling fans, with shared bath, $12-$20; with private bath, $20-$30; 77-0274) is also a good, clean place to stay. It's above the SANSA airline office, about 300 meters from the oceanfront.

One block to the south of the above hotels, **Cabinas Helen** (cold water, private bath, table fans; $12-$20; 77-0504) are built off the back of a family's house and have a nice atmosphere. On the same street, **Villas Cruz** (private bath, ceiling fans, kitchen, veranda; $40-$50; 77-0271, fax: 77-0050) are a good value and are fancier than most accommodations in Quepos.

The luxurious new **Hotel Kamuk** (hot water, private bath, air-conditioning; $60-$80; 77-0379; fax, 77-0258), on the main street facing the ocean, breaks from the sleepy, banana-port-of-the-past feeling of Quepos. The third floor features an international restaurant.

Hotel Mario (cold water, private bath, ceiling fans, screens; $12-$20; 77-0339), across from the health center 100 meters from the ocean, is rather dark, but its rooms are clean.

Hotel Mar y Luna (cold water, table fans; with shared bath, under $7; with private bath, $7-$12; 77-0394) is fairly clean. Upper rooms have windows and shared baths. Lower rooms have private baths. **Hotel Malinche** (cold water, private bath, table fans; $12-$20; 77-0093) has some nice touches in its decor, and **Hotel Ramus** (cold water, private bath, table fans; $12-$20; 77-0245) is okay, too. The above three are located in the block west of the bus terminal.

The real deals are on the periphery of Quepos, away from the ocean. You don't want to swim at the beach in Quepos, anyway, because it's polluted. Most are located near the church and *cancha de fútbol* (soccer field), about four blocks inland.

Cabinas Ana (cold water, private bath, ceiling fans; $12-$20 for up to 5 people; 77-0443, 23-5567) are 200 meters from the northwest corner of the soccer field. Not much atmosphere, but clean and a good value. On the northeast corner of the soccer field, **Cabinas Doña Alicia** (cold water, private bath, ceiling fans; $7-$12; 77-0419) are an excellent deal. Each cabin, built by friendly local people, has three rooms.

Hotel Ipakarahi (cold water, private bath, table fans, ceiling fans; $12-$20; 77-0392), 500 meters north of the church, has closets, desks, beautiful wood ceilings, and tiled bathrooms—attention to detail one does not often find in budget cabinas. There's a grungy looking workshop at the entrance, but once you get past that, the hotel is nice.

A popular place for both tourists and locals, **Restaurante Isabel** (open all day), in the next block after La Buena Nota, offers a full menu. The **Soda Ana**, a few doors down, has good, cheap *casados*. Owned by a transplanted *gringa* married to a Tico soccer hero, **El Gran Escape**, next door has some of the best food in town. Mexican food is their specialty, but they also serve hearty American breakfasts and desserts like Triple Suicide Brownies. Our favorite place to stop for a *refresco* in Quepos is **El Kiosko**, a small, open-air place on the oceanfront three blocks from La Buena Nota.

The market at the bus terminal is a good place to grab a quick bite to eat and to stock up on fruits and vegetables. The **Quepoa** on the south side of the market has tasty seafood. Toward the ocean from the market is **Pizza Gabriel,** which has good food and is run by a friendly local owner.

MANUEL ANTONIO LODGING AND RESTAURANTS   We will mention facilities in order of their appearance on the road between Quepos and Manuel Antonio.

With a beautiful vista above Quepos, **Villas El Tucán** (ceiling fans, full kitchen; $100-$120; no phone) are one- and two- bedroom houses with giant porches. Next door, sharing the same lovely view, **Restaurante La Arcada** (6:30 to 10 p.m.) serves Italian specialties.

Cabinas Pedro Miguel (cold water, ceiling fans, private bath; $20-$30; 77-0035) are funky rooms—some with kitchens—in a tranquil setting 1 kilometer from Quepos and 100 meters from the main road. They are overpriced but very hospitable. The European-owned **Hotel Plinio** (hot water, private bath, ceiling fans, screens; $50-$60 including breakfast; 77-0055, fax: 77-0558), across the road, has comfortable, wood-panelled rooms off a wide veranda with hammocks, and is surrounded by lush foliage. It has one of the most popular dinner restaurants (open daily for breakfast and dinner) in Manuel Antonio, featuring delicious pasta, lasagna, eggplant parmigiana, and pizza. Its homemade bread is worth a trip in itself. Call for reservations.

The German-owned **Hotel El Mirador del Pacífico** (hot water, private bath, ceiling fans, screens; $40-$80; phone/fax: 77-0119) has big bright rooms with verandas and offers help with planning vacations and making transportation arrangements. **Mimo's Hotel** (hot water, private bath, ceiling fans and air-conditioning, screens, kitchen, pool with jacuzzi; $60-$80 including breakfast; $40-$50 in off-season; phone/fax: 77-0054) has spacious and elegant rooms.

Farther down the road on your right is **Bahías** (open evenings year-round, all day during the high season; 77-0350) a bar/restaurant featuring seafood, 46 varieties of tropical cocktails, and wonderful music: tangos, vintage jazz, good stuff. There is live music on weekends. The new **Bahías Hotel** (hot water, private bath, air-conditioning; $90-$100; $40-$50 in off-season; 77-0350, fax: 77-0279) features a square bathtub right next to the bed, some with jacuzzis. Next door, **Galería Atelier** features fine art from Perú and Ecuador, including amazing paintings on glass, ceramics, and textiles.

The French-owned **Sula Bya-ba** (hot water, private bath, ceiling fans; $50-$60; 77-0597, fax: 77-0279) looks rather Japanese, with two walls that are full screens. Next on the left is the entrance to **El Salto** (hot water, private bath, ceiling fans, pool; $80-$100 including breakfast, dinner, and nature tour; 77-0130, fax: 41-2938), overpriced cabinas on a hilltop with a 360-degree view of the Quepos area and the coast in the distance. El Salto has horses to ride and a bar/restaurant. The cabinas are about 700 meters from the main road.

At the crest of the hill on the left is the Canadian-owned **El Lirio** (hot water, private bath, ceiling fans; $70-$80; 77-0403; Apdo. 123, Quepos), spacious, well-designed rooms with a distant sea view that are slightly overpriced. **Hotel Las Charruas** (hot water, private bath, ceiling fans, screens, refrigerator; $60-$80; phone/fax: 77-0409), across the road, has rather dark, overpriced rooms and an unfriendly Uruguayan steak house.

Hidden Village Cabinas (cold water, private bath, ceiling fans, screens; $40-$50; with kitchen, $60-$80; 77-0090) are located below the roadway, so they have no view. They are nice but are also overpriced. **Villas las Amapolas** (hot water, private bath, ceiling fans, screens; $60-$80) have a jacuzzi, kitchens, and lovely private terraces with bamboo furniture. The owners are friendly local people.

The Norwegian-owned **Villas Oso** (hot water, private bath, ceiling fans; $50-$80, depending on size; 20 percent off-season discount; phone/fax: 77-0233) have terraces, views, big screened windows, and kitchens. Recommended.

The 32-room **Divisamar** (hot water, private bath, air-conditioning, pool; $70-$80; 77-0371, fax: 77-0525) is one of the largest hotels on the hill. It has a restaurant and a family atmosphere. The best rooms are on the upper floors. Across the street is the **Barba Roja** (open 7:30 a.m. to 12 midnight; closed Monday), a favorite with visitors because of its gringo-style lunches and dinners, such as burgers, nachos, and BLTs, and its sinful desserts—try the macadamia pie a la mode! Above the Barba Roja is the **Mamaya Gallery** (open 4 p.m. to 9 p.m.; closed Monday), with tasteful exhibits of local artisanry.

Just before the main road heads down toward Manuel Antonio are the elegant villas of the **Hotel Mariposa** (hot water, private bath, ceiling fans, pool; no children under 15; $180-$200 including gourmet breakfast and dinner; 77-0355, fax: 77-0050), which has beautiful views from private balconies and excellent service. Down a steep dirt road, 1 kilometer to the right from the Mariposa, is **Makanda-by-the-Sea** (hot water, kitchen; $100-$180; 77-0442; Apdo. 29, Quepos), secluded villas with a sunset ocean view in a reservelike atmosphere. Recommended.

Back on the main road are **El Dorado Mojado** (hot water, private bath, air-conditioning, screens, kitchen; $120-$140 including breakfast; 77-0368), which has no view, and **Altamira Inn** (cold water, shared bath, ceiling fans; $20-$30; 77-0477), a small bed-and-breakfast. Next on the right are the comfortable and well-designed **Villas Nicolas** (hot water, ceiling fans, screens, kitchen, pool; $90-$100; $80-$90 for smaller rooms without views; 77-0375, phone/fax: 77-0538), with private terraces and beautiful views. Recommended. **Villas El Parque** (77-0096, fax: 77-0538), 50 meters back toward Quepos, is owned by the same people and also has fantastic views.

Next on the left is the French-owned **Hotel Byblos** (hot water, ceiling fans, air-conditioning, pool with jacuzzi; $140-$220 including breakfast and dinner; 77-0411, fax: 77-0009). Its spacious cabinas are set in a forest below the restaurant. Management can be unfriendly. **Hotel Villas Los Mogotes** (hot water, private bath, ceiling fans, air-conditioning, pool; $90-$100 including breakfast; larger villas with kitchens, $80-$150; phone/fax: 77-0582) was the summer home of the late singer Jim Croce. It's tastefully decorated and has good ocean views and jet ski rentals. The rooms directly above the restaurant can be noisy.

Condominios Costa Verde (hot water, private bath, ceiling fans, screens, kitchen; $70-$100; 23-7946, 77-0584, fax: 77-0560) have views. You won't miss Costa Verde—they have several signs and entrances on both sides of the road. **La Quinta** (cold water, private bath, ceiling fans, pool; $50-$60; with view and kitchen, $60-$80; 77-0434; Apdo. 76, Quepos) is quiet, with private terraces and beautiful views of the park from its spacious grounds. The elegant French restaurant **La Brise**, at the entrance to La Quinta, has reasonably priced entrées.

Hotel Arboleda (cold water, private bath, ceiling fans; $80-$90; with kitchens, $100-$120; 77-0092, fax: 77-0414), has a restaurant and rows of cabinas on a hill, some with ocean views, and others nearer the beach. It's somewhat overpriced compared to other hotels in the area but is reasonable in the off-season and close to the beach. The **Iguana Azul Restaurant**, after the entrance to Hotel Arboleda, is built on a hillside with a beautiful view. It uses very little grease in its cooking.

The **Karahé** has three kinds of cabinas. The older ones (hot water, ceiling fans, refrigerator; $80-$90; 77-0170, phone/fax: 77-0152) have magnificent views, but you have to walk up more than 100 steps to get to them and they are not as well maintained as the others; the newer rooms near the road (hot water, air-conditioning; $90-$100) have terraces; the junior suites (hot water, air-conditioning; $100-$120), which also have terraces, are across the road, between the pool and the beach. Breakfast is included in all rates.

BEACH AREA LODGING AND RESTAURANTS   Now we're down at the beach, where the less expensive cabinas are. All of them have off-season discounts. **Cabinas Piscis** (cold water, private bath, ceiling fans, screens; $30-$40; 77-0046) are surrounded by shade trees and have a little trail to the beach. Their small restaurant serves *comida típica*. **Hotel Delmar** (cold water, private bath, table fans; $30-$40; 77-0543) is next on the left.

The **Restaurant Mar y Sombra** is the traditional place to eat on Playa Espadilla. It is about 500 meters from the park entrance. Espadilla is known for its dangerous rip currents. **Cabinas Ramirez** (cold water, private bath, table fans; $20-$30; off-season discount; 77-0003) is next door. The more secure ones have metal bars and padlocks but are stuffy and dark; others have better ventilation, but tend to be noisy.

On the way to the park you'll see the **Del Mar Bar** on the beach, which rents surfing and snorkeling equipment. A road to the left by Del Mar Bar goes to the following places: **Cabinas Espadilla** (cold water, private bath, table fans, refrigerator; $20-$40; 77-0416) are clean and light. Some have hotplates. Across the road is the **Costa Linda** (with shared bath and no fans, $7-$12; with private bath, table fans, and kitchen, $30-$40; 77-0304), a youth hostel with small stuffy rooms. The ones in the back have more ventilation. The restaurant (open all day) has reasonably priced meals served in a simple, pleasant atmosphere. It specializes in fresh fish and salad.

The **Vela Bar** (cold water, ceiling fans; $20-$40; with kitchens and hot water, $40-$50; 77-0413) offers seafood and vegetarian specialties with a Spanish touch. Cabinas in the back have locked wooden security boxes. The new **Hotel Villabosque** (hot water, private bath, ceiling fans, air-conditioning; $60-$80; 77-0401) is a solidly built two-story building. The rooms have satiny pink bedspreads and curtains. **Cabinas Los Almendros** (with cold water and ceiling fans, $30-$40; with hot water and air-conditioning, $40-$50; 77-0225), on the left, are clean and quiet and have a good restaurant.

We couldn't see **Cabinas Irarosa** (cold water, private bath, table fans; $7-$12; no phone) because they were all occupied, but they look neat from the outside. As you come out again onto the road to the park, right on Playa Espadilla, you'll see **Cabinas Manuel Antonio** (cold water, private bath, ceiling fans; $12-$20; 77-0212, 77-0255), which is run-down and has a party atmosphere. **Hotel Manuel Antonio** (cold water, private bath, no fans, no screens; 77-0212, 77-0255) on the left, has bright, sunny rooms and is a good value for budget travelers. There are camping spots with bathrooms next door.

GETTING THERE: *By Bus:* A direct *San José–Manuel Antonio* bus ($4.70) leaves the Coca Cola at 6 a.m., 12 noon, and 6 p.m., returning at 6 a.m., 12 noon, and 5 p.m. Buy tickets in advance on weekends and holidays and purchase return tickets as soon as you arrive. The Quepos ticket office is open Monday through Saturday, 7 to 11 a.m., 1 to 5 p.m.; Sunday, 7 to 11 a.m., 1 to 4 p.m.). This bus will pick you up at your hotel on its way from Manuel Antonio to Quepos, but you must be out on the road to flag it down. Do not let anyone but the bus driver load or unload your baggage. Try to keep it with you if possible. Things have been stolen from the luggage compartment. There is one driver on this route who makes the trip in three hours, a fact which defies conventional concepts of space and time. We have heard of several people who have become quite religious on his bus.

San José–Quepos buses leave from the western end of the Coca Cola at 7 and 10 a.m., 2 and 4 p.m., returning at 5 and 8 a.m., 2 and 4 p.m. (23-5567, 77-0263; $3). These buses are slow and make many stops. The trip takes four hours. Watch out for pickpockets at the Coca Cola. From Quepos, take a 20-minute bus ride (20 cents) 7 scenic kilometers to the entrance of the park. It leaves at 5:45, 8, 9, and 10:30 a.m., 12:30, 3, and 5 p.m., and returns 20 to 30 minutes later. Service is continuous on weekends during the dry season.

Quepos–Puntarenas buses leave at 4:30 a.m. and 3 p.m., returning at 5:30 a.m. and 2:30 p.m. All of the above buses pass by Playa Jacó, an hour and a half from Quepos.

Buses leave Quepos for Dominical and San Isidro de El General at 5 a.m. and 1:30 p.m., returning from San Isidro at 7 a.m. and 1:30 p.m. You can now travel to Quepos or Jacó in style with the **Americana V.I.P. Coach Service** (22-8134, 77-0017, 28-0867 nights; $30 one way, $55 round-trip). It leaves the Gran Hotel Costa Rica (Avenida 2, Calle 3 in San José) at 7 a.m. on Monday, Wednesday, Friday, and Sunday, arriving in Manuel Antonio four hours later, and returning the same days at 3 p.m. These luxury Greyhound buses have 24 reclining airline seats, carpeting, air-conditioning, a bathroom, stereo, and TV with VCR. Continental breakfast is provided on the way down, a drink and appetizers are offered on the way back, and a cash bar is available.

By Boat: Manuel Antonio is included in the itinerary of the luxurious **Temptress Cruise** (20-1679, 31-0832, fax: 20-2103; 800-336-8423), which spends a week sailing from Palo Verde National Park in Guanacaste to Drake Bay, Corcovado, and Isla del Caño and comes complete with naturalist guides. **Drake Bay Wilderness Camp** (phone/fax: 71-2436) also offers transportation from Quepos to Dominical in taxi and from there to Drake by boat as part of its package deals.

By Car: The trip takes about three and a half hours if you take the Atenas turnoff and drive the narrow, winding road through the Aguacate mountains. This route is scenic and gives you a glimpse of rural life. You can buy sugarcane juice and fruit along the way. If you feel more comfortable with better highways, go all the way to Puntarenas, follow the signs to Jacó, and continue on to Quepos. It only takes a half hour longer even though it looks much farther on the map. The last 24 kilometers before Quepos are in the process of being paved. Call La Buena Nota (77-0345) for the latest information.

By Air: SANSA flies to Quepos (33-0397, 33-3258, fax: 55-2176; $11.50 one way) Monday through Saturday at 8 a.m., returning at 8:35 a.m. It's a 20-minute flight. Buy tickets at least two weeks in advance during the dry season. There are also 3 p.m. flights, depending on the season. SANSA will transport you from its San José office (Calle 24, Paseo Colón) to the airport, and a private bus ($2) will deliver you to your hotel in Quepos or Manuel Antonio, and pick you up to get you to your return flight. **Travelair** has flights to Quepos (32-7883; $30 one way) at 7 a.m. daily, returning at 7:50 a.m., with a 4:10 p.m. flight, returning at 5 p.m., earlier in the rainy season.

Rental cars are available through most hotels in the area, but it's best to arrange for them in San José and pick them up in Quepos.

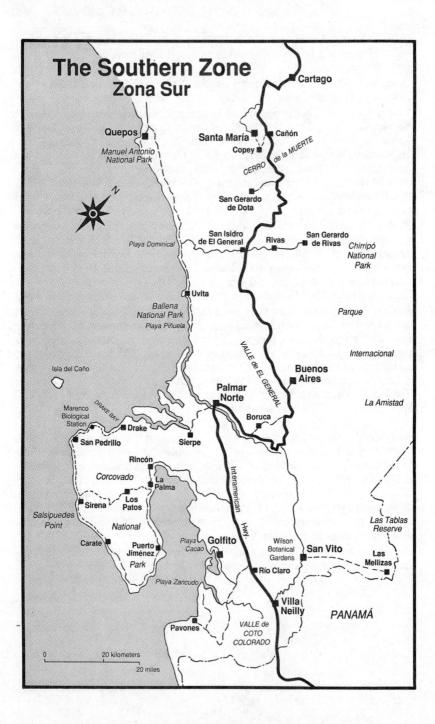

The Southern Zone
Zona Sur

Cartago

Quepos

Manuel Antonio National Park

Santa María

Cañón

Copey

CERRO de la MUERTE

San Gerardo de Dota

N

Playa Dominical

San Isidro de El General

Rivas

San Gerardo de Rivas

Chirripó National Park

Uvita

Ballena National Park

Playa Piñuela

Parque

Internacional

Isla del Caño

Buenos Aires

La Amistad

Palmar Norte

Marenco Biological Station

DRAKE BAY

Drake

San Pedrillo

Sierpe

Boruca

VALLE de EL GENERAL

Rincón

Corcovado

La Palma

Interamerican Hwy

Las Tablas Reserve

Sirena

Los Patos

Salsipuedes Point

National

Carate

Puerto Jiménez

Playa Cacao

Golfito

Wilson Botanical Gardens

San Vito

Las Mellizas

Park

Río Claro

Playa Zancudo

Villa Neilly

PANAMÁ

Pavones

VALLE de COTO COLORADO

0   20 kilometers

20 miles

TWELVE

Southern Zone

Costa Rica's Southern Zone encompasses the southern half of coastal Puntarenas Province (from Playa Dominical to the Osa Peninsula, to Punta Burica
on the Panamanian border), as well as the mountainous southern half of
San José Province and inland Limón Province, including Chirripó National
Park and La Amistad International Park, which extends across the border
into Panama. It is a part of Costa Rica that many Ticos have never visited.
In this small country, the high mountains seem an almost impenetrable barrier. Yet for hikers, naturalists, anglers, and those who want to get off the
beaten track, this area has a tremendous amount to offer.

Despite its reputation nationally as a center of agroindustry (bananas, pine-
apples, palm oil, coffee), it has a larger percentage of national parks and
forest reserves than any other region of Costa Rica. It also has the largest
concentration of indigenous people, especially the Guaymis and Borucas,
centering around the town of Buenos Aires, south of San Isidro de El General.
Because the area is not really on the tourist trail, budget accommodations
are plentiful and of much higher quality than elsewhere in the country.

The Interamerican Highway, which becomes San José's Central Avenue,
crossing the city from west to east, turns right at Cartago to connect the
Central Valley with the Zona Sur, or Southern Zone. It winds into the mountains that surround fog-shrouded Cerro de la Muerte, the highest pass on
the Interamerican Highway. These mountains were the scene of the begin-
nings of the 1948 Civil War—the late Don Pepe Figueres's farm, *La Lucha
Sin Fin* (The Endless Struggle), is located off this road (see Chapter One).

There is a small monument to those who lost their lives in that conflict in
the plaza of **Santa María de Dota**, down a road to the right at Empalme.

Day hikers will enjoy a trip to **Copey**, a small town in the mountains above
Santa María, about an hour south of Cartago. Its fresh, brisk climate at 7000
feet makes for an exhilarating walk through the hills of native oak. Treat

yourself to a trout lunch at William Rodríguez's *soda* and buy tart, crispy local apples for dessert.

You can visit Don Fernando Elizondo's well-developed **trout farm** and rent horses from Chema, his next-door neighbor. Chema rents one **room** (shared bath; under $7 including breakfast; no phone) with a beautiful stained-glass window and might know of other houses to rent. Ask him about hiking, biking, and horseback tours around Copey, and to Manuel Antonio National Park, Río Macho Reserve, and the high altitude plateau of Cerro de las Vueltas.

GETTING THERE: You can catch the bus to Santa María from San José (Calle 21, Avenida 16 bis; 27-3597; $1) at 6 a.m., 9 a.m., 12:30 p.m., 3 p.m., and 5 p.m. Buses return to San José from the main square in Santa María at 6 a.m., 9 a.m., 1 p.m., and 4 p.m. The trip takes about two hours.

To get to Copey, take a San Isidro bus (Calle 16, Avenidas 1/3) to Cañón del Guarco, kilometer 58 on the Interamerican Highway. (You'll see the little yellow markers on the side of the road that tell you how many kilometers you are from San José.) From Cañón it's 7 kilometers downhill on a dirt road to Copey. Santa María is another 7 kilometers downhill. You can either walk or hitchhike. It's customary in that region for drivers to offer rides to people on the road.

To the left from the Cañon del Guarco church on the Interamerican Highway is the road leading to **Genesis II**, a private cloud forest reserve 2360 meters (7500 feet) above sea level, where quetzales can be observed. Visitors stay in rather dank rooms ($460 for two for a minimum three-day stay, including meals; $12-$20 per day for students with valid ID; fax: 21-2053) on the bottom floor of the owner's house. Rates include transportation to and from the San José Airport. Volunteers who spend five hours a day constructing nature trials pay $50/week for room and board and stay in primitive huts (bathrooms are in the main house). It's a minimum six-week commitment. Fax Steve and Paula Friedman for information.

The new **Albergue Tapantí** (heated water, private bath; $30-$40; fax: 22-0436), which has good beds and a restaurant, is on the Interamerican Highway going south from Cañón.

After you pass it, you'll soon see the lush vegetation become stunted and then diminish as you wind around the Cerro de la Muerte. When taking this trip, dress in layers and try to go early in the day, before fog and rain reduce the visibility to zero. This can happen even in the dry season. Landslides are also a very real danger during heavy rains.

In **San Gerardo de Dota**, Don Efraín Chacón and his family rent cabinas at **Albergue Rio Savegre** (heated water, private bath; $20-$30/person including three meals; 71-1732), and provide delicious homemade meals for anglers and nature lovers on their *finca* (farm). At 1900 meters (6300 feet), the temperature averages 10°C (50-55°F) in this narrow mountain valley. Don Efraín takes advantage of the crisp weather to grow apples and peaches.

Quetzales can be observed there, especially during their nesting season in April and May. Trout abound in the chilly waters of the Río Savegre, which passes the farm. Be sure to call ahead for reservations. To get there, take a San Isidro bus from San José and ask to be let off at the *"entrada a San Gerardo."* The turnoff is at the 80-kilometer mark on the Interamerican Highway. The Finca Chacón is a 9-kilometer downhill hike from there. Don Efraín can pick you up if you call him ($12 round-trip). If you are traveling there by car, make sure you have four-wheel drive or at least a powerful engine, because the road is extremely steep and narrow. Recommended.

The **Valle de El General** is one of Costa Rica's natural jewels. When the fog clears after you pass Cerro de la Muerte, the surrounding small towns in the valley offer beautiful flowers and a lovely climate.

The town of **San Isidro** is the gateway to Chirripó National Park and Playa Dominical. The clean, new **public market** in San Isidro is a delight, offering an array of beautiful fruits and vegetables. There is also a new museum, gallery, and theater complex surrounding **Café el Teatro** (closed Sunday), a nice little restaurant 200 meters west and 75 meters north of the church. The **Bar Chirripó** and **El Tenedor** on the Parque Central are also good places to eat.

There are several clean and inexpensive hotels in town, such as **Hotel Chirripó** (heated water, no fans; with shared bath, under $7; with private bath, $7-$12; 71-0529), **Hotel Amaneli** (heated water, private bath, table fans; $12-$20; 71-0352), and **Hotel Iguazú** (both private and shared baths; $12-$20; 71-2571). Make sure your room is not facing the Interamerican Highway, as trucks and buses pass all night. Six kilometers south of San Isidro, on the left, is the large, comfortable **Hotel del Sur** (private bath, air-conditioning, TV optional, pools; $20-$30; 71-0233), with gardens, tennis courts, playground equipment, and a restaurant.

GETTING THERE: Comfortable buses leave San José for the three-hour trip to San Isidro once an hour from three bus companies along the same block (Calle 16, Avenidas 1/3; 23-3577, 22-2422, 23-0686; $2.50). Buy tickets in advance, especially on weekends and holidays. Buses back to San José leave hourly.

CHIRRIPÓ NATIONAL PARK

San Gerardo de Rivas is a small mountain village at the entrance to Chirripó National Park. Even if you are not up to climbing the mountain, the scenery is beautiful and birds of all kinds are abundant. You can even see quetzales halfway up the mountain, although it's best to go with a guide who can show you where they nest. There is a small **hot spring** in a lovely natural setting at the top of a hill less than a kilometer from San Gerardo, and you can hike to nearby waterfalls. Ask for directions at your hotel.

Francisco Elizondo offers simple, clean lodging at his newly constructed **Posada del Descanso** (cold water, shared bath, $7-$12 including meals),

400 meters past the ranger station in San Gerardo. He is a font of information. His brother Rafael creates wonderful folk art, carving pieces of wood into all kinds of creatures. Don Francisco's wife cooks for guests. Let her know in advance what you want and when. This is one of the few *campesino* places that serves a lot of vegetables. The views are great and the price is right. Some cabinas have bunk beds, others have double beds.

Cabinas Marín (under $7), next to the ranger station, have a couple of rooms in their *soda*/house/*pulpería*, and **Cabinas Chirripó** (heated water, shared bath; under $7), farther up the road near the church, have three rooms on a hillside under their *soda*/house/*pulpería*.

To reserve yourself a space in San Gerardo de Rivas, call 71-0433, ext. 106, the only phone in town, and leave a message for the cabinas of your choice, saying at what time you'll call back. Hopefully someone will be at the phone at that time. All of the cabinas also rent horses for the trip up the mountain during the dry season and can take you to explore the San Gerardo area at any time of the year.

Pensión Quetzal Dorado ($7-$12/person including meals; 71-0433, ext. 109) is a three-hour hike from the village of Herradura, which is 3 kilometers from San Gerardo. We weren't able to go there, but apparently it has a great view, offers access to Cerro Urán and Chirripó, and rents horses.

Most people I talked with before venturing off to **Chirripó** told me about their own experiences on the mountain. Many Costa Ricans have climbed it once but won't ever go again. True, the trek can be painful, tiring, frustrating, and freezing, but it's so satisfying to reach the summit, which, being the highest peak in southern Central America at 3819 meters, is really the top of this part of the world. A trip to Chirripó, with only one day at the summit, will take a minimum of five days, including transportation to and from San José.

The week before Easter is the Ticos' favorite time to climb Chirripó, because they are on vacation and the weather is usually dry. At any time of year, call Parques Nacionales (33-4160) three days in advance to reserve a spot. For general information call the office of the Reserva Biológica Amistad (71-1155), of which Chirripó is a part, in San Isidro.

To climb Chirripó, check in at the ranger station, near the final bus stop. There you register and pay the nominal entrance and overnight fees. They give you a pamphlet with a map and a chart that shows the altitude of each landmark on the climb. If you want to be able to know exactly where you are or if you're planning to explore any of the neighboring peaks or valleys, we recommend you buy a good, large-scale, topographical map. Unfortunately, Chirripó is at the intersection of four different sections of the topographical map, so you might have to buy all four parts to get the whole picture.

The summit area is above timberline, so once you get there you can always see where you are as long as inclement weather and fog do not envelop you. Watch out for lightning. Be sure to bring:

> Warm clothes and a warm sleeping bag. It gets very cold at night—3°C (43°F). If the ranger is around, he can lend you blankets. I slept in a Polarguard sleeping bag with one blanket inside it, another on top, another underneath, all my clothes on, and a friend beside me. I was almost warm.
>
> Binoculars to look for birds and to look out into the distance from the tops of mountains and ridges.
>
> Snacks for the hikes. Dried bananas and peanuts are good for energy when you're climbing. Carrots proved to be our lifesaver on the Cuesta de Agua. They quench your thirst and give you something to do slowly and steadily as you climb that never-ending hill.
>
> A poncho to keep you dry during the multiple rainshowers that occur daily.
>
> A water bottle, at least one liter per person, to replenish all the liquid you'll lose sweating.
>
> A kerosene or alcohol burner if you want to cook. Because of recent forest fires, building fires in the park is no longer allowed.

The first day is long and grueling. Hikers make the 14 straight uphill kilometers to the huts in anywhere from seven hours to two days. It took us 11 hours. We left at 4:30 a.m., while it was still dark. We took the *Thermometer* shortcut, which is supposed to shorten the trip by an hour. You walk up the road from San Gerardo, veering right at the two forks and passing over two bridges. It's about 500 meters to a sign that says *Sendero al Cerro Chirripó* and points up—climb over the fence and head straight up through the steep pasture. Stay to the left of the forest, pass through an opening in the fence at the top of one false summit, and continue along the ridge until you get to the next fence. The whole climb from the sign to this last fence should take 30 to 45 minutes.

There you will find the trail. It's well marked. Signs every 2 kilometers give the altitude and distance to the summit. Subtract 4 kilometers for your distance to the huts, as they are below the summit. You will be slapping flies, sweating, and slipping on your long haul, but if you can take your mind off the strain, you'll really enjoy your surroundings.

The trail climbs through a dense cloud forest, where *jilgueros* (goldfinches) sing their amazing song—which sounds like it's blown through a flute made of glass. The song is simple, but very fine. The birds like to stay up in the highest treetops, so they're difficult to spot. The *jilguero*'s natural habitat is the cloud forest. Sadly, as people destroy the cloud forests in Costa Rica, they are destroying the *jilguero* as well.

The first opportunity to get water on your climb is at a stream off the trail from a point 15 minutes past a sign saying *Llano Bonito*. This is four or five hours into the hike. After the stream comes **La Cuesta del Agua**, which is the longest haul of them all—it took us three hours to climb. It ends at **Monte Sin Fé** (Faithless Mountain), where you walk into a new kind of forest. When we were there it was drier and the trees were shorter with less green foliage. Green, orange, and yellow moss hung from the grey lichen-covered branches and wagged in the wind like furry beards. Almost 5000 acres of Chirripó, including Monte Sin Fé, were destroyed in April 1992 by a fire, which is believed to have been started by careless campers near the shelters.

The next major landmark is the **refugio natural**—a big cave where five people could sleep if it's raining, up to ten if it's not. A stream next to the cave was dry when we were there in February. This cave is only an hour and a half from the huts, so try to continue on. You have to climb **La Cuesta de los Arrepentidos** (Repentants' Hill), then the trail traces around the side of a mountain. When the view opens up you can see **Los Crestones** on the top of a ridge straight ahead. These are huge, sharp rocks that look like they were folded accordion-style. The huts are in the valley just below them.

Arriving at the huts is a relief. The third, the yellow one, is where you should try to stay. It has a wooden floor and a good wood stove. If you're lucky, someone will have a pot of water boiling and will offer you a cup of hot tea.

Mornings are clear in the summer until 9 a.m. or so, then the valley fills with fog. Wisps of fog drift in until they crowd together and form dense clouds. Visibility minimizes, and at 2 or 3 p.m. it rains for about 45 minutes, so be sure you're on the trail by dawn. Besides avoiding the fog and rain, you'll get to enjoy this pretty time of day—the sun touches the frost-covered leaves and grasses, the ice melts, the plants stretch, and whole meadows squeak softly.

There are many places to explore. Of course you should go to the summit of Chirripó, an hour and a half up the same trail. You pass through the **Valle de los Conejos**, where no rabbit has lived since a destructive fire in 1976. *Lagartijas* (little lizards) occupy the valley. Each lizard has a different sheen that perfectly matches the rock it suns itself on. On the top of Chirripó you can see both the Pacific Ocean and the Caribbean Sea if the clouds haven't rolled in by the time you get there. There's a register to sign in a metal container wedged between the rocks in the summit cairn. Right below Chirripó is **Lago San Juan**. You can swing by it on your way down. It's fun to take a quick swim, and there are ideal sunning rocks on the lake's banks.

The lake-filled **Valle de las Morenas** is on the other side of the peak, with a hut where you can stay. Ask for its key at the San Gerardo park station before you set out. If you want to continue hiking in that direction, you can pass over Cerro Urán and continue along the **Camino de los Indios**, a trail known and used almost solely by the local Indians. Talk to Parques Nacionales in San José and hire a guide for this hike. You can also climb

King fisher

Urán and take the Camino de los Indios back through another valley to San Gerardo. Again, you should talk to Parques Nacionales beforehand and take a good map.

Other day-hike possibilities are **Cerro Ventisqueros**, the second highest mountain in southern Central America, whose trail takes off from the main trail a bit below the Valle de los Conejos. It is supposed to be a relatively easy hike. You can also hike from the huts to Los Crestones. The top of the ridge is reached by going up to the left of Los Crestones. Follow the ridge left to **Cerro Terbi**, a mild half hour. There's a register in the cairn stones there, too. To make it a round trip, continue on the ridge a few hundred meters and descend on a trail that goes through a steep chimney and ends up in Valle de los Conejos. You can also continue walking along Terbi's curving ridge, ascending and descending the peaks, and go down into Valle de los Conejos when you get tired.

Note: When you go on your day hikes, take a map, a compass, a sweater, a rain jacket, snacks, and water.

GETTING THERE: From the market in San Isidro, buses leave for San Gerardo de Rivas at 5 a.m. and 2 p.m. The trip takes an hour and a half. When asking which of the many buses to take, specify San Gerardo de *Rivas*, because there's another San Gerardo. To be able to start your hike before dawn, arrive a day early and spend the night in San Gerardo de Rivas. The 10:30 a.m. bus from San José will get you to San Isidro in time to catch the 2 p.m. bus to San Gerardo.

By Car: It's about 45 minutes from San Isidro to San Gerardo de Rivas. Take the paved road which you'll see going uphill on your left just south of San Isidro. It's 9 kilometers to the town of Rivas. San Gerardo de Rivas is 11 kilometers on good gravel roads from there.

PLAYA DOMINICAL AND
PARQUE NACIONAL BALLENA

The scenery along the unfinished Costanera Sur Highway south of Playa Dominical is reminiscent of California's Big Sur coast—with lush tropical vegetation, of course. Someday the highway will connect Dominical with Palmar Norte near the Osa Península. Swimming at the long beach at the village of Dominical can be quite dangerous, but the warm, reef-protected waters of Ballena National Park, half an hour's drive to the south, are perfect for swimming and snorkeling. Accommodations are more reasonable here than in Manuel Antonio (see the Central Pacific Zone chapter), and the views from some of the hillside lodges are just as beautiful.

Note: If you are planning to cook, bring food from the beautiful market in San Isidro, as there is not much available in Dominical.

As you approach Dominical from San Isidro, you follow the peaceful Río Barú. If you go right instead of left to cross the bridge into the village, you'll come, in about a kilometer, to **Hacienda Barú**, where you can rent horses for a trip to the hacienda's private rainforest reserve. The hacienda also rents a small three-bedroom house (heated water, table fans, ceiling fans, kitchen; $30-$40; 71-1903, fax: 71-0441) about 400 meters from the beach.

Go north along the same road and you'll come to the gas station, where you can buy tide tables, fishing supplies, film, topographical maps, and *The Tico Times*. It also rents boogieboards and beach umbrellas and has clean bathrooms.

Near the Río Barú, 400 meters inland from the village, are the clean and well-built **Cabinas Río Mar** (hot water, private bath, ceiling fans; with kitchenettes, $30-$40; with two bedrooms and full kitchens, $80-$90; 71-2333, fax: 71-2455). More cabinas are under construction.

As you enter the village of Dominical, you'll see **Cabinas Willdale** (heated water, private bath, table fans, ceiling fans, screens; $12-$20; 71-1903, fax: 71-0441), which are clean and peaceful and have nice touches like reading lamps, writing tables, and hammocks overlooking the estuary. **Rancho Memo** (71-0866), on the left, has good food in its shady restaurant and rents both rooms (shared bath; $12-$20) and a whole house ($30-$40; $150/week). It has the only public phone in town and is the official bus stop.

Cabinas Coco (cold water, shared bath, table fans; under $7; 71-2555) are clean and small and run a disco on weekends. **La Residencia** (heated water, shared bath, ceiling fans, screens; $12-$20; 71-2175), on the left, also has clean, small rooms.

Pisces Pacific Boat Tours (71-1903, 21-2053) has sportfishing trips ($375/day) and overnight trips to Isla del Caño and Drakes Bay, and rents a house as well. **Cabinas Nayarit** (cold water, table fans, ceiling fans; with shared bath, under $7; with private bath, $7-$12; $30-$50 for houses; 71-1878), 400 meters down the road to the right, are clean and located on the beach.

Cabinas Roca Verde (cold water, table fans, screens; with shared bath, $7-$12; with private bath, $12-$20; 71-1414), which have a restaurant, are about a kilometer south of the village where a small estuary intersects with the beach. There are nice tidepools and rock outcroppings.

About 4 kilometers south of the Roca Verde, a road to the left climbs up to **Escaleras**. There are several new places to stay on this road that have breathtaking views. The only problem is that you have to have a four-wheel-drive vehicle or a horse to get there. The road conditions are on the brink of being improved, so check with **Selva Mar Reservation Service** (71-1903, fax: 71-0441) to see what the situation is.

Just past the road to Escaleras, you'll find **Cabinas Punta Dominical** (heated water, private bath, ceiling fans, screens; $20-$30; 25-5328, fax: 53-4750), on a rocky point overlooking the ocean. The cabinas are well designed, private, comfortable, tranquil, and fanned by ocean breezes. They have hammocks, a restaurant, horses, and great views. If you have the time and can get reservations in advance, it is really worth the trip (about four hours from San José including rest stops). Although there is a beach north of Punta Dominical, there are a lot of fishing boats there, and the river is polluted, so swimming is not recommended.

All of the following places can be booked through the Selva Mar Reservation Service (71-1903, fax: 71-0441):

About 3.5 kilometers south of Punta Dominical on the left are **Cabinas Escondidas** (private bath, natural ventilation; $30-$40 including breakfast; 71-1903, fax: 71-0441). Each of the three cabinas is in its own secluded setting, with beautiful views, a nearby hidden beach with large tidepools, and guided nature walks back into the jungle. Here you'll find true tranquillity. The owners are receptive to the individual needs of their guests, and gourmet meals are prepared upon request.

✪ **Finca Brian y Milena** (screens; $60/two people including meals and tour; no charge for children under ten) offers a hiking or horseback tour to their farm, which is planted with 65 species of exotic fruits, nuts, vegetables, and spices. They also offer a four-day trek to the **Salto Diamante**, a triple waterfall, with meals in friendly *campesino* homes ($160/two people). You must be in good shape for this. A wood-fueled hot tub awaits guests after their trek.

✪ **Bella Vista Lodge** (solar-heated water, shared bath, natural ventilation; $30-$40 including breakfast) has a beautiful view of the ocean from high atop the Escaleras road. Accommodations are simple but comfortable, and the lodge has a wide, breezy veranda from which to enjoy the view, an inexpensive restaurant, and horseback tours to nearby waterfalls. They will pick you up in Dominical for an extra fee.

Villa Cabeza de Mono (kitchen, pool, maid service; $80-$150) sleeps five to seven and comes complete with food supplies and its own version of the beautiful Escaleras view. It's a nice place to retreat from the world for a while.

Restaurant El Manú (35-6895), 2 kilometers from the main road, is built over a rocky stream and is cool and shady. It serves healthful California-style food and rents well-designed cabins and villas with swimming pools.

A half hour's drive south of Dominical is **Parque Nacional Ballena**. It protects the largest coral reef on the Pacific side of Costa Rica and the Ballena Islands, where humpback whales are seen with their young between December and April. Local boatmen can take you out to the reef for **snorkeling, skindiving, fishing,** or **birdwatching**. Frigate birds, ibises, and brown boobies all nest on Isla Ballena. The best-equipped boat ($35-$40/hour), with canopy and individual seats, can be booked through the Selva Mar service, or leave a message for León Victor Gonzales at the *pulpería* in Uvita (71-2311).

The ocean at Parque Ballena is gentle and at bathtub temperature. The ranger station is on the beach to the right of the main road. At low tide you can walk out to good snorkeling spots on the reef at the north end of the park. There is a natural swimming pool in the rocks there. You can also hike, drive, or boat down to **Playa Piñuela** to the south, one of the prettiest areas of the park. Camping is allowed. You can get water at the park administration.

As you turn right toward **Uvita** from the Costanera Sur highway, you'll see **Soda La Cooperativa** (open daily, 7 a.m. to 2 p.m.) on your left. It's very clean, with good food and service. A few hundred meters inland from the same intersection is the *pulpería* of the Diez family, who will show you how to get to the beautiful natural **waterfalls** and **pools** on the Río Cortezal, which runs through their farm.

Selva Mar has a **tour** ($75/person) that includes breakfast and horseback riding on Rancho La Merced (an old hacienda north of Uvita where you can see wildlife near the mangroves), a boat tour of Ballena Park, and lunch on the beach. It is topped off with a cool swim in the Río Cortezal pools.

Selva Mar will also connect you with the Duarte family, who will take you on horseback up to their **farm**, where you can see how sugar is made in an ox-powered *trapiche* (sugar mill) and get an overview of traditional *campesino* life. Birders will find this trip rewarding, as it covers a wide range of habitats and altitudes. Fees ($65/2) for the trip help the Duartes preserve their remaining rainforest.

GETTING THERE: Buses leave San Isidro de El General daily for Uvita, at 7 a.m. and 3 p.m., passing through Dominical an hour and a half later. The return bus passes Dominical around 7:30 a.m. You can also take a 7 a.m. or 1:30 p.m.

bus from San Isidro through Dominical and up the coast four hours to Quepos. Buses leave Quepos for San Isidro at 5 a.m. and 1:30 p.m. Check local bus schedules by calling Memo's Restaurant (71-0866) in Dominical.

By Car: Dominical is about 45 minutes from San Isidro on a paved road with potholes. The Costanera Sur is still unpaved but is in good condition, although the rough gravel is hard on tires. Roads between Quepos and Dominical are unpaved but in good condition.

Boruca is a small town cradled in a green valley in the southwestern part of Costa Rica. The countryside is beautiful—you can walk up the red dirt trails for views across mountains, valleys, and rivers.

The Borucas offer a glimpse into the traditions of Costa Rica's indigenous peoples. For instance, they traditionally celebrate the new year with the *Fiesta de los Diablitos*, a dramatic reenactment of the war between the Spanish conquistadores and the Indians in which the Indians win. (Native peoples throughout the Americas share the *Diablitos* tradition, though usually their drama represents a war between the Spanish and the Moors.) The *Diablitos* are men disguised as devils. One man is the bull. The *Diablitos* taunt the bull with sticks, and he prances around and chases them. Costumes are fashioned from burlap sacks and balsa-wood masks carved by Borucan artisans.

The group, accompanied by a drummer and a flute player, meets on a hill the night of December 30. At midnight, a conch shell sounds, and they run down the hill into town. They spend the whole night going from house to house, giving a short performance at each, then relaxing to enjoy the *chicha* and tamales they are offered. The group visits most houses in town that night and during the next three days. The third day of the fiesta the *Diablitos* symbolically kill the bull. A huge bonfire reduces the bull to ashes.

Except for such traditional fiestas, the pace of life in Boruca is slow and steady. Men leave town early in the morning to work small *fincas* (farms) in the nearby hills. Women usually stay at home. They weave naturally dyed cotton yarn on simple looms tied around their waists, making belts, purses, and small tablecloths. Men carve expressive masks out of balsa wood. Both women and men carve elaborate scenes onto large, hollow *jícaras* (gourds).

If you are interested in these traditions or just in getting to know the life of this small town, you would probably enjoy visiting Boruca. Opportunities abound for joining soccer games, teaching new games to children, and meeting people. You should know Spanish and be willing to conform to small-town life for the duration of your visit. Many families are willing to take in visitors for a few days. Ask the people on the bus, then ask around town. Expect a lot of curiosity about yourself and your gear. Beware of becoming a gringo Santa Claus. Showering gifts is not a good precedent to set for future visitors nor for the people of the town, who learn to expect undue generosity from gringos they barely know.

GETTING THERE: It takes a whole day to get to Boruca from San José. Take the 8:30 a.m. bus from the Zona Sur station (Avenida 18, Calle 4; 21-4214) to Buenos Aires or to the *bomba* (gas station) along the Interamerican Highway, 1 kilometer out of town. A school bus leaves Buenos Aires at 1:30 p.m., stops at the *bomba* soon after, and arrives in Boruca (18 kilometers up and down a mountainous dirt road) at 3:30 or so. Or you can get off the Zona Sur bus at the *Entrada de Boruca*, about 30 minutes past the *bomba*, and walk 8 kilometers up the path that takes off to the right of the highway. The hike takes about two hours.

GOLFITO

The port town of Golfito has a gorgeous setting—lush, forested hills surrounding a deep bay on the Golfo Dulce with the misty outline of the Península de Osa in the distance.

Because there is frequent plane service to Golfito, it is a good jumping-off place for touring the southern part of Costa Rica—Corcovado National Park on the Osa Peninsula, the Wilson Botanical Gardens and Amistad International Park near San Vito, the surfer's mecca at Pavones, and the small, isolated, and interesting eco-tourism projects that surround the Golfo Dulce.

Golfito itself has been spruced up a bit in the last few years. Many new hotels have opened due to the influx of Central Valley shoppers, who visit the **Depósito Libre,** a huge outdoor mall with air-conditioned shops that are filled with *electrodomésticos* (household appliances) and luxury items.

The government established the town as a duty-free port in 1990. Ticos are allowed to buy $400 worth of merchandise every six months. The imported items are still sold with a hefty tax, which will not make them of much interest to tourists, but does make them cheaper than in San José. If consumer fever infects you, know that foreigners are allowed to buy as much as they want, but anything beyond the $400 limit will be transported by free-port authorities to the customs station of your choice. Shoppers come mainly on weekends, so during the week Golfito is relatively empty, except before Christmas.

The town is stretched along one main road squeezed between the gulf and the mountains, which are covered by virgin forest and have been made into a wildlife and watershed reserve. There are several trails through the reserve, good for 45-minute to one-and-a-half-hour hikes. The northern part of town is the Zona Americana. United Fruit administrators once lived in this quiet neighborhood in big wooden houses on stilts, surrounded by large lawns and gardens.

Buses run along the road between the northern and southern parts of town, stopping at both the *depósito* and near the airport. Taxis are plentiful, and it costs about 50 cents to travel anywhere in town.

The southern part of town is called the Pueblo Civil and is a noisy collection of bars, restaurants, and hotels. It feels much more like a crowded, active port than does the tranquil, distinguished Zona Americana. The 75-foot church and the large, brick-lined square at the center of town are part of the set of the Warner Brothers–Enigma Pictures film *Chico Mendes*, which covers the life story of the Brazilian rubber tapper union president who was assassinated in 1988 for his efforts to save the rainforest and its peoples. Filming is scheduled to start at the end of 1992. The church and the square will be donated to Golfito after the picture is finished.

The following facilities and attractions are presented in order of their appearance north to south:

Hotel Sierra (pools; $60-$80 including breakfast; 75-0666, fax: 75-0087), next to the airstrip, offers the only luxury accommodations in the area and is quite nice, with a disco, restaurant and bar, and tours. **Cabinas Casa Blanca** (cold water, private bath, table fans, screens, parking; $7-$12; 75-0124), 350 meters south of the *depósito libre*, is a refurbished house with cabinas on the first floor and the owner's living quarters above. They have a family atmosphere.

Across the street, **Hospedaje Familiar** (shared bath, table fans, air-conditioning, $7-$12; 75-0217) offers rooms in a house with kitchen privileges. **Jardín Cervecero Alamedas** (open daily, 8 a.m. to 12 midnight) is a traditional two-story home with the ground floor made into a cheery restaurant. Its specialty is seafood, and it claims to have "the coldest beers in Costa Rica," which it serves in frosted glasses. **Hotel Costa Sur** (cold water, private bath, ceiling fans; $12-$20; 75-0871, fax: 75-0832), next door, is a pleasant place to stay.

Hotel Del Cerro (both heated and cold water, ceiling fans, screens; downstairs rooms with shared bath, $7-$12; with private bath, $12-$20; 75-0556, fax: 75-0551), across from the tip of the old United Fruit dock, has a great view of the bay, lots of plants, original art on the walls, and a restaurant with friendly service. The French-owned **Centro Turístico Samoa del Sur** on the waterfront rents boats, bikes, and cabinas ($30-$40; 75-0233, fax: 75-0573), but its real claim to fame is **Le Coquillage**, a thatch-roofed, open-air restaurant featuring pizzas, seafood, and a happy atmosphere. It is somewhat pricey but very good.

El Uno (private bath; under $7), 25 meters north of the municipal dock, is very basic and inexpensive. (The rooms do not have windows.) The rooms of the **Hotel Golfito** (cold water, private bath, ceiling fans; 75-0047) are a bit dark, but are a good value. It is 25 meters south of the dock. **Restaurante La Eurekita** (open daily, 6 a.m. to 10 p.m.) is one of the most popular restaurants in town with both locals and tourists. It has a good view of the bay and serves generous and delicious natural fruit drinks.

Hotel Delfina (75-0043), 200 meters south of the dock, is divided in two. If you stay in the cheaper south half (shared bath; under $7), try to get a room with windows and be aware that almost everyone who stays there wakes up at 4 a.m. to catch a bus. The other half (cold water, private bath; with table fans, $7-$12; with air-conditioning, $12-$20) is more modern and probably more quiet.

The **Sanbar Marina** (75-0874), to the south, offers jet boat rental and fishing, snorkeling, and scuba-diving excursions. Going out on its 40-person fishing barge ($75/day including lunch and refreshments) is one of the cheapest fishing trips available in Costa Rica. Sanbar Marina also rents rooms on a nearby island.

Off the coastal road, in the heart of the Pueblo Civil, is **Hotel Costa Rica Surf** (heated water; with shared bath and ceiling fans, under $7; with private bath and table fans or air-conditioning, $7-$12; 75-0034), which proclaims itself the "Gringo Aid Station." The rooms are dark. It has a restaurant/bar and a real estate office below and hosts American Legion meetings the first Tuesday of every month. **El Surfari**, also located below the rooms, sells souvenirs, hand-painted shirts made by local artisans, Central American crafts, and gold nuggets from the Osa Peninsula. It also has tourist information and can tell you about rentals in the area.

At the entrance to town, **Las Gaviotas** (heated water; with fans and shared bath, $20-$30; with air-conditioning and private bath, $30-$40; with kitchen, $40-$50; pool; 75-0062, fax: 75-0544) is right on the water's edge with a dock for visitors' boats. Scarlet macaws preen themselves in the gardens. There is an outdoor covered restaurant specializing in excellent seafood, and the cabinas have private porches. (The town bus makes its last stop here.) **El Gran Ceibo** (private bath, table fans, ceiling fans; $12-$20; 75-0403), across the street, has nice, neat rooms.

Across the water on Puntarenitas Spit is the **Jungle Club**, which is reputed to serve good, moderately priced meals. Many yachts are anchored in the restaurant's little bay, attesting to its popularity. If you're not a yachter, hire a boat at the municipal dock for the short ride.

You might also consider taking a boat-taxi to **Captain Tom's Place**, at Playa Cacao. Captain Tom is a one-legged expatriate whose boat broke down a few decades ago. His home is carefully strewn with chunks of sea lore: magic realism at its best. It's worth visiting him just to check out the quarters. His wife, Rocío, serves up Jungle Burgers for a reasonable price. Their **Shipwreck Hotel** (cold water, no fans, kitchen facilities; $7-$12/person) is housed in a beached 62-foot trawler. Each "room" has its own creative design and paperback library. The baths are in Tom and Rocío's house 50 meters away. They will also rent you a tent for camping in their front yard.

To the northeast, **Cabinas Palma** (cold water, private bath, natural ventilation; $20-$30; 75-0357, fax: 75-0373) are quiet, breezy, aesthetically designed, and a good deal. They offer boat services and canoes to use. **Restaurant Siete Mares,** nearby, is recommended for good seafood at reasonable prices.

Note: Because of the currents, the water is cleaner on Playa Cacao than on other parts of the bay. In fact, you shouldn't swim in other parts of the bay. You can get to Playa Cacao either by water taxi or by a road that goes around the bay.

Rainbow Adventures Lodge (solar-heated water; $80-$100 including transportation from Golfito and three meals; $60-$80 without meals; no charge for children under four; 75-0220, U.S. fax: 503-690-7750), 35 minutes by boat west of Golfito at Playa Cativo on the Golfo Dulce, is a lovely, pristine nature preserve. The beautifully designed lodge and two-bedroom cabins are furnished with antiques and silk rugs and decorated with freshly cut flowers from the surrounding gardens. The lodge honors dietary preferences, and the cabins have kitchens. The preserve is great for swimming, snorkeling, fishing, and birding. The lodge offers free anchorage, showers, and water for yachts.

About halfway to Playa Cativo is **Casa Orquídea,** a private botanical garden overlooking the sea that grows edible plants as well as ornamentals. A jungle trail for birders takes about 45 minutes to walk. You can visit Casa Orquídea through Zancudo Boat Tours (see below).

GETTING THERE: *By Bus:* Golfito buses leave San José (Calle 4, Avenida 18; 21-4214) at 6:30 a.m. ($4, indirect) and at 11 a.m. and 3 p.m. ($5, direct). It's a seven-hour trip. Or you can take any Zona Sur bus to Río Claro, where the road to Golfito leaves the Interamerican Highway. *Villa Neilly–Golfito* buses pass through Río Claro hourly. It's a half-hour trip. Tracopa has buses back to San José ($5) at 5 a.m. and 1 p.m.

By Air: You can avoid the long, winding (though scenic) bus ride by flying SANSA to Golfito (33-0397, 33-3258, 21-9414; $20 one way) Monday through Saturday at 6 a.m. There is also a flight on Wednesday, Thursday, and Friday, which leaves San José at 1 p.m. and lands in Golfito at 1:40 p.m. Flights return at 7 a.m. and 2 p.m. Make reservations and buy tickets in advance, and be aware that the schedules change often. Travelair leaves San José for Golfito (32-7883, fax: 20-0413; $57 one way) daily at 8:40 a.m., returning at 10:10 a.m. by way of Palmar Sur.

By Car: Follow the Interamerican Highway from San José to Río Claro and turn right. The trip takes about seven hours. If you want to do the trip in two days, San Isidro de El General or even Playa Dominical are good places to stay overnight.

Playa Zancudo, on a strip between the ocean and the Coto River, is one of the Zona Sur's most popular beaches during the dry season, though you'd never know it during the rainy season, when adjectives to describe the place range from peaceful to boring. The fine black-sand beach stretches for kilometers, and the surf is gentle. Its good fishing attracts many North American visitors and residents.

Hotels and cabinas are plentiful on this beach. At the center of town, across the road from the dock, is **Estero Mar** (75-0056). It is a lively bar during rainy season and has the only public telephone in town. It has been known to rent rooms when all of the other places are full. **El Coquito** (cold water, private bath, no fans; $7-$12), 200 meters to the south of Estero Mar, rents small cabinas with windows that unfortunately are not oriented towards the sea and therefore miss the cool breezes.

Los Almendros (cold water, private bath, ceiling fans, good screens; $12-$20; 75-0515), 400 meters north of Estero Mar, has comfortable cabinas with nightlamps and a good restaurant that caters to the middle class. It has boats and arranges river, bay, and ocean fishing trips. Nearby, **Dee** and **Steve Lino** (75-0268) run a charter fishing business with the latest equipment and a 29-foot sportfishing boat. Call them directly or make reservations through Los Almendros.

North of Los Almendros is **Río Mar** (private bath, fans; $7-$12), pleasant, inexpensive cabinas well placed between ocean and river. With windows facing the beach, **Cabinas Zancudo** (cold water, private bath, ceiling fans, good screens; $7-$12; 77-3027) are simple and pleasant.

The ✪ **Cabinas Sol y Mar** (cold water, private bath, ceiling fans; $20-$30; for secluded "honeymoon" suites, $30-$40; 75-0353) has cabinas and a restaurant and has been highly recommended for its friendliness, good food, tranquillity, and creative design. It is a 25-minute walk south of Zancudo. **Zancudo Boat Tours**, next door, provides boat service from Golfito. It will also take you to the best snorkeling spots; to Pavones; to the Casa Orquídea botanical gardens; and down the Río Coto to see birds, crocodiles, monkeys, and otters. Let them know your travel plans in advance, because boat travel depends on the tides. Zancudo also rents surfboards, boogieboards, and a paddle boat for the back canals.

GETTING THERE: There is a *Golfito–Zancudo* bus during the dry season. The trip is two and a half hours. Ask around in Golfito's Pueblo Civil for time and location. Boatloads leave from the municipal dock of Golfito for Zancudo ($2-$3/person) Monday and Friday at 12 noon and return from Zancudo around 6 a.m., usually with the high tide. On the other days, hire a boat at the municipal dock of Golfito ($15-$20/boatload). Local boats provide transportation from Zancudo to Golfito ($1-$2). They either go via the sea or take a shortcut through the Atrocha, a natural canal through mangroves in which many birds and sometimes alligators can be seen.

Pavones is highly publicized in surfer magazines for having the longest wave in the world. It draws throngs during the rainy season, when the waves are largest. On peak days, expect between 50 and 80 surfers in the water. If you don't surf, try another beach (such as nearby Zancudo). Pavones is crowded and not suited to body surfing or swimming. The area has recently been the site of some Wild West-like confrontations involving drug trafficking and land disputes.

In Pavones, there are four simple rooms above the cantina, the **Pavón Tico** (shared bath, no fan; under $7). It sometimes annexes rooms in other houses across the street. The *pulpería* next to the soccer field also rents a few rooms (under $7). Doña María Jiménez, who lives 400 meters east of the school (which is 200 meters north of the cantina), has two cabinas and rents horses. There are no phones in Pavones.

GETTING THERE: *By Bus:* Take a bus at 2 p.m. near the municipal dock in Golfito or hire a jeep-taxi ($50-$60). The ride, along bumpy dirt roads and across the Río Coto by ferry, can take up to two and a half hours, depending on the state of the road and your means of transportation. Buses leave Pavones for Golfito at 5 a.m.

By Car: Take the Golfito-Rio Claro road about 10 kilometers to the turnoff for Conte. It's about 15 kilometers to Conte on a gravel road, then turn right and it's another 10 kilometers to the beach. The short ferry ride across the Rio Coto starts when you get there. The trip takes about two hours.

Two kilometers south of Pavones, along the dirt road that follows the coast to the border with Panama, is **Bahía Pavones Lodge** ($12-$20/person including breakfast; no phone). The lodge is well situated, 50 meters from the shore, with a wooden deck built onto the top of a towering rock right on the beach. Rooms in the main building (shared bath, screens) are simple and small. The cabinas (private bath) are a bit larger, with their own porches. The kitchen serves dinner and prepares cold lunches. Make arrangements to stay there through the Tsunami Surf Shop on Avenida Central in Los Yoses, San José, next to Azafrán. They are sometimes willing to rent rooms to people who just show up, but don't count on it.

Three kilometers south of Bahía Pavones Lodge, high up on a jungle-covered hillside, is ✪ **Tiskita Lodge** (private bath; $50-$60/person, double occupancy, including three meals). The rustic but comfortable cabins all have superb views of the ocean and are cooled by sea breezes. This would be our choice for the perfect honeymoon spot. Agronomist Peter Aspinall has planted 100 varieties of tropical fruits from around the world there, which attract many birds and monkeys. Trails wind up and down the mountain backdrop, and there is a 20-meter waterfall close to the cabins. Packages including charter flights and guided nature walks are available through Costa Rica Sun Tours (55-3518, 55-3418, fax: 55-4410).

From Pavones, one can take a **boat to Playa Zancudo**, about an hour away by sea. It is several hours by land, if it is dry season and the roads are passable. Walter Jiménez, who anchors his boats and himself near the school, will take passengers ($35/boatload to Zancudo; negotiable rates for other destinations).

CORCOVADO NATIONAL PARK

The **Península de Osa** reaches out of southwestern Costa Rica into the Pacific Ocean. Its large virgin rainforests receive 4000 millimeters of precipitation a year. For years, Osa's incredible wealth of tropical flora and fauna was protected from human destruction by the peninsula's isolation from the rest of the country. Then a lumber company moved in, more settlers came, and sports hunters began killing endangered animals in large numbers. Scientists urged the creation of a national park to protect the peninsula, and in 1975, 108,022 acres in its western corner were declared Corcovado National Park.

Corcovado contains eight unique habitats, ranging from mountain forest to swamp. In the park, scientists have identified at least 500 species of trees, 285 birds, 139 mammals, 116 amphibians and reptiles, and 16 freshwater fishes.

Corcovado used to harbor another kind of inhabitant: *oreros* (gold panners), who lived in the jungle and sifted for their fortunes in the park's rivers. Few struck it rich, but most at least made a living. The Banco Central set up a special office in Puerto Jiménez to buy the gold, which the country used to help pay the interest on its huge foreign debt. But due to massive unemployment in the region, the gold panners' numbers grew so much that their activity started causing real destruction. The silt from their panning was filling up the rivers and the lake in the park's basin. In 1986, the park service and the Costa Rican Civil Guard physically removed all of the gold panners, promising them an indemnity for their lost jobs. After a year without payment, the *oreros* camped out in protest in the city parks of San José until the government came through with the checks they had promised. Panning activity has started again, this time in the forest reserve bordering Corcovado. Two thousand families are now making their living in this way. Even though it is destructive, the park service has decided to let it go on instead of risking the panners working in Corcovado itself.

A surge in population is threatening the delicate ecological balance of the unprotected forests in the Osa Peninsula. *Campesinos* have moved in and started burning and cutting back the jungle for space to build their houses and cultivate small plots of land. An expanding national population, a shortage of available land elsewhere for cultivation, and a new road with bridges built by the U.S. Army Corps of Engineers in 1989 are all factors encouraging settlement.

This situation is a microcosm of what is happening all over the tropical world. The shortage of land is so serious that clearing and colonizing the jungle seems like the only alternative to many people. But rainforest soil is very poor when there's no forest covering it: once the trees are gone, the rainforest's self-fertilization by dead leaves, plants, and animals stops, and the soil becomes infertile. When it rains, the soil erodes and silt fills the rivers.

Since there is little biomass left to absorb excess moisture, floods become a problem.

The jungle plays many critical roles. It provides a habitat for thousands of animals that would die without it. Its trees produce oxygen and chemicals that are extracted for use in medicines like morphine, codeine, and quinine. It conserves the humidity of the land and protects watersheds.

Visiting the Península de Osa is a good way to learn firsthand about the conflict between the conservation of natural resources that humans need in the long-term, and the short-term options that many people consider their only means of survival.

Now, thanks to international support for Costa Rica's conservation efforts, the **Fundación Neotrópica** (53-2130) (see Chapter Two) is starting to address this problem through its BOSCOSA project. Costa Rican conservationists are realizing that they must create their own models for sustained development, rather than relying on techniques developed in countries with different cultural and economic patterns. They are forging a new understanding of human and environmental issues as one and the same. In-depth studies have been done of the needs of *precarista* (squatter) communities in the Osa Peninsula, and strong relationships between BOSCOSA workers and the people are being established. Through studies of animal and plant species that grow in forest reserves, new crops and livestock projects are being experimented with to provide solutions for both people's needs and environmental problems. Call for more information.

Corcovado National Park's **administration office** (78-5036, fax: 78-5011) is next to the Banco Nacional in Puerto Jiménez. Call ahead if you are going to the park to tell them how long you want to stay and whether you will need meals and lodging. (All guard and research stations within the park provide rooms and meals if you give sufficient notice.) They prefer that you call them at least a week in advance. During the dry season you can

camp fairly comfortably, but be aware that the beaches are infested with *purrujas*, perhaps the most aggravating of Costa Rican insects. Do not plan to just sack out on the beach—bring a tent. Fees to camp or stay at the stations are minimal. Bring mosquito nets, insect repellent, long socks, several changes of cotton clothing, a swimsuit, a flashlight, a water bottle, snacks, and two pairs of hiking boots or running shoes, or rubber boots.

A small, friendly town, **Puerto Jiménez**, is the gateway to Corcovado. There are good white-sand beaches just south, beyond the second point that juts out into the gulf.

The meeting place in Puerto Jiménez is **La Carolina** (fax: 78-5073), a small outdoor *soda* right on the main street. It has now formalized its status as an information center by getting a fax machine. You can buy plane tickets there, make hotel reservations, and arrange for local transportation.

LODGING **Cabinas Marcelina** (private bath, table fans; under $7; no phone) is simple now but might expand in the future with more luxurious cabinas. The friendly owners can set guests up for horse rides, gold-panning expeditions, and fishing trips.

The most comfortable place to stay in Jiménez is **Cabinas Manglares** (cold water, private bath, ceiling fans, screens; $7-$12; 78-5002), which has a restaurant, a shared cooking area, and a monkey and an alligator in permanent residence. It's a five-minute walk from downtown, near the airport. Go 300 meters down the main street from the soccer field then make a left before the church, two blocks past Cabinas Marcelina. Make a right, cross the little bridge (look for the alligator in the water on the left), and Manglares is around the bend.

On the way into town from the dock, **Cabinas Brisas del Mar** (private bath, table fans; under $7; no phone) are simple and have windows facing the gulf. **Vivero y Jardín Joyosa** (cold water, shared bath, no fans; under $7; no phone), near the Texaco station, has very basic bunk-bed accommodations. The owners can give you information on reforestation and other ecological projects.

Next to the dock, **Agua Luna** is a well-appointed restaurant in a series of *ranchitos* (round, indigenous-style buildings with pointy, thatched roofs). It is more expensive than the simpler restaurants in town, but the food is good.

South of Puerto Jiménez are three interesting eco-tourism projects:

Tierra de Milagros (no smoking; $20-$30; off-season discount; fax: 78-5073) is a nature preserve and reforestation project 20 kilometers south on the road to Corcovado. It has a friendly counterculture atmosphere, and its accommodations are minimal, to put the least distance between you and nature: open-air *ranchos* with hammocks, no electricity, a central primitive shower, and toilets. Bring your own linens. Vegetarian meals ($10/day) supplemented by fresh fish are served. There are trails to the beach and nearby waterfalls. The preserve arranges hiking and horseback trips and welcomes work-exchange volunteers. Tierra de Milagros is located 45 minutes south of Puerto Jiménez by taxi, or 20 minutes by water taxi from Playa Sombrero.

Bosque del Cabo (private bath, $50-$60/person including meals; 22-4547, 22-7338, fax: 78-5073) is very remote, with a spectacular view of the ocean from above Playa Matapalo, at the southern tip of the Osa Peninsula. There is a beautiful waterfall with scarlet macaws nesting above its pool, a lovely cove, and a creek. Cabins are spacious and private. They also offer guided horseback tours.

Costa Rica Expeditions' ☻ **Corcovado Tent Camp** (cold water, shared bath, natural ventilation; $30-$40/person including meals; 57-0766, 22-0333, fax: 57-1665) is on the beach 1.5 kilometers west of Carate, at the southern border of Corcovado National Park. Lodging is in ten-by-ten-foot tents that are eight feet high in the center. You can also get a package with round-trip charter air transportation ($400/person); packages with SANSA transportation are less expensive.

GETTING TO PUERTO JIMÉNEZ: Buses leave San Isidro de El General at 5:30 a.m. and 12 noon for Puerto Jiménez. It's a five-hour trip. You can also intercept the *Villa Neilly–Puerto Jiménez* bus at 7 a.m. or 3 p.m. at Chacarita (Piedras Blancas) on the Interamerican Highway, by taking any Zona Sur bus from San José.

By Car: Follow the Interamerican Highway to Piedras Blancas and turn right about 50 kilometers to Puerto Jiménez.

By Air: Aeronaves de Costa Rica flies from Golfito to Puerto Jiménez (75-0278; $7.50) daily at 6 a.m. and 2 p.m.

GETTING TO CORCOVADO NATIONAL PARK: *By Air:* You can rent a small, five-passenger **plane** that will fly you directly to Sirena, the main research station inside the park. From Golfito, take **Aeronaves de Costa Rica** (75-0278; $110/planeload). From San José, take **SAETA** (32-1474, 32-9514; $400/planeload). Many of the nature tour companies listed in Chapter Three have guided tours to Corcovado.

From Puerto Jiménez there are two ways to enter Corcovado National Park. The most convenient entrance is to the north via **La Palma**. Transportation to La Palma from Puerto Jiménez or the Interamerican Highway is quick and easy. A bus leaves Puerto Jiménez at 5:30 a.m. for La Palma. It's an hour-long trip. From La Palma it's a 12-kilometer, three-hour walk to the park's northeastern entrance at **Los Patos**, crossing the Río Rincón 19 times. The trail in this stretch is a narrow gravel road. When vehicles pass, the drivers often offer rides to hikers. The worst stretches of the whole trip are immediately before and after Los Patos, where the trail can be swampy and slippery, especially in the rainy season. Call park headquarters in advance to arrange for room and board at the Los Patos guard station.

After Los Patos, there are 6 kilometers of steep trails through high mountain forests, then 14 kilometers of flat walking through low, dense rainforest to the research station at Sirena. The trail is clearly marked, but at some river crossings you have to check up- or downstream for where the trail takes off again. Some of the rivers can be thigh-deep in the rainy season.

You might want to bring a machete, because the trail is narrow and there are overhanging branches. Be careful not to walk into poisonous spiders, whose webs span the trail, and bring repellent and plenty of patience for the horseflies. Other members of the animal kingdom you might meet are frogs, morpho butterflies, tapirs, ocelots, and monkeys.

The other way to enter Corcovado from Puerto Jiménez is via **Carate**, on the southern coast of the Osa Peninsula. Look for Cirilo Espinosa at the *pulpería* next to La Carolina in Puerto Jiménez. He drives a truck to Carate Monday and Saturday mornings ($4.50), returning anytime after 10 a.m. Have patience if something goes awry and hold on tight—the road gets progressively worse as the trip goes on. On other days, a taxi ($45-$60/carload) can be rented. Make arrangements through the park office. If you'd rather walk, it's about an eight-hour trip, with no stores along the way.

At Carate, turn right and walk along the soft sand beach about 45 minutes to the **La Leona** ranger station. You can eat and spend the night here if you check with the park administration office beforehand. (Don't swim—there are sharks and the current is strong.)

The walk from La Leona to Sirena spans 15 kilometers and takes about four or five hours. It is almost entirely along the soft sand beach. You must do it at low tide, because you walk around a couple of rocky points covered at high tide. There is a rusty shipwreck at Punta Chancha, with huge engines scattered around the rocks.

A bit later you reach Salsipuedes (Get-out-if-you-can) Point, with a pretty cave hollowed out of the coast. At some of the rock points there are trails that cut inland for a few hundred meters. The best way to find them is to start looking as soon as the coast looks impassable. The Salsipuedes trail gives you a break from the soft sand for a kilometer or two, but lather yourself up with repellent before starting into the jungle.

There are many monkeys along this trail. You will probably see scarlet macaws singing raucously and winging awkwardly through the sky. *Pizotes* (coatimundis) also come to the coast frequently. If you bring a machete you can take a break along the way to open up a coconut for a refreshing *agua de pipa*. After you cross the Río Claro, cut in either on the Sirena trail, or at the airstrip a bit farther down.

Sirena is a large research station populated by eco-tourists and biological researchers who are mostly from the United States and Europe. There are several kilometers of nature trails around Sirena that unfortunately are becoming severely eroded due to overuse and poor maintenance. Do not bathe in the ocean, as there are sharks, but as long as you look out for crocodiles you can swim in the nearby Río Claro and Río Sirena.

If you want to reward yourself after your wet, buggy time in Corcovado, consider spending a night or two in one of the resorts at Bahía Drake (see below), half an hour by boat from **San Pedrillo**, the northwestern entrance station. The resorts will pick you up from there.

The walk from Sirena to San Pedrillo is 25 kilometers: 15 along wide, flat, hard beach, 7 through rainforest, and 3 weaving between beach and coastal jungle. The entire walk can take six to seven hours. Make sure you walk the beaches at low tide. We hiked the first stretch, along the beach, at night. If you want to sleep comfortably, bring a tent, as the *purrujas* are terrible there.

One kilometer from the Sirena research station is the Río Sirena, the deepest (three to four feet in the rainy season) river with the strongest current that you'll have to cross on this hike. After that, it's about two hours to the Río Corcovado, which has a sandy bottom and is two feet deep at low tide. Two hours later is the Río Llorona, comparable to the Corcovado. If you walk at night as we did, you'll note some mysterious fog there. A couple of hundred meters later is the Piedra Arco, a huge rock arch covered with greenery. Soon after, a poorly marked trail cuts off into the jungle. Around the rocky point you'll find La Llorona, a 100-foot waterfall that cascades onto the beach. Don't be fooled by the tiny waterfall that you see immediately after leaving the sandy beach; continue on another 15 minutes to get to La Llorona. Do not attempt this except at low tide.

The trail through the rainforest climbs steeply at first, then rises and descends to creeks along the way. Much of it is level, winding through the jungle. For the most part it is a good, wide path, but watch the ascents and descents, because there the trail is eroded and slippery. A couple of hours later, you descend back to a beach. It's another hour to the Río San Pedrillo. With long legs you can jump it near the mouth; otherwise, test the waters and wade. If you want to keep walking, take the trail that follows the coast to Bahía Drake, 10 kilometers away.

Marenco Biological Station (cold water, shared bath, natural ventilation; $60-$80 including meals; $30-$40 for children), about 5 kilometers north of Corcovado on the Pacific, is dedicated to "conservation, education, tourism, and adventure." Naturalists enjoy Marenco because they have a chance to see rainforest, river, and sea wildlife all in the same area. Some even take off their binoculars long enough to enjoy snorkeling. A half-hour hike through a series of lovely rocky coves ends at the Río Claro, where a deep natural pool lends itself to a refreshing freshwater swim. One of Costa Rica's first eco-tourism projects, the Marenco Biological Station has resident biologists to help visitors understand the intricate ecological relationships there. The cabinas, simple and well designed, overlook the Pacific and the

Isla del Caño. Meals are delicious and wholesome, served family-style. Marenco offers tours to the northern part of Corcovado, hiking from San Pedrillo to La Llorona waterfall.

Because of Marenco's isolated location, transportation is coordinated through its office in San José (21-1594, fax: 55-4513; Apdo. 4025, 1000 San José). A four-day, three-night tour (around $575) includes food, lodging, air and boat transportation from San José, as well as guides.

DRAKE BAY

Drake Bay, purported to be where Sir Francis Drake anchored and set foot in Costa Rica in 1579, is about ten minutes north of Marenco by boat. The bay is calm, with many sailboats and yachts anchoring there. Four types of whales visit the bay. Fishing is excellent along the coast. There are four North American-run lodges on Drake Bay, and several new Tico-owned budget places. All offer ocean fishing trips and guided tours to Corcovado and Isla del Caño.

❂ **Drake Bay Wilderness Camp** (solar heated water, ceiling fans; $50-$60/person including three meals; $40-$50 in tent-cabins; phone/fax: 71-2436; English and German spoken) is right on the beach with nice cabinas, a shady campground, and good American-Tico-style food. Snorkeling is good both right at the camp and ten minutes away at Punta San Josesito. The camp will lend you masks and fins, and canoes for exploring the Río Agujitas, known for its needlefish. You can canoe up the river in search of monkeys, then relax in the giant tidepools near the lodge. Package deals including transportation from San José or Quepos are available (call or fax for information).

Across the Río Agujitas is ❂ **El Caballito del Mar** (cold water, private bath, ceiling fans; $50-$60/person including meals; phone/fax: 31-5028), which specializes in scuba diving. For early birds, they serve coffee at 5 a.m. Dinners at its restaurant include complimentary wine.

Overlooking the ocean, ❂ **La Paloma Lodge** (cold water, bathtub, natural ventilation, screens; $50-$60/person including meals; 39-0954, 39-2801) is built on top of a hill above the other lodges. Thatched-roofed family-size cabinas, perched on stilts, are breezy and have porches and lofts. The owners pride themselves on the personalized service they give their guests. Tours and free use of snorkeling gear and on-shore fishing equipment are available.

Slightly to the south of La Paloma Lodge is the Canadian-owned ❂ **Cocalito Lodge** (cold water, private bath, natural ventilation, screens; $50-$60/person including meals; fax: 75-6291, Canadian phone: 519-782-4592), which has a good swimming beach directly in front of its cabins. The hotel has planted botanical gardens designed to attract birds and monkeys. Its restaurant specializes in grilled and barbecued seafood served by candlelight.

The hotel offers scuba-diving packages in conjunction with the *Adventuress* (call or fax for information).

North of Río Agujitas, toward the town of **Drake** (pronounced "Drah-kay" in Spanish) are the budget places. **Casa Mirador** (cold water, private bath, natural ventilation; $12-$20/person including meals; 27-6914) has basic but nice accommodations and good food atop a hill with a beautiful view. ❂ **Albergue Jinetes de Osa** (cold water, shared bath; $20-$30/person including meals; 53-6909; English spoken) offers bunk beds and can arrange for you to stay with *campesino* families on excursions into the interior. **Cabinas Cecilia** (cold water, shared bath; $12-$20/person including meals; leave message: 71-2436) has two rooms with six bunk beds in each. They provide transportation from Sierpe ($7.50) for a minimum of four people, and have a trip to Isla del Caño ($15) plus other guided hiking and camping trips.

Río Sierpe Lodge ($50-$60/person including meals and transportation from Palmar; 20-2121, fax: 32-3321), 15 miles down the Sierpe River toward Drake Bay, offers rustic accommodations for anglers, naturalists, and scuba divers. Fishing and diving excursions include guides and all equipment. Hiking and horseback tours are also available.

GETTING THERE: Your lodge will arrange transportation for you from San José if you wish.

By Bus: If you want to get there on your own, take a bus to Palmar, which leaves San José (Calle 4, Avenida 18; 21-4214) at 5 a.m. and 7 a.m. The trip takes five and a half hours.

By Air: Or you can take a plane to Palmar. SANSA (33-0397, 33-3258, 21-9414, fax: 55-2176; $20) leaves Monday, Wednesday, and Friday at 10:30 a.m. Travelair (32-7883; $50) leaves daily at 8:40 a.m. with a stop in Golfito, arriving in Palmar at 10:45 a.m. From Palmar, you then take a bus or taxi to Sierpe, a village on the Sierpe River 20 minutes away.

You have to go down the river a couple of hours and out into the ocean to get to Drake Bay. The crossing from the wide river mouth into the ocean is dangerous and must be done according to the tides by an experienced skipper. The lodges will send one to pick you up in Sierpe. There are dugouts that take local people in and out inexpensively, but they are usually overloaded and have been known to capsize at the river mouth. If you want to risk it, ask around at the sleepy port of Sierpe. Faster boats, called "especiales" can take five or six passengers (usually $60-$75/boatload). Be sure to agree on a price before you get in—there are many local boatmen competing for your business, so you should be able to get the going rate. It is usually cheaper and less complicated to get back to Sierpe, because you can find Drake people that are going into town and share traveling expenses with them. The going rate for tourists is $15 per person.

The adventurous can arrange to go by horseback inland to Rancho Quemado, where a car (the White Knuckle Special) can take you to the town of Rincón on the Golfo Dulce. Check at Cabinas Cecilia (see above).

A more elegant solution is the **Temptress cruise** ($1495 for a six-night cruise; 20-1679, U.S. phone: 800-336-8423), which includes Drake Bay, Corcovado, and Isla del Caño in its itinerary.

If you need to spend the night in **Sierpe**, the new gringo-run **Hotel Pargo Rojo** (hot water; with ceiling fans, $12-$20; with air-conditioning and refrigerator, $20-$30; 75-6092) has a balcony overlooking the river. They will pick you up at the airport and arrange transportation to Drake Bay. There is also the **Hotel Margarita** (shared bath; under $7) in a big white house near the dock.

Restaurante Las Vegas serves good fish and chicken, and **Rosita's** is popular for *comida típica*.

If flying to Palmar, the best place to stay in is the **Casa Amarilla** (cold water, ceiling fans; with shared bath, under $7; with private bath, $7-$12; 75-6251), next to the Plaza de Deportes in Palmar Norte. The upstairs rooms have balconies. It is often full, so make reservations. **Hotel Xenia** (cold water, shared bath, ceiling fans; under $7; 75-6129), 150 meters north of the bus stop, is clean and has good beds, but is a bit run-down and dark. **Restaurante Chan Jeng**, underneath the local disco, has good food. The airport is in Palmar Sur, 2.5 kilometers across the Rio Térraba. There are usually taxies around when flights come in.

SAN VITO

The Villa Neilly–San Vito road was built by the United States in 1945 before the end of World War II as a strategic protection point, since the area is due west of the Panama Canal. The gravel road rises so sharply that in 20 minutes, Villa Neilly's heat is forgotten in the cool, misty mountains that lead to **San Vito** (3150 feet above sea level). Immigrants from post-war Italy founded San Vito in the early 1950s. In the last few years its population has doubled, to 37,000. It's a clean, modern town nestled in a high mountain valley.

San Vito has several clean, inexpensive places to stay. **Cabinas Las Mirlas** (heated water; under $7; 77-3054), next to the Ministry of Agriculture office, are perched among fruit trees overlooking a creek. **Hotel El Ceibo** (heated water, private bath; $12-$20; under $7 in older rooms; 77-3025), in back of the *Municipalidad*, is very clean and attractive and has a good restaurant. The rooms in the back have nice views.

Albergue Firenze (heated water, private bath; $7-$12; 77-3206), down a road to the left at the entrance to town from the Río Térraba road, are basic but nice. About 100 meters down the same road are **Cabinas Las Huacas** (heated water, private bath; $7-$12; 77-3115), which are clean and new and have a disco on weekends.

The ☺ **Wilson Botanical Gardens** (closed Monday), 6 kilometers uphill from San Vito on the Villa Neilly road, is a great place to learn about the trees and plants you'll be seeing throughout Costa Rica. Their self-guided tour booklet ($2) provides a wealth of information about the palms, aroids, bromeliads, ferns, heliconias, and marantas that form the main collections in the 25 acres of cultivated grounds. Many other plants are also featured in the lush design of the gardens, inspired in part by the great Brazilian horticulturist, Roberto Burle-Marx. A trip through the greenhouses is another treat—they're filled with plants from around the world that are threatened with habitat loss and extinction. Some 278 species of birds inhabit the gardens and the 342-acre forest reserve surrounding them. Five miles of trails offer mountain vistas, overlooks into rainforest canopy, and hikes to the lovely, rocky pools of the Río Jaba (banana leaves placed on the pools' rocks make them slippery enough to slide on).

Many fascinating botanical and agroecological experiments are being done at the garden, and it is also a center for innovative methods of community development. You can tour the grounds for $4.50 (half day), $6 (full day), or $12 (full day plus a hearty lunch). Lodging is $40-$50/person including excellent meals, in dormitory-style rooms with heated water and shared bath; $60-$80/person in attractive new cabins with heated water and private bath; $20-$30 for students and researchers. There are discounts for residents. Reservations must be made in advance through the Organization for Tropical Studies (40-9938, 40-5033, fax: 40-6783). For more information write Gail Hewson Gómez (Jardín Botánico Wilson, Apdo. 73, San Vito, Coto Brus 8257).

GETTING THERE: *By Bus:* A direct bus to San Vito leaves San José at 2:45 p.m. from Tracopa (Calles 2/4, Avenida 18; 21-4214, 77-3410). It's a five-hour trip. Buy tickets in advance. Indirect buses (a seven-hour trip) leave at 6:15, 8:15, and 11:30 a.m. This route is paved all the way and crosses the Río Térraba on a ferry (five minutes) at Paso Real, east of Palmar Norte. Most of these buses pass the Botanical Gardens after a stop in San Vito. Check with the driver. Return buses are at 5 a.m. (direct), 7:30 a.m., 10 a.m., and 3 p.m. The Tracopa office in San Vito is around the curve from the *Municipalidad* (city hall). *San Isidro–San Vito* buses leave at 5:30 a.m. and 2 p.m., returning at 6:30 a.m. and 1:30 p.m.

You can take the *San Vito–Villa Neilly* bus to the garden at 7 a.m. and 1 p.m., or take the *Villa Neilly–San Vito* bus at 6 a.m., 1 p.m., or 3 p.m. A taxi from San Vito is about $2.50.

By Air: You can charter a five-passenger plane to San Vito, or fly to Golfito with SANSA ($20) or Travelair ($50) and take a taxi ($40) to the Botanical Garden.

By Car: The San José–San Vito trip takes five hours: two and a half hours to San Isidro, after which the road straightens out a bit, then one and a half hours to the Río Térraba ferry ($1.50), then another hour to San Vito. Be sure not to miss the turnoff to the ferry at Paso Real. You'll see the river on your left, then you'll pass the ferry landing down below before you see a small sign indicating the road to San Vito. Once in San Vito, turn right onto the main street and follow it 15 minutes more to the Botanical Garden.

Parque Internacional La Amistad extends over the Talamanca mountains from the southern border of Parque Nacional Chirripó down into Panamá. It is the largest park in the country (192,000 hectares). Comprising eight life zones, La Amistad is one of the richest ecological biospheres in Central America.

Preliminary surveys indicate that two-thirds of the country's vertebrate species are found in this park. It is an important refuge for animals that require large areas for hunting, foraging and reproduction, like the jaguar, margay, and puma. Some of these animals are not protected anywhere else in Costa Rica.

Hiking deep into the park should only be undertaken by experienced tropical trekkers. The animals are wild, the paths are few, and the topography is abrupt. North Americans have been known to suffer from hypothermia there. But hiking in the Las Tablas forest reserve at the entrance to the park is safe and rewarding.

The Sandí family at **Las Tablas** farm receives visitors and will give you an excellent lunch or dinner at their farmhouse, if you let them know a few hours beforehand. You can camp in their pasture, but beware of unseasonal rains. They grow apples, peaches, apricots, and passion fruit and use water-generated electricity. Quetzales can be observed, and you can hear the unmistakable sound of the bellbird. Four-wheel drive and chains are needed to get up there in the rainy season, but a regular car can make it to the Río Cotón in the dry season, where you can park and walk about a kilometer to the farm. It takes about two and a half hours to drive there from the Wilson Botanical Gardens. Check with the Wilson Gardens staff for current information about Las Tablas. You can get a taxi to drive you there and back for about $45 for the whole day. Horses and guides can be arranged for at Las Tablas farm.

Isla del Coco (Coco Island), 500 kilometers off the Pacific Coast, boasts 200 dramatic waterfalls, many of which fall directly into the sea. Because the island is uninhabited, animals there are not afraid of humans. The fairy terns find humans so interesting that they hover about them curiously.

Although its geological origin remains a mystery, scientists believe Isla del Coco is a volcanic hot spot at the center of the Cocos tectonic plates. The Coco Island finch is a subspecies of the finch endemic to the Galapagos Islands that prompted Darwin's questions about evolution. Several species of birds, lizards, and freshwater fish are found nowhere else on earth. Whereas on mainland Costa Rica there are so many species that the behavior of each is highly specialized, on Isla del Coco individual birds of the same species will have different feeding habits—very interesting from an evolutionary standpoint. Some 77 nonendemic species, mainly seabirds, can also be observed.

European sailors probably first discovered the island in the 1500s. Many early visitors were pirates who rested and restocked fresh water there during their expeditions. They named the island after its numerous coconut palms, but apparently enjoyed the coconuts so much that there are almost none left today. Passing boats placed pigs, deer, and goats on the island to provide meat for return voyages. Having had no predators, these animals now constitute the majority of the wildlife there.

There are two main tales of buried treasure on the island. The Portuguese Benito Bonito, "The One of the Bloody Sword," is said to have buried his fabulous treasure there. At the time of Peru's wars of independence from Spain, the aristocracy and clergy entrusted their gold and jewels to Captain James Thompson, who promised to transport their riches to a safe port. Thompson disappeared with the loot and is supposed to have hidden it on Isla del Coco. Although many treasure hunters have searched the island, no one has found anything yet.

Hunting for gold doubloons might not be rewarding at Isla del Coco, but scuba divers find it rich in natural treasures. The ship **Okeanos** (20-1679, in U.S.: 800-348-2628) takes scuba divers to the island for ten days of heavy-duty diving ($2495/person not including airfare). The **Temptress** takes tourists to all the coastal national parks and reserves with a biologist guide. Contact Parques Nacionales (57-0922) for current access information.

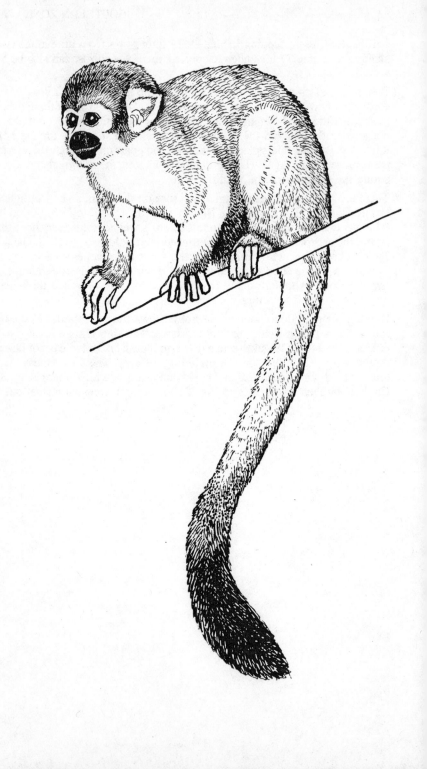

THIRTEEN

Staying Longer

OPTIONS FOR RESIDENCY

Securing permanent residency in Costa Rica is a complicated and increasingly difficult process. Temporary residency can be obtained by students in registered university or language school programs, by volunteers with the U.S. Peace Corps (or its Canadian, European, or Japanese equivalent), and by members of church-affiliated service groups.

To live here on a permanent basis you must either have a lot of money to invest in starting your own company—*inversionista* (investor) status—or apply for *pensionado* or *rentista* status. *Pensionados* must receive at least $600/month from Social Security or from a qualified pension or retirement plan. *Rentistas* must prove that they have investments guaranteeing them a monthly income of $1000.

You may apply for permanent residency while in Costa Rica, but you will need to supply the following documents: birth certificates for you and your dependents; all marriage and divorce certificates; naturalization certificates (if applicable); and a letter from your home police department certifying that you have no criminal record.

Pensionados will need to obtain a letter from Social Security or their pension or retirement plan verifying that the pension is for life and that the stated monthly amount will be paid out in Costa Rica. The pension plan must have been in existence for at least 20 years and the company must provide a statement of incorporation and economic solvency, certified by a CPA, which in turn must be authenticated by a Costa Rican consul. References from two banks with which the pension plan deals must also be provided.

Rentistas are required to submit a letter from their bank or recognized investment company stating that the amount of monthly income received from investments is stable, permanent, and irrevocable, and that income from these investments will be paid out in Costa Rica for no less than five years. The company providing the income must have existed for more than tnree years and must supply statements of incorporation, economic solvency, and bank references, the same as with the pension plans mentioned above.

Signatures on all foreign documents have to be notarized and the notary's signature must be authenticated by the county commissioner or secretary of state. The Costa Rican consul nearest to the place where the documents were issued will authenticate the commissioner's signature. This costs $40 per document. All documents must be translated into Spanish by a translator approved by the Costa Rican Ministry of Foreign Relations.

In addition, all candidates for permanent residency must submit two copies of their passport, one copy of each dependent's passport, and twelve passport-size photographs (six front and six profile) for each person involved. Candidates are also required to sign a sworn statement that they will live in Costa Rica at least four months a year, and must submit to a chest x-ray for tuberculosis, as well as blood tests for venereal diseases and AIDS.

Pensionados must provide fingerprints and photographs before they can receive residency permits, so that their identities can be checked by Interpol. This is done in an effort to exclude criminals, who may present falsified police documents.

Both *pensionados* and *rentistas* can set up their own businesses, but they cannot be employed by someone else. Each month, their $600 or $1000 must be converted into *colones*. Until recently, this entitled them to import their belongings into the country duty-free, but that privilege no longer exists. Now taxes must be paid on shipments of household furniture, appliances, and vehicles.

If all of this sounds complicated, expensive, and frustrating, it is. However, it's just the tip of the iceberg if you want to live or do business in Costa Rica. Do not plan to do your residency application yourself unless you have plenty of patience to deal with lines, national holidays, lunch breaks, misunderstandings, offices that have moved from where they were a month ago, impossible-to-find phone numbers, and so on. If you've got comfortable shoes and love to meditate or read novels while waiting in line, you'll find *trámites* (bureaucratic machinations) just your cup of tea. If you are nervous and impatient or have fallen arches, you will suffer.

Presently, there are about 2000 bona fide *pensionados* and *rentistas* living in Costa Rica. The best place to get current information is through the 950-member **Asociación de Pensionados y Rentistas** (Apdo. 700-1011, San José; 33-8068, fax: 22-7862).

For $900, the association will handle all the paperwork and running around necessary to secure either of the above residencies, taking from two to four months. Private lawyers can charge up to $2000 for the same services and take up to two years. Once you get your residency through the Asociación, you automatically become a full member and are eligible for many other services, as well as medical insurance offered by the Costa Rican Social Security System (in the ICT building mezzanine, Avenida 4, Calle 5). Even though Social Security health care is light years ahead of the medical systems in most Latin American countries, its clients must deal with long lines, short appointments, and delays lasting months between referral and delivery for x-rays, ultrasounds, operations and other diagnostic treatment services.

WAYS TO WORK

The Costa Rican government doesn't want foreigners to take jobs from Costa Ricans. Therefore, most foreigners are not allowed to work unless they are performing a task that Ticos cannot do. But with some thought, you might be able to discover a skill you have that will help you establish temporary residency (*residencia temporal*). Qualified teachers are needed at the English-, French-, Japanese-, and German-speaking schools in San José. English teachers are often needed by the various language institutes. The National Symphony needs musicians; *The Tico Times* needs reporters.

Doctors, lawyers, architects, and engineers are plentiful here and are protected by powerful professional associations that make entry difficult for foreigners.

Retired businessmen can join the **International Executive Service Corps** (IESC), a private, nonprofit firm sponsored in part by AID (Agency for International Development). They have a skills bank in Stamford, Connecticut, that matches volunteers with Third World companies needing consultants. Volunteers are paid living expenses only. Besides the U.S., eight other "developed" countries have similar organizations (IESC, Apdo. 70 Centro Colón, San José; 33-9855).

LEGAL ADVICE

If you live here and have a business or buy land, sooner or later you will need to hire a lawyer. Here are our guidelines for choosing one in Costa Rica:

> Shop around. There is usually no charge for meeting and consulting with a lawyer. Find someone you respect and can communicate with easily. Often your paperwork will be handled by law students working in the lawyer's office, and they will be the ones you end up having to communicate with, so be sure to meet them, too. Probably the most important person to have a trusting relationship with is the secretary. Some lawyers are always "not there" or "in a meeting" according to their secretaries. You can call for *weeks* and never get to talk to them.

> Get recommendations from other residents. Find a lawyer in the field you are interested in with whom people have had positive experiences. *Licenciados Xs* may be terrific international lawyers, but you

can bet their specialty isn't residencies, so don't expect them to be good at it.

Don't go to someone because they're a "nice guy" or somebody's friend. "Honest and efficient" is better than nice. Costa Ricans are always nice, even if they are irresponsible and slow.

Legal fees vary greatly. Some very good lawyers charge more because they know that what they do is far superior to the run of the mill. If you have the money, it is worth every penny to have a good lawyer here. Of course, just because a lawyer charges more does not mean they are good. Some very reliable lawyers are not all that expensive. Guidelines have been established to govern legal fees. These guidelines have been published in the *Gaceta* (the legal government newspaper). You can make a copy from the archives of the Biblioteca Nacional, or ask the Colegio de Abogados (Bar Association) for the going rates.

Most legal work does not get done unless you keep tabs on your lawyer. Educate yourself on rules and regulations. Do not sit back and expect that everything is humming along now that *Licenciado X* has your affairs in his capable hands. Check and double check, ask to see receipts, ask to see your *expediente* (file). Watch out if the lawyer tells you *"Tranquilo. No hay problema. No se preocupe. "* ("Relax. No problem. Don't worry.") This is Costa Rican for "Don't make me think about it."

Whether you have a good lawyer or a mediocre one, things still take a long time to get done here. So, as long as you know that things are *en trámite*, enjoy the relaxed pace and take a couple of long weekends yourself.

REAL ESTATE AND INVESTMENTS

According to an article in *The Tico Times,* "...the potential investor in Costa Rica should beware of ALL glib, 'fact-filled,' English-speaking promoters flogging ANYTHING, whether it's gold mines, beach property, condominiums, agribusiness, or mutual funds. Unfortunately, Costa Rica has long been a haven for con artists, whose favorite targets are trusting newcomers. This doesn't mean, however, that legitimate investment opportunities don't exist, in agribusiness as well as in other areas. They do, and it's unfair to tar all projects with the same brush. Would-be investors here, like everywhere else, are advised simply to move cautiously, ask lots of questions, and check with well-established, reputable companies before parting with any money. That way, investors can be confident of making a good choice."

For real estate and business opportunities you might subscribe to *The Tico Times*, Apdo. 4632, 1000 San José, CR; from U.S. and Canada: Dept. 717, P.O. 025216, Miami, FL 33102, USA; weekly, 32 pages, $45/year. A trial subscription is available for $16.50.

You can also contact the **American Chamber of Commerce of Costa Rica,** Apdo. 4946, 1000 San José, CR; 33-2133, fax: 23-2349.

RENTING

Houses and apartments in San José rent from about $200/month and up. Suburban and country houses can rent for as little as $150/month. Luxury condominiums or estates can rent for $1000-$1200/month or more. "Unfurnished" usually means without stove or refrigerator as well as without furniture.

As you will see from the cagelike appearance of most houses, Costa Ricans do not trust each other very much, and you shouldn't either. Most people do not leave their homes unoccupied at all. That means you have to pay a maid or housesitter if you want to go away for an evening or a weekend, unless your house is very, very secure. Currently, $1.25 to $1.50 per hour is considered good pay for maids and housesitters. Neighbors can tell you what the incidence of robberies is in your area, and having a good neighbor who will watch out for you is invaluable.

SCHOOLS

Costa Rica has free public education, but few foreigners are content to send their children to public schools. Like most government institutions, the schools are understaffed. Teachers are underpaid, and there is an emphasis on boring, repetitive, rote learning. Even parents who feel their children might be "enriched" by the experience of being in a completely Spanish-speaking classroom usually end up at English-speaking or bilingual private schools after a few weeks. Ticos who can afford it also send their kids to private schools, which include students of many races and nationalities.

Many parents want their children to come away from Costa Rica speaking Spanish. Spanish lessons from native speakers are included in the curriculum at English-speaking schools. Children are also often motivated by the friendships they make at school or in their neighborhood to learn Spanish. In other words, they will learn Spanish without having to be subjected to the public school system.

The English-language private schools are excellent, and many parents feel that their children are more academically stimulated here than in the public schools at home. They follow the U.S. academic year and prepare students for acceptance in foreign as well as Costa Rican universities.

Costa Rica Academy. Pre-kinder through grade 12. West of Cariari Country Club. Apdo 4941, San José; 39-0376, 39-0974.

Country Day School. Pre-kinder through grade 12. Escazú. Apdo 8-6170, San José; 28-0873, fax: 28-2798.

The European School. Pre-kinder through grade 6, will expand to high school in the future. Behind the Universidad Nacional in Heredia. Apdo. 177 Heredia, CR; 37-3709, fax: 31-7583.

International Christian School. Pre-kinder through grade 12. Apdo. 3512, San José, Barrio Escalante; 25-1474.

Marian Baker School. Pre-kinder through grade 12. Apdo. 4269, San José. San Ramón de Trés Ríos, east of San José; 34-3426, fax: 34-4609.

Bilingual private schools are usually less expensive and also prepare students for U.S. college acceptance. They follow the Costa Rican academic year, which begins in March and ends in November.

Anglo-American School. Primary. Apdo. 3188, 1000 San José; 25-1729, 25-1723.

Blue Valley School. Primary. Apdo. 561, 2050 San Pedro, CR; 25-6703, fax: 53-7708.

Canadian International School. Pre-kinder through grade 3. A grade will be added each year. Apdo. 622, 2300 San José, CR; 24-2844. Located in Curridabat, east of San José.

Centro Educativo las Vistas. Pre-kinder through grade 3, in Escazú. Apdo. 3702, 1000 San José, CR; 28-1763.

Colegio Humbolt. Kinder through grade 12. Classes in German and Spanish. Rohrmoser; 32-1455.

Colegio Internacional SEK. Pre-kinder through grade 10. Apdo. 963, 2050 San Pedro, CR; 53-1231, fax: 53-9762.

Colegio Metodista. Kinder through high school. Located in San Pedro and Sabanilla. Apdo. 931, 1000 San José; 25-0655.

Escuela Británica. Kinder through grade 10. Located in Pavas. Apdo. 8184, 1000 San José; 22-0719, fax: 32-7833.

Liceo Franco-Costarricense. Classes in French, English, and Spanish. Concepción de Trés Ríos, east of San José; 79-6616.

Lincoln School. Kinder through grade 12. Moravia. Apdo. 1919, San José; 35-7733, fax: 36-1706.

Saint Anthony School. Primary. Apdo. 29, Moravia; 35-1017.

Saint Benedict. Primary. Apdo. 142, 2350 San Francisco de Dos Ríos, CR; 27-9504.

Saint Clare. Junior high, high school. Apdo. 53, 2150 Moravia, CR; 35-7244.

Saint Francis. Kinder through grade 12. Moravia. Apdo. 4405, 1000 San José; 35-6685.

Saint Joseph's Primary. Apdo. 132, Moravia; 35-7214.

Saint Mary's School. Kinder-6th. Apdo. 229, 1250 Escazú, CR; 28-2003.

Santa Monica Primary. Apdo. 53, 2150 Moravia, CR; 35-4119.

Saint Peter's Primary. Apdo. 302, 2100 Curridabat, CR; 35-4119.

Teocali Academy. Pre-kinder through grade 9. Apdo. 186, 5000 Liberia, Guanacaste; 66-0273.

LABOR RELATIONS FOR DOMESTIC HELP

All domestic employees have the right to social security benefits from the *Caja Costarricense de Seguro Social*, maternity benefits set by the Ministry of Labor, a Christmas bonus, and severance pay.

Whether live-in or not, a domestic employee is entitled to the minimum wage set by the Ministry of Labor (23-7166). However, this wage is disastrously low—about $90 per month at current rates of exchange. Ask around for the going rate in your neighborhood. Live-in help can be required to work not more than 12 hours a day, and other employees eight hours. The employee has a half-day off each week, a 15-day paid vacation after 50 weeks of continual service, and half-days on January 1, Holy Thursday, Good Friday, May 1, September 15, and December 25. If an employee works these days, then an additional half-day salary must be paid. Days off should be previously scheduled.

New employees must be registered with the *Caja,* in the fifth-floor Department of Inspections (23-9890). The employer must bring identification, such as a passport or residency *cédula*, the employee's *cédula*, and the facts about the job and wages. The employer then receives a computer form, which is used to make the monthly payments to the *Caja* (19.5 percent of the monthly wages). Employees receive a paper giving them the right to the *Caja's* services (health care, maternity care, pensions). The monthly payment may be made by a messenger. If you lack a messenger, lines at the *Caja* seem shortest between 10:45 and 11:15 a.m.

A pregnant employee is entitled to one month off before the baby's birth and three months afterwards, with half of her monthly wage. Pregnancy is not a legal reason for dismissal.

The *aguinaldo* (Christmas bonus) is paid to employees who have worked from December 1 through November 30. It is equivalent to one month's salary. Most employers pay the *aguinaldo* early in December.

If the employer has cause to dismiss an employee, the employee must be paid unused vacation time, the proportionate *aguinaldo*, and all wages due. The employer must also document the dismissal with the *Caja*. If the employer must lay off help for reasons other than performance (i.e., leaving the country), employees must be given prior notice, unused vacation pay, the *aguinaldo*, and wages due, plus severance pay (one month's pay for every year of work). Should an employee decide to leave, the employer is not obligated to pay severance pay.

HEALTH CARE

The Social Security system makes low-cost medical care available to those who need it, but doctors also have their private practices in the afternoons. A gynecological exam including Pap test costs around $15; a sonogram costs about $25; a complete cardiac stress exam runs about $45. Dental care is also considerably less expensive here than elsewhere. All of the above services are available to foreigners.

Facelifts and other plastic surgeries cost a fraction of what they do elsewhere, and postoperative care is also a lot cheaper.

Well-qualified alternative medicine practitioners such as acupuncturists, homeopaths, chiropractors, and massage therapists are also available here and charge less than their northern counterparts. Ask at the **Center for the Creative Arts** (82-8769) in Santa Ana or the **Clínica de Bienestar Corporal Integree** (Avenida 14, Calles 1/3; 33-3839) and check *The Tico Times*. Homeopaths are listed in the phone directory.

Casa de Campo ($52/day including food, lodging, and therapy; 29-5309) is a private alcoholism/drug addiction treatment center with a fully bilingual staff. There are also several English-speaking chapters of AA and NA in Costa Rica.

The low cost of health care and labor make full-service custodial care of the elderly less expensive. **Golden Valley Hacienda** (43-8191) near Alajuela, offers specialized care for Alzheimer's patients, and **Villa Confort Geriatric Hotel** (21-8773) in La Uruca provides a comfortable atmosphere for its elderly residents, who just need help in everyday living. Both are in converted homes 10 to 20 minutes from San José. The monthly cost ($1500 double occupancy; $1700 single) includes round-the-clock care, meals, laundry, physical therapy, and music therapy.

RECOMMENDED READING

BOOKS

Abrams, Harry. *Between Continents, Between Seas: Precolumbian Art of Costa Rica.* New York, Harry Abrams, 1981.

Baker, Bill. *The Essential Road Guide for Costa Rica.* 1992. 800-881-8607.

Bell, John. *Crisis in Costa Rica: The Revolution of '48.* Austin, The University of Texas Press, 1971.

Biesanz, Mavis, Richard, and Karen. *The Costa Ricans.* Englewood Cliffs, NJ, Prentice-Hall, Inc., 1987.

Bonilla, Alexander. *La Situación Ambiental de Costa Rica.* San José, Ministerio de Cultura, Juventud y Deportes, 1985.

Boza, Mario. *Costa Rica National Parks.* San José, Editorial Heliconia, 1992. Hardbound, 333 pages, bilingual text, beautiful photographs.

Boza, Mario. *The National Parks of Costa Rica.* San José, Editorial Heliconia, 1987. Softbound, 112 pages, bilingual text, beautiful photographs.

Carr, Archie. *The Windward Road.* Gainesville, Florida State University Press, 1979.

Cornelius, Stephen E. *The Sea Turtles of Santa Rosa National Park.* San José, Fundación de Parques Nacionales, 1985.

DeVries, Philip. *The Butterflies of Costa Rica.* Princeton University Press, 1987. 327 pages, 50 color plates.

Edelman, Marc and Joanne Kenen. *The Costa Rica Reader.* New York, Grove Weidenfeld.

Gallo and Mayfield. *The Rivers of Costa Rica.* Menash, 1988. Color photographs, maps, hydrographic tables.

Glassman, Paul. *Costa Rica.* Moscow, VT, Passport Press, 1991.

Golcher Valverde, Federico, et al. *Investors Guide to Costa Rica.* San José, Costa Rican-American Chamber of Commerce, 1992.

Gómez, Luis Diego. *Vegetación y Clima en Costa Rica.* San José, UNED, 1987. Two volumes, 21 maps.

Howells, John. *Choose Costa Rica: A Guide to Wintering and Retiring.* San Rafael, CA, Gateway Books, 1992.

Janzen, Daniel, Editor. *Costa Rican Natural History.* Chicago, University of Chicago Press, 1983.

Palmer, Paula. *Wa'apin Man.* Editorial Costa Rica, 1986.

Palmer, Paula. *What Happen, A Folk History of Costa Rica's Talamanca Coast.* San José, Ecodesarrollos, 1977.

Palmer, Sanchez, Mayorga. *Taking Care of Sibo's Gifts, an Environmental Treatise.* Asociación de Desarrollo Integral de la Reserva Indígena Cocles/ Kekoldi, San José, 1991. Apdo. 170 Sabanilla Montes de Oca, 24-6090, fax: 53-7524.

Perry, Donald. *Life Above the Jungle Floor.* San José, Don Perro Press, 1991. 170 pages, index, 52 color photographs.

Searby, Ellen. *The Costa Rica Traveler.* Occidental, CA, Windham Bay Press, 1991.

Skutch, Alexander F. *Birds of Tropical America.* University Press of Texas.

Skutch, Alexander F. *Helpers at Birds' Nests.* University of Iowa, 1987.

Skutch, Alexander F. *The Imperative Call.* University Presses of Florida.

Skutch, Alexander F. *Life Ascending.* University Press of Texas.

Skutch, Alexander F. *Life of the Woodpecker.* Ibis Publishing Co., Santa Monica, CA.

Skutch, Alexander F. *A Naturalist on a Tropical Farm.* University of California Press.

Skutch, Alexander F. *Nature Through Tropical Windows.* University of California Press.

Skutch, Alexander F. *Parent Birds and their Young.* University Press of Texas.

Stiles, Gary. *Field Guide to the Birds of Costa Rica.* Ithaca, NY, Cornell University Press, 1988.

Young, Allan. *Field Guide to the Natural History of Costa Rica.* San José, Trejos Hermanos, 1983.

PERIODICALS

Mesoamérica. Published monthly by the Institute for Central American Studies, Apdo. 300, 1002 San José, Costa Rica. Phone: 33-7112, fax: 33-7221.

The Tico Times. Apdo 4632, San José. From U.S. and Canada: Dept. 717, P.O. 025216, Miami, FL 33102, USA; weekly, 32 pages, $45/year, 3-month trial subscription $16.50. Phone: 22-8952, fax: 33-6378.

VIDEOS

Costa Rica: Making the Most of Your Trip. Practical information on travel, shopping tips, health care: 1 hour, 36 minutes, $35 including shipping. In CR: 28-0266, in U.S.: Marshall Productions, P.O. Box 534, Carlsbad, NM 88221.

Costa Rica Today. Aspects of Costa Rican life for both tourists and potential residents: 1 hour, $30. In CR: 59-7946, in U.S.: Carlos Thomas, P. O. Box 5042, Dept. TT, New York, NY 10185.

Costa Rica Video. VHS, 34 minutes, $25 including shipping. Megaview Productions, 255 North El Cielo, Suite 155, Palm Springs, CA 92262.

This is Costa Rica. 35 minutes, $25. Features all tours offered by Swiss Travel Service, Apdo. 7-1970, 1000 San José, CR, 31-4055.

Notes from the Publisher

An alert, adventurous reader is as important as a travel writer in keeping a guidebook up-to-date and accurate. So if you happen upon a great restaurant, discover a special locale, or (heaven forbid) find an error in the text, we'd appreciate hearing from you. Just write to:

Ulysses Press
P.O. Box 3440
Berkeley, CA 94703

* * *

It is our desire as publishers to create guidebooks that are responsible as well as informative.

We hope that our guidebooks treat the people, country and land we visit with respect. We ask that our readers do the same. The hiker's motto, "Walk softly on the Earth," applies to travelers everywhere . . . in the desert, on the beach, and in town.

* * *

Index

Also Available From Ulysses Press

HIDDEN BOSTON AND CAPE COD
This compact guide ventures to historic Boston and the windswept Massachusetts coastline. 228 pages. $7.95

HIDDEN COAST OF CALIFORNIA
Explores the fabled California coast from Mexico to Oregon, describing over 1000 miles of spectacular beaches. 468 pages. $13.95

HIDDEN FLORIDA
From Miami to the Panhandle, from the Keys to Cape Canaveral, this award-winning guide combs the state. 528 pages. $14.95

HIDDEN FLORIDA KEYS AND EVERGLADES
Covers an area unlike any other in the world—the tropical Florida Keys and mysterious Everglades. 156 pages. $7.95

HIDDEN HAWAII
A classic in its field, this top-selling guide captures the spirit of the islands. Winner of the Lowell Thomas Award. 480 pages. $14.95

HIDDEN MEXICO
Covers the entire 6000-mile Mexican coastline in the most comprehensive fashion ever. 444 pages. $13.95

HIDDEN NEW ENGLAND
A perfect companion for exploring from Massachusetts colonial villages to the fog-shrouded coast of Maine. 564 pages. $14.95

HIDDEN PACIFIC NORTHWEST
Covers Oregon, Washington, and British Columbia. Seattle sightseeing, Oregon beaches, Cascades campgrounds, and more! 528 pages. $14.95

HIDDEN SAN FRANCISCO AND NORTHERN CALIFORNIA
A major resource for travelers exploring the San Francisco Bay Area and beyond. 444 pages. $14.95

HIDDEN SOUTHERN CALIFORNIA
The most complete guidebook to Los Angeles and Southern California in print. 516 pages. $14.95

HIDDEN SOUTHWEST

Explores Arizona, New Mexico, Utah, and Colorado, describing Native American sites, campgrounds and desert adventures. 504 pages. $14.95

CALIFORNIA: The Ultimate Guidebook

Definitive. From the Pacific to the desert to the Sierra Nevada, it captures the best of the Golden State. 504 pages. $13.95

DISNEY WORLD AND BEYOND
The Ultimate Family Guidebook

Unique and comprehensive, this guide to Orlando's theme parks and out-lying areas is a must for family travelers. 300 pages. $9.95

DISNEY WORLD AND BEYOND: Family Fun Cards

This "guidebook you can shuffle" covers Orlando's theme parks with a deck of 90 cards, each describing a different ride or exhibit. $7.95

DISNEYLAND AND BEYOND: The Ultimate Family Guidebook

The only guidebook to cover all Southern California theme parks. Includes three chapters of daytrip possibilities for families. 240 pages. $9.95

FLORIDA'S GOLD COAST: The Ultimate Guidebook

Captures the tenor and tempo of Florida's most popular stretch of shore-line—Palm Beach, Fort Lauderdale and Miami. 192 pages. $8.95

LAS VEGAS AND BEYOND: The Ultimate Guidebook

Takes in the Las Vegas casinos and shows, then ventures out from the city to natural hideaways and to four national parks. 240 pages. $9.95

THE MAYA ROUTE: The Ultimate Guidebook

Travel the route of the ancient Mayans. Yucatan Peninsula, Belize, Gua-temala, and Honduras are explored. 300 pages. $12.95

FOR A FREE CATALOG OR TO ORDER DIRECT   For each book send an ad-ditional $2 postage and handling (California residents include 8% sales tax) to Ulysses Press, 3286 Adeline Street, Suite 1, Berkeley, CA 94703. Or call **800-377-2542** or 510-601-8301 and charge your order.

ABOUT THE AUTHORS

Beatrice Blake has lived in Costa Rica for 12 years. In 1985 she rewrote *The Key to Costa Rica*, which her late mother Jean Wallace had originally published in 1978, and has updated it yearly since then. It has been on the *Publishers Weekly* list of travel bestsellers for three consecutive years. Beatrice now lives in Brooklin, Maine, with her husband and two children.

Anne Becher is a free-lance journalist and translator (M.A., Hispanic Linguistics). In addition to co-authoring *The New Key to Costa Rica*, she co-edits a bilingual literary magazine, *The Underground Forest—La Selva Subterránea*. She has travelled the full length of the Americas, by land, and currently lives in Costa Rica with her husband, Joe and young son, Jacob.

ABOUT THE PHOTOGRAPHER

Writer and photographer Allan Seiden travels widely from a homebase in Honolulu, Hawaii, where he lives with his wife, Mahchid, and their daughter Martine. His award-winning work has appeared in magazines and newspapers around the world. His most recent project is a comprehensive, illustrated large format history of Hawaiian royalty titled *Hawaii...The Royal Legacy*. Seiden is a member of both the Society of American Travel Writers and the American Society of Media Photographers.

ABOUT THE ILLUSTRATOR

Deirdre Hyde is an illustrator working out of Costa Rica. A graduate of the University of Reading, England, with a degree in Fine Arts and Philosophy, her work has taken her throughout Central and South America, West Africa, and Spain. Her main focus is on conservation themes and she works closely with conservation groups such as World Wildlife Fund. Hyde is painting for conservation.